MW01055939

ReFocus: The Films of Wallace Fox

ReFocus: The American Directors Series

ReFocus is a series of contemporary methodological and theoretical approaches to the interdisciplinary analyses and interpretations of neglected American directors, from the once-famous to the ignored, in direct relationship to American culture—its myths, values, and historical precepts.

Titles in the series include:

ReFocus: The Films of Preston Sturges
Edited by Jeff Jaeckle and Sarah Kozloff

ReFocus: The Films of Delmer Daves
Edited by Matthew Carter and Andrew Nelson

ReFocus: The Films of Amy Heckerling
Edited by Frances Smith and Timothy Shary

ReFocus: The Films of Budd Boetticher
Edited by Gary D. Rhodes and Robert Singer

ReFocus: The Films of Kelly Reichardt
E. Dawn Hall

ReFocus: The Films of William Castle
Edited by Murray Leeder

ReFocus: The Films of Barbara Kopple
Edited by Jeff Jaeckle and Susan Ryan

ReFocus: The Films of Elaine May
Edited by Alexandra Heller-Nicholas and Dean Brandum

ReFocus: The Films of Spike Jonze
Edited by Kim Wilkins and Wyatt Moss-Wellington

ReFocus: The Films of Paul Schrader
Edited by Michelle E. Moore and Brian Brems

ReFocus: The Films of John Hughes
Edited by Timothy Shary and Frances Smith

ReFocus: The Films of Doris Wishman
Edited by Alicia Kozma and Finley Freibert

ReFocus: The Films of Albert Brooks
Edited by Christian B. Long

ReFocus: The Films of William Friedkin
Steve Choe

ReFocus: The Later Films and Legacy of Robert Altman
Edited by Lisa Dombrowski and Justin Wyatt

ReFocus: The Films of Mary Harron
Edited by Kyle Barrett

ReFocus: The Films of Wallace Fox
Edited by Gary D. Rhodes and Joanna Hearne

edinburghuniversitypress.com/series/refoc

ReFocus
The Films of Wallace Fox

Edited by Gary D. Rhodes and Joanna Hearne

Dedicated to
Tom Brannan of Marietta, Oklahoma
and to Wallace Fox, Jr., and all the family and descendants of
Wallace Fox

Edinburgh University Press is one of the leading university presses in the UK. We publish academic books and journals in our selected subject areas across the humanities and social sciences, combining cutting-edge scholarship with high editorial and production values to produce academic works of lasting importance. For more information visit our website: edinburghuniversitypress.com

Edinburgh University Press Ltd
The Tun—Holyrood Road
12 (2f) Jackson's Entry
Edinburgh EH8 8PJ

Typeset in 11/13 Ehrhardt MT by
IDSUK (DataConnection) Ltd

A CIP record for this book is available from the British Library

ISBN 978 1 3995 0563 5 (hardback)
ISBN 978 1 3995 0565 9 (webready PDF)
ISBN 978 1 3995 0566 6 (epub)

Contents

Figures

Notes on Contributors

Andrew H. Fisher received his Ph.D. in History from Arizona State University and is currently Associate Professor of History at William & Mary, where he teaches courses on modern Native American history, environmental history, and the American West. His first book, *Shadow Tribe: The Making of Columbia River Indian Identity* (2010), examines off-reservation communities and processes of tribal ethnogenesis in the Columbia Basin of the Pacific Northwest. His current project is a biography of the Yakama actor, technical advisor, and activist Nipo Strongheart.

Jacob Floyd (Muscogee [Creek]/Cherokee) is an assistant professor in the School of Visual Studies at the University of Missouri. His research focuses on Indigenous self-representation on screen, and he is currently working on a book manuscript about Native actors' negotiations in Hollywood publicity and labor titled *DeMille Indians: The Native American Experience in Classical Hollywood* (forthcoming).

Joanna Hearne is the Jeanne Hoffman Smith Professor in the Film and Media Studies department at University of Oklahoma. She also taught for many years at the University of Missouri, where she was the founding director of the Digital Storytelling Program. She has published two books in Indigenous media studies—*Native Recognition: Indigenous Cinema and the Western* and *"Smoke Signals": Native Cinema Rising*—as well as articles on Indigenous cinema history, animation, and digital media. She received a National Endowment for the Humanities Fellowship in 2017 and served as a Fulbright Canada Research Chair in Culture and Society at the University of Alberta in 2019.

David J. Hogan worked as an entertainment journalist in Los Angeles before spending thirty years in Chicago book and magazine publishing. As an executive editor and publisher, he specialized in film, the 1950s and 1960s, the American Civil Rights Movement, World War II, military aviation, and the American West. He has worked with notables who include Walter Cronkite, Myrlie Evers-Williams, Herman Spertus, Tom Hayden, Senator Daniel K. Inouye, Maureen O'Hara, and John S. D. Eisenhower. Hogan is engaged by the aesthetics and cultural significances of vintage horror and science fiction, comic shorts, and film noir. He is working on his tenth book of film history, and has published essays in books devoted to Edgar Ulmer, Joseph H. Lewis, Budd Boetticher, movie Expressionism, and neglected B-movies. Hogan lives with his wife Kim in Arlington Heights, Illinois.

Murray Leeder teaches at the University of Manitoba. He is the author of *Horror Film: A Critical Introduction* (2018), *The Modern Supernatural and the Beginnings of Cinema* (2017) and *Halloween* (2014), and editor of *Cinematic Ghosts: Haunting and Spectrality from Silent Cinema to the Digital Era* (2015) and *ReFocus: The Films of William Castle* (Edinburgh University Press, 2018). He has published in such journals as *Horror Studies*, *The Canadian Journal of Film Studies*, *The Journal of Popular Culture*, *The Journal of Popular Film and Television*, *Film Journal* and *The Journal of Communication and Languages*.

Gary D. Rhodes (Cherokee) currently serves as Associate Professor of Film and Mass Media at the University of Central Florida, Orlando. He is the author of *Emerald Illusions: The Irish in Early American Cinema* (2012), *The Perils of Moviegoing in America* (2012), and *The Birth of the American Horror Film* (Edinburgh University Press, 2018), and is the editor of such anthologies as *Edgar G. Ulmer: Detour on Poverty Row* (2008), *The Films of Joseph H. Lewis* (2012), and *The Films of Budd Boetticher* (Edinburgh University Press, 2017). Rhodes is also the writer-director of such documentary films as *Lugosi: Hollywood's Dracula* (1997) and *Banned in Oklahoma* (2004). His latest book, co-authored with Robert Singer, is *Consuming Images: Film Art and the American Television Commercial* (Edinburgh University Press, 2020).

Sara Rutkowski is an assistant professor of English at the City University of New York: Kingsborough Community College. She is the author of *Literary Legacies of the Federal Writers' Project: Voices of the Depression in the American Postwar Era* (2017), and has published various essays on Depression-era and postwar American writers and the cultural and political contexts of twentieth-century global literature. She is currently working on editing a collection of essays about the Federal Writers' Project.

Marlisa Santos is Professor in the Department of Humanities and Politics and Honors College Faculty Fellow at Nova Southeastern University. Her research focuses on film noir and classic film studies. She is the editor of *Verse, Voice, and Vision: Poetry and the Cinema* and the author of *The Dark Mirror: Psychiatry and Film Noir.* She has also published numerous articles on various topics such as Cornell Woolrich, film noir aesthetics, the James Bond franchise, and American mafia cinema, and on directors such as Ida Lupino, Martin Scorsese, Edgar G. Ulmer, and Joseph H. Lewis.

Michael L. Shuman is a Senior Instructor in the Department of English at the University of South Florida. He teaches courses in the Professional & Technical Writing program and coordinates the department's internship program. While primarily teaching technical communications, his research interests include film studies, especially film noir of the late 1940s and early 1950s, the psychoanalytic theory of Otto Rank, and contemporary speculative fiction. His analysis of film tropes and popular music, "Dracula's Deuce: How Horror Films Haunt Garage and Surf Music," appeared in the Fall 2017 issue of *Weird Fiction Review*. He is Deputy Editor of *The Mailer Review*.

Robert Singer is a retired Professor and Deputy Executive Director of Liberal Studies at the CUNY Graduate Center. He received a Ph.D. from New York University in Comparative Literature. His areas of expertise include literary and film interrelations, interdisciplinary research in film history and aesthetics, and comparative studies. He co-edited *Zola and Film* (2005), *The Brooklyn Film* (2003), and co-authored the text, *The History of Brooklyn's Three Major Performing Arts Institutions* (2003). He is the co-author, with Gary D. Rhodes, of *Consuming Images: Film Art and the American Television Commercial* (2020).

Phillip Sipiora is Professor of English and Film Studies at the University of South Florida. He has lectured nationally and internationally on twentieth-century literature and film and is the Founding Editor of *The Mailer Review*. He is the author or editor of five books and has published approximately three dozen scholarly essays, including readings of Stanley Kubrick, Billy Wilder, Joseph H. Lewis, Edgar Ulmer, Ida Lupino, and Robert Wiene. He is the editor of *Ida Lupino, Filmmaker* (2021) and author of "Criticism" in *Norman Mailer in Context* (2021).

Wallace Fox, Chickasaw filmmaker

Introduction: Wallace Fox and the B Film

Joanna Hearne and Gary D. Rhodes

> Beyond the industrial structures and the typical glossy Hollywood cinema . . . there is another entire category of American fictional feature films created and shown under different conditions. These are the B-movies, also called "quickies," "cheapies," "low-budget," or simply "budget films," even "C" or "Z" films . . . B films occupied an equally important role in Hollywood; to concentrate upon the A would emphasize the art of a few films and elide the basis of production, the underlying commercial and artistic means by which the industry survived—as well as the vast quantity and range of films offered to spectators during the studio era.
>
> Brian Taves, "The B Film: Hollywood's Other Half"[1]

> In asking "hakarʉ marʉʉmatʉ kwitaka?" [who is bullshitting who?] we have to remember: movies are movies, reels of data captured on camera, never to be trusted and producing multitudes of incommensurable interpretive possibilities. We also have to remember: movies are far more than that, something far-reaching, endless, and rooted in ancient traditions of storytelling and storied tales.
>
> Dustin Tahmahkera, "Hakarʉ Marʉʉmatʉ Kwitaka?: Seeking Representational Jurisdiction in Comanchería Cinema"[2]

> How have Native Americans participated in the creation of films in the twentieth century?
>
> Liza Black, *Picturing Indians*[3]

Bringing together two streams of film history from the quotations above—at the intersection of B film history and Indigenous film history—we find one answer to Cherokee historian Liza Black's question in the life and career of Wallace Fox, the youngest member of the first family of Indigenous filmmakers in Hollywood. Born in Purcell, Indian Territory (later Oklahoma) on March 9, 1895, Wallace (or "Wally") Fox began his Hollywood career as an assistant director in 1921. The film was *The Invisible Fear*, directed by Fox's brother Edwin Carewe. After working as an actor and later director, Carewe ascended to major studios as the producer-director of such films as *Resurrection* (1927), *Ramona* (1928), and *Evangeline* (1929). Some of Carewe's films were written by the third brother, scenarist and scriptwriter Finis Fox. Together, Edwin and Finis became major Hollywood players, and part of the social scene of the 1920s.[4] By contrast, Wallace Fox did not appear at Tinseltown parties, at least not so far as the Los Angeles press noticed. Nor did Fox become a director at major studios. From his directorial debut in 1927 with *The Bandit's Son*, a western starring Bob Steele, Fox spent over two decades working in what became known as B-movies.

Our anthology tracks several analytical approaches to the B film career of Wallace Fox: his work within distinct film genres, his work across the B film industry, and his work in the context of his Chickasaw Nation citizenship. At times these approaches converge and can be understood in conversation, as when we consider Fox's westerns, while at other times they diverge, as in considerations of Fox's horror films or East Side Kid dramedies. The highly codified, constrained production system of the B film industry left little room for the Indigenization of genre films in the way that contemporary Indigenous directors have undertaken with independent feature films, such as Jeff Barnaby's 2019 zombie film *Blood Quantum*, or Georgina Lightning's 2008 gothic ghost story *Older than America*. Fox represents something of a hidden Indigenous presence in the history of the genre film—hidden especially because he did not "Indigenize" the B film genre system so much as occupy a managerial role within it as a director and sometimes producer who, due to the rigidity of the B film studios and their budgets at mid-century, had little control over its scripts. Even if he had wanted to, without control of scripts, Fox could not have made oppositional work within the B film system. But he could, and did, have a career making genre films, and he seems to have thrived in that milieu despite (or perhaps because of) its limitations. The chapters here focus on the work he made within that system—westerns, horror, serials, and more—showing us the contours and necessarily varied career of an Indigenous person directing mainstream, low-budget studio films during the era of classical Hollywood cinema.

As editors, we come to this anthology from two different backgrounds, our work converging in a manner not unlike Fox's life and career. Gary D. Rhodes is a citizen of the Cherokee Nation who grew up in the Chickasaw Nation of

Figure I.1 *Bullets for Bandits* (1942), directed by Wallace Fox.

Oklahoma. He has written about Native Americans in the cinema, both in scholarly publications and in op-eds for popular audiences, but much of his research concentrates on American film history, specifically the classical Hollywood era and B-movies in which Fox spent the bulk of his career. Joanna Hearne is a non-Indigenous scholar of Indigenous media history, whose work often involves attention to re-crediting Indigenous participants in the film industry as well as archival recovery of Indigenous film texts.

WALLACE FOX AND THE B-MOVIE SYSTEM

When we speak of B-movies, we are speaking of low-budget cinema, but more specifically the kind of low-budget films produced in Hollywood during the 1930s and 1940s. Film historian Brian Taves defines them this way:

> First, they were to fill the bottom half of a double bill. Second, B's had leads with moderate, questionable, or unknown box-office appeal, such as second-string cowboy stars. Third, budgets and shooting schedules were more limited [than A films], and B's were usually made in three

> weeks or as little as one week. Fourth, the running time ordinarily ranged from fifty-five to seventy minutes.[5]

While westerns were core to the "poverty row" studios that produced B-movies, other genres came to the fore as well, including comedy, drama, and horror. Certainly it is possible to identify auteurs amongst the large number of B-movie directors, most notably figures like Edgar G. Ulmer and Joseph H. Lewis. But most of these filmmakers hardly fit that description. Consider instead Taves's description of the successful B-movie director:

> Many individuals were shunted into careers dominated by B's because of their consistent effectiveness in filming efficiently and smoothly. They became typecast, in a sense, not for lack of talent, but precisely because of their demonstrated skill. Turning out pictures rapidly on low budgets required rare abilities: knowing exactly what shots were necessary, editing in the camera without wasting footage on full coverage or more than a few takes, quickly arranging the lighting and camera angles to conceal the cheapness of the sets, eliciting or giving an effective performance with few rehearsals, and covering such disadvantages with fast pacing and shadowy lighting. These abilities were highly prized and might well lead to a continuation in the B realm, but seldom advanced one to the A's.[6]

This context—the strictures and systems of B film production—frames our discussion of Wallace Fox, who directed approximately eighty films, as well as short subjects and serials, before spending the last four or five years of his career directing low-budget television programs.

Fox was not an auteur. By contrast, we herald him in part because he is an avatar of most B-movie directors, an example of what was special about them: the ability to helm successful low-budget films year after year, genre after genre. And to create at least some films that still resonate with audiences decades later. During his lifetime, Wallace Fox was never as noteworthy or as praised as his two famous brothers, whose careers came to an end with talkies in the early 1930s.

But prior to his death in 1958, when his B-movies began appearing on television, and certainly since his demise, Wallace Fox has experienced something his brothers never did. Not fame, but repeat viewings, over and over again. The fact that so many of his sound movies fell into the public domain—as large numbers of B-movie studios went out of business and never renewed their copyrights—meant that they became popular for TV stations to program. Late-night viewers might see one of Fox's Monogram horror films such as *The Corpse Vanishes* or *Bowery at Midnight*, for example. By the 1980s, some of them became available on inexpensively produced home video formats. By the 1990s, some appeared on DVDs on sale for as little as $1. Thus, with regard to studying B-movies, access is both limited and extensive. It is limited due to the general lack of surviving company paperwork, as is available for major studios like Warner Bros. Fortunately, the project of digitizing film industry trade publications has helped expand the historical archive, as the "poverty row" film companies did receive regular coverage in them. With regard to extensive access to B-movies, the fact that most of them are public domain means that viewing them—even if in sometimes poor-quality prints—is extremely easy to do. Hundreds of such movies populate YouTube, for example.

In addition to the wide accessibility of his films, the Wallace Fox legacy has also been fueled by ongoing interest among movie buffs in genres like westerns and horror, as well as in the stars of his films, such as Bela Lugosi, B-western film star Johnny Mack Brown, and the young actors who played tough-talking urban teen characters in Monogram Studio's *East Side Kids* film series. As a result, Fox's films have remained visible and relevant in a manner that his brothers' work has not.

Examining film directors of the classical Hollywood era is both exciting and challenging. Much effort has been expended on locating auteurs and heralding their unique styles, particularly given the constraints of studio-era filmmaking. That Orson Welles directed such films as *Citizen Kane* (1941) is all the more amazing given that—as Frank Capra once said in the mid-forties—there were only a few directors with the power to choose their own projects. Scholarly consideration of such studio-era auteurs as Welles and Hitchcock is crucial, but can minimize the fact that most directors largely adhered to overarching studio styles, helming films that they were told to make. Here is the world of, for example, Archie L. Mayo, W. S. "Woody" Van Dyke, and Victor Fleming. Though Fleming was the director of such important movies as *The Wizard of Oz* (1939) and *Gone with the Wind* (1939), he was not as much an auteur as he was a talented studio director.

If anything, B-movie directors were even further hampered in terms of power, as some described in conversations with Gary D. Rhodes. Joseph H. Lewis, for example, repeatedly spoke about his lack of choice of story material to direct for B-movie studios in the forties, as well as severely limited budgets and shooting schedules. "Seven days!" he would marvel in retrospect, thinking about how quickly he directed some of those films. Gerald "Jerry" Schnitzer, who wrote many B-movie scripts in the forties—including *Bowery at Midnight* (1942) which Wallace Fox directed—learned he was supposed to write a project for actor Bela Lugosi on Friday; he had to deliver the finished script on Monday. He had no choice over the genre, and he had only 48 hours to write it. Schnitzer also talked about the fact that it was B-movie producers like Sam Katzman who held the power, not the writers and directors, with Katzman not only choosing which individual films and film series to make, but even at times becoming involved with particular dialogue on given movies: a brash, cigar-smoking micromanager. He was also someone who, realizing the changing audience landscape of World War II, saw a need to make movies specifically targeted towards women and children.

Studies in B-movies are at once expansive and limited, meaning that much scholarly work has been undertaken on B genres like horror and film noir, particularly as they relate to a few directors that have—despite the aforementioned limitations—been viewed as auteurs, such as Edgar G. Ulmer and Joseph H. Lewis.[7] Engagement with their work has varied in approach and methodology, ranging from psychoanalytic criticism to neo-formalist aesthetic analysis. That said, there remains a dearth of work on the industrial practices of the B-movie studios, a term that may itself be problematic. As Schnitzer told Rhodes, "studios" like Monogram and PRC weren't really studios; they were mainly comprised of company offices, with personnel renting studio space as needed.

In the B-movie industry, most directors were not auteurs, any more than they were at the major studios. The companies producing B-movies often masked the individuality of their directors in favor of the consistency of genre products. As a result, there has not been enough focus on individuals within the B film system. We focus on Fox in part to emphasize that even in such restricted industrial contexts, those working within it *were* individuals, despite their lack of authorial control.

WALLACE FOX AND INDIGENOUS HOLLYWOOD

In addition to being an exemplar of a successful director of low-budget B-movies, Wallace Fox is distinctive because of his Indigenous identity as an enrolled citizen of the Chickasaw Nation. He and his family members are all listed on the Dawes Commission of Final Rolls (the "Final Rolls of Citizens and Freedmen of the Five Civilized Tribes"), and trace their Chickasaw lineage, through their mother Sallie Priddy, to their mixed-blood ancestor John McLish, who appears in histories of the Chickasaw as a translator and treaty signatory, and who traveled, during Removal, from the Chickasaw homelands in Mississippi to the Indian Territory in 1837. McLish had close ties with Chickasaw Nation leadership and the powerful Colbert family, and even generations later, Wallace's eldest brother Finis was active in tribal and Territory politics, serving briefly as a legislator in the Chickasaw government.

Thus, although Wallace was only a young child during the family's time in Indian Territory—his mother died when he was five, and his father remarried and moved the family to Texas sometime before 1906—he grew up in a politically engaged environment at a moment of intense pressure on the Chickasaw

Nation, immediately prior to the formal dissolution of the tribal governments in Indian Territory on the eve of the 1907 admission of Oklahoma to U.S. statehood. He and his parents and brothers lived through some of the events, like the settler land runs of the 1890s, so often (mis)represented in later films; they would have discussed not only local but also national Indian policy. These federal policies changed radically during their lifetimes, from the early twentieth-century assimilationist policies of land allotment and tribal government dissolution; through the pressure for reform in the late 1920s leading to the 1934 Indian Reorganization Act advocating tribal and territorial reorganization; to the late 1940s and early 1950s Termination and Relocation policies which attempted to terminate tribal governments and collective landholdings once again.

The Fox brothers came from an intermarried family of relatively wealthy lawyers, stockmen and landowners, and could pass for white; they were highly mobile physically and socially at a time when the movements of people from other Native nations were often restricted by reservation Indian agents or superintendents who had the power to control the off-reservation travel of individual tribal members. Like his elder brothers, Wallace Fox traveled widely in his youth, enlisting in the Navy in 1911 and serving in World War I. Passport records show him traveling back to the U.S. from Istanbul upon his discharge in 1918. By 1920 he had joined his brothers in Los Angeles, where Edwin Carewe was directing films and Finis Fox working as a scenarist. Unlike Native American actors in the Hollywood studio system, Wallace Fox and his brothers held positions of industrial importance; once Carewe retired from acting to direct and produce full time, the brothers worked behind the camera rather than in front of it. They were proud of their Chickasaw Nation citizenship and of their youth living in Indian Territory—both Finis Fox and Edwin Carewe often mentioned it in their interviews and press materials—but they never played Indian for the camera.

In mid-century Hollywood from the late 1920s through the early 1950s, images of Indians were ubiquitous on American screens and consistently narrated Indian demise. Decades of scholarship have parsed these stereotypes—from Robert Berkhofer's 1978 *The White Man's Indian: Images of the American Indian from Columbus to the Present*, which outlined the historical trajectory of "noble" and "savage" images of Indians, to the work of Jacquelyn Kilpatrick (*Celluloid Indians*), M. Elise Marubbio (*Killing the Indian Maiden*), Armando José Prats (*Invisible Natives*), and others.[8]

Productions during Wallace Fox's career in classical Hollywood imagined Indians not only through these longstanding stereotypes but also in terms of production cycles that engaged with policies and political discourse, such as the pressure to reform the Indian boarding schools in the 1920s (the subject of Paramount's prestige films, *The Vanishing American* in 1925 and *Redskin* in 1929) and the assimilationist pressure of the postwar period through the mid-1950s (framed as integrationist in "pro-Indian" westerns such as *Devil's Doorway* and *Broken Arrow*, both 1950). The 1930s and 1940s, Fox's own peak decades, saw the rise of the B-western, the singing cowboy, and the talkies in which Indian characters spoke in broken English or not at all, even as they provided a major source of on-screen action and stunts. Outside of a few projects that attempted to represent pre-contact Native life—such as *Nanook of the North* (1922), *Daughter of Dawn* (1925), and *The Silent Enemy* (1930)—Indian characters were always represented in relations of hostility or loyalty to white settlers, and in some stage of decline or vanishing.

In contrast to the "vanishing Indians" on screen, Indigenous participants were alive and well and professionally active in Hollywood at mid-century. Most Indigenous performers specialized in playing Indian roles, or were hired onto productions as consultants, such as Nipo Strongheart and Chief Yowlatchie (Daniel Simmons), both Yakama, Mohawk actor Jay Silverheels, and Molly Spotted Elk (Mary Alice Nelson, Penobscot). Seneca scholar Michelle Raheja has developed an expansive definition for performative "redfacing" to indicate "the process and politics of playing Indian," whether the performer is Native American or non-Native (indeed, makeup artists frequently applied bronze skin makeup to both, as Liza Black's research has shown).[9] Many Native actors had their own professional and social networks in Los Angeles, but studios also hired large numbers of non-professional Native extras when shooting westerns on or near reservation lands. In both cases, performers used what power they had to negotiate for better pay and labor conditions, and some actors, like Victor Daniels (Chief Thunder Cloud), used promotional materials to leverage small interventions in the larger patterns of Hollywood representation and messaging.[10]

Wallace Fox would have constantly navigated this complicated space of film conventions as a Chickasaw director working within the extremely narrow limitations of the Hollywood studio system in general and the strictures of the B-film production pipeline in particular (which precluded certain kinds of variation even as it was predicated on producing prolific versions). Raheja describes such Indigenous negotiations as "visual sovereignty," a way of "thinking about the space between resistance and compliance wherein filmmakers and actors revisit, contribute to, borrow from, critique, and reconfigure" film conventions, "while at the same time operating within and stretching the boundaries created by these conventions."[11]

Recovering the career of Wallace Fox contributes, then, not only to the history of the B film but also to the history of Indigenous Hollywood, where behind the images of Indian erasure on screen, we also find ample evidence of "Indians in unexpected places" (to use Phil Deloria's phrase).[12] One of those places is that ur-story of vanishing Indians, the 1936 George Seitz version of

The Last of the Mohicans, a production for which Wallace Fox served as an Assistant Director. Should we begin to think about this film differently with the knowledge that a Chickasaw director was involved in the production? At the very least, we can no longer see it solely through the lens of onscreen stereotypes; re-recognizing and re-crediting the stories of Indigenous presence within the very industry that produced images of Indians vanishing shows us the contours of the system in a new way—its "working environments, representational boundaries, and conditions of possibility."[13] At the same time, as a director and sometimes producer, Fox was not defined by his identity as so many Native performers were; he was not limited to westerns or to films on Indian subjects but rather ranged as widely in genre work as the B-film industry allowed. For example, much scholarship in Indigenous film history has tracked the dynamics of creative control whereby non-Indigenous directors dictated representations of Indigenous peoples on screen; Fox's films occasionally instantiate the opposite configuration, in which a Chickasaw filmmaker orchestrates the consolidation of urban Irish-American identity and values on screen, as in the *East Side Kids* series. Yet across the contradictions in Fox's Chickasaw background and his representations of the bowery, "survival is the name of the game" (see Sipiora's chapter in this volume).

In *Kings of the Bs* (1975), Todd McCarthy wrote persuasively that:

> In accord with Henri Langlois' policy at the Cinémathèque Française, that every film ever made deserves to be saved because of the constantly changing perspective of history, we determined to reach back (some might say down) into film history as far as possible, to disregard temporarily the upper crust, to let qualitative considerations, by and large, surface where they may, perhaps to illuminate the business side of the art form for a change, and, hopefully, partially fill a gap in film history, to study the American B (and C and Z) movie.[14]

In opting to compile an anthology on Wallace Fox, we share the same perspective, hoping to build on prior literature by investigating an important but largely forgotten director, one who helped anchor the industry for over a quarter of a century, not because of his heritage as an Indigenous person, but largely in spite of it.

In this volume, we present twelve essays on the film career of Wallace Fox, beginning with three that explore different eras and concerns that surface in his westerns, the genre in which he worked more often than any other. Andrew H. Fisher inaugurates the volume with his chapter "Between Compliance and Resistance: Mapping the Careers of Wallace Fox and Nipo Strongheart in Early Hollywood," which importantly places Fox's career within the context of his era.

Figure I.2 *Gunman's Code* (1946), directed by Wallace Fox.

Joanna Hearne's "Indian Agents and Indigenous Agency at Universal" explores *Wild Beauty* (1946) and *Gun Town* (1946), both of which depict Native American characters on screen. They invite us to re-examine the potential for Raheja's "visual sovereignty" in the work of an Indigenous director embedded within the Hollywood system. Both films make heroes of Indian agent characters and activate discourses of friendship and hostility between settlers and tribes in their storylines, looking toward the resurgence of social commentary in sympathetic westerns and frontier *noir* films from major studios in the 1950s, while also adopting some of the gender politics of the singing cowboy films of the 1930s.

In Chapter 3, "Neglected Western Traditions and Indigenous Cinema in the 1945–46 Series Westerns of Wallace Fox," Jacob Floyd examines Fox's westerns of a later period, specifically those starring Kirby Grant. In addition to examining Fox's use of stock footage against its initial purpose, Floyd provides insight into how the Grant film series demonstrates neglected and progressive traditions.

Chapters 4, 5, and 6 move the discussion to the horror genre, in which Fox worked only rarely, but quite memorably, particularly given how much attention the work of Bela Lugosi and Lon Chaney, Jr. still receives. In "*The Corpse Vanishes* and the Case of the Missing Brides" Gary D. Rhodes analyzes how

The Corpse Vanishes (1942), with Bela Lugosi, activates generic past practice, resulting in the convergence of three important trajectories of horror entertainment: (A) the intrepid and fast-talking female newspaper journalist who investigates and documents weird goings-on that, (B) under scrutiny invoke the vampiric more than the scientific, all being the work of (C) a bizarre and insane family. Here is a brew that percolates with more possibilities than any test tube in the mad scientist's laboratory, combining elements of the past into a unique formula that was prescient of horror movies to come.

In "'Like a crazy nightmare': Noirish Vampirism and Deviance in *Bowery at Midnight*" Marlisa Santos interrogates another of Fox's collaborations with Bela Lugosi, one in which surrealistic, logic-stretched aspects of the film set it apart from conventional B-picture horror fare and place it squarely as a weirdly compelling *noir*, in the same—albeit less polished—vein as Boris Ingster's *Stranger on the Third Floor* (1940) and Jacques Tourneur's *Cat People* (1942). From the opening scenes showing Lugosi as a seemingly charitable soup kitchen proprietor, Fox capitalizes on viewer associations with his vampire roles, making the ensuing narrative about underground criminal networks, drug addiction, and class privilege much deeper than those of typical scare features and displaying the unapologetically violent, logic-averse, and morally ambiguous elements of film noir that would come to define the cycle.

Murray Leeder concludes the trio of horror film chapters with "Voices and Vaults: *Pillow of Death*." In it, Leeder argues for the last of Universal's Inner Sanctum series, *Pillow of Death* (1945), with Lon Chaney Jr., as an unusual and ambiguous treatment of the cinematic supernatural. After establishing the film's place within traditions of films involving spiritualism, the chapter provides close readings of three scenes in which characters investigate apparently supernatural phenomena. The chapter observes that ambiguous uses of POV shots and sound cues place the film formally within Tzvetan Todorov's category of the Fantastic, even as the script on its own seems more inclined towards the Fantastic-Uncanny.

In Chapter 7, on "Wallace Fox and America's 'Career Girls,'" David J. Hogan investigates the director's work in what was sometimes called the "women's picture." His chapter looks at those movies—*The Girl from Monterrey* (1943), *Career Girl* (1944), and *Men on Her Mind* (1944)—as 1) discrete creative projects; 2) exemplars of America's growing interest in working women; and 3) revealers of American attitudes about women. For Hogan, Fox's career-girl trilogy focuses on professional ambition, much as Fox himself diligently pursued his professional career, coping endlessly with challenges posed by minuscule budgets, and laboring to succeed.

Fox's work with the "women's picture" was not limited to feature films, however, as Sara Rutkowski researches with "She Made Her Own Deadline: Fox's *Brenda Starr, Reporter*." One of the last "cliffhanger" serials produced by Columbia Pictures, *Brenda Starr, Reporter* (1945) caps the era of the "girl reporter" film, a fashionable genre throughout the 1930s and early 1940s. But unlike other girl reporters portrayed as fast-talking hardboiled heroines whose encounters with their male counterparts bristle with sexual tension, Brenda Starr is notably wholesome and soft-edged. Nevertheless, she is also a driven and daring sleuth, who proves she can excel in a dangerous man's world. Rutkowski's chapter examines how the particular commercial, cultural, and aesthetic demands of the film serial format helped to create a unique version of the girl reporter as one which embodied the contradictions inherent in a burgeoning postwar society: namely, the desire both to contain women in acceptable, feminine roles and to relish their capacity for independence and ambition.

In Chapter 9, Phillip Sipiora presents "*Bathos* in the Bowery," which interrogates Fox's films in the *East Side Kids* series, an innovative collective portrait of urban New York adolescence that was produced between 1941 and 1945. These films were not unlike other contemporary portraits of rebellious youth, but what distinguishes the work of Fox is his ingenious demonstration of youthful rebellion in a complex weave of bathos and pathos that systematically reveals penetrating sociological insight into the complex, challenging cultural arena of an urban homeland during wartime. Many films from this era were patriotic efforts to boost national morale, and others appealed to respite or escapism from the stresses of war. Fox's films, however, are much more than a gesture of distancing the nation from the trauma of current events. There are common performative and cultural threads running through them, particularly Fox's deft use of intertwined bathos and pathos to entertain as well as articulate his subject matter with somber gravity.

Chapter 10 provides insight into Fox's major foray into science fiction. Michael L. Shuman's "Infernal Devices: Wallace Fox's Aeroglobe, Cosmic Beam Annihilator, and the Pit of Everlasting Fire" inspects the 1947 serial *Jack Armstrong: All American Boy*. For juvenile audience members just beginning to comprehend the puzzle and complexity of the adult world, Fox's serial provides an alternative, and simpler, solution to the problematic mechanics of living while inspiring both the thrill of heroic temperament and the wonderment of scientific progress. Fox appropriated the conventions of the B-movie serial format and, with an extensive career of producing thrills and suspense on a low budget, directed a chapter play that met the stated goals of the format admirably and, perhaps, more consistently than Hitchcock, Lang, or Chaplin fulfilled their own A-movie ambitions.

Robert Singer concludes the current volume by exploring the final stage of Fox's career, which unfolded in the nascent medium of television. Chapter 11, "A Fox in the Wild: *Ramar of the Jungle* and the Crisis of Representation," specifically delves into *Ramar of the Jungle* (1953–1954). Fox's episodes and the entire series have been pejoratively classified as ideologically circumscribed, even embarrassing narratives. Singer contends that Fox's *Ramar* episodes are not as easily catalogued as markedly racist and merit reassessment. National and international media productions from the postwar era invite intergeneric, alternative readings of the socio-political matter, while acknowledging obvious controversies. For Singer, these are *problematic*, not superficial, narratives.

Collectively, it is our hope that the essays that comprise *The Films of Wallace Fox* will add meaningfully to studies of B-movies and classical Hollywood as well as expand the purview of Indigenous film history to include B-films. Wallace Fox exemplifies the convergence of these film forms and genres that might otherwise be regarded as distinct or even disparate. While audiences and researchers from these fields begin with different kinds of working knowledge and expectations, bringing distinct approaches into juxtaposition can expand the horizons of both readerships and help all of us to reclaim the history and work of one of the first Native American film directors.

NOTES

1. Brian Taves, "The B Film: Hollywood's Other Half," in Tino Balio, *Grand Design: Hollywood as a Modern Business Enterprise, 1930–1939* (Berkeley: University of California, 1993), 313.
2. Tahmahkera, Dustin, "Hakarʉ Marʉʉmatʉ Kwitaka? Seeking Representational Jurisdiction in Comanchería Cinema," *Native American and Indigenous Studies* 5:1 (Spring 2018), 103.
3. Liza Black, *Picturing Indians: Native Americans in Film, 1941–1960* (Lincoln: University of Nebraska Press, 2020), 13.
4. See Joanna Hearne, *Native Recognition: Indigenous Cinema and the Western* (Albany, NY: SUNY Press, 2012), 151–2.
5. Taves, 314.
6. Ibid., 330.
7. See, for example, Gary D. Rhodes (ed.), *Edgar G. Ulmer: Detour on Poverty Row* (Lanham, MD: Lexington Books, 2008) and Gary D. Rhodes (ed.), *The Films of Joseph H. Lewis* (Detroit, MI: Wayne State University Press, 2008).
8. Robert F. Berkhofer, *The White Man's Indian: Images of the American Indian from Columbus to the Present* (New York: Vintage, 1979); Jacquelyn Kilpatrick, *Celluloid Indians: Native Americans in Film* (Lincoln: University of Nebraska Press, 1999); Armando José Prats, *Invisible Natives: Myth and Identity in the American Western* (Ithaca, NY: Cornell University Press, 2002); M. Elise Marubbio, *Images of Native American Women in Film* (Lexington: The University Press of Kentucky, 2006).
9. Michelle Raheja, *Reservation Reelism: Redfacing, Visual Sovereignty, and Representations of Native Americans in Film* (Lincoln: University of Nebraska Press, 2011), xxi; Black, *Picturing Indians*.
10. See, for example, new work on Cherokee humorist Will Rogers, Winnebago performer and activist Lilian St. Cyr, and Yakama consultant Nipo Strongheart, among others: Amy M. Ware, *The Cherokee Kid: Will Rogers, Tribal Identity, and the Making of an American Icon*

(Lawrence: University Press of Kansas, 2015); Linda M. Waggoner, *Starring Red Wing! The Incredible Career of Lillian St. Cyr, the First Native American Film Star* (Lincoln: University of Nebraska Press, 2019); Andrew H. Fisher, "Tinseltown Tyee: Nipo Strongheart and the Making of Braveheart," *American Indian Culture and Research Journal* 42:3 (2018), 93–118; and Nicolas G. Rosenthal, "Representing Indians: Native American Actors on Hollywood's Frontier," *The Western Historical Quarterly* 36:3 (2005). Two recent special issues on Indigenous representation and performance include the *American Indian Culture and Research Journal* on Indigenous representation, edited by Nic Rosenthal and Liza Black (42:3, 2018), and an In-Focus dossier on "Indigenous Performance Networks: Media, Community, Activism" in the *Journal of Cinema and Media Studies*, edited by Joanna Hearne with contributions from Christine Bold, Jacob Floyd, Kiara Vigil, Karrmen Crey, Jaqueline Land, and Dustin Tahmahkera (60:2, 2020).

11. Raheja, 193.
12. Philip Deloria, *Indians in Unexpected Places* (Lawrence: University Press of Kansas, 2004).
13. Hearne, "Introduction," *Journal of Cinema and Media Studies* 60:2 (2020), x. See also Hearne on re-crediting in *Native Recognition*, 179–215 and 265–6.
14. Todd McCarthy, "Introduction," in Todd McCarthy and Charles Flynn (eds), *Kings of the Bs: Working within the Studio System* (New York: E. P. Dutton, 1975), xii.

CHAPTER I

Between Compliance and Resistance: Mapping the Careers of Wallace Fox and Nipo Strongheart in Early Hollywood

Andrew H. Fisher

During the early decades of the twentieth century, Hollywood seemed to be full of chiefs but not enough Indians. Thanks to the popularity of the western genre, the film industry supported a veritable council of celluloid chiefs and sachems, who competed for work and sometimes jealously checked each other's bona fides. Many were not mere charlatans or pretenders, but popular expectations compelled them to adopt colorful stage names and even to assemble whole personas of dubious authenticity. Among the notables were Chief Big Bear, Chief Black Hawk, Chief Blue Eagle, Chief Buffalo Child Long Lance, Chief Francis Sitting Eagle, Chief Red Fox, Chief Running Horse, Chief Standing Bear, Chief Thunderbird, Chief Young Turtle, and at least three Chief White Eagles. Others performed under such imposing titles as Chief Darkcloud, Chief John Big Tree, Chief Many Treaties, Chief Strongheart, and Chief Yowlachie.[1] By the late 1920s, "Hollywood Indians" had become so commonplace that a Wyoming newspaper could sarcastically describe them as a distinctive type:

> He is a male person, so eager for work "in the movies" that he even jumps at the chance to take off his clothes, dab 95 percent of his body surface with an unpleasant red compound that is disagreeable to wear—besides temporarily ruining [the] bathtub—and run about the Hollywood environs with a thousand of his kind, wearing only a few feathers, in blazing sun or shivering cold.[2]

There were some women as well, including Princess Redwing and Princess Tsianina Red Feather. The latter, a Cherokee-Creek singer, reportedly caused a local "Indian shortage" in the fall of 1927 when she summoned all the Native performers in town to participate in a four-night extravaganza of "ceremonials" at the Hollywood Bowl.[3]

Thanks to this pageant, director Wallace Fox had difficulty finding sufficient extras to wrap up the shooting of FBO's *The Riding Renegade*, starring cowboy actor Bob Steele. According to the *Roosevelt Standard*, Princess Tsianina's event at the Hollywood Bowl took virtually all of the Indians away from the studios and made it necessary for Steele and Fox to "combine the hinterland of Hollywood for three days to get enough Indians for the scenes in the production." Apparently, Fox could not wait for the pageant to conclude and chose not to participate himself, despite his Chickasaw ancestry and the good cause to which it contributed; namely, "to raise funds to build an Indian village near Los Angeles where the vanishing Americans can carry on their arts and crafts."[4] He had a schedule to keep, and he would soon acquire a reputation for finishing his movies on time and under budget.[5]

The Riding Renegade, which opened in February 1928, was Fox's third film as lead director and one of six he released that year alone. Such a high rate of productivity did not lend itself to auteurism, artistry, or concern for authenticity. It also suggests the different choices made by one Native film professional at a time when Hollywood expected and rewarded stereotypical presentations of Indianness both on and off screen. While his brothers Edwin Carewe and Finis Fox collaborated to create *Ramona* (1928), a lavishly produced and critically acclaimed epic about the plight of California Indians, Wallace Fox began a long and prolific career churning out B-movies. Between 1927 and 1938, he directed sixteen westerns and served as assistant director on *The Last of the Mohicans* (1936). Of those films, only the latter and *The Riding Renegade* featured Native Americans in any significant way. The rest were conventional B-westerns, with bandits, kidnappers, robbers, or rustlers as the villains and Indians conspicuously absent. Significantly, Native Americans provide heroic backup in *The Riding Renegade*, but none of Fox's early movies made them the protagonists or the focal point of the story. If he was interested in advancing what Michelle Raheja calls "visual sovereignty," it is not readily or consistently apparent within his body of work.[6] Whether we should read that choice as capitulation to the dominant discourse of early American cinema, or whether Fox's career encourages us to expand our understanding of Indigenous filmmaking, is one of the central concerns of this chapter.

Fox presents a particularly interesting case because, unlike many of his contemporaries, he did not engage in obvious forms of "redfacing" either as a director or as a member of the Los Angeles Indian community. Most Hollywood Indians of his generation worked in front of the camera, taking the roles assigned them by the cinematic conventions and cultural discourses of the day. They played their part as Savages or Noble Savages, Vanishing Red Men, and Romantic Primitives in scenarios written by and for members of the dominant society. In public appearances as well, they often donned paint and feathers to satisfy the expectations of white audiences, which generally assumed their inherent backwardness and imminent demise. As Raheja notes, these acts of redfacing performed cultural and ideological work with subversive potential, "even if they lead through what appears to be negative self-fashioning." Especially in the early twentieth century, she argues, Hollywood Indians often functioned as "trickster figures" who simultaneously enacted and critiqued stereotypical representations of Indianness. Fox presents an even more ambiguous and ambivalent figure, one who "illustrates the intricacy of archival retrieval in the face of the complex histories of Native presence in the film industry and in film audiences across the span of the twentieth century." On the one hand, he had clearer connections to a living Indigenous community than did some of those who gathered at the Hollywood Bowl, and he could readily access the Native networks that permeated Los Angeles. On the other hand, Fox often passed as white and largely passed up the opportunity to use his Chickasaw heritage as a promotional vehicle.[7]

Unfortunately, his reasons for doing so are opaque, as he did not leave behind a collection of personal papers or publications and did not receive much attention from the contemporary press. We simply cannot know with certainty how he perceived himself and his work in Hollywood. What is clear from Fox's filmography is that he managed to find steady employment directing movies during a period when Native Americans generally had little creative control within the film industry. Fox certainly faced powerful constraints in the form of western genre conventions and B-movie production standards.[8] As a director, though, he may have enjoyed a level of power in the studio that most Hollywood Indians could only imagine. Unlike James Young Deer, and to a lesser extent his brother Edwin, Fox did not use that position to create alternative images and narratives concerning Native Americans. For the most part, his early films had no overt pedagogical purpose, activist agenda, or artistic pretensions to match the likes of *Ramona*. Yet, insofar as Fox had the ability to select and shape his productions, he avoided indulging the popular appetite for tropes of Indian savagery and doomed nobility. As such, he escaped the confines of Raheja's "virtual reservation" and resisted the typecasting of Native film professionals. In that sense, we can see Fox as a trickster, shielding himself and his people from the colonial gaze even as he made movies that otherwise suited dominant assumptions about the American West and prevailing tastes in western cinema.[9]

Regardless of his personal motives and perceptions of his own work, Fox deserves recognition as a pioneering Native filmmaker during the Golden Age of American cinema. He was part of a much larger cohort of Hollywood Indians, but one of only a handful to rise beyond the rank of actor or extra in the early decades of the twentieth century.[10] The Fox brothers were particularly successful in that regard. Edwin and Wallace became directors, while Finis wrote numerous screenplays and directed one film. Other Indians of their generation worked as technical advisors, which provided opportunities to engage in a kind of artistic activism. Although they lacked creative control, they could nudge movie productions in the direction of greater authenticity, accuracy, and sympathy in their representation of American Indian cultures and histories. Native technical advisors rarely received much attention or credit, but their invisible labor in film studios represented an early attempt to exert Indigenous influence over the narrative and to communicate ideas with potential to empower Native Americans. Even when they failed to do so, their presence complicates and enhances our understanding of the Hollywood Indian. "They were there," argues historian Liza Black, "and that should matter at least as much as the discursive battle going on over filmic representations of Indians."[11]

One of these unsung activists was Nipo Strongheart, a celluloid chief who came to Hollywood during the Silent Era and stayed for more than forty years. He never became famous and often struggled to earn a living, yet he worked on numerous productions through the heyday of the Western genre and made meaningful contributions to several proto-revisionist Indian films. It was often frustrating work, because it required negotiating the paradoxical demands of Hollywood studios. Some producers and directors sought the stamp of authenticity for their films by hiring Native technical advisors, who presumably possessed special knowledge of Indian cultures. Once on the job, though, these technical advisors frequently struggled against their employers' preconceived notions of Indianness. "For filmmakers," writes Black, "Native employees had to present ideas and cultural objects radically different from anything with which white Americans were familiar, yet those ideas had to simulate or build on what white people already believed they knew about Indians." As someone determined to challenge these assumptions, Strongheart provides an interesting counterpoint to Fox, who occupied a different part of "the space between resistance and compliance" wherein Native film professionals engaged with settler society's expectations.[12]

Taken together, their careers allow us to see Hollywood Indians as agents of film history, rather than merely as objects of the colonial gaze. Moving beyond studies that emphasize settler constructions, scholars such as Liza Black, Philip Deloria, Jacob Floyd, Joanna Hearne, Michelle Raheja, Linda Scarangella McNenly, and Kiara Vigil have started to investigate how Native Americans themselves disrupted the dominant discourse and negotiated the terms of representation. Like other "contact zones" where Indigenous people engaged with non-Indigenous audiences and expectations, the movie industry presents "a site for the investigation of agency and of the negotiation of social meanings and representations of Native identity."[13] Such investigations are crucial to overcome the logic of elimination that still dominates both Hollywood films and academic studies concerning Native Americans in the movies. As Black explains,

> Failing to document Indian presence in film implicitly endorses the myth of the vanishing Indian, thereby implying that Indian people did not survive settler colonialism. Recognizing Indian involvement in films decolonizes film studies and challenges the unexpectedness of their presence in twentieth-century films.[14]

Fox and Strongheart alike worked within the constraints of a studio system that marginalized Indians, but with different means and ends, and with different public personas. While Strongheart eagerly played Indian and pursued representational reform through prestige pictures, Fox downplayed his Native identity and labored in the relative obscurity of the B-movie system. Neither is widely known today, even among film scholars, and only Strongheart routinely receives mention in the same breath as other Hollywood Indians. It is my contention that Fox warrants inclusion in a cohort that, to quote Raheja, "set the stage for later generations of Indigenous artists who would borrow from, contest, and operate in dialogue with images produced by this first generation of film actors and directors."[15]

WALLACE FOX

Fox and Strongheart came of age at a time when the future of Native Americans seemed in doubt—indeed, when most whites assumed Indian people would soon die out as distinct cultures within the United States. From the 1880s to the 1920s, federal policies pushed to complete the settler colonial project of elimination through religious conversion, compulsory education, and land redistribution. In the name of "Americanization," mission and boarding schools attempted to strip away the languages and customs of Native children, so that they could be remade in the white man's image. The 1887 Dawes Act intensified the assault on Indigenous families and communities through the allotment of reservations and the sale of "surplus" lands to non-Indians. Meanwhile, world's fairs and Wild West shows presumably gave Americans and Europeans their last opportunities to see the "Vanishing Race" in all its primitive splendor, at least until motion pictures began recording Native cultures for posterity. In 1894, Thomas Edison shot the first footage of American Indians in his New Jersey studio. Specifically, he filmed Lakotas supposedly performing the Ghost Dance, which just a few years earlier had triggered the carnage of the Wounded Knee Massacre. Modern technology would ostensibly help preserve the final, fleeting vestiges of a people unable to adapt to modernity.[16]

Fox was born soon after Edison premiered his new Kinetoscope. On March 9, 1895, Frank Marion and Sarah Priddy Fox had their third son in the town of Purcell, located within the Chickasaw Nation in Indian Territory. Wallace's father was a former Confederate officer turned farmer, businessman, and lawyer, who had settled in the area during the 1870s. His mother was a "half-breed" Chickasaw, in the parlance of the time, and the daughter of a prominent local cattleman. In the language of blood quantum, the federal government's pseudo-scientific system of racial classification, their boys were one-sixteenth Chickasaw. The 1900 U.S. census identified them as "Indian," but it is unclear how much they learned about Chickasaw culture and history before entering the Euro-American school system. Their mother had a college education, and both Finis and Jay (later Edwin Carewe) attended university when Wallace was still a boy. He went to military school in San Antonio, Texas, and by 1910 he and his parents had temporarily relocated to Corpus Christi. Finis served several terms in the Chickasaw Nation's legislature during Wallace's youth, though, so he likely grew up with some awareness of the challenges facing their people.[17]

Around the turn of the century, the Chickasaws and other tribes in Indian Territory found themselves once more in the path of American expansion. During the 1830s, Chickasaw leaders had accepted removal from their ancestral homelands in present-day Mississippi with the understanding that they could live undisturbed in their new home. By the early 1890s, however, white settlers had begun pressing on the nation's borders and squatting on its land. Two years before Fox's birth, the Secretary of the Interior reported the presence of some 49,000 whites and only 3,000 Indians within Chickasaw territory. The region quickly became notorious for banditry and lawlessness because tribal governments lacked jurisdiction over non-Indian intruders and federal law enforcement was thin on the ground. In 1895, several mixed-race gangs committed a string of robberies, murders, and rapes across Indian Territory. Perhaps childhood stories of those wild and wooly days influenced Fox's later cinematic interest in western outlaws and gave him an imprimatur of authority on the subject. The greatest crime being perpetrated, though, was the theft of tribal lands in Indian Territory. In 1897, the Atoka Agreement compelled the Choctaws and Chickasaws to take allotments and provided for the opening of their "surplus" acreage for sale. The following year, the Curtis Act ratified that agreement and paved the way for Oklahoma statehood by abolishing tribal courts, establishing public schools, and extending federal jurisdiction over the former Indian Territory.[18]

On the Dawes Rolls, which enumerated the people eligible for tribal enrollment and allotments, the Fox brothers appear as "Chickasaw by Blood." Given their ancestry and background, they could have made passable celluloid chiefs. Certainly, other Hollywood Indians made do with less, wringing every last drop of cachet and credibility from highly attenuated or even imaginary bloodlines. For the most part, though, the available evidence suggests that the Fox siblings rarely drew attention to their Native heritage. By 1920, when a census enumerator visited Wallace and his wife Cleo Easton at their Los Angeles address, he identified himself as white. Newspaper stories almost never noted his Chickasaw affiliation—even when he was out scouring the Hollywood Hills for Indian extras—and he did not present himself as a chief. By contrast, the Chickasaw actor William F. Harrison regularly performed as Chief Young Turtle in plays and pageants around Los Angeles. He likely represented the Chickasaws at the Hollywood Bowl pageant, along with a young opera singer known as Princess Lou-scha-enya, the "Hummingbird of the Chickasaws." She was neither a true princess nor "full-blooded," but savvy Hollywood Indians often claimed both a pure bloodline and a royal lineage because it enhanced their appeal to white audiences.[19]

The Fox brothers were not ashamed of their Native ancestry, and they invoked it selectively to help promote particular movies or underscore their authority on Indian subjects. In 1927, for example, *The Los Angeles Times* interviewed Finis Fox regarding his script for Edwin Carewe's remake of *Ramona*. "Very appropriately," the reporter wrote, "the adapter of 'Ramona' to the screen has a little of the red man's blood in his own veins. And Finis Fox is very proud of his descent from the peace-loving Chickasaws." His youngest brother Wallace echoed that sentiment in 1945, following the release of *Song of the Range*, when a newspaper story said that Wallace was "proud of a percentage of Choctaw" and "claim[s] that a dash of Indian helps to put zip into a 'western.'" As the mistaken tribal affiliation suggests, reporters and critics may well have exaggerated or even invented such statements to suit their own essentialist notions of Indian identity. However, it is probable that these declarations of pride accurately reflected the brothers' own views as well as their knack for promotion. Like other Hollywood Indians of their day, the Foxes had adapted to white society and lived far from home. After they settled in Los Angeles, whatever ties they had to the Chickasaw community in Oklahoma grew more tenuous, and being Indian became more abstract. Just "a dash" of Chickasaw blood was enough to pitch certain movies without having it circumscribe or define their larger body of work.[20]

Although the racial position and politics of the Fox brothers are difficult to discern in the absence of much direct evidence, we can speculate based on their background and the dominant discourse among Native American intellectuals at the time. During the early 1920s, when the brothers launched their film careers, the rhetoric of pan-Indian leaders generally emphasized universalist themes of racial progress and uplift. Members of the Society of American Indians (SAI) differed over the merits of specific policies and the desirability of full assimilation, but they largely agreed that their "race" could and must become full, competent citizens of the United States. "In formulating their positions," argues Lucy Maddox, "the SAI spokespersons had essentially to demonstrate to their audience, especially their white audience, that Indians were not constrained or determined by their racial identification." Prominent among these spokespersons were representatives of the "Five Civilized Tribes" of Oklahoma, such as Cherokee writer John Milton Oskison and Chickasaw politician Charles Carter. Oskison urged the public to embrace the "modern Indian" as a "new man," one who remained "Indian only in blood and traditions." Carter, who briefly served on the Chickasaw Council before winning election as a Democrat to the U.S. House of Representatives, helped pass the Indian Citizenship Act of 1924. For them, race was not a permanent bar to Native American advancement, as it seemed to be for African Americans. Rather, as Oskison wrote optimistically, "prejudice simply does not exist among people who can make or mar a career . . . The Indian who fits himself for the company of those at the top will go up. He will go up swiftly and surely as his white brother."[21]

Such sentiments would have appealed to the Fox brothers as they fitted themselves to ascend the professional ladder into the upper echelons of Hollywood society. By presenting as "civilized" Indians, practically white in both appearance and culture, they forsook the allure of "full-blooded" celluloid chiefs but also escaped the stigma associated with visible markers of racial difference. They could pass as white people, if they chose to do so, yet still lay claim to special knowledge of Indians through their family history and "blood memory." That liminal position—simultaneously precarious and privileged—had been staked out by elite members of the Five Tribes almost a century before the Foxes arrived in Hollywood. As the light-skinned children of a "mixed-blood" Chickasaw and a former Confederate soldier, they likely grew up sensitized to the importance of emphasizing their white ancestry within a local racial hierarchy that accorded few rights to African American freedmen and their descendants. Within the Hollywood Indian community as well, white admixture passed muster while allegations of black ancestry produced scandal and disgrace, as demonstrated by the sad fate of Chief Buffalo Child Long Lance. The Fox brothers could expect to "go up," as Oskison said, if they did not make too much of their Native heritage in a world that still placed Indianness at odds with modernity.[22]

And up they went. By the early 1930s, Wallace Fox was happily hobnobbing with other movie moguls at the exclusive Embassy Club and Montmartre Café, located on a glitzy section of Hollywood Boulevard. He was among 117 studio notables arrested there in October 1931, when the Los Angeles vice squad raided the establishments to shut down an illegal gambling operation. In some newspaper stories, Fox was one of the few mentioned by name, in the same breath as actors Harry Carey and Joseph De La Motte, directors Robert G. Vignola and Robert Hill, theater manager Marvin Park, and orchestra leader Gene Morgan. Such illustrious (if bad) company suggests that Fox had indeed reached the higher rungs of Hollywood society just a few years after his directorial debut. He had also achieved acceptance as something other than a curiosity. Significantly, none of the newspaper coverage made an issue of his Native heritage or even mentioned it. Despite the presence of illegal alcohol and even "drunks" passed out under gaming tables, there were no smirking, suggestive references to his Indian ancestry. He was simply a director, one of the boys, arrested at a studio "stag party" where bigwigs talked business over cards and roulette.[23]

At the same time, Fox's "dash" of Indian blood gave him an entrée to the "Native hubs" that united the diverse and diffuse American Indian community in Los Angeles. Building on Renya K. Ramirez's ethnographic concept, which emphasized the connections between urban centers and distant reservations, Jacob Floyd suggests that Native hubs also formed within metropolitan areas. In Los Angeles, commercial, intellectual, and social networks radiated out from Hollywood like spokes on a wheel, serving "to connect Native people separated from each other by the physical and subjective geographies of urban life." These hubs had begun to form even before the film industry relocated to California, as Native people from across the state and beyond moved to the City of Angels in search of employment. The 1920 federal censuses listed 183 Indian adults and 35 children in Los Angeles County, while an untold number of others escaped enumeration or chose—like Wallace Fox—to pass as white. By 1930, the official population of Native Americans had grown to 236 adults and 133 children, with around 20 percent hailing from Oklahoma. Others came and went periodically, like Humming Bird and her Osage husband, perhaps carrying news from back home to friends and relatives in Los Angeles.[24]

As the Indian community grew, its disparate members developed overlapping associations that provided both personal comfort and professional opportunity. During the 1920s, Native actors began hosting regular parties or "powwows" at their homes, which often became hubs in their own right. A 1926 gala at Luther Standing Bear's house in Culver City reportedly attracted more than 2,000 guests, including "Indians from every part of Los Angeles," and one wonders if the Fox brothers made an appearance. Hollywood Indians also joined or founded an array of charitable and fraternal organizations, such as the American Indian Order and the Wigwam Club. These groups witnessed their share of debate and scandal, often surrounding issues of race and sex, but they gave Hollywood Indians additional venues in which to socialize and network. Starting in 1928, the Wigwam Club hosted an annual picnic in Sycamore Grove Park, where people from many different tribes mingled and sampled each other's foods, dances, and handicrafts. That same year, Edwin Carewe announced plans for his own "ultra-exclusive screen colony club" composed of "the ultra-Americans of filmdom . . . an ultra-American being defined as one with American Indian ancestry." Among those invited to join were Will Rogers, Monte Blue, Al Roscoe, Finis Fox, and Wallace Fox.[25]

Fox may have tapped into these social networks when searching for Indian extras to appear in *The Riding Renegade*. That production was the only one of his early films to feature Indians as a plot device, and it is notable that he took the time to track down Native performers. Many B-western directors would not have bothered, as studios routinely hired non-Indians to play both leading roles and background parts. In 1926, western actor William S. Hart complained that, "since the motion pictures have become controlled by business interests they do not go in for the real thing so much. They use Mexicans for Indians and there a great many Mexicans in this country."[26] Even so, film audiences and critics appreciated seeing real Indians and praised productions that featured them as more authentic, even as they often heaped derision on the Native actors themselves. Witness a review of George B. Seitz's 1925 epic, *The Vanishing American*, which applauded the fact that

> Indians, themselves, act parts of considerable importance. Indian babies play Indian baby roles, and in one case a child so young it could not speak plainly was required in several minutes of camera close-ups, and it is one of the favorite stories of Seitz—that of the tedious time experienced in feeding the little Redskin chocolate candies in between scenes to keep it good humored and awake.

The reviewer went on to say, "Almost every moment of it you believe. This is true because almost every foot of its action may very well have happened. And most of it actually did happen."[27] Paramount shelled out big money to shoot that film on location in Navajo Country, though, whereas B-movie directors had to make do with low budgets and local resources.

Why did Fox make the effort to track down Native extras for a film that lacked not only the overhead but also the artistic aspirations of *The Vanishing American* or *Ramona*? One intriguing possibility is that he knew hiring non-Indians could antagonize his compatriots in the Hollywood Indian community. In 1926, Indian actors had organized the War Paint Club, which despite its stereotypical name pursued the serious mission of advancing their interests within the film industry. Initially headquartered in the home of Mary and Daniel Simmons, who performed as White Bird and Chief Yowlache, the club assembled a list of "authentic" Native performers for distribution to the studios. The club's purpose was to ensure employment for actual Indigenous people, rather than "pretendians," as well as to save the studios from potential embarrassment by the employment of charlatans. In effect, Floyd explains, "it became a casting agency for Native talent, and White Bird was its casting director," reputedly able to procure as many as 150 Indians at short notice. By 1927, when Famous Players-Lasky Corporation handed Fox his first directing assignment, he must have known about the War Paint Club and may have sympathized with its grievances. If so, calling White Bird on the phone would have been the practical way to go about locating Indian extras for his production.[28]

Unfortunately, because no copies of *The Riding Renegade* have survived, it is difficult to assess the level of verisimilitude Fox achieved in terms of casting and costuming those extras. According to one newspaper story about the production, the script called specifically for Apaches, but the promotional materials show generic Plains tribesmen in buckskins and feathered war bonnets. Advertisements and reviews simply refer to them as Indians, and the film's setting is described vaguely as "the Western bad lands" or "desert." In any case, Fox did not employ more than a "score" of cowboys and Indians, though he apparently used them effectively "to give the proper background to this thrilling story." None of them are credited, so we cannot know which tribes they came from or whether their names appeared on White Bird's list of approved Native performers. We also do not know the wages they received for their work, which goes to the question of whether Fox prioritized his budget over the demands for pay equity coming from the War Paint Club. He certainly followed studio practice in hiring non-Indians for the two named Native characters. The role of Chief White Cloud went to Nicholas Tamborello, an Italian American who performed as Nick Thompson, while a Greek immigrant called Pedro Regas (or Riga, born Panagiotis Thomas Regaskos) played the part of Little Wolf (Figure I.1).[29]

White Cloud and Little Wolf are not the protagonists of *The Riding Renegade*, but it is unique among Fox's early films in affording Native Americans a significant and sympathetic place in the story. The hero, Bob Taylor (played by Bob Steele), is the son of a sheriff but "runs away from home to become a wanderer of the wastelands." After he saves the life of Little Wolf out in the desert, the young man's tribe adopts Bob, causing his own father to disown him for "going native." He then discovers that bandits have been robbing the Indians, and he sets out with Little Wolf to foil the gang's latest plot to stick up a stagecoach carrying a strongbox and Bob's love interest, Janet Reynolds. The duo secures Janet and the strongbox, only to have Sheriff Taylor arrest them for robbery, which allows the villains to escape with the loot after wounding Little Wolf. The sheriff soon realizes his error and goes in pursuit of the bandits, but they take him prisoner and are about to kill him when Bob and his Native friends come to the rescue. The Indians, not the cavalry, save the day. Still, wrote one reviewer, "Steele is the whole show. He is a three-ring circus in himself, riding, roping, shooting and making love with the same fine grace and skill he displayed in his previous picture."[30]

Although neither original nor bold in its positive treatment of Native Americans, *The Riding Renegade* stands nearly alone among Fox's early

Spirit of the West Film
at the Hippodrome Today

BOB Steele in "The Riding Renegade"

The spirit of the great West, with its hardy pioneers, Indians and cow boys, has been successfully transferred to the screen in "The Ridinhg Renegade," an FBO Western picture starring Bob Steele, which is now on view at the Hippodrome theatre. In the cast supporting young Steele are Lafe McKee, Bob Fleming, Ethan Laidlaw, Nick Thompson and Pedro Riga.

Figure 1.1 Newspaper advertisement for *The Riding Renegade*, *Bakersfield Morning Echo* (Bakersfield, California), 4 February 1928.

films in its engagement with themes of racial transgression and "going native." The trope of the white man who befriends Indians, or becomes one of them, was already familiar to contemporary audiences. They would not have found shocking promotional taglines such as "Red Man or White!" or "Why did he turn renegade and live with the Indians?" In focusing on the injustices done to Indigenous peoples and the power of racial prejudice, however, *The Riding Renegade* echoed other, more famous films of the Silent Era in their calls for reform. It was thus of a piece with both *Ramona* and the Meriam Report, which in 1928 publicized the scandalous state of Indian affairs in the United States. That parallel alone hardly qualifies Fox as an activist director, as his film also aligns with other contemporary westerns that told stories of white absolution and cultural appropriation. *The Riding Renegade* was also effectively a one-off for Fox, though *Trapped in Tijuana* (1932) flirted with issues of boundary crossing and interracial love. Even so, the film can be read as an act of "aesthetic diplomacy," one of the few instances in which Fox overtly talked back to colonial discourse and in defense of Native Americans.[31]

The bulk of his own cinematic output over the next ten years was devoted to comedic shorts, romantic adventure films, and B-westerns. Of the latter, the majority were conventional cowboy and gunfighter movies such as *Near the Trail's End* (1931), *Powdersmoke Range* (1935), and *The Mexicali Kid* (1938). None of them depicted Native Americans or referenced Indian issues, except for an allusion in *Trapped in Tijuana* to Mexican Yaquis who are wrongfully accused of kidnapping an American boy. Their general absence from Fox's early productions constitutes a form of erasure, but it can also be explained more benignly or even interpreted as a kind of passive resistance. As a cog in the B-movie machine, Fox may not have exercised much control over which films he directed or the scripts that studio producers chose to make. He also likely recognized that B-westerns did not offer much space for grand artistic or political statements. They were intended as cheap entertainment, and he excelled primarily at making them cheaply. In the process, he made a good living for himself and avoided the pitfall of being branded an "Indian director" in a business that barely allowed Native people to act. If he turned away from artistic activism, though, he also refused to indulge the dominant society's insatiable appetite for images of Indian dysfunction, savagery, and stoicism in the face of inevitable annihilation. From that perspective, Fox also engaged in redfacing "as a kind of virtual, visual prophylactic that keeps Native American cultural and spiritual practices somewhat sacrosanct, or at least hidden from the white tourist gaze."[32]

That does not fully absolve him of complicity in the perpetuation of problematic tropes, however, as seen through his involvement with the 1936 screen adaptation of *The Last of the Mohicans*. To be fair, as an associate director to George Seitz, Fox had limited creative influence on the production. It is also true that James Fenimore Cooper's original story gave them little room to maneuver around the biggest stumbling block in Native American cinema—the Vanishing Indian myth—even if Seitz had been so inclined. The film trips over many of the others as well. Set against the backdrop of the French and Indian War, it features a heroic white Indian (Hawkeye) and his noble savage allies (Chingachgook and his son Uncas), an evil savage villain (Magua), and a pair of damsels in distress (Alice and Cora, the daughters of a British colonel). Ultimately, the good guys win, but at great cost to themselves and the movie Indian's image. Uncas dies after saving Cora, his newfound love, and she leaps to her death in grief. Thus, a lasting cross-race romance is averted and the extinction of the Mohicans is assured, while Hawkeye and Alice survive to build a bright future on the American frontier. Fox could hardly have altered the film's ending or underlying message, but he did collaborate with Seitz in bringing this saga of settler colonialism to the screen.

Without access to production records, it is difficult to say precisely how Fox contributed to what some critics have called the most successful film adaptation of Cooper's novel. Most likely, he used his logistical expertise and managerial skills as a maker of B-movies to help the production run as efficiently as possible. Perhaps Fox even deserves a share of the glory that went to assistant director Clem Beauchamp, who received an Academy Award nomination for his work on the film. If Fox had a hand in casting decisions, he might also claim some credit (albeit indirectly and negatively) for the subsequent formation of the Indian Actors Association (IAA), which succeeded the War Paint Club in 1936. According to Bill Hazlett, a Blackfeet who served as the Association's first chairman, "when [the studios] were casting *The Last of the Mohicans*, some of us noticed that Indians were underbidding each other just so they could get work." The IAA organized to "stop the movie producers from encouraging and allowing this price cutting," and it went on to achieve some important victories for Native performers in Hollywood. Did Fox side with labor or management in this dispute? Was he upset or conflicted when, as usual, non-Indians landed all the credited Native roles? We may never know the answer to these questions. Judging from Fox's cinematic oeuvre, however, it seems safe to conclude that advancing Indian causes either locally or nationally took a back seat to making movies and making a good living in Hollywood.[33]

NIPO STRONGHEART

In contrast to Wallace Fox, for Nipo Strongheart, the play was the thing wherein to capture the conscience of the nation. During a career that overlapped temporally with Fox's, Strongheart self-consciously embodied the Indian imaginary for the express purpose of asserting Native rights and challenging white racism, while also affirming his own identity. Born in May 1891 to a white father (George Mitchell) and a Yakama mother (Leonora Williams), Strongheart began life as George Mitchell, Jr., a "mixed-blood" who spent most of his childhood far from the Yakama reservation in south-central Washington. The lifelong process of embracing and embellishing his Native heritage began in 1902, when he and his father signed on as trick riders with Buffalo Bill's Wild West Show. By his own account, the troupe's Lakota performers dubbed him Nipo (supposedly derived from Nee-Hah-Pouw, "Messenger of Light") after he fell from a horse, then "came back" from the dead. The translation is incorrect, but he stuck with it and later added both the title of chief and the surname Strongheart, probably after seeing the eponymous William DeMille play that he would later help remake for the screen. This knack for appropriation and invention remained a hallmark of his career after he left the Wild West in 1904 to work in theater. By 1917, he had appeared in productions of *The Heart of We-to-Na* and other plays that reputedly "interpreted the romance and poetry of the Red Man with skill and fidelity." American entry into World

War I brought additional opportunities to perform as a paid lecturer on behalf of bond drives and military recruiting, which "Chief" Strongheart parlayed into regular employment on the lyceum and Chautauqua circuits.[34]

During the early 1920s, life on the lecture circuit gave him the chance to blend performance with political action, as well as to connect with Native communities around the United States. His rigorous touring schedule made him an ideal field representative for the Society of American Indians, an intertribal organization broadly committed to racial uplift and policy reform. Part of Strongheart's mandate was to cultivate support among influential whites and distribute petitions in support of Indian citizenship. During his travels, however, he also visited reservations and other Indigenous enclaves to report on their needs, recruit members, and render whatever assistance he could in the moment. These experiences opened his eyes to the severe problems confronting Indian Country in the 1920s, and enabled him to claim expertise as an ethnographer, which became part of his résumé in Hollywood. He then fed his observations back into his lectures, using specific examples of government corruption and mistreatment to sharpen his critique of the "Indian Bureau System." His penchant for naming names repeatedly got him into trouble with the Office of Indian Affairs—including threats of arrest and his temporary dismissal from the Chautauqua circuit in 1923—but it also infused his performances with a purpose higher than mere entertainment. Shrugging off the danger to his career, he defiantly declared, "I am still *going on and my arrows are dipped in truth* and they make mighty weapons against the enemy."[35]

Strongheart also began acting in movies during this period. After appearing in early pictures with the Philadelphia-based Lubin Company around 1905, he took a series of uncredited roles in western shorts such as *The White Chief* (1908), *The Bandit King* (1912), and *The Crisis* (1916). He also claimed to have advised David Belasco on the screen adaptation of *The Heart of Wetona* (1919), but the exact nature of his contributions is murky. These productions steeped Strongheart in the melodramatic mode that framed cinematic portrayals of the "Vanishing Red Man," and he grew to resent such films and the people who made them. In 1920, for example, he rejected the advances of the "Wyandote Indian Film Corporation" when it "tried to rope [him] into buying stock and go out soliciting trade for them. . ." Although the company's representative purported to be "a half breed Wyandote [*sic*]," Strongheart thought she looked "very much from the place where the shamrock grows. Anyway they try to tell me that they are going to make movies about Indians and their primitive life. I can see another mind poisoning movie that will make a savage of my dear Red Brothers." His own racial assumptions and insecurities aside, he recognized that Native Americans needed to get behind the camera if they hoped to shift the discourse concerning their past, present, and future in America.[36]

His big break came in 1925, when Cecil B. DeMille's studio hired him as the technical advisor for its remake of the 1914 film adaptation of *Strongheart*. It was one of several movies chosen to establish DeMille's reputation as an independent producer, and he recruited top talent from his former company to ensure its success. True to Hollywood form, a non-Indian star named Rod La Rocque landed the leading role, with Tyrone Power cast as his father. Strongheart, who sometimes mocked his own small stature and thinning hair, no longer looked "Indian" enough to play the strapping hero. While his onscreen presence was limited to the minor part of "Medicine Man," he had important things to do behind the scenes.[37]

One of his first assignments as technical advisor was to help select a title that would distinguish the movie from the original screen version. A few days after he signed the contract, production editor Elmer Harris asked "our Indian friend" what he thought of the title *Braveheart* as an alternative. Strongheart was initially non-plussed, stating that he had "never heard of that as the name of an Indian," whereas his own surname connoted the virtues of "patience, courage, bravery and sacrifice." Of the other possibilities they discussed—including *The American*, *Race*, *The Red Barrier*, *The Savage Gentleman*, *Red and White*, *This Civilization*, and *"But Not Our Women!"*—he actually preferred *The Redskin*.[38] Despite the term's pejorative connotations, Strongheart saw it as a more authentic choice:

> He said that the term—Redskin—is used in the Indian sign language to indicate the red man as against the white man. In the sign language, the white man is indicated by a gesture across the forehead, meaning that the white man wears a hat. The Redskin is indicated by rubbing the forefinger of the right hand on the back of the left hand, and indicates the color of the Indian's own hide.[39]

They finally settled on *Braveheart*, which Strongheart conceded "might be a good title as well as a name for the hero" (Figure 1.2). As a technical advisor, he lacked the creative control that he had possessed on the lecture circuit, but he would not stop trying to push the production in the direction of greater verisimilitude.[40]

Strongheart's commitment to constructing a historically authentic and politically pointed narrative shows most clearly in his work on the screenplay. Here again, however, his contributions were overshadowed by others who received greater compensation and credit. In March 1925, DeMille's studio had hired continuity writer Mary O'Hara (later famous for the children's novel *My Friend Flicka*) to create three scripts for a total of $18,000, one of which became *Braveheart*. In her autobiography, the "Queen Bee" makes no mention of Strongheart or the film, but a publicity photo shows

Figure 1.2 Mary O'Hara and Nipo Strongheart in a publicity photo for *Braveheart*, 1925 (Yakima Valley Museum, Yakima, WA; 2002-850-665).

them together, with her holding the script. While the exact nature of their collaboration remains fuzzy, Strongheart's fingerprints are literally all over the screenplay. Trying to ground the story in Yakama culture and history, he added details that only he could have known and even crafted whole scenes that ended up on the cutting room floor. Hollywood compromised Strongheart's vision—as it has so often done with Native artists—yet that hardly negates his agency within the production.[41]

His influence on O'Hara's screenplay is most evident in the film's setting and storyline. In the original draft, the movie opens with a scene depicting the 1855 council that produced the Yakama Nation's treaty and reservation—not an event widely known or a tribe often (ever?) featured in Hollywood films. Washington Territorial Governor Isaac I. Stevens and his secretary are shown interpreting the treaty terms to the fourteen signatory chiefs, including their nominal "head chief," Kamiakin. Speaking through sign language, he agrees to surrender their land but explicitly reserves their rights to salmon, game, berries, and roots. Stevens readily agrees: "It shall be as you say. The fish, the game, the roots and berries everywhere shall be yours forever." Kamiakin does not trust him, however, so he insists upon three "immortal witnesses" to the agreement; the Sun, a snow-capped mountain (Ta-ho-ma, or Mt. Rainier), and the Big River (the Yakama name for the Columbia). Stevens has that written into the treaty too: "[A]s long as the sun shines and the mountain stands and the river flows the Redskin shall hunt and fish at his accustomed places and keep peace with the white man." All of these details came from Mid-Columbia Indian oral traditions concerning the Stevens treaties, which Strongheart had learned about from his contacts on the reservation. Working through them, he grafted Yakama concerns onto a script that originally had nothing to do with them.[42]

The original screenplay also contained ethnographic markers that further root the film in the Columbia Basin and show Strongheart's hand. Early scenes of an Indian village included shots of salmon drying on racks in traditional Plateau fashion, women pounding and packing fish into buckskin parfleches, and a dog knocking over a cradleboard without hurting the infant. Strongheart added these touches to illustrate Native ingenuity, a recurring theme in his lectures, as well as to teach the audience about his own people. He sent Harris detailed descriptions of popular Plateau pastimes such as stick game and horseracing, and he furnished O'Hara with Sahaptin language translations for the names of the principal Indian characters. Apparently, she chose not to incorporate them, but the writing team took his advice seriously. As one note on the third draft said, "All cross marks by Strongheart. Better see on all these things, some are wrong and others incorrect and could stand much improvement." We can only imagine his frustration when the editors eliminated most of the cultural background and the opening council scene. Although the press book called the film "a colorful romance of the Northwest," nowhere does it specifically identify Braveheart's people as Yakamas. Still, thanks to Strongheart's interventions, there is little chance of mistaking them for the Apaches, Comanches, Navajos, and Sioux that populate the majority of early westerns.[43]

In his quest for historical authenticity, Strongheart went so far as to scout shooting locations on and around the Yakama reservation. He promptly sent a telegram to a friend and contact in the area, Lucullus V. McWhorter, requesting photographs of "local scenes" that could inform the screenplay and potentially appear in the film. McWhorter responded enthusiastically with images and ideas for the script, and he urged Strongheart to lobby for a shoot in the Yakima Valley. "Practically every feature of tribal life can be staged," he wrote, "from the *travos* [*sic*] and pack-horse to the aristocratic automobile; from the rush-mat lodge . . . to the two story dwelling of modern structure." Strongheart's inventory of "essentials for an Indian camp" included modern props like cars and iron stoves as well as traditional items. The Yakamas would thus appear as a living culture, with one foot firmly planted in the present, not as generic movie Indians in ersatz paint and feathers. Both men had seen enough of the Wild West to grow tired of its conventions and stereotypes, especially what McWhorter called "the posing of the self-conscious Indian." As he told Strongheart (himself a self-conscious poser), "I think that you are correct wherein the Sioux contingent with its sameness . . . is depicted in the various shows." Staging the movie in Yakama country would offer something "original and unique" to the producers, not to mention personal rewards for Strongheart. If "Brother Nipo" could pull off the move, McWhorter promised, "then you will be solid with our people here, and no mistake." Bringing the movie home would be Strongheart's ticket to authenticity and acceptance by his mother's tribe.[44]

In the end, though, nothing turned out as he hoped it would. He did not travel to the Northwest, and the company never reached the Yakima Valley. Nature itself seemed to conspire against the production. On September 12, Strongheart sent a letter to McWhorter sheepishly explaining that a portion of the cast and crew had come as far as Portland and Astoria, only to be deterred by forest fires and a flood on the Upper Columbia that "scared the company out." Unable to film because of the thick smoke, director Alan Hale headed back to Los Angeles after waiting two weeks for better conditions. He managed to get some footage, but most was of such poor quality that it had to be redone in Sonoma County, California, in the fall. Strongheart came up from Hollywood with a contingent of Plains Indian extras to shoot the required outdoor scenes. The setting was much different from the "Land of the Yakimas," and he felt "heart sick" about the failure to deliver on a promise to his people. There would be no triumphant homecoming for him. Still, to borrow a line from *Smoke Signals*, the finished film got about as close to "Dances with Salmon" as one could expect from Hollywood at that time.[45]

For all his frustrations and failures, Strongheart succeeded in framing an original picture that evoked the Yakama Nation's contemporary fight for justice. Finished in December 1925, *Braveheart* pays homage to the original play but takes the story into new territory. The hero attends college and plays football, but he goes there for the specific purpose of acquiring the legal knowledge necessary to defend his tribe's fishing rights against a rapacious cannery owner. The principal villain is Hobart Nelson, who uses intimidation and violence to drive Braveheart's people away from their traditional fisheries. During his time at the fictional Strathmore College, Braveheart wins the big game and the heart of Nelson's daughter Lucie, whose life he had saved earlier in the film. In doing so, he earns the enmity of Nelson's son, Frank, an open racist who also plays football for Strathmore and frames Braveheart for passing the team's signals to the opposition. He is expelled from school and banished from his tribe, yet he continues to represent his people in court and ultimately wins their case. He then saves them from destruction at the hands of the U.S. Cavalry when the savage Ki-yote, a jealous rival for future leadership of the tribe, tries to start a war by abducting Lucie. After killing Ki-yote in a duel, Braveheart does the noble thing and lets Lucie go (against her wishes) because their races cannot mingle. He then returns to his people and marries the maiden Sky-Arrow, who has loved him from the start.

Even as this resolution reaffirms the trope of the Noble Savage and the theme of doomed interracial romance, *Braveheart* ends with a message of Indigenous persistence. The law upholds the tribe's treaty, and so they will continue to fish in perpetuity. It is a dramatically different ending from those seen in most Indian movies of the Silent Era, particularly *The Vanishing American*, against which DeMille's film competed for audience attention. Based on Zane Grey's novel of the same name, the 1925 Paramount production is considered a cinema classic and a textbook example of the titular trope. The original story shares many dramatic conventions with *Strongheart* and *Braveheart*, including a Native protagonist who uses his college education to defend his people, an interracial love affair, and an uprising of not-so-noble savages triggered by the actions of a nefarious white villain. As the title loudly proclaims, though, *The Vanishing American* presumes the final demise of Indians as the inevitable price of progress. The hero, Nophaie, accepts the necessity of assimilation into Euro-American society shortly before dying from a gunshot wound. This conclusion, argues Jacquelyn Kilpatrick, "allows the viewer to 'tolerate' the Native Other, even feel deep sympathy, but without responsibility since the Indians are soon to be no more." Braveheart, by contrast, lives to lead his people into the future.[46]

Although the film earned disappointing returns at the box office, Strongheart made it the centerpiece of his résumé and his evolving persona as an expert on all things Indian. He began advertising his services as a technical advisor in the Studio Directory and often identified himself as a friend of Cecil B. DeMille, though there is no evidence that the two men ever spoke directly. Unfortunately, studio employment dried up during the Great Depression as the film industry contracted and the western genre hit hard times. Throughout the 1930s, Strongheart struggled to get contracts, and to make ends meet he often had to work part-time in Hollywood costume shops and as a seasonal carrier for the Postal Service. He also kept a foot in the world of live performance as a paid organizer of Indian pageants in the Los Angeles metropolitan area. During World War II, his reputation as "a recognized authority on the American Indian" landed him a position as chair of the American Indian War Finance Committee, which produced patriotic festivals designed to sell war bonds. When the war ended and movie production cranked up again, he returned to the studios and enjoyed a period of steady employment over the next ten years. By 1956, he took credit for technical advising on the films *Canyon Passage* (1946), *Black Gold* (1947), *The Outriders* (1950), *Young Daniel Boone* (1950), *Westward the Women* (1951), *Across the Wide Missouri* (1951), *The Painted Hills* (1951), *Lone Star* (1952), *The Half-Breed* (1952), *Pony Soldier* (1952), *The Charge at Feather River* (1953), and *Rose Marie* (1954).[47]

His involvement with these productions spanned a range of activities in the studio and on shoots across the West. In addition to costuming and location scouting, he trained actors and extras in military skills such as horsemanship and saber maneuvers, supposedly based on his own experience in the U.S. Cavalry. His claims regarding military service are undocumented and dubious, but they were ultimately less important to his résumé than were his carefully burnished credentials as an ethnographer and an authentic Indian himself. As he told producer-director Nunnally Johnson in 1958:

> It has been my privilege to reside with numerous Tribes and Nations of the American Indian People, having been assigned by the United States Government in the translation of Language, Music and Mythology for the Smithsonian Institute, Bureau of American Ethnology, and the WAR Department.[48]

Although such statements certainly stretched the truth, Strongheart understood that Hollywood accepted and even invited bold acts of self-invention and self-promotion. The important thing was to get the job, earn the salary and the experience, and thereby be in a position to portray Native Americans as accurately and sympathetically as possible.

Strongheart's most important contributions in that regard came as a writer and coach of Indian dialogue. Going beyond the linguistic suggestions he had made for *Braveheart*, he crafted entire passages employing Indigenous languages rather than the broken English common in most contemporary westerns. For *The Outriders*, an MGM production featuring Navajos as well as some Apaches and Pawnees, he wrote the dialogue and taught the actors how to pronounce their lines properly. It was, he later joked, "not an easy task to coach some movie people to speak an Indian language while they are still unable to speak their own." He could not speak Yakama fluently, much less Navajo or Pawnee, but he apparently did develop a command of both Plains Indian sign language and the Chinook Jargon historically used for cross-cultural communication on the Northwest Coast. Those skills came in handy for the film *Across the Wide Missouri*, which Strongheart personally considered "better than any of the pictures made so far." While shooting on location in Colorado, he provided many hours of dialogue coaching and sign language instruction to the principal actors (all non-Indian) Clark Gable, Ricardo Montalban, Mariah Elena Marquesa, James Whitmore, Jack Holt, Carol Naish, John Hodiak, and John Hartman. Technically, Chinook Jargon is not an Indigenous language and was not spoken on the Great Plains, where the film is set. For a western movie made in the early 1950s, however, its integration into the script represented a significant step toward the authentic and respectful depiction of Native Americans on screen. Instead of inarticulate grunts, or the guttural "heaps" and "hows" typically heard in Hollywood movies of the time, audiences would hear a historical Indian tongue. Moreover, non-Indian actors would have to learn that language from the Indian technical advisor who wrote their lines.[49]

Of course, in terms of audience response, it is impossible to measure the effects of Strongheart's creative interventions. None of the motion pictures that he worked on became major commercial or critical successes, and film historians rarely comment on them. As part of a broader movement to reframe Native Americans in cinema, however, Strongheart scored some minor victories. In 1948, for example, President Steve Broidy of Allied Artists wrote a letter to the National Congress of American Indians (NCAI) commending his work on *Black Gold*. In turn, the NCAI bestowed its first Tolerance Award on the film for portraying Native American history "truthfully" and "creating a warm spirit of tolerance for the American Indian." Broidy said, "Your west coast representative, Nipo Strongheart, was an important figure in making this picture authentic and instilling the proper spirit in the depiction of the Indian characters." Two years later, Twentieth Century-Fox released *Broken Arrow*, commonly (if mistakenly) regarded as the first revisionist Indian film of the postwar period. Strongheart did not work on that production but helped bring similar sensibilities to *Across the Wide Missouri*, *Pony Solider*, and other westerns of the early 1950s that showed Native Americans in a more positive light.[50]

Strongheart's work shines a spotlight on the hidden history of Native creativity in Hollywood, reminding us that Indians and other Indigenous peoples have always been more than mere performers in settler colonial fantasies. Well before the 1970s, when Vine Deloria, Jr., urged Indians to engage in self-representation, Strongheart was striving to shape cinematic narratives that would educate non-Indian audiences and encourage better treatment of Native Americans. His accomplishments were relatively small and his frustrations many, but he never stopped trying to swim against the stream of myths and stereotypes flowing out of Hollywood. Others swam with it. Two years after Strongheart's death in 1966, the Chickasaw technical advisor Rodd Redwing (nephew of Princess Redwing) complained, "I've got the worst job in the world. I teach cowboys how to kill Indians." Although he recognized that the films he helped produce got the history wrong, he saw nothing to be done about it. "I've found out we won practically all the battles. The white man didn't beat us, he starved us out." Still, sighed Redwing, "you can't combat lies."[51] Strongheart would have disagreed. He was among the first Native film professionals to recognize an essential truth about movie making: If Indigenous artists ever hoped to see full and fair representation of their peoples on screen, they would have to get behind the camera before they got in front of it.

CONCLUSION

Nipo Strongheart and Wallace Fox were both Hollywood Indians, part of a diverse and dynamic community engaged in the making and remaking of societal expectations for Native Americans. They chose different career paths, though, and they staked out different positions in the space between compliance and resistance that comprised the virtual reservation of the early movie industry. For Strongheart, film offered a means of challenging racist attitudes, correcting biased narratives, and calling the public to action. As a technical advisor and writer, he tried to advance not only the cause of visual sovereignty, but also the goals of Indian citizenship and tribal treaty rights in the United States. To achieve those ends, he often engaged in "Indian play" and thus played into some of the very stereotypes and tropes that still haunt Native Americans.[52] Even so, artistry and authenticity mattered to Strongheart because films had to inspire and inform as well as entertain if they were to effect societal change. As with many other Native performers, his commitment to aesthetic diplomacy spilled over into public speaking, pageants, and other community events that drew on his experience with live entertainment.

Wallace Fox took a different road, and definitely the one less traveled by Hollywood Indians of his time. As a director, he possessed greater creative control than did Indian actors and technical advisors, though still limited by the financial and technical constraints of B-movie production. With a few exceptions, he did not use that power to make films about Native Americans or Indigenous issues. He also seems to have eschewed the sort of redfacing or Indian play that characterized the professional lives and personas of so many contemporaries, perhaps because it could have resulted in professional confinement on the virtual reservation. While Strongheart struggled to flip the script in the western genre—and periodically struggled to find employment with the studios—Fox worked more steadily and ultimately made a larger variety of movies. The western remained his bread and butter, but he enjoyed the freedom to range beyond it, as the other chapters in this volume show. Fox's low profile, coupled with his lack of artistic or activist aspirations, has reduced his visibility and legibility as an Indigenous filmmaker. If Edwin Carewe belongs in that category, however, then certainly we must also count his brother among the first Native artists to carve out a niche in Hollywood.

What did Fox and Strongheart make of each other and their respective bodies of work? Once again, the historical record provides no solid answers, as there appears to be no evidence that they interacted either personally or professionally. They moved in different (if overlapping) circles and labored in different parts of the film industry, making different films for different audiences, with different ends in mind. One suspects that Strongheart would not have thought much of Fox's movies, if he ever saw them, because they did not actively challenge the cinematic conventions and cultural discourses that marginalized Native Americans. To court an old western cliché, though, the town was big enough for the both of them. Our vision of Indigenous filmmaking in early Hollywood should be equally capacious.

NOTES

1. Diane MacIntyre, "A Golden Quiver of Native Americans from the Silent Era," *The Silents Majority: Online Journal of Silent Film* (mdle@primenet.com, 1997), print copy in Library and Archives of the Autry Museum, Los Angeles, CA, MS. 641, The Richard Davis or Chief Thunderbird Collection, Box 2, Folder "Correspondence, Grace Slaughter (great-granddaughter) and Susan Shown Harjo (great-granddaughter)."
2. *Jackson's Hole Courier* (Jackson, Wyoming), April 5, 1928, 4.
3. "Shortage of Indians Troubles Director," *The Roosevelt Standard* (Roosevelt, Utah), May 31, 4; "Indian Dance to Be Outstanding," *Los Angeles Times*, September 4, 1927, B10.
4. "Shortage of Indians Troubles Director."
5. Ibid. As Brian Taves notes, critics have generally denigrated and dismissed B directors as lesser talents within the film industry, yet they often possessed valuable skills that helped underwrite a studio's bottom line: "Many individuals were shunted into careers dominated by B's because of their consistent effectiveness in filming efficiently and smoothly. They became type-cast, in a sense, not for lack of talent, but precisely because of their demonstrated skill. Turning out pictures rapidly on low budgets required rare abilities: knowing exactly what shots were necessary, editing in the camera without wasting footage on full coverage or more than a few takes, quickly arranging the lighting and camera angles to conceal the cheapness of the sets, eliciting or giving an effective performance with few rehearsals, and covering such disadvantages with fast pacing and shadowy lighting. These abilities were highly prized and might well lead to a continuation in the B realm, but seldom advanced one to the A's" ("The B Film: Hollywood's Other Half," *History of the American Cinema*, Encyclopedia.com, https://www.encyclopedia.com/arts/culture-magazines/b-film-hollywoods-other-half (accessed 8 April 2021).
6. As Michelle H. Raheja explains in *Reservation Reelism: Redfacing, Visual Sovereignty, and Representations of Native Americans in Film*, "visual sovereignty recognizes the complexities of creating media for multiple audiences, critiquing filmic representations of Native Americans, at the same time that it participates in some of the conventions that have produced these representations . . . Under visual sovereignty, filmmakers can deploy individual and community assertions of what sovereignty and self-representation mean, and through new media technologies, frame more imaginative renderings of Native American intellectual and cultural paradigms. . ." (Lincoln: University of Nebraska Press), 200.
7. Raheja, 20–1; Joanna Hearne, *Native Recognition: Indigenous Cinema and the Western* (Albany, NY: SUNY Press, 2012), 3.
8. On the constraints that Fox faced as Poverty Row director, see Joanna Hearne, "Indian Agents and Indigenous Agency at Universal," this volume.
9. Raheja, 43–4. According to Taves, "Most B directors could not revise the script, had little say in choosing a cast or crew, and were seldom involved in the editing." Within the constraints of the form, however, "resourceful filmmakers, especially directors and cinematographers, were sometimes allowed to be more creative than in A's" ("The B Film").

10. Philip J. Deloria, *Indians in Unexpected Places* (Lawrence: University Press of Kansas, 2004), 231–3.
11. Liza Black, *Picturing Indians: Native Americans in Film, 1941–1960* (Lincoln: University of Nebraska Press, 2020), 4–6.
12. Black, 192; Raheja, 193.
13. Kiara M. Vigil, *Indigenous Intellectuals: Sovereignty, Citizenship, and the American Imagination, 1880–1930* (New York: Cambridge University Press, 2015), 3; Linda Scarangella McNenly, *Native Performers in Wild West Shows: From Buffalo Bill to Euro Disney* (Norman: University of Oklahoma Press, 2012), 8–10. McNenly follows Mary Louise Pratt and other theorists in defining contact zones as "(post)colonial spaces of interaction by multiple participants with various agendas involving unequal power relationships, but with the possibility of agency by marginal groups." They entail "a two-way process of interaction and cultural production," not a one-way street paved entirely by the dominant group (11).
14. Black, 36.
15. Raheja, 45.
16. Raheja, 35.
17. "Biographical Sketch of the Fox Brothers," Tribal Writers Digital Library, Sequoyah National Research Center, <https://ualrexhibits.org/tribalwriters/artifacts/FoxBrothers_Biography.html>; U.S. Census Bureau, *1900 United States Federal Census, Township 6, Chickasaw Nation, Indian Territory*, p. *30*, Enumeration District 0155, FHL microfilm *1241849*, Ancestry.com, <https://www.ancestrylibrary.com/discoveryui-content/view/74959959:7602?> (accessed April 12, 2021); Mary Jo Turner, "Historical Highlights," August 23, 1962, *The Purcell Register* (Purcell, OK), 2.
18. "More License Tax Correspondence," *The Purcell Register* (Purcell, OK), December 8, 1893, 1; Reports of Agents in Indian Territory, *Annual Reports of the Commissioner of Indian Affairs*, 1895 (Washington, DC: Government Printing Office, 1896), 157–8; M. Kaye Tatro, "Allotment," *The Encyclopedia of Oklahoma*, Oklahoma Historical Society, <https://www.okhistory.org/publications/enc/entry.php?entry=AL011> (accessed January 23, 2021).
19. Chickasaw by Blood, Card 1374, Search the Dawes Final Rolls, 1898–1914, Oklahoma History Center, <https://www.okhistory.org/research/dawesresults.php?cardnum=1374&tribe=Chickasaw&type=by%20Blood> (accessed January 23, 2021); U.S. Census Bureau, *1920 United States Federal Census*, Los Angeles Assembly District 63, Los Angeles, California, Roll T625_106, p. 13B, Enumeration District 154, Ancestry.com (accessed April 12, 2021); "Tribes Well Represented," *Los Angeles Times*, April 3, 1927, A1; "Indian Couple Here to Lend Aid on Film," *Los Angeles Times*, July 18, 1930, A5. On the importance of being considered "full-blood" for Indian performers, see Kiara Vigil, *Indigenous Intellectuals* and Linda M. Waggoner, *Starring Red Wing!: The Incredible Career of Lilian M. St. Cyr, the First Native American Film Star* (Lincoln: University of Nebraska Press, 2019).
20. "Ramona Found to Be True Modern, Says Finis Fox," *Los Angeles Times*, October 2, 1927, C12; "Proud Indians," *The Havre Daily News* (Havre, MT), 3.
21. Lucy Maddox, *Citizen Indians: Native American Intellectuals, Race, and Reform* (Ithaca, NY: Cornell University Press, 2005), 54–7, 62; "Charles David Carter," *The Encyclopedia of Oklahoma*, Oklahoma Historical Society, <https://www.okhistory.org/publications/enc/entry.php?entry=CA066> (accessed January 26, 2021); Oskison quoted in Maddox, 64, 66.
22. Donald A. Grinde, Jr. and Quintard Taylor, "Red vs Black: Conflict and Accommodation in the Post Civil War Indian Territory, 1865–1907," *American Indian Quarterly* 8:3 (Summer 1984), 211–29; Donald B. Smith, *Chief Buffalo Child Long Lance: The Glorious Impostor* (Red Deer, AB: Red Deer Press, 1999), 50. Grinde and Taylor note that, among

the Five Tribes, the Choctaws and Chickasaws were the most hostile to freedmen and sought to either expel them or limit their socio-economic mobility. Sylvester Long, who adopted the stage name Chief Buffalo Child Long Lance and co-starred in *The Silent Enemy*, claimed Cherokee and Croatan ancestry. He was actually the son of former African American slaves, however, and he killed himself in March 1932 after rumors of his black heritage threatened to destroy his career.

23. "Hollywood Film Notables Seized," *The Capital Times* (Madison, WI), October 2, 1931, 5; "Lady Luck Deserts Her Devotees in Hollywood," *Los Angeles Times*, October 2, 1931, A8; "Supper Club Trial Launched," *Los Angeles Times*, December 8, 1931, 10.
24. Renya Katarine Ramirez, *Native Hubs: Culture, Community, and Belonging in Silicon Valley and Beyond* (Durham, NC: Duke University Press, 2007), 3; Jacob Floyd, "On Hollywood Boulevard: Native Community in Classical Hollywood," *Journal of Cinema and Media Studies* 60:2 (Winter 2021), 163–8; Nicolas G. Rosenthal, *Reimagining Indian Country: Native American Migration & Identity in Twentieth-Century Los Angeles* (Chapel Hill: University of North Carolina Press, 2012), 21–4; "Indian Couple Here to Lend Aid on Film," *Los Angeles Times*, July 18, 1930, A5.
25. Rosenthal, 44–5; Raheja, 32–4; Richard Davis to Red Fox St. James, June 9, 1925, Library and Archives of the Autry Museum, Los Angeles, CA, MS. 641, The Richard Davis or Chief Thunderbird Collection, Box 2, Folder 31; "Ultra-American," *Stockton Daily Independent* (Stockton, CA) March 9, 1928, 4.
26. Rosenthal, 42.
27. "Zane Grey Film of Indians in Cutting Room," *Oakland Tribune* (Oakland, CA), September 20, 1925, 67.
28. Rosenthal, 44; Floyd,.
29. "Shortage of Indians Troubles Director," 4; "Mystic," *Petaluma Argues-Courier* (Petaluma, CA), August 6, 1928, 3; "'Riding Renegade' at the Hippodrome," *Bakersfield Morning Echo* (Bakersfield, CA), February 3, 1928, 4; Full Cast and Crew, *The Riding Renegade*, IMDB, <https://www.imdb.com/title/tt0019323> (accessed January 24, 2021).
30. "Mystic," 3; "'Riding Renegade' Brings Back Days of Flaming West," *The Chico Enterprise* (Chico, CA), June 1, 1928, 6.
31. "Temple Theater," *Alton Evening Telegraph* (Alton, IL), October 19, 1928, 11; "Bob Steele as 'The Riding Renegade,'" *Herald-Recorder* (Arroyo Grande, CA), April 5, 1928, 5; Raheja, 19.
32. Raheja, 21–2.
33. Hazlett quoted in Rosenthal, 44.
34. Andrew H. Fisher, "Tinseltown Tyee: Nipo Strongheart and the Making of Braveheart," *American Indian Culture and Research Journal* 42:3 (2018), 96–9.
35. Maddox, 9–14; Thomas G. Sloan to Nipo Strongheart, January 29, 1924, Folder 20–13, Yakama Nation Library, Toppenish, WA [hereafter YNL]; Thomas Bishop to Floyd L. Mathews, December 30, 1922, Folder 18–92, YNL; Nipo Strongheart to Lucullus McWhorter, January 21, 1921, Folder 114–1, Click Relander Collection, Yakima Valley Regional Library, Yakima, WA, [hereafter Relander Collection], 4, emphasis in original.
36. Fisher, 99–100; Nipo Strongheart Diary, March 16, 1920, YNL.
37. Scott Eyman, *Empire of Dreams: The Epic Life of Cecil B. DeMille* (New York: Simon & Schuster, 2010), 212–16; L. M. Goodstadt to Fred Kley, Miss Rosson, Mr. Stevenson, June 10, 1925, Box 259, Folder 9, MSS 1400, Cecil B. DeMille Papers, Brigham Young University, Provo, UT [hereafter DeMille Papers]; Executive Meeting Minutes, December 12, 1925, Box 259, Folder 9, DeMille Papers, 3.
38. Elmer Harris to Cecil B. DeMille, May 12, 1925, Box 259, Folder 12, MSS 1400, DeMille Papers; Barrett Kiesling to Cecil B. DeMille, May 6, 1925, Box 259, Folder 17, MSS 1400, DeMille Papers.

39. Harris to DeMille.
40. Barrett C. Kiesling to George Harvey, May 19, 1925, Box 259, Folder 17, MSS 1400, DeMille Papers; Barrett C. Kiseling to Cecil B. DeMille, June 3, 1925, Box 261, Folder 15, MSS 1400, DeMille Papers; Charles Beahan to Cecil B. DeMille, May 14, 1925, Box 261, Folder 13, MSS 1400, DeMille Papers.
41. Cecil B. DeMille to L. M. Goodstadt, March 24, 1925, Box 259, Folder 9, MSS 1400, DeMille Papers; L. M. Goodstadt to Mr. Stephenson, June 5, 1925, Box 259, Folder 9, MSS 1400, DeMille Papers; Elmer Harris to Cecil B. DeMille, March 27, 1926, Box 264, Folder 15, MSS 1400, DeMille Papers; Executive Meeting Minutes, December 31, 1925, Box 259, Folder 1, MSS 1400, DeMille Papers; Mary O'Hara, *Flicka's Friend: The Autobiography of Mary O'Hara* (New York: G.P. Putnam's Sons, 1982), 145–58.
42. Original screenplay of *Braveheart*, Folder 23–1, YNL, 1–5; Andrew H. Fisher, "This I Know from the Old People: Yakama Indian Treaty Rights as Oral Tradition," *Montana, The Magazine of Western History* 49 (Spring 1999): 2–17.
43. "Notes for Mr. Elmer Harris. May, 12th 1925," Folder 23–11, YNL; Third draft of screenplay for *Brave Heart*, Folder 23–3, YNL; "Catching Catchlines for use in Advertising Rod La Rocque's 'Braveheart," Press Book, Folder 23–7, YNL.
44. Bigfoot [Lucullus McWhorter] to Nippon Strongheart (telegram), May 5, 1925, Folder 22–75, YNL; Big Foot to Strongheart, May 5, 1925, Folder 22–73, YNL, 1–3; Big Foot to Strongheart, May 12, 1925, Folder 22–73; Essentials for and [*sic*] Indian Camp, Folder 23–17, YNL, 1–2; Big Foot to Strongheart, May 22, 1925, Folder 22–72, YNL.
45. Brother Nipo to Big Foot, September 12, 1925, Folder 114–1, Relander Collection, 1–3, emphasis in original; "Big Bunch of Movie Actors Come," *Healdsburg (California) Tribune*, September 28, 1925, 2; "Healdsburg People Attend Entertainment at Guerneville," *Healdsburg (California) Tribune*, October 1, 1925, 2.
46. Jacquelyn Kilpatrick, *Celluloid Indians: Native Americans in Film* (Lincoln: University of Nebraska Press, 1999), 29–33.
47. *Studio Directory*, April 1931 (Los Angeles, CA: Stenographic Service of Hollywood, 1938), Unprocessed papers of Strongheart Collection, Yakama Nation Museum [hereafter YNM], 1; H. E. McCroskey to Jack Gain, July 28, 1933, YNM; Ben Arid to C. M. Vandenburg, September 18, 1935, YNM; E. J. Fostines to Nipo Strongheart, December 12, 1945, YNM; Nipo Strongheart to Sam Marx, October 31, 1956, YNM.
48. Nipo Strongheart to Nunnally Johnson, June 9, 1958, YNM.
49. Nipo Strongheart to Russell B. Adams, April 30, 1949, YNM; Nipo Strongheart to Mahdah Brown, October 10, 1950, YNM; Dialogue Coaching schedules for *Across the Wide Missouri*, YNM.
50. Steve Broidy to N. B. Johnson, September 14, 1948, YNM.
51. Mary Blume, "Redwing Bites Dust Again, Again, Again," *Los Angeles Times*, May 25, 1968, 17, Vertical File Mass Media—Films and TV, Autry Museum, Los Angeles.
52. The concept of "Indian play" comes from Lisa K. Neuman's *Indian Play: Indigenous Identities at Baycone College* (University of Nebraska Press, 2013). Similar to Raheja's idea of redfacing, it describes the complex cultural and ideological work of Native performers who employ stereotypical representations in order to engage non-Indian audiences and thereby "create a space for counterhegemonic discourse" (23).

CHAPTER 2

Indian Agents and Indigenous Agency at Universal: *Wild Beauty* (1946) and *Gun Town* (1946)

Joanna Hearne

Scholarship on the sympathetic western has rightly presumed the studio system to be a non-Indigenous project. Most Indigenous actors had little power to influence the scripts they were hired to perform (if they had any lines at all) or the social practices of production itself. While some directors claimed to have Indigenous heritage, such as James Cruze and Victor Fleming, most such stories are not only apocryphal but also conflate two related but distinct forms of Indigenous identity: Indigenous heritage (a Native American ancestor) and tribal enrollment—that is, citizenship in a specific Indigenous nation. Wallace W. Fox and his brothers Finis Fox and Edwin Carewe (stage name for Jay Fox)—citizens of the Chickasaw Nation—are among the very few Native people to occupy positions of creative control in Hollywood, working behind the camera rather than in front of it.

Like his older brothers, Wallace Fox was born and raised in the Chickasaw Nation in Indian Territory (later Oklahoma) just before the transition to statehood, and along with their father Frank M. Fox, all three brothers are named and identified as Chickasaw on the 1907 "Final Rolls of the Citizens and Freedmen of the Five Civilized Tribes of the Indian Territory," or Dawes Rolls. With their intermarried family origins—enrolled members of the Chickasaw Nation but with white settler ancestry as well—the brothers could have "passed" as white, but chose not to hide their Chickasaw identities. Finis Fox had been active in the Chickasaw legislature before moving to Los Angeles, and Edwin Carewe, especially, publicized his Chickasaw heritage as part of his marketing campaign for his 1928 film adaptation of *Ramona*, about California settlement and injustices towards Native Nations. Yet the brothers' identities were neither accomplished facts nor stable platforms but rather were produced in contexts of instability, coming out of the multiple displacements of settler immigration,

Chickasaw Removal, and frequent family relocations that ultimately led them to the multi-ethnic metropole of Los Angeles.

While Fox directed films across a number of genres, his work for Universal in the mid-1940s included many B-western films, a few of which involve or directly address "Indian subjects." This chapter takes up two such films, *Wild Beauty* and *Gun Town*, both 1946, asking whether and how the post-WWII B-film industry, with its highly commercialized organizational constraints, offered a space for progressive (though not necessarily transgressive) work for those who could wield the conventions of the genre. Both *Wild Beauty* and *Gun Town* make heroes of Indian agent characters and activate discourses of friendship and hostility between settlers and tribes in their storylines, looking towards the resurgence of social commentary in sympathetic westerns and frontier noir films from major studios in the 1950s (beginning with films like *Broken Arrow* from Twentieth Century-Fox and *Devil's Doorway* from MGM, both 1950) while also adopting some of the gender politics of the singing cowboy films of the 1930s. These instances might also be considered moments of what Chad Allen calls "treaty discourse," or the articulation of nation-to-nation relationships in their narrative politics, and—in the case of *Gun Town*—with redfacing in its self-referential commentary on Hollywood's systems of racial masquerade.[1]

Figure 2.1 Wallace Fox's *Gun Town* (1945).

Fox's sympathetic westerns of 1946—a historical moment of federal power and propaganda as the country emerged from WWII—present Indian agents as heroes of frontier supervision and even, in the case of *Wild Beauty*, paternalistic benevolence. The films' preoccupation with the nation-state and with Indian agents as the settler nation's explicit representatives foregrounds a colonial managerialism, imagining a frontier in need of federal authority. The politics of sympathetic representations presented through individual character trajectories reflect an institutional politics of U.S. administration, bringing everyone—Native tribes and settlers alike—into the purview of the settler nation-state and its governing structures. This dynamic, by which representations of settler sympathy function as strategies of containment, is well established in the scholarship on images of Indians. As with Indigenous critiques of federal structures of limited recognition for Indigenous sovereignty, we can critique sympathetic images in the B-western for the ways in which they contribute to what Glen Coulthard calls "a lie of capitalism that dresses up exploitation in liberal inclusion."[2] Sympathetic images are not signs of progress but rather complex artifacts emergent from specific historical and industrial conditions; in B-film genres, they are articulated within systems of settler colonial containment, and Wallace Fox was embedded in this system not as a change-agent but rather as an operator, wielding technical rather than narrative control.

The Fox brothers worked the levers of the industrial film production system but were also hemmed in by it. In the post-WWII context, for Wallace Fox, agency took the form of accommodation rather than refusal—he was an institutionalist, unlike his more ambitious, sometimes audacious elder brother Edwin Carewe, and he directed the stories he was given. As essentially a middle manager in the business-oriented hierarchy of the low-budget genre system, his control involved logistics and technical choices around lighting, takes, and stock footage. He was also a military veteran, having served in WWI, and like other Native men who served in the military, Fox may have had a strong sense of national service. He must also have been a practical person and a realist—a daily requirement of his work producing low-budget films on a tight schedule. The B-film genre system is tied to razor-thin profits and a nimble business model, so, unlike his brothers, Wallace Fox's career involved more humility than stardom.

Although he couldn't change the B-system itself, he largely stuck with sympathetic representations of Indians on screen. The politics of sympathy in Fox's mid-1940s westerns track the close working relationship of Hollywood and the U.S. government from the war years. The postwar cinematic government agents (in films like *T-Men*, 1947) make heroes of the supervisory arm of the nation state; in Universal's 1946 westerns, the ideal frontiersman is a government agent, not an individual cowboy or vigilante gunslinger but rather a figure backed by federal bureaucracy and holding managerial authority—a teacher, detective, and Indian expert rolled into one. Historically, federal Indian agents (especially during the early reservation period so often represented in westerns) were agents of genocide—often politically appointed through the spoils system and profiting from delivery of inadequate rations and other forms of corruption. Yet in Universal's 1940s westerns, these figures are rehabilitated as the films throw their weight behind U.S. administrative power, even as government itself was the engine of resource extraction on Indigenous lands (especially, in the post-WWII moment, uranium mining). Sympathetic representations of Indians naturalize the settler state as, in exchange, the state authority is legitimated. Yet these politics have at times been a useful tool for Native Nations to wield; like sovereignty itself as a legal concept imported from Europe, tribes also used federal trust relationships to defend against more local and state-level depredations, and sympathetic representations could influence viewers while also shielding Indigenous communities from the intrusions of a national gaze.

Thus these productions offer a window, however opaque, into Fox's work as both an Indigenous director and a career director within a conformist, profit-driven, hierarchical studio system, and at a particular moment in the larger post-World War II production of images of Indians. In this they can also offer a case study for thinking about how the B-movie industry might or might not function as a site for Indigenous agency in media production. Can the lenses of Indigenous image studies and production studies allow us to see content in a new way (even if Fox might not have chosen to see his work this way)? What might a method for such a recovery look like? With their adherence to genre codes and their jokey and sometimes hokey theatricality, Fox's B-westerns look more like other genre films from his time, and much less like the corrections and re-alignments by Indigenous documentary filmmakers (such as Neil Diamond's *Reel Injun*, 2009) or the Indigenizing work of contemporary Native-directed, independent genre films (such as Jeff Barnaby's *Blood Quantum*, 2019, or Georgina Lightning's *Older than America*, 2008). While scholarship in Indigenous media studies often attends to the ways in which Native directors resist or intervene in systems of Hollywood misrepresentation, from all evidence Wallace Fox worked steadily within the low-budget studio system for the whole of his career without seeming to fight it from within. Rather than the investment in historical accuracy and cultural authenticity that critics and audiences sometimes expect Native filmmakers and activists to deliver, and far from the "discourse of sobriety" in documentary or tone of activism around re-shaping cinematic images of Indians, Fox's films evince an intimacy and ease with B-film production and aesthetic conventions. Just as no performance is sustained by the performer alone, Fox's work was highly situated across complex and shifting industrial structures. Reading his surroundings (just as Amy Ware interprets Cherokee performer

Will Rogers's home interiors to find evidence of his allegiance to Indigenous arts), we find evidence towards recovery, one that attends to issues of both identity and directorial auteurism, yet also recognizes the overarching power of the system—especially for B-film production—in relation to both.[3]

Working at the intersection of Indigenous media studies and media production studies, this chapter explores Fox's productions' potential for what Seneca scholar Michelle Raheja calls "visual sovereignty," or "the space between resistance and compliance" in the work of an Indigenous filmmaker in relation to the larger systems of visual representation and film production, circulation and reception.[4] In the case of Wallace Fox, this space was exceedingly narrow, and the ways in which we can understand him to be "speaking" through his films are limited as well. His working environment in the B-film industry at mid-century comprised a highly systematized commercial production complex that dictated harsh budgetary restriction, extraordinarily tight shooting schedules, and contractual precarity. Vicki Mayer, Miranda Banks, and John Caldwell remind us that media researchers must strike a balance between "describing media workers as the creators of popular culture and as functionaries in the service of capitalism," even as we recognize how media workers "shape and refashion their identities in the process of making their careers in industries undergoing political transitions and economic reorganizations."[5] Unlike current production studies as established by Caldwell and others, however, ethnographic methods, interviews, and the kind of ample digital material provided by DVD extras and bonus features are not an option for this historical research. Because Wallace Fox did not leave personal papers in print archives, we lack direct access to his own voice through correspondence; it's impossible to know for sure what he himself thought of his work, and to what extent he saw his Chickasaw identity and Indian Territory upbringing as an influence on his sympathetic western B-films—but we can propose possibilities.

While we may not be able to access Fox *himself* through his films, it's significant that he produced these sympathetic westerns at a moment when the discourse around Indigenous peoples in the United States was shifting radically, even as the industrial structures through which Fox exercised limited power were also changing, all of which affected his production of commoditized images of Indians for popular consumption. Beyond the individual trajectory of Fox's career, his productions have implications for film and Indigenous media history, suggesting an earlier beginning to the mid-century cycle of sympathetic westerns. Fox's sympathetic western productions are marked by the historical contexts of low-budget studio operations, B-movie and western genre alignment with post-WWII federal Indian policy shifts and policy questions, and cultural representations of a specific form of settler colonialism—the federal management of western lands, resources, animals and people. Sympathetic B westerns of the 1940s visualized these issues within the genre-based narrative forms of frontier family formation, surrogate and re-configured families, custodial transfer of children, and preoccupations with systems of childrearing and assimilationist education. These new ways of understanding the representational politics of sympathy and the production of sympathetic B-western film cycles connect Wallace Fox (and his brothers) to a larger dynamic of continuing liberalism in Hollywood, enfolding a Chickasaw family of filmmakers within the auspices of a national and seemingly progressive agenda encoded within the images of Indians in that most anti-Indian of film genres, the western.

FOX AT UNIVERSAL

Looking closely at productions like *Gun Town* and *Wild Beauty* helps us see not only how B-westerns worked in general in the mid- and late 1940s, but also how elements of Universal's studio production system (budgets, schedules, stock players, etc.) intersected with narrative, thematic, and aesthetic elements of filmed stories and images of Indians. Working with this tension—between production finance and schedule details and the larger resonance of the film's stories (keeping "the whole equation of pictures" in mind)—also allows us to explore Fox's career as an Indigenous director in a non-auteurist way, yet with an eye to his craftsmanship within negatively defined conditions (e.g. budgetary austerity, hierarchical management, and formulaic genre conventions).[6] Fox is not often mentioned in connection with larger circuits of Indigenous workers in Hollywood, although Andrew Fisher's chapter in this collection points to his inclusion in his brother Edwin Carewe's plans for a "screen colony club" for filmmakers with American Indian ancestry.[7] Scholars of Indigenous Hollywood have revealed extensive networks of Indigenous performers in Los Angeles, as seen, for example, in Michelle Raheja's work on groups like the DeMille Indians and the off-screen activism of Italian actor Iron Eyes Cody, and Liza Black and Nicolas Rosenthal on the Los Angeles Native American actors' community. Such work demonstrates the ways in which Native actors made lateral connections among themselves, sometimes using that solidarity to seek more traction and power over their working conditions.[8] From the available evidence, the Fox brothers made fewer connections to other Indigenous film industry workers and performers outside of a few stars and prominent directors, even as they maintained their Chickasaw identity as a point of pride and translated their family bonds into professional collaborations. Wallace Fox often worked with his brothers in the early part of his career and was involved in many of Carewe's 1920s productions, although as the youngest of the Fox brothers his career (perhaps due to this later timeframe or other reasons) generally did not involve the close partnership that Edwin Carewe and Finis Fox seemed to have on productions like *Ramona* (1928) and *Evangeline* (1929).

Fox had a long apprenticeship in the studio industry and working with his brothers, but his career as a director gained traction after his elder brothers retired (Carewe's last film appeared in 1934). Before his stint at Universal, Fox had directed short sponsorship films for GE and other companies, and served as assistant director on major studio productions such as George Seitz's 1936 version of *The Last of the Mohicans* (starring Randolph Scott and distributed by United Artists). He had worked in RKO's cutting and camera departments, and eventually directed his first feature for RKO, the 1935 *Powdersmoke Range* (shot on location and starring Harry Carey), which won him a director's contract with the company.[9] He went on to make a series of feature films for RKO through the 1930s, as well as *East Side Kids* comedies for Monogram, and many westerns for both Monogram and Columbia. By the time he moved to Universal, he was "journeyman director" and quite experienced at directing outdoor action films on a shoestring budget.[10]

Fox's work at Universal was probably facilitated by career B-film producer Ben Pivar, who made some westerns over his career with Buck Jones and others, but was mostly known for his low-budget horror films. The two might have met at Columbia, where both had worked previously. As an executive producer at Universal, Pivar oversaw Fox's first films for the studio—including the 1944 production of *Riders of the Santa Fe* (in which Rod Cameron replaced longtime Universal player Johnny Mack Brown as the lead), and the late winter 1945 production of the Lon Chaney horror film *Pillow of Death*, Fox's only non-western for the studio. Fox worked under contract for Universal Pictures for two years, from 1944 through 1946, as director and associate producer on nine films (of which seven were ultra-low-budget series). His first film for Universal was typical of what would follow: the eight-day shoot for *Riders of the Santa Fe* in early June of 1944, with a total production budget of $54,600 (although the production went over this budget by about $3,600). The following summer of 1945, he directed four films: *Code of the Lawless*, *Bad Men of the Border*, *Trail to Vengeance*, and *Gun Town*, all shot in 6–8 days for budgets ranging from $51,000 to $58,000 (earlier in February and March of 1945 he had also directed the horror film *Pillow of Death* for Universal, a 12-day shoot for a much larger budget of $133,500). The films must have been financially successful enough to justify further studio resources, since Fox's final summer of shooting for Universal involved a jump in the base budgets for the series to $65,000 for the June and July 8-day productions of *Rustler's Roundup* and *Lawless Breed*, and, that same summer, the stand-alone film *Wild Beauty*, which involved not only a longer shoot (12 days) and travel to the location, but also a $150,000 budget. Fox delivered this film at a substantial savings, $4,000 *under* budget, a feat that must have impressed executive producers at the studio.[11]

The years at Universal represented a move up for Fox, and coincided with a period of growth for the studio as well; between 1944 and 1946, Universal's net profits increased by almost 17 percent and the studio planned several expansions.[12] This prosperity for a minor studio accounts for the added resources for the western series unit, from an almost impossible target of $55,000 to a slightly more manageable $65,000 (although production costs still frequently went over this more capacious budget). In part, the studio's success in churning out films with "slick production values" on tiny budgets rested on teams of experienced craftspeople, including not only stock players but also veteran cinematographers and directors (B-film scholar Thomas Reeder lists Wallace Fox among the B-movie "luminaries" working with Pivar at Universal, including Phil Rosen, Lew Landers, William Nigh, Charles Lamont, Roy William Neill, George Waggner, Harold Young and James Hogan).[13] The contract talent—lead and stock players—improved while working together on cycles of western series productions—Johnny Mack Brown was replaced by Rod Cameron in 1944–1945, and later Kirby Grant, all playing alongside former vaudeville comedian Fuzzy Knight.

Fox's key task as a B-film director—getting a film in on time and on budget—took real hustle. The experienced teams at Universal were efficient, but according to Reeder,

> it was the director who was on the firing line for these productions, with Pivar breathing down his neck every step of the way to ensure that everything was kept on schedule and within budget. Only the heartiest and organized of individuals could function within the Draconian constraints imposed.[14]

Production files from Universal reveal the hard push at the end of scheduled shoots, with days ending very late. On the last day of shooting *Riders of the Santa Fe* on June 14th, 1944, the company worked from 8:00 a.m. until 10:25 p.m. and shot seventeen pages' worth of material. On one of his last films for Universal—*The Rustler's Round-Up*—production records again show long days (ending at 9:25 p.m. and 10:40 p.m.) at the end of the eight-day shoot.

If B-film directors bore the brunt of stressful production schedules, their salaries didn't show it. Fox's compensation did eventually rise, but initially Universal picked him up for a song. For his first film, *Riders of the Santa Fe*, Pivar brought him on for a three-week contract at $350/week, or a total of $1,050 (with Pivar making $600 as executive producer, associate producer Oliver Drake making $1,500, and contract talent Fuzzy Knight making more than any of them at $1,850). On the feature film *Pillow of Death*, Fox made a directorial fee of $1,500, while Pivar made $2,500 as executive producer, and both their salaries were dwarfed by star Lon Chaney's flat rate fee of $10,000. Directing and producing *Wild Beauty* was the only time Fox made more than his contract talent, with a $3,000 flat fee and $4,000 producer's fee (and an additional $500 for secretarial support). How did these financial and schedule pressures translate to the cultural production of post-WWII B-westerns, their images of Indians and Indian agents? And how do their tight budgetary and management systems affect how westerns talk about race, gender, and identity? Fox's economies of production created intertexts with other films through use of stock footage, the need to stay current with trends like noir aesthetics, and the ability to borrow and genre-blend to reach multiple audiences in a single hour.

THE INDIAN AGENT IN THE POST-WWII MOMENT

Identities matter in the western. Identity play around race, gender, and Indigeneity in frontier encounters are at the heart of the genre, fraught with cultural conversations and sometimes deeply coded messages about contemporaneous interethnic social relations. In his book on westerns of the 1930s, Peter Stanfield departs from previous structural interpretations of the western genre as a "frontier myth" and instead emphasizes 1930s westerns' inheritance of vernacular song forms from blackface minstrelsy and the genre's alignment with the South, arguing that 1930s series westerns instantiate an "ideological displacement that relocates concerns of Southern identity onto the terrain of the Western: the Southerner crosses the divide that separates him or her from the American commonwealth by being transformed into a Westerner."[15] Laying out a persuasive case in his chapter "Dixie Cowboys," focusing on late-1930s B-westerns, he suggests that the "accommodation of contradiction and conflict is achieved through the means of *disguise*" in which "Westerns operate . . . as a mask for the South" and "for the Union as a whole."[16]

In Wallace Fox's post-WWII, mid-1940s series westerns, however, the primary concern and principal engine is not the "home under threat" or "economic dispossession" of the family home, as in the Depression-era series westerns Stanfield describes, but rather the proper management (and exploitation) of western territory and its natural resources and populations—the films focus on wild horses, white laborers, and Native tribes. Further, Fox's 1940s westerns feature heroes who are not Southerners transformed into Westerners (as we see in storylines like *The Squ*w Man*, *The Virginian*, and *Riders of the Purple Sage*, or the dissolute but noble gambler in *Stagecoach*).[17] In *Wild Beauty* and *Gun Town*, the hero is also not a freelance cowboy, a farmer, a gun for hire, or a local sheriff—he's an Indian agent, an employee of the federal government's Bureau of Indian Affairs, under the auspices of the Department of the Interior. Whether intervening in an environment of corruption (in *Gun Town*) or functioning as an administrative agent (in *Wild Beauty*), the Indian agent is a frontier functionary who has a boss in Washington, giving his intervention the weight and authority of federal control over local power struggles. His presence triggers a relationship of frontier to metropole that we see awkwardly on display in later sympathetic western films as well, such as Ford's *Cheyenne Autumn* (1964) with its inserted studio shots of Edward G. Robinson as Secretary of the Interior Carl Schurz attempting to navigate governmental bureaucracy on behalf of displaced, starving Cheyenne.

The history of this figure of the Indian agent in sympathetic westerns—the representations Wallace Fox might have had in mind while shooting *Wild Beauty* and *Gun Town*—is apparent in Paramount's *The Vanishing American* (1925) and *Redskin* (1929), films in which Indian agents feature prominently and negatively as figures in need of reform. In *The Vanishing American*, the Indian agent is irredeemably crooked, greedy, and lecherous, so intent on profiting from his position that he is a menace to the reservation and everyone on it. In *Redskin*, the agent, who doubles as an enforcer of boarding school discipline, is overly punitive and inflexible, but ultimately swayed by the gentling influence of his love interest, the schoolteacher. Fox would have seen these high-profile prestige productions, as he was active in Hollywood in the 1920s and his elder brother Edwin Carewe's Indian drama, *Ramona*, came out in 1928. Established screenwriter Adele Buffington, who wrote the script for *Wild Beauty*, would also likely have seen them; she too was active in the industry by the 1920s and wrote the scenario for the 1926 sympathetic Indian drama *The Test of Donald Norton*, about a mixed-race romance. In both *Wild Beauty* and *Gun Town*, the governmental Indian agent is caught up in a heterosexual romance plot when a frontier woman, engaged to the wrong man (the capitalist villain) finds the agent to be a more promising romantic partner.

Indian agents are a version of federal agent particular to the operations of Indian Affairs, western land settlement, and land management; they were first employed under the War Department, and then later under the Department of the Interior. Indian agents are key figures for plots involving land, Indian reservations, and federal Indian policies, as they are instantiated in western genre stories. Indian agents are also signals that the story at hand is not about Indian wars or the frontier per se, but rather that post-1871, early reservation period when treaties were no longer being negotiated, frontier wars were within recent memory, and protective laws and treaty promises were in place but regularly broken in cycles of corruption, abuse, and reform. Like reservation teachers, Indian agents represent U.S. control over Native tribes, policies of assimilation, and settler colonial presumption of management; the presence of an Indian agent in a western raises representational questions about how settler colonial nations treat not only Indigenous nations but also other minority populations—a potent question in the aftermath of WWII and the Japanese–American internment camps in the West. The B-films in this postwar moment valorize the Indian agent in a political climate of assimilation, a moment of tension between separation of tribes (in the reservation system) and integration (through assimilationist boarding schools, the Relocation policy, the military, and other institutions); in the wake of genocides and injustices, in the face of differences, how will different peoples live together?

The westerns of the 1940s featuring Indian agents represent a shift away from the themes of 1930s series films, which have no equivalent to the Indian agent figures as they are instantiated in Universal's films. These films represent, instead, a re-engagement of the sympathetic discourse so prevalent in the 1920s around Native peoples and Native-settler relations, through references in expository dialogue alluding to the language of policy reform materials in the popular press. As in films from the 1920s—*The Vanishing American*, *Redskin*, and others—the films cultivated an image of informed sympathy and advocated reform (which, in their storylines, also mark the Indian agent as a good frontier detective and a good romantic partner). Establishing Native communities as fundamentally non-threatening and friendly to settlers in *Wild Beauty*, and as justifiably provoked in *Gun Town*, also subtly advocates for federal Indian policy reform and for federal over state or local authority in tribal negotiations and land use. The figure of the Indian agent makes these films' critiques of capitalist extraction specific to the West, even as films emerge from a for-profit studio system (itself an extractive industry in the far west).

Fox's work at Universal resonated with and contributed to other kinds of national discourse around the post-World War II renegotiation of Indigenous participation in civic life: the Relocation policy, problems of re-integrating returned Native soldiers, restrictive voting rules in reservation states, and shifting attitudes towards assimilation, education, and federal management of tribal and public spaces in the West (including resources like wild horses and grazing rights, minerals, and oil). The B-film production system in the 1940s—the structuring institution for Fox's career—intersects with this context of postwar U.S.-tribal politics, when emergent cold war ideology contributed to shifting federal Indian policies, especially the integrative, assimilationist policies of Relocation and Termination.

Fox's series westerns in the mid- to late 1940s came out just before an explosion of sympathetic pro-Indian westerns from major studios, including the breakthrough films *Broken Arrow* from Twentieth Century-Fox and *Devil's Doorway* from MGM. Both films were begun prior to 1949 (and Elliot Arnold's novel *Broken Arrow*, from which the film was adapted, was published in 1947), so the timing between Fox's "Indian agent" films with Universal and the 1950 resurgence of sympathetic westerns from major studios is quite close. Only three years separate the B-western and A-western production cycles—the B-film industry's short shooting and production schedules allowed them to pivot faster toward new trends than the major studios. As Stanfield does for singing cowboy westerns of the 1930s, critics such as Slotkin, Lenihan, and Cripps have aligned the representation of the frontier with the South in these mid-century films, arguing that the representations of Indians and of mixed-race romance in *Broken Arrow* and *Devil's Doorway*, along with other examples, allegorize Southern race relations at the dawn of the Civil Rights era. Steve Neale provides a counter-voice to this trend, arguing against reading cinematic representations of Indians solely as "empty signifiers" or "ethnic stand-ins" for non-Native minorities.[18] In addition to the prominent issues specific to Native Americans in this period—especially the shift in federal policy towards assimilation and the termination of the federal trust relationship with tribes—there were other western issues brewing, such as the mid-1940s sagebrush rebellion (both *Devil's Doorway* and *Shane* feature conflicts driven by land use and grazing rights).[19] The thematics of *Wild Beauty* and *Gun Town* prefigure the early 1950s cycle, focusing on the character of the Indian agent just as the federal government prepared for a shift in policy. In each of these films, sympathetic Indian characters and plotlines arc signs in a larger screen semiotic—they represent a nostalgic love of place threatened by the contemporary evils of capital, a relationship mediated by heroic federal managers. While it's impossible to draw a line directly from Wallace Fox's personal politics—of which we know almost nothing—to his films' images of Indians and representation of Indigenous issues, what is visible in the texts are larger discourses that are both specific to federal Indian policy and western land debates, and also address national tensions in order to advocate for a broad, fundamentally left-liberal agenda centered around equal rights. The universalizing discourse of the films enables this progressive positioning, however, by eschewing both the historical corruption of actual Indian agents and the distinctive rights to self-governance and homelands inherent in Native sovereignty.

WILD BEAUTY

Wild Beauty tells the story of an enlightened doctor and Indian agent, Dr. Dave Morrow (Don Porter), newly arrived schoolteacher Linda Gibson (Lois Collier), and a Native boy, Johnny, (Robert "Buzz" Henry in redface), who ultimately work together to save a wild horse herd from a heartless industrialist's (Gibson's erstwhile fiancé) plan to slaughter the horses and sell the hides for shoe leather. Screenwriter Adele Buffington specialized in western-genre films and had frequently written for Universal's western series starring Johnny Mack Brown (a few of which Fox directed).[20] In *Wild Beauty*, Buffington and Fox create a sympathetic advocacy picture directed to youth and family audiences, foregrounding a seemingly progressive agenda from within the constraints of a B-film production system by combining visual and dramatic elements of a horse story with the expository strategies of the social problem film.

This mode of sentimental storytelling works toward multiple ends, as the formulaic structures and logics of genre narrative enable coincidences and narrative turns to satisfy two contradictory impulses at once: validating the perspectives of the disenfranchised—Indigenous peoples, children, and the non-human world—and reinforcing a frontier system of federal oversight and hierarchy. The story tracks closely with larger cycles in U.S. cultural production for mass audiences, including renewed attention to animal companions in coming-of-age stories and to the impacts of resource extraction in western lands. Premised on questions about how Native peoples and lands will be governed within the settler nation-state, the film advocates for protection of reservation resources from exploitation by appealing, through the figure of the Indian agent, to a structure of imagined imperial benevolence in the form of the Department of the Interior—that is, the federal administration's Bureau of Indian Affairs.

In *Wild Beauty*, the Indian agent—with his goals of Native assimilation and economic improvement—represents a point at which settler colonialism resembles imperialism. He is (and the schoolteacher is) raised and educated in an urban metropole and sent as an emissary to the farther reaches of the territory newly understood as the United States, ostensibly in a service role but one with great authority over a subjugated—and also aestheticized—Indigenous population. Along with its emphasis on bureaucratic, medical, and educational supervision of tribes, the film narrates a romance among the managerial class in a modernizing West, with the implied adoption of an Indian child at the center of the story's reconfiguration of family. The Native child comes in for great concern and attention in this story; as a contested figure, he instantiates the way Indian child welfare remained at the heart of Indian affairs in the popular imagination. *Wild Beauty* does this at the intersection of two genres with different modes of address—while the story of a boy and his horse engages youth audiences through narrative strategies of plot and character, the Indian agent figure (and other off-screen experts conveyed through images of books and texts) registers another more expository, didactic mode, evoking the social problem film.

The story's engine is the settler wardship of Johnny, who at the film's opening is being raised by trading post operator Barney Skeets (George Cleveland) and the Indian agent Dr. Dave Morrow. By the film's end, Linda Gibson and Dr. Morrow have become a couple and formed a substitute family for Johnny; in the interim, the motherless Johnny heals an injured colt and re-unites it with its mother and the wild herd, re-emphasizing the centrality of custodial transfer and substitute parenting to this story of frontier family formation.

As a horse story, and on the heels of cultural touchstones such as Walter Farley's novel *The Black Stallion* (1941) and the film *National Velvet* (1944, from the novel by Enid Bagnold in 1935), *Wild Beauty*'s left-liberal interest in racial equality and government protection of western lands takes the form of attention to interspecies relationships and children's worlds. Close-up shots make an individual personality of the central horse character, Wild Beauty (a strategy audiences would have been familiar with from the visual treatment of horse celebrities like Gene Autry's Champion, Roy Rogers' Trigger, and the Lone Ranger's Silver), as well as the dog, Corky. Both animals perform stunts that direct the action of the film (as when Wild Beauty opens a corral to free his herd). His close-ups are intercut with long shots of wild horse herds, emphasizing both his individuality and his representation of a population of western wild horses. The wild herd footage is recycled from the 1935 Universal film *Stormy*, directed by Lew Landers, which was shot partly on location in the painted desert area near Tuba City, Arizona (a Navajo crew rounded up large numbers of wild horses for the production). The film's re-use of this footage—and its larger narrative hinging on protecting wild horse herds on reservation land—points to further intertextual influence from the 1925 Paramount film *The Vanishing American*, an artifact of the strongly reformist discourse in an earlier sympathetic Indian drama cycle in the late 1920s. *The Vanishing American* also focused on Navajo by means of expository sequences (in an extended prologue), Indian agent and schoolteacher figures, and the rounding up of wild horses on the reservation for military use in World War I. *Wild Beauty* takes up not only plot points and the style of mixed narrative and expository modes from *The Vanishing American*, but also a similar assimilationist discourse, using its horse story as a whisper-thin allegory for a post-WWII liberal politics of racial integration.

When Dr. Morrow first questions Johnny's dedication to healing the colt, he frames it in social terms: "Why set your heart on him, Johnny, he's of an outlaw breed!" To which Johnny responds, "But you don't understand, Dr. Dave—if Wild Beauty's my friend, he'll make them all my friends." That settlers can be friends "with an outlaw breed" encodes a form of "treaty discourse," as Chadwick Allen has articulated it in his analyses of *The Lone Ranger*—a discursive site where the nation-to-nation diplomacy and social relations between Native Americans and settlers can be rehearsed—here through the mediated, representational space of the screen.[21] This sequence also foregrounds the way the film presents individual friendships that exemplify larger relationships—Wild Beauty functions as a synecdoche for the herd, a representative and "composite picture" of a particular type—so that systemic change can be narrated at the level of personal relationships. In parallel to Wild Beauty's journey from "outlaw breed" to "friendship and understanding" with Johnny, the schoolteacher Linda Gibson initially calls Johnny a "little savage," but her companion Sissy Cruthers re-frames our view of him to see that "that little Indian *is* cute isn't he—just like a picture out of the book the professor gave you." That book, the imagined text

"Children of the Arizona Indian," read aloud alongside several expository monologues by Dr. Morrow, foregrounds hierarchies of institutionalized settler expertise that interrupt the story's forward action and shift its address to the didactic tone of the social problem film (its earnest presentation in sharp contrast to the theatricality and playfully ironic tones of *Gun Town*). Even as he acts to correct and shape the behavior of the young white schoolteacher, Dr. Morrow's speech advocates for American Indian assimilation as a form of "responsibility towards the Indian, and his problems . . . to help them learn our ways, so they can exist side by side with us." Morrow's only solution to "the Indian and his problems"—the problem of co-existence in their territory with settlers—is assimilation ("learning our ways"), represented narratively in the struggle over raising Johnny.

This contested education is visualized in several schoolhouse scenes, as Gibson wrangles the incorrigible Johnny ("I'm afraid that's one youngster you'll never corral in a schoolroom, Ms. Gibson!") into her classroom. The spectacles of Native patriotism (as the children sing "My Country 'Tis of Thee") resemble those in *The Vanishing American*, although the children are not in uniform. This orderly setting, and the Doctor's "Field Hospital No. 3, U.S. Office of Indian Affairs" (along with his habit of re-naming people, so that "Wasa Wininama" becomes "Winnie"), are marked as colonial spaces and strategies, in contrast to the adobe buildings and the carefully placed background images of women weaving and grinding corn in town. Later scenes show Johnny in the classroom, and the film seems to assure audiences that they can have it both ways—to honor Johnny's "wild" nature and also to incorporate him into assimilationist schooling. This narrative of guardianship and amalgamation is given closure visually through an image of familiar reconsolidation as Dr. Morrow and Linda Gibson form an adoptive family for Johnny.

Dr. Morrow's extended speech explicitly asks viewers to understand individuals as a representative of type, a form of abstraction: "To understand these people it's best to begin by trying to live close to the ones you meet in the daily pursuit of your work. You'll find that they represent something of a composite picture of them all. . ." The subsequent montage sequence creates a setting that feeds a touristic fantasy of the southwest, including scenes of sheep herding, carding wool, and weaving rugs while also tracing the rug through stages of production, turning Navajo culture into a commodity for tourist consumption. With an emphasis on hard economic circumstances, the speech concludes with the hope that white America will "cultivate sufficient understanding and national decency to help them build their cultures into industrial successes, or at least an equitable standard of living." Gibson compliments him on this "complete account." The importance of the authoritative, thorough narrator to the legitimization of settler colonial management in this story aligns it with public rhetoric of Indian policy and policy reform, such as the 1928 Meriam

Report that was so important to the 1920s sympathetic film cycle, while also resembling John Ford's frequent depictions of a Washington bureaucrat in the Indian Affairs office in his 1964 film *Cheyenne Autumn* (a film that also imagines the settler family's temporary adoption of a Cheyenne girl in its closing images).

This rhetoric, while impossibly condescending, is presented as preferable to the raw capitalist exploitation formulated by the film's villains. They position the wild horses variously as a waste ("not good for anything, even the redskins' great economic plan") and a national resource worth protecting ("but boss, ain't you kind of messing with Uncle Sam? Them horses belong to the reservation"). The film's villainous pair—aspiring retail shoe magnate Gordon Madison (Robert Wilcox) and cattle rancher John Andrews (Dick Curtis, the stock player of villains for the series)—bond over Andrews' complaints that Indians are no longer "willing to work for what they're worth" because they've had "too much dang education for the breed," "stuffin' the redskins with a lot of high falutin' notions about improving their so-called culture." The cattleman's willingness to slaughter the horses (and kill Native people in the process) marks his villainy in contrast to Dr. Morrow, who couldn't find the heart to shoot the injured colt even when he didn't think it could survive its injuries. Indians, too, would (according to the cattleman) "never go for mass slaughter like that" even if it brought them economic wealth. The rough talk of the film's villains, and their subsequent violence, makes the film's case for why federal oversight is necessary to keep the most ruthless and most racist aspects of capitalist extraction at bay. Through this contrasting rhetoric, Fox's film advocates a politics of federal trust status and protection for Native peoples and their resources, foregrounding a discourse of equality and development but only within a context of assimilation—a limited postwar "progressive" position that cedes power to the federal government.

GUN TOWN

Where *Wild Beauty* combined a horse story with the social problem film, *Gun Town*, performing a similar feat of genre-blending, mixes the new aesthetics of film noir with the crooner tradition of B-westerns. If *Wild Beauty* looks back to the didactic solemnity of *The Vanishing American* in 1925 and forward to *Cheyenne Autumn* in 1964, *Gun Town* adapts the 1930s singing cowboy film while anticipating the social commentary of frontier noir films like MGM's *Devil's Doorway* (1950). Authenticity—historical, representational, or otherwise—was not the goal for *Gun Town*, which is, in every way, all about performativity, acting, and masquerade in the playground of the imagined West. At the same time, however, this tonally complex, low-budget series film anticipates trends in the genre years early—a sympathetic stance towards Indigenous issues, strong women characters, and elements of noir visual and narrative style complete with night shooting, a cynical detective hero and a femme fatale. Its A-film equivalent might be John Ford's *My Darling Clementine*, also 1946, also notable for its noir elements, but *Gun Town* was made on extraordinarily different budgetary terms and with lighter, more playful and theatrical tones interwoven. But, as with the urban settings of noir, on the frontier strangers can appear out of nowhere, it's hard to know who is who, and only the government agent can flush out disguised corruption.

Fox directed *Gun Town* and also served as its associate producer, with production taking place during six days in August of 1945, on a tight budget of $51,000. By this point Kirby Grant was heir to the lead role in the series (after the departure of former leads Johnny Mack Brown and Rod Cameron).[22] The film's story tells of frontier corruption in Gun Town. Saloon owner Lucky Dorgan (Lyle Talbot) covertly sabotages his fiancé's pending contract with Wells Fargo stage lines. The incoming Indian agent Kip Lewis (Kirby Grant) sorts it out, revealing through frontier-style detective work that white men in Lucky's employ are masquerading as Native warriors in order to disrupt the road-building project. It's a complex plot—if Lucky's fiancé "Buckskin" Jane Sawyer's (Louise Currie) work crew doesn't finish the road construction on time, Gun Town will lose the mail franchise, which automatically breaks her potentially lucrative contract with Wells Fargo. Lucky takes various steps to sabotage her operation so that another company, Transcontinental, can take over Gun Town's contract (and pay him a substantial kickback). This rather abstract discourse sketches a vague, largely off-screen matrix of corrupt companies that the characters allude to in tossed-off comments in order to support (however thinly) the dramatic action on screen. As with other B-westerns, the production relies on this spectacle and the characters to carry things along largely on their own. And they do—saloon singer-entertainer Belle Townley (Claire Carleton), along with white villains dressed in redface, pull off various musical, theatrical, and attack stunts in order to distract and disrupt Buckskin's road work crews. Kip and Buckskin eventually discover the ruse, but in desperation, Lucky precipitates a real Indian attack, a cover for his own heist further camouflaged with redface disguises, but this too is foiled and Lucky is killed by his erstwhile fiancé. The playful tone of the film's opening scenes is gone by the end—the staged attacks have become real ones, and Gun Town is destroyed.

The film opens with a song, "A Cowboy's Happy," sung by Belle, who faces the audience from the window of a moving stagecoach. Former vaudeville performer Fuzzy Knight, a fixture at Universal, plays stagecoach driver Ivory Keys, who attempts to join in (to Belle's dismay). Joking that "Ivory Keys missed his calling," Ivory says that "when my old man said he wanted me to go on the stage, I reckon he meant stage*coach*!" The audience has its cue: this western vehicle is a performative space. Accompanied by onscreen music (the banjo player is beside Belle in the stagecoach), the song is about how a cowboy is happy when "the trail is wide and he can ride." While the song constructs the "happy cowboy" on the wide trail, there are actually no cowboys in the scene. The white male hero that everyone is singing about is absent. But when the stagecoach is ambushed—apparently by Indians—we are primed for his delayed entrance, riding up over a ridge to see and rescue the runaway coach. In another exceptional coincidence, Buckskin happens to see the whole event from her wagon, which enables her to provide an eyewitness account at a critical moment in town. Kip isn't the happy cowboy of the song, however; rather, he's a cynical government employee, an Indian agent. As the film moves from horse opera to noir during its hour runtime, the figure of the Indian agent brings federal authority and an ability to read clues to a frontier space of confused identities where the practice of "playing Indian" is revealed to be a mask for capitalist corruption.

The interruption of Belle's performance turns out to have been a performance as well, an orchestrated, fake "Indian attack": Belle and Lucky had planned her big entrance into Gun Town with the "runaway stagecoach" saved by three men. But once Kip drives the stage into town, the gathered crowd suspects that he himself may have hijacked it, and a lynch mob attempts to hang him (perhaps registering the early noir influence *The Ox-Bow Incident* of 1943). Kip is saved by Buckskin, who intervenes in the shouting with her bullwhip and a challenge ("did you see it? Well I did"), hopping up on the hanging platform as if it's a stage. Belle and Lucky watch the action as if it's a show as well, commenting to one another, "That crowd is turning the hero into a villain!" and "Looks like everyone wants to get in the act," concluding at the end that "the show's ending just as we planned it, with the dirty work being blamed on the Indians." Melodramatic coincidence—the chance encounters on the frontier that create opportunities for athletic stunt-filled rescues and interventions in ongoing action—aligns with another aspect of melodrama: mistaken and faked identities that await revelation. The space of masquerade so often opened up by the frontier envisioned in B-films contradictorily imagines both the identity play of costumed performativity and also the seemingly reliable "tells" that evidence an underlying stable identity. These tells, once recognized and taken as clues, become the solution to a frontier mystery. This preoccupation with identities is evident in the film's strong women characters as well—Claire Carleton as the hard-nosed saloon singer Belle and Louise Currie as the tough, observant sharpshooter Buckskin; "both are easily the life of this party," according to the March 15, 1946 *Hollywood Reporter* review.[23] Davey, Buckskin's little brother, is taken in by Belle's act despite being warned that "she's only acting, Davey," but he's able to see through his own sister's tomboy act, assuring Kip that "deep down beats a feminine heart." Here the film draws a line between what's "only acting" and what's "deep down"—between performative identities and real ones—assuring audiences that such a line *can* be drawn.

Partly because of their budgetary austerity, B-westerns turn to inexpensive aesthetic strategies like reflexivity and complex plotting, engaging in a different register from the more serious key of A-list westerns from prominently named directors. As Scott Simmon writes, the B-western "form as a whole is unable—or refuses—to take itself as solemnly as the A western."[24] In B-films, problems and conflicts are worked out via theatrical traditions of costume, coincidence, performance, and melodrama, codes and conventions of the stage. With its sequences of heavily expository dialogue supporting convoluted plots, Simmon argues, B-westerns rely on "a knowing theatricality, complicitous with the audience;" "the clash between the genuine landscapes and the theatrical performance adds to the form's inadvertent surrealism. The B-western always seems to be threatening to break the fourth-wall convention and to let its audiences in on the joke."[25]

We can also expand on Peter Stanfield's argument that B-westerns inherit the performative and musical qualities of American minstrel traditions—and we see this especially in actors who moved from the minstrel stage to B-film production, like Fuzzy Knight—to understand the communicative mode of B-films as they engage in representations of playing Indian. Where Stanfield sees in the B-western's minstrel roots an allegorical coding of Southern race relations (as discussed above), Fox's B-westerns of the 1940s featuring the Indian agent hero strongly suggest the films' alignment not only with the South but also with the West—with frontier or treaty relations between Native peoples and settlers. The dynamics of playing Indian as an onscreen machination—not through casting, as in the common practice of redfacing, but in the form of a plot device—is a cinematic story trope that dates at least to John Ford's *The Iron Horse* in 1924, where the lead villain, a white man, masquerades as Cheyenne, and of course harks back much further to the iconic, originary Indian play of the Boston Tea Party. Dakota historian Phil Deloria describes the paradox of playing Indian as a uniquely American strategy for creating a national identity while reaching for authenticity in the face of the anxieties of industrialism and modernity: "the self-defining pairing of American truth with American freedom rests upon the ability to wield power against Indians—social, military, economic and political—while simultaneously drawing power from them."[26]

Gun Town renders this process of redfacing both visible and villainous—making a practice already steeped in ambivalence yet more so through a critique of playing Indian that also perpetuates it. That this onscreen practice is reproduced—even as it is condemned—by a Chickasaw director further compounds *Gun Town*'s already politicized pressure on creating, re-creating, recognizing, and re-recognizing identity as the primary work of its frontier story. Deloria writes that "even as Indian play has been an invasion of the realities of native people, it has been an intercultural meeting ground upon which Indians and non-Indians have created new identities, not only for white Americans, but for Indians themselves."[27]

Gun Town offers three very distinct scenes where characters present ideas about Indians for the audience to weigh. In the first, Kip and Buck characterize Indians as victimized but potentially deadly frontier fighters, a national liberal framework representing Native grievances, and potential violence, as justified reactions to settler incursion. Kip reveals his purpose in Gun Town after Buckskin offers him a job working for her: "Well, I've already got one boss, the Department of the Interior." "Oh, Indian Affairs!" Buckskin replies, "So that's why you got so upset over the attack on the stage." Kip has doubts about the apparent Indian attack on the stage, "because I just came from a long powwow with the Apaches." Buckskin notes that "hard feelings are brewing all along the frontier" and Kip replies with a brief, bitter speech about Native rights, as a camera re-framing to close-up underscores the importance of this view of frontier relations: "That's the way they are . . . shy back and watch more and more settlers moving in, killing their game, taking over all the best land, fencing them out. Then one fine day when everything looks peaceful. . ." Buckskin agrees: "Yeah I know, that's the way it was back on the Bighorn years ago." The serious tone of this exchange deals the audience an abrupt turn away from the theatrical play of the film's opening, pivoting toward a discursive mode more appropriate to the social problem film and to the western genre's more somber treatments of frontier trauma, presaging the climactic action—a story that began with a "fake" Indian attack will end with a "real" one.

The second scene, an exchange between Kip and Ivory about the stage robbery, takes place as they swap jokes and play music together in the unused stagecoach. Unlike the serious-minded tone of the previous scene, here the men return to a space of comedy and performativity. Regarding B-western performances, Simmon points out how "acting in westerns begins as a series of codified gestures and conventional poses" and "leans towards the presentational rather than striving for the representational."[28] B-western narratives rely on these conventions to form a system of racial and gender markers, which organize the genre's characteristic tension between fixed and free-flowing models of identity. As Kip ponders how the tribe could have attacked the stagecoach unseen, he free-associates, banters, and puns: "Maybe he flew on! Coulda been a Crow Indian!" Ivory chimes in, "Hey I got it, it waren't no live Indian at all, it were an Indian spirit . . . don't ya see? What would a live Indian want to steal money for? He ain't got no use for it. . ." "You know," replies Kip, "You've tickled a pretty good clue out of that music box."

Ivory's fantasy, that Native people exist outside of settler cash economies, is reinforced in other westerns, such as Mann's 1950 film *Winchester 73* in which Indian characters engage in trade but are left out of the circulation of cash (or gold) altogether. In *Gun Town*, Kip and Ivory's jocular code-play activates seemingly arbitrary "stage rules," invented for B-film plots and perhaps inherited from the general investment in such systems that powered the minstrel stage, around race and gender identity (e.g. Indians wouldn't steal money because they don't use money). That a Native director is being paid (though paid poorly) to produce this story about Indians not needing money not only belies the clue upon which the whole charade hinges, but also returns us to Phil Deloria's cautious assessment of playing Indian as a survival strategy for Native culture brokers. Deloria writes that

> in the early twentieth century, Indian people participated in the making of Indian Others as never before . . . yet the fact that native people turned to playing Indian—miming Indianness back at Americans in order to redefine it—indicates how little cultural capital Indian people possessed at the time. Such exercises were fraught not only with ambiguity, but with danger. Mimetic imitations could alter political, cultural, and personal identities in unanticipated ways.[29]

In the third and last scene in which Native people form the primary subject of conversation—the lead-up to the climactic Indian attack—Lucky characterizes Indians derisively as passive pawns inclined to drunkenness and subject to white manipulation. The masquerade has already been revealed, after a dramatic chase (Buckskin wipes paint off an injured man's face: "This is a white man, Sheriff!" But Kip says, "I'm not surprised. I figured they were white men masquerading as Indians," as if this were a common strategy on the frontier). However, in the closing act, Lucky precipitates a "real" Indian attack out of desperation, as cover for his last-ditch attempt to get rich by robbing the bank: "We'll wait till the Indians get going good, and then we'll join 'em; nobody'll ever know the difference." His followers ask how he convinced the Apache to attack. "Easy," he replies, "I told the Apaches a posse was being formed to clean out their village, because the stagecoach robberies were being blamed on them—those kegs of firewater did the rest!" Lucky's raw, racist stereotype, coded in the film as villainous but not as inaccurate, presents Native people as pliable, vulnerable to alcohol, and easily misled. However, Buckskin's white road crew workers are similarly cast as a malleable crowd, prone to manipulation by theater and to overstaying at the saloon, and they are similarly capable of violence in the opening scenes when they quickly form a lynch mob. As much as *Gun Town* reflects on performance, it is also interested in audiences, and how they can be duped by shenanigans on stage; in the film's world, both working men and Native people have a crowd mentality and are easily manipulated. Lucky's kind of identity play is presented as a contrast to Ivory's, and while it is uglier, it works by the same rules.

While there are many identifiable elements of noir in *Gun Town*—like *T-Men*, it features cynical federal agents in the detecting role, a transgressive femme fatale, and a vision of capitalist rot as private interests are twisted and distorted by corruption—its peak noir moment comes with the visual aesthetics of the extended Indian attack at the film's close. Gun Town is left devastated, but viewers are assured that with the rotten parts burned away, the foundation can be rebuilt—it's a bleak ending for a film that began with a song about happy cowboys. The chiaroscuro light, shadow, and silhouette of the night shooting, with fire effects and a largely dark screen, call up an off-kilter world of visually abstract chaos. Critics praised this powerful final sequence, but diverged over whether to attribute it to Fox's production: the *Hollywood Reporter* asserts that while "the footage WAS spectacular," the "epic night raid" was "stock, no doubt." The *Daily Variety*, however, credits the footage to the cinematographer ("Maury Gertsman's camera"), commending his "punchy handling" of both the chase sequences and torch-lit attack.[30] Fox often began his western series films for Universal with a moving camera and, like his brothers, he knew how to shoot a disaster scene—in fact, he may have learned to manage smoke effects from his elder brother Edwin Carewe, who used fire and smoke very skillfully in the settler attack scenes of *Ramona* in 1928. However, in this case, it was stock—Fox frequently used stock footage, as he did for the wild horse herd scenes in *Wild Beauty*. He made extensive use of recycled footage from the 1941 Universal film *Badlands of Dakota* for the dramatic finale of *Gun Town*, as Jacob Floyd discusses in detail in this volume.

B-westerns made up for their anemic budgets not just with sensationalism—stunts, songs, pratfalls, and general outrageousness—but also with imaginative and conceptual sophistication. In *Gun Town*, reflexivity is cheap, and easy to work into the narrative around scenes of spectacle. While clearly influenced by westerns that featured singing, Fox seems less interested in aligning the genre codes with Southern tensions, and more interested in characters playing Indian, as well as in the work of detection to uncover the manipulations of frontier masquerade through "tells" and clues. And rather than the earnest belief in assimilation proposed in *Wild Beauty*, *Gun Town* is preoccupied with performative and unstable identities.

CONCLUSION

Fox was deeply embedded in western genre production and wholly engaged with its requisite spectacle and action, fluent in the earlier stage conventions of melodrama and minstrelsy that informed its performative traditions, and conversant with its images of Indians. Across these tonally complex low-budget films that hit American screens in 1946, we can ask what kind of problems are posed to be solved in these story worlds. How do the villains talk about Native people, and how do the Indian agent heroes talk about them? Problems of frontier corruption involve extractive capitalism in both, and in each case the Indian agent makes a case for federal government presence, surveillance, and protection, asking viewers to invest in the idea of the modern nation-state. In *Wild Beauty*, corrupt settlers deride what might have been perceived (or misperceived) by audiences as racial uplift (education and economic development), and the film's government mouthpiece advocates for adoption and assimilationist education for Native children. In *Gun Town*, corruption works by disguise, and the agent's task is to detect and protect, relying on his knowledge of the rules and tells of frontier identity.

In the midst of these ambiguous portraits of a confusing and cacophonous frontier, Fox's own navigation of plot and production within Universal's complex system—and his degree of agential power within it—remain just out of reach. From the scraps and managerial traces of production files and resonant texts produced in tightly scripted and controlled circumstances, what we can recover here suggests a negotiation of administrative power no less for Fox himself within the studio system than for the Indian agents in the plots of his movies. The parallels across mode of production and text invite us to re-center and re-examine Indigeneity and Indian images both in front of the camera and behind it, recognizing within the settler colonial frameworks of mid-century motion pictures the potential for intercultural space, one which necessarily often subsumed the personal politics of director, cast, and crew into a generalized national discourse communicable in the lingua franca of genre. But the discursive work of genre is far from apolitical, and can be—and was, here—bent towards a left-leaning rhetoric of equality, a broadly liberal "treaty discourse" in the genre-blending communicative modes of the B-western. This postwar cinematic promotion of federal administrative power functioned both to contain Indigenous sovereignty and, sometimes, to shore up the power of Indigenous nations to push back against discriminatory state and local laws. For all the convolutions of the budget studio's commercial imperatives, Wallace Fox's career presents a fascinating case of an Indigenous director producing images of Indians from within the heart of the system.

NOTES

1. Chadwick Allen, "Hero with Two Faces: The Lone Ranger as Treaty Discourse" *American Literature* 68 (1996), 609–38; Michelle Raheja, *Reservation Reelism: Redfacing, Visual Sovereignty, and Representations of Native Americans in Film* (Lincoln: University of

Nebraska Press, 2011), 20. See also Angela Aleiss, *Making the White Man's Indian: Native Americans and Hollywood Movies* (Westport, CT: Praeger, 2005).

2. Quotation is from Joanne Barker, "Confluence: Water as an Analytic of Indigenous Feminisms," *American Indian Culture and Research Journal* 43:3 (2019), 30.
3. Amy M. Ware, *The Cherokee Kid: Will Rogers, Tribal Identity, and the Making of an American Icon* (Lawrence: University Press of Kansas, 2015).
4. Raheja, 193.
5. Vicki Mayer, Miranda J. Banks, and John T. Caldwell, "Introduction, Production Studies: Roots and Routes", in Mayer, Banks, and Caldwell (eds), *Production Studies: Cultural Studies of Media Industries* (New York: Routledge, 2009), 2.
6. Thomas Schatz, *The Genius of the System: Hollywood Filmmaking in the Studio Era* (New York: Henry Holt and Company, 1988).
7. Andrew Fisher, "Between Compliance and Resistance: Mapping the Careers of Wallace Fox and Nipo Strongheart in Early Hollywood," this volume.
8. Raheja, 1, 102; Nicholas G. Rosenthal, "Representing Indians: Native American Actors on Hollywood's Frontier," *The Western Historical Society* 36:3 (2005): 329–52; Liza Black, *Picturing Indians: Native Americans in Film, 1941–1960* (Lincoln: University of Nebraska Press, 2020).
9. "Wallace Fox is Winner of Director's Contract," *The Washington Post*, September 1, 1935, M3.
10. Thomas Reeder, *Stop Yellin', Ben Pivar and the Horror, Mystery and Action-Adventure Films of His Universal B-Unit* (Albany, GA: BearManor Media, 2011) 358.
11. USC Special Collections, Universal Pictures Production Files, #1465 "Bad Men of the Border"; #1459 "Code of the Lawless"; #1469 "Gun Town"; #1524 "Gunman's Code"; #1522 "Lawless Breed"; #1397 "Riders of the Santa Fe"; #1519 "Rustler's Round-Up"; #1467 "Trail to Vengeance"; #1513 "Wild Beauty."
12. Reeder, 365.
13. Ibid., 367.
14. Ibid., 367.
15. Peter Stanfield, *Hollywood, Westerns and the 1930s: The Lost Trail* (Exeter: University of Exeter Press, 2001), 5.
16. Ibid., 195.
17. Joanna Hearne, *Native Recognition: Indigenous Cinema and the Western* (Albany, NY: SUNY Press, 2012); Stanfield, 206–7.
18. Steve Neale, "Vanishing Americans: Racial and Ethnic Issues in the Interpretation and Context of Post-War 'Pro-Indian' Westerns," in Edward Buscombe and Roberta Pearson (eds), *Back in the Saddle Again: New Essays on the Western* (London: British Film Institute, 1998), 8–28; Joanna Hearne, "The 'Ache for Home': Assimilation and Separatism in Anthony Mann's *Devil's Doorway*," in Peter C. Rollins and John E. O'Connor (eds), *Hollywood's West: The American Frontier in Film, Television, and History* (Lexington: University Press of Kentucky, 2005), 126–59.
19. Karen R. Merrill, *Public Lands and Political Meaning: Ranchers, the Government, and the Property between Them* (Berkeley: University of California Press, 2002); "Federal Policy, Western Lands, and Malheur," *BlogWest* January 7, 2016. Available at <https://blogwest.org/2016/01/07/federal-policy-western-lands-and-malheur/5> (January 6, 2018).
20. Fox had made quite a few films from Buffington's scripts; active in the industry as a founding member of the Screen Writers Guild, Buffington advocated for original screenplays over adaptations and was at the height of her career in the 1940s.
21. Allen, 611.
22. USC Special Collections Universal Pictures #1469, file 09170, "Gun Town."
23. "Gun Town," *Hollywood Reporter*, March 15, 1946.

24. Scott Simmon, *The Invention of the Western Film: A Cultural History of the Genre's First Half-Century*, (Cambridge: Cambridge University Press, 2003), 174.
25. Ibid.
26. Philip Deloria, *Playing Indian* (New Haven: Yale University Press, 1998), 7, 191.
27. Ibid., 187.
28. Simmon, 174.
29. Deloria, 125. Michelle Raheja similarly describes "redfacing" as "ambivalent cultural and political work" that could both protect Native performers and simultaneously lead them to "negative self-fashioning," 21.
30. "Gun Town," *Hollywood Reporter*, 15 March 1946; "Gun Town," *Daily Variety*, March 15, 1946.

CHAPTER 3

Neglected Western Traditions and Indigenous Cinema in the 1945–1946 Series Westerns of Wallace Fox

Jacob Floyd

When one talks about western movies, a set of specific imagery, cultural and gender politics, and generic conventions come to mind: the individual rugged male hero, Calvary rides, and epic southwestern vistas. While apparent across many western films, this iconography acquired added weight through its presence in significant film studies, such as Jim Kitses's oft-reprinted list of western motifs based upon binaries he believed were central to the genre (individual/community, nature/culture, West/East, etc.) that all stem from one foundational opposition: the wilderness versus civilization.[1] While significant to the development of various strains of film studies, from auteur studies to semiotics, these genre studies privileged the same kind of western films: the exceptional films made by a small group of auteurs. In fact, Kitses's taxonomy, often applied to the entire genre, was created to address the work of only a handful of auteur directors. Yet, the western film genre is far more varied and contradictory than we may immediately assume and exceeds any simple formulation of its contents. Nowhere is this more evident than in the B-westerns of the 1940s. In this chapter, I will discuss six western films directed by Wallace W. Fox over the course of one year that illustrate a different western tradition: one that challenges and complicates the conventional notions of westerns through progressive themes that emphasize the importance of collective civic action against corrupt institutions. Through their repeated motifs and themes, these films illustrate a neglected and richer history of the genre at a time of cultural and industrial change.

Additionally, while examining Fox's films sheds light on a neglected tradition of western genre filmmaking, his films also suggest the influence of another tradition: his Native American heritage. Fox was a Chickasaw working in the genre most tied to Native (mis)representation. On the surface, these films, in their plots and motifs, resemble other B-westerns of his era; however, taking his Native background into account when reading his films, specifically his use of recycled footage from other films, suggests a subtle Indigenous critique of the foundational assumptions of the genre, and foreshadows an approach of contemporary Indigenous media makers. Revisiting Fox as a genre director provides us with a richer view of the western genre. Reclaiming Fox as a Native filmmaker presents new possibilities in what we consider to be Indigenous film and suggests a longer lineage of Native filmmaking approaches.

THE 1945–1946 SERIES WESTERNS

"Series western" describes the films produced by an industrial practice in which directors and stars were contracted by a studio to make a series of western films, usually six or seven, over a short period of time and on limited budgets. While ostensibly B-pictures, part of the attraction of these films to studios was their versatility in film programs (they average just under an hour in runtime), and they occasionally received top billing, especially in middle America.[2] The series of films examined here were produced and directed by Fox for Universal and starred Kirby Grant. They are: *Trail to Vengeance*, *Bad Men of the Border*, and *Code of the Lawless* (all 1945), *Gun Town*, *Lawless Breed*, and *Gunman's Code* (1946). This series was the only one in Fox's career that he both produced and directed, suggesting that these are the films over which he had the most creative control.

The war years saw major shifts in the Hollywood studio system generally, and in Universal's operations specifically. In 1940, the five major studios agreed to limit the practice of block booking, and as a result focused their efforts on major A-picture productions, leaving the B-picture market to the minor major studios, namely Universal and Columbia. Unlike the majors, these minor majors did not own their own theater chains, and thus more programmatic content like serials, shorts, and B-pictures, became significant forms of income.[3] The stature of series westerns is suggested by the announcement of Universal's 1945–1946 slate of films in which Fox and Grant's series is listed third-to-last behind all of its other feature films and only ahead of serials and short-subjects.[4]

In 1937, J. Cheever Cowdin took over Universal from its founder, Carl Laemmle. An investor uninterested in the operations of the studio's filmmaking, Cowdin hired Nate Blumberg to be the head of studio production. Later inspired by the unprecedented success of Abbott and Costello's programmatic comedy output, Bloomberg focused on repeating what had proven successful, and to "parlay every success into formula," a practice "evident in virtually all its in-house productions."[5] Fox was a prolific and efficient genre director and his talents suited Blumberg's Universal model. According to Wheeler Dixon, as a veteran of Monogram and serial production, Fox was "used to short schedules and tighter budgets" and "was trained to keep an eye on the budget and keep things moving."[6]

Before exploring the formula at work in these films, we must first discuss the problem of authorship. In this chapter, I attribute the series to Fox, though even if all industrial material were available it would be impossible to determine who was most responsible for a certain decision in a film. Eight screenwriters[7] were credited with involvement in the six films discussed here, though far more were likely involved, and several films borrow elements from other films whose screenwriters went uncredited.

The number of screenwriters would suggest a diversity of material, but the films in this series go beyond mere similarity; they feel like the same film. The resemblance between them may be attributed to studio practice, similar to that found in the story of Warner Bros. "Keeper of the Bs," Bryan Foy. According to Richard Maltby,

> in the late 1930s . . . he [Foy] is supposed to have kept a pile of about 20 scripts on his desk. Each time his unit completed a movie, its script would go back to the bottom of the pile. Over a period of about a year, it would gradually work its way to the top. Then it would be dusted off and given to the scriptwriter to rewrite.

For Maltby, Foy's story (he suggests it has merit enough to be more than apocryphal), "illustrates the cost-effectiveness of Hollywood's system of constructing familiar fictions that fulfilled their audiences' requirement that movies be 'just like . . . but completely different' from each other."[8]

To overemphasize these elements as predetermined by the studio, or suggest that existing content merely needed to be plugged into new films, underplays the creative role of a director, even within the rigors of studio Hollywood. The primary role of a director is on-set decision making, even if they, in the Hollywood production system, must, "fight narrowly for what he thinks is achievable."[9] That these films make the same decisions over and over again and that Fox was the one constant creative force involved in them suggests that he had some degree of responsibility for their content. The reality is that these films were determined by a negotiation between studio practice, financial limitations, audience response, producers, unit heads, screenwriters, and Fox (as director and producer), so that when I write "Fox's film" I am referring to the result of that negotiation, in which Fox played a significant role.

FORMULA

There are five recurring themes and motifs in the films in this series: First, mistaken and concealed identities; second, a complication of western gender norms; third, contrasting effective communal efforts and reactionary mob violence; fourth, a critique of unbridled capitalism; and fifth, a tension between federal and local government. Combined, these themes and motifs emphasize the importance of collective action, especially by those in society who may otherwise be marginalized.

Each film in this series more or less conforms to the following formula: a stranger (Kirby Grant) rides (usually via stagecoach) into a frontier town in the midst of civic unrest, and in nearly all of them, his arrival is interrupted by some action foreshadowing the larger corruption he will find once he reaches his destination. In each instance, his identity is either unknown or deliberately withheld, even from the audience. He encounters a woman who is seeking to reform the town (usually played by Jane Adams), and a musically talented oaf who becomes his sidekick (Fuzzy Knight) and acts as his comedic foil. The civic strife is the result of internal corruption by a local business owner who incites the death of a family member of one of the main characters. Grant investigates this murder, and after a series of convoluted events, implicates the corrupt official. Grant, who reveals himself as an agent of the federal government, apprehends this figure after a fistfight, but the figure escapes his capture and unleashes violence onto the town. In the midst of this violence, the town is nearly destroyed, and the figure is killed or driven away in the violence. The town is restored through civic action though the fate of the villain may be left uncertain. Structurally, each film features at least two songs, a stagecoach robbery, two fistfights, and a horse chase.

Grant's off-screen persona, or lack of one, plays a part in these films. As Universal was shifting its production philosophy, it was also searching for a reliable series western star. Bob Baker, Johnny Mack Brown, and then Tex Ritter had all successfully anchored Universal's series western output. But Universal declined to renew Brown's contract and Ritter left for PRC in 1944, leaving an opening. In part, the turnover as Universal's series western lead was made more manageable by the consistency of Fuzzy Knight who had acted as foil to Baker, Brown, and Ritter. When Grant took over the reins, he would be the familiar face for the audience.[10]

The risk in casting Grant was that he was a relative unknown. In a report in *Motion Picture Herald* about *Gun Town* a theater manager in Gentry, Arkansas asked, "Who is Kirby Grant? My patrons ask me who he is. They don't know him around here and that hurts business. It proves that western names mean something at the box office."[11] While potentially precarious as a box-office draw, Grant also provided Universal and Fox with a unique opportunity. While other series stars came with existing personas tied to specific performance styles and themes, Grant offered Fox a blank slate. These films would develop Grant's persona, and if successful, turn him into Universal's new western star.

The anonymity of Grant as an actor and the absence of an existing persona are exploited in the very structure of these films. In each film, Grant is a stranger arriving into town. Nobody knows who he is and he actively conceals his identity. Audiences likely assume he is the hero because he is the star of the film, or through his reaction to the event that interrupts his arrival. For example, in *Code of the Lawless*, Grant goes out of his way to assist a character he witnesses being shot. Interestingly, Grant's hero's anonymity is not utilized for suspense, and his identity is not provided as privileged information to the audience. Rather, Grant's anonymity as persona and his character's anonymity within the narrative are utilized to play with identity and social dynamics tied to identity.

Code of the Lawless displays the instability of identity in these films because while mistaken and concealed identities are a common motif in the series, in this film, masquerade is an extended part of the plot. The film introduces us to the town of Pecos in Arizona Territory, a frontier town exploited by the Hilton Corporation, which is the settler's only source of goods and protection. Chad Hilton, Jr., the long-lost son of Hilton's elderly CEO Chadwick Hilton, sends a letter announcing he will arrive to meet his father for the first time. Hilton Sr., isolated in his mansion and unaware of the rampant exploitation of Pecos, is being taken advantage of in his old age by his assistant, Lester Ward. When Ward shoots Chad before he arrives in town, Carter (Grant) comes to his aid and takes him to recover at Bonanza Featherstone's (Fuzzy Knight) shack, and when Bonanza is not looking, Carter steals Chad's identifying documents and assumes his identity. Carter then arrives in Pecos pretending to be Chad, to the delight of Chadwick Sr. and the consternation of an understandably suspicious Lester. While the assumed identity adds intrigue, and mild farce, among the characters, the initial result is destabilizing to audiences because we do not know who Carter is; it seems out of character for a series western star to play an identity thief. In fact, Ward is later exposed as a forger before we find out Carter's true identity, suggesting that hero and villain are both frauds to some extent. It is extremely late in the film's climax that Carter reveals he is a special agent of the Department of the Interior sent to investigate Pecos, and he apprehends Ward.

The use of disguise and the prevalence of plots containing mistaken and concealed identities are common in series westerns. The commonality of this trope has been attributed to the possibility of the frontier, that in the West you can be anyone. Generally, such possibility is seen as the reinvention of the Easterner in the West, a place that does not abide by the strict social codes of the more "civilized" part of the country.[12] Such reinvention is contrasted in *Rustler's Round-Up* as Pinkerton (Knight) and Bob Ryan (Grant) meet in a stagecoach riding into the lawless town of Rawhide. Pinkerton has only read about the West, but hopes to reinvent himself as a famous lawman like Bob Ryan, the man he does not know he's sitting next to. Ryan pretends to be someone else hoping to get "away from things." In this film, as in all of the films in this series, we do not know who Grant is until later in the film, often at the climax. These reveals may feel like a *deus ex machina*, but they serve more of a thematic than narrative purpose as they illustrate how a town treats outsiders. Grant's characters, while all ultimately powerful figures, withhold their authority until after they have suffered injustice at the hands of suspicious locals. Grant's initially mysterious character is not the only prominent social outsider in this formula. In each film, Grant's hero is aided by a woman reformer and a musical sidekick who are also situated on society's margins. These films are a cinema of outsiders: the hero is an outsider, his accomplices are outsiders, and it is the entrenched elite that are the villains.

Immediately upon arriving in town, Grant's character encounters civic unrest and a woman who is leading an effort to reform her corrupt town. In *Rustler's Round-Up*, Bob Ryan (Grant) immediately encounters Jo (Jane Adams) outside of a saloon, where she is canvasing for votes for an election that is ending in a matter of minutes. Jo is working to elect an honest sheriff to replace a puppet installed by the Todd Brothers, three local ranchers who own most of the town. Jo is emblematic of this reformer character in the series, and while Grant plays an authority figure that apprehends the villain, it is the reformer character who spearheads actual, large-scale change against corruption, usually at great personal cost. After the initial election fails, Jo's father is murdered by the Todds in an attempt to rustle his cattle. Grant and the Fuzzy Knight character investigate and solve this injustice, but it is Jo who focuses on the systemic problems of the town that create an environment for such injustice to occur.

The reformer is also capable of providing action and spectacle. In *Round-Up* Jo performs the majority of the film's horse-riding stunts. Laura Horak has noted the prevalence of the "cross-dressed chase," action sequences borrowed from stage melodramas and utilized as cinematic spectacle in which "a young woman steps in for an incapacitated man, navigates a series of outdoor spaces faster than the men who pursue her, and shows off her horseback-riding skills." Horak notes the height of this trope's popularity was during an early transitional period in film history, drawing upon the popularity of cinematic chase films, and notes that despite the figure's brief popularity "after 1913, cross-dressing heroines became rare," as cross-dressing shifted from melodramatic to comedic trope."[13] The chase sequence in *Round-Up*, like many of the subtle subversions in the films in this series, conforms to this older melodramatic tradition while altering it to become a critique. In the film, after her father is shot, Jo races to seek help. In the middle of her dramatic ride, Ryan (Grant), our presumptive hero, sees her riding and assumes her horses have gone wild and races to stop them. Rather than talking to him, or asking him for help, Jo effortlessly steals his horse and continues her ride. The classic structure of the "cross-dressed chase" is still there: a woman's father is incapacitated and she must take it upon herself to get help. Yet, Ryan becomes just another obstacle for her to overcome. The tone of the scene, and especially the musical scoring, does not play the scene for laughs but instead suggests this is a heroic act that overcomes the misguided intent of the film's protagonist.

These films also differ from the earlier trope in that the "cross-dressed" characters are not necessarily cross-dressing (in fact, the only cross-dressing by way of disguise is done by men in this series). In stage melodramas and early films women, as what Horak terms "female-bodied men,"[14] undertake their action in disguise as men. While we may assume cross-dressing is always inherently transgressive, Horak argues that in these instances it should "be considered conservative as it implies that women must stop being women in order to achieve agency."[15] By this point in the development of series westerns, this figure is no longer in disguise. While these women have family connections to the victims of crimes, they are typically economically independent. As Stanfield observes, "what is striking in these films is precisely how unmotivated and 'natural' the independent and economically active woman is."[16] Nevertheless, even in other B-westerns from this era, the strong women in traditionally masculine roles still receive comment from other characters, as novelty, generally to draw distinctions between the East and West. By contrast, over the six films in this series no such remarks are made; characters do not comment or seem surprised by a strong woman. While the reformer character does not dress in disguise, they still often exhibit traits or markers considered masculine; for instance, Jo is named Josephine, but goes by Jo and dresses in a man's top.

Additionally, a key aspect of the older melodramatic "cross-dressed chase" trope was that a woman's agency was "a necessary expedient during a temporary disruptive period, which dissolves as soon as the period is ended."[17] In these films, no such dissolution occurs. In fact, in a film like *Gun Town*, Jane, presented as a natural and unquestioned business leader, is the figure most tied to the formation and civic consistency of the town. In *Round-up*, Jo does not hold such a lofty position, but she is still present in and a part of two different, and important, male-dominated institutions in the town: the saloon and the court.

Gender non-conformity is not exclusive to the reformer character. Each film features a sidekick whom Grant meets at some point in the film's opening moments. Grant's sidekick (played by Fuzzy Knight) in these films is a musically talented misfit who acts as his comedic foil and partner in investigations, but also challenges societal norms, including gender norms. Most notably, in *Trail to Vengeance*, Hungry (Fuzzy Knight) orders by mail, and also makes his own, women's perfume, an act that the film presents as an endearing trait. In *Gunman's Code*, the two cross-dress in order to ambush a group of raiders, a move played as legitimate investigative work instead of as comedic situation. This is perhaps Fox's biggest departure from classical Hollywood norms where characters coded as Queer were typically villainous or untrustworthy.

As Brower observes in a Queer reading of classical westerns, in such films minority characters, including those marked as sexually transgressive, are not only mistreated by the narratives but also "these characters' marginal status is paired with some crime or transgression" that is used to justify their exclusion from the community. As she notes, "one way or another, elimination of marginalized characters becomes morally justified and expected in the course of the typical western plot."[18] In Fox's films, these marginalized characters are the film's heroes, the ones crucial to changing the corrupt local systems.

In these films, the three characters fight local institutions corrupted by evil businessmen. In this respect, the films reiterate a common theme from this strain of westerns: that operations on the frontier, far from the influence of civilization, have become corrupted and wild. However, the failure at the heart of the towns in these films does not seem to be proximity to wilderness, and the danger is not a threat from without. Rather, the emphasis is on the greed of individuals replacing community control and betterment. This aspect of the formula is portrayed with macabre humor in *Trail to Vengeance* where a mortician, appropriately named Horace Glumm, blackmails a local banker to steal away the mortgages of local townspeople. Death and economic exploitation are combined in the film, and the film's morality suggests that one is worse than the other, as Dorothy (Jane Adams) tries to persuade Jeff Gordon (Grant) of the innocence of her father, who was framed for the murder of Gordon's brother and the theft of his mortgage, by saying, "he might kill, but steal?" The connection between murder and economic dispossession is reiterated in another scene, where, after ordering the assassination of another character, Glumm tells his henchmen, "I have become very greedy, Bully. I want another body." The culture of greed reaches its absurd end as corporate greed is mirrored by Glumm's quest for more work: lives become commodity, a means to financial ends.

As individuals have corrupted the local institutions, the films in this series argue that collective action is the only effective remedy. The films deny the effectiveness of both individual action and vigilante justice. Most notably, in nearly every film, Kirby Grant's hero apprehends the villain only for them to escape. Grant's one-on-one showdowns are ineffective at best, and at worst allow the villain to regroup with their gang to launch an assault on the town.

The assumption in each of these films is that local governments are prone to reactionary politics and corruption, and it is a strong federal government, represented by Grant's character as almost always a U.S. marshal or government agent, that acts as a check on civic order. Grant's character is often more than anything a detective who is passionate about due process. Even after he identifies the corrupting element in a town, he waits until he has performed an investigation in order to collect enough evidence to convict the villain. Grant's fidelity to due process and the justice system is contrasted with the reactionary mob violence incited by local businesspeople. In this case, Grant's heroes subvert a central aspect of the A-western film hero who is presented as a marginal figure able to act (often violently) outside of accepted laws in order to preserve the tenuous social order on the frontier. As Butler notes, "B-movie cowboys . . . possessed the ability to slide between society and wilderness, excelling in each sphere" and "become—completely and without irony—bandits for the sake of law and order."[19] Grant's heroes are not only operating within the justice system, they represent it and enforce its perpetuation.

PERFORMATIVITY

The formula present in Fox's films demonstrates the ways in which the B-westerns of this era differed from their A-counterparts and highlights conceptions about the content of the western film. Another significant difference is that despite, or rather because of, their often rigid formulas, series westerns have a playful, performative address and narrative instability. According to Steve Neale, "the concept of verisimilitude is central to an understanding of genre,"[20] and by "verisimilitude" he means that in every genre, there are horizons or probability: the chance that something happens, as well as how "proper" this action is within the genre. Both the probability and proper-ability of events within genres reflect societal norms and expectations. It is in verisimilitude that the series western most differs from the A-western film, as the series western has its own concept of proper action.

One explanation for this difference is the importance of its stars. While true of essentially all of classical Hollywood, because of series westerns' quick turnaround time and the need to differentiate remarkably similar products, they relied heavily on the appeal of their stars and those stars' unique ability to perform spectacular actions. The foregrounding of performance in series westerns was so central to these films that Peter Stanfield argues that series western stars "are best viewed not as 'actors' but as 'performers'"[21]; audiences went to see Johnny Mack Brown's athletic prowess, or to hear Gene Autry sing. The genre's focus on spectacle and performativity allows for actions and events which would not be considered proper in A-westerns, and as such the series western has its own mode of narrative address. Unlike A-pictures, series westerns privileged performance and spectacle as much as plot or character psychology. The formulaic nature of the plots was mirrored in the films' use of stock characters, which were often little more than avatars of star personas; Fuzzy Knight plays Fuzzy Knight characters who differ mostly in character name only.

This is not to say that, while formulaic, series westerns were simple: the plots of these films are incredibly complicated, especially considering their

60-minute runtimes. Nor should they be dismissed as films for children, a common misconception. These films were primarily "aimed . . . at working-class audiences"[22] and to appeal to their audiences more directly, B-westerns "incorporated current events into the plot and action", including those from the "Depression, dust bowl, and New Deal."[23] While westerns often provided escapist entertainment during the war, Loy notes that during the war, because the Office of War Information and Office of Censorship were focused primarily on major studio release and feature films, B-westerns often "escaped the censor's stamp and remained above the struggle between the federal government and Hollywood studios,"[24] allowing them more freedom to include potentially controversial themes of the genre: "lawlessness or class and racial conflicts."[25] The allusion or appeal to contemporary events and anxieties is a staple of genre storytelling, though here it connects with the genre's more direct mode of address to its audience, one developed during the 1930s, and a mode of address that Gene Autry attributed to his success as a "New Deal Cowboy."[26]

Autry may have seen his success in his ability to "tackle the same problems" that faced his audience,[27] but it was music that was central to his films, and the element most copied by Universal. Music is an important element of spectacle but also as address in the films of this series, though none would be generically easy to categorize as musicals. Each film contains two to three songs presented in varying degrees of reflexivity, meaning that they are more or less motivated by performance in the film's narrative. For instance, the opening number of *Gun Town*, performed by Fuzzy Knight while driving a stagecoach, is more reflexive because at this point in the film we are not yet aware of our relationship to the film and its rules, and the song's presence is motivated after the fact, when we are told that Fuzzy's character wanted to be on the stage, not "on the stage." Also in *Gun Town*, the songs by Belle Townley (Claire Carleton) are far less reflexive and more motivated because she is a visiting performer at a local saloon. Yet, while the majority of the musical numbers fall on the more conservative side of this reflexive spectrum, they serve similar purposes to musical numbers in musicals. Belle's performance in *Gun Town* pushes the narrative forward as it reveals her seduction of the local workers. Similarly, Jo's opening song in *Rustler's Round-Up* situates the election and her desire for change before Bob Ryan arrives.

Musical numbers foreground performance in these films, both narratively and in the *mise en scène*. Belle, and her corrupt counterpart Lucky, discuss their evil plot in theatrical terms, and this framing appears to motivate the *mise en scène* of the film, as Fox frames the two watching characters enact their plan as if it were a performance. Also in *Gun Town*, the local sheriff models himself after Wild Bill in dress and action. In *Round-Up*, Bryan (Grant) and Pinkerton (Knight) solve the mystery of Jo's father's murder by acting out what may have happened.

Whereas the performative register merely suggests a conservative form of reflexivity,[28] there are small moments of actual reflexive moves, that, like the performative register, address the series western film's audience. In *Gunman's Code* there is an unexpected scene in which Hungry (Fuzzy Knight) breaks the fourth wall and addresses the audience directly. As far as fourth wall breaks go, the scene is subtle, but telling. Jack (Kirby Grant who is investigating a series of stagecoach robberies) exits frame left to follow and talk to Lara (Jane Adams playing a potential romantic interest and a woman trying to clear her brother's name). Yet the camera does not follow Jack, rather it stays with Hungry/Fuzzy who looks to the audience and says, in exasperation: "women." Played for laughs, the break acts as punchline (one of the oldest punchlines there is). Yet it reveals a knowledge and convention on the part of the audience. That Hungry is frustrated with Jack's actions suggests that he has deviated from the important aspects of the plot, a plot known all too well by the audience, and that Hungry/Fuzzy can confide to his audience that he's tired of the convention. Fuzzy is performing for the audience, but also relating to them, suggesting that his comic relief relies on a relationship to the audience.

Knight's characters are the most performative figures and act as surrogates for the audience. Like the audience, Knight's characters want to be western heroes. In *Rustler's Round-Up* this desire is made explicit, as he plays a character who acts the way western heroes do in the books he reads, but becomes an actual hero by following and imitating the actions of Grant's character. Grant models how to be a hero and Fuzzy models how to apply what the audience has seen. This modeling is highlighted by Loy who suggests that B-westerns, through their modes of address, in tackling issues relevant to current events, as multimedia works engaged with radio shows and comics, and especially to their younger fans, "were valuable components in the political socialization milieu of children."[29] While Loy oversimplifies the audience of these films as primarily children, and acknowledges that more study needs to be done on their social role, his analysis does suggest that through their address, and in these performative techniques, these films connected with their audiences in a more direct way than their big-budget counterparts.

FOX AS NATIVE FILMMAKER

The presence of an Indigenous filmmaker in classical Hollywood presents a fruitful complication of our conception of Indigenous cinema and its history. Indigenous filmmaking is typically considered a relatively recent development, one made possible by civil rights movements, the rise of independent filmmaking, film festivals, and technological democratization. Yet, Fox had a prolific career across classical Hollywood. A central characteristic of Indigenous film and videomaking has been the deconstruction of popular images from Hollywood, specifically western movies, so what do we make of a Native filmmaker producing Hollywood westerns? Lastly, Indigenous filmmaking is seen to exist outside of the main flows of worldwide filmmaking; yet, here was a Native director working for a Hollywood studio. How might we consider Fox an Indigenous filmmaker when he challenges some of the central characteristics of Indigenous filmmaking?

A popular framing of Indigenous filmmaking is Maori filmmaker Barry Barclay's concept of Fourth Cinema, which expands the Three Cinema model: Hollywood as First Cinema, auteur and national art films as Second Cinema, and the postcolonial cinemas of Third Cinema. According to Michelle Raheja, Fourth Cinema, as a theorization of Indigenous filmmaking, "has its roots in specific Indigenous aesthetics with their attendant focus on a particular geographical space; discrete cultural practices; social activist texts; notions of temporality that do not delink the past from the present or future; and spiritual traditions."[30] Raheja links this definition to the following quote from Barclay:

> If we as Maori look closely enough and through the right pair of spectacles, we will find examples at every turn of how the old principles have been reworked to give vitality and richness to the way we conceive, develop, manufacture, and present our films. It seems likely to me that some Indigenous film artists will be interested in shaping films that sit with confidence within the First, Second, and Third cinema framework. While not closing the door on that option, others may seek to rework the ancient core values to shape a growing Indigenous cinema outside the national orthodoxy.[31]

Barclay, like many others, prioritizes the idea expressed at the end of this quote; to identify a unique Indigenous cinema and show how it stands in opposition to other models of filmmaking. While Barclay endorses that approach, to shape a cinema that addresses the specific and local needs and interests of Indigenous communities in its practices, he does not "close the door" on Indigenous involvement in other models of cinema.

Where Barclay suggests that Indigenous filmmakers "will be interested" in First Cinema, Fox, as an Indigenous director in studio Hollywood, presents a past tense "were" that connects to the present and near future, as Indigenous filmmakers begin to more prominently occupy space in First Cinema. We need to revise how we approach Indigenous cinema to consider the works of filmmakers in multiple "cinemas," to consider the franchise superhero films of Taika Waititi along with his nationally funded work, or the FX on Hulu television work of Sterlin Harjo along with his festival films or documentaries made for Muscogee (Creek) and Seminole communities. Looking back to Wallace Fox as an Indigenous filmmaker might help inform such a revised approach.

It may appear thorny to draw upon the experience of a historical director to inform the present, but such an approach is a common one in Native conceptions of time. Mark Rifkin has argued for a "Temporal Sovereignty," the need to conceptualize Indigenous experience outside of histories dictated by settler narratives and markers.[32] One of the major influences for Rifkin's work is to go beyond the view of a modern/traditional binary in which Natives in modernity are seen as less than; anachronisms of a more "authentic past." Drawing upon the phenomenology of Merleau-Ponty and the works of Indigenous philosopher Dale Turner, Rifkin suggests that "tradition" be characterized as "distinctive ways of being-in-time" that "emerge from material processes of reckoning with an environment and are open to change while helping provide an orientation and background for everyday Native experience."[33] Applied to film history, we may see Fox not as an anomaly, but rather as someone who presents a way of being Indigenous in response to a specific set of "material processes" in the film industry.

In this case, perhaps a more appropriate view of Indigenous cinema, or Fourth Cinema, would be similar to Deleuze's enigmatic "soul of cinema,"[34] less of a chronology than an approach, as Deleuze's works were not so much histories as studies of strains of cinema that utilized specific ways of thinking and experiencing time throughout the development of film history. Likewise, a study of Native cinema would be less interested in taxonomy than in the ways Indigenous filmmakers attempted to assert their Indigeneity in different contexts and historical moments, that is, the work of finding commonalities in their responses to different "material processes", or "tradition." Perhaps Fourth Cinema comprises its own framework outside of the Three Cinema model, but it may also exist within First, Second, and Third Cinema in that Indigenous approaches, aesthetics, and practices can be found, to varying degrees, within all three cinemas, even the most acute version of its First: the Hollywood Studio system.

Industrial practice and limitations, the intervention of other producers and screenwriters, and generic convention all likely informed the aspects of Fox's films discussed in this chapter. However, we must also account for the possibility that his Native heritage may have influenced, or inflected, his series westerns. Additionally, there is one technique that Fox uses in these films that we associate with far newer media forms: recycling footage. A curious, and understudied, aspect of B-movies from this era is the use and reuse of existing stock footage. The use of stock footage was likely a result of an interplay between a story necessity (these films needed a third act action sequence), audience expectation (this act would need to be visually spectacular), and economic reality and wartime scarcity (they did not have the time or budget to shoot epic scenes, and studios could reuse footage until audiences got tired of it). But Fox's use of this footage serves more than a utilitarian purpose, regardless of which of the above reasons were most important at the time. In the context of Fox's films, stock footage is occasionally used ambivalently, and in some instances against its original purposes, a practice that foreshadows a significant attribute of contemporary Indigenous filmmaking.

The climax of *Code of the Lawless* features stock footage of a massive, wagon-led land run.[35] In its initial usage, we presume the footage was used to convey the excitement and open possibility of the frontier. Such moments are also central to the absent presence and erasure of Indigenous people in the genre, but in this film, the footage is framed as a mistake, an error precipitated by deception. A corrupt, local official has bribed a prospector to claim he has found gold in hopes of diverting the electorate so that they will miss a key election that would free them of the Hilton Corporation's exploitation. The resulting run is a fool's gold rush; the settlers rushing from their civic duties to an opportunity that does not exist. It is not a triumph, but a folly.

Whereas *Code of the Lawless* uses only one significant recycled action sequence, *Gun Town* is comprised of large amounts of recycled footage, and displays Fox's most striking use of the technique. In *Gun Town*, Lucky Dorgan is trying to gain control of Gun Town by robbing his business partner Buckskin Jane's stagecoach lines. While performing the robberies, Dorgan and his henchmen dress as Indians. Their plan is to blame a local tribe for the attacks, and set a local mob upon them. Kip Lewis (Kirby Grant) is an Indian agent who knows the tribe is peaceful and innocent, and apprehends Dorgan. However, Dorgan's henchmen, conveying the real news about the town mob to the tribe, lead an attack on Gun Town. The footage from *Gun Town* is almost entirely derived from *Badlands of Dakota*, a 1941 Universal film by Alfred E. Green. A film that straddled the line between A and B western, *Badlands* provides a contrasting example of the genre to Fox's film. While *Badlands* is largely a comedy, and like many B-westerns contains an excess of comedic relief, the film takes its commitment to western mythology rather seriously, if a bit a historically: Wild Bill, Calamity Jane[36], and General Custer all appear in the film.

The films have similar major plot points, but differ in how those plot points fit into the overall plot and theme of the film. Whereas *Gun Town* concerns business and civic treachery, *Badlands* is a love triangle between two brothers, Jim and Bob Holliday, and Anne, a woman they knew growing up "back east." In the film, Bob has been living in Deadwood since its inception and tasks Jim, an Easterner who travels from St. Louis, to fetch Anne so the two can be married. However, on the trip back to Deadwood, Jim and Anne fall in love and are married. In his anger, Bob secretly joins the McCall brothers, two criminals who have been carrying out raids on stagecoaches disguised as Indians. Meanwhile, at the suggestion of Bob, in hopes that as a fish out of water he will be killed in the line of duty, Jim is appointed sheriff of Deadwood. Eventually Jim grows into his job, cleans up the town, and ultimately fends off an attack by the Sioux.

Badlands uses the two brothers to explore one of the classic western movie binaries: it contrasts Jim, the civilized Easterner, with Bob, who has become corrupted by living in the West. The difference between the brothers and what they represent is articulated by Anne during a speech in which she tells Jim that it will not be people like Bob but "common people like us who will tame the west" and that "real pioneers build homes and raise families." Making the Edenic imagery of the frontier explicit she closes by noting that she and Jim will be the ones who "replenish the earth." The contrast reaches its climax when Jim confronts Bob, who is dressed as an Indian, robbing the bank, and asks if Bob was an outlaw before he came back from St. Louis.

In *Gun Town*, the Bob character, Lucky Dorgan, is driven to crime not by rejected romance or because of his time on the frontier, but out of greed. He wants Jane's share of control in the town's business. Kip Lewis, who partially replaces the Jim character, travels back and forth between East and West, and in the end it appears he may be traveling again, leaving the future of the town in the hands of Jane. Importantly, unlike Anne who will "tame" the West through a nuclear family and by building homes, Jane, Kip suggests, will rebuild Gun Town through community; its people not its buildings.

The use of recycled footage appears to have determined crucial aspects of the *Gun Town* story. Because *Badlands* included Wild Bill and Calamity Jane as characters, characters that look like them are present in the recycled action sequences. Yet, because these sequences were filmed in wide shots, and their costumes are all that can be discerned by viewers, Calamity Jane becomes Buckskin Jane, who wears a similar outfit, and the Sheriff dresses like Wild Bill. What's more, instead of simply including Bill and Jane as characters in *Gun Town*, which would have been as historically inaccurate as their versions in *Badlands*, their counterparts in *Gun Town* deconstruct their iterations in *Badlands*. In *Badlands*, Wild Bill is presented as an aging figure of an older, wilder West. His purpose in the film appears to be to comment on the dangers of the frontier and pass his mantle on to Jim as the new hero in Deadwood. In *Gun Town*, Wild Bill becomes the Sheriff, credited only as "Sheriff," which suggests how important he is to the film. The Sheriff of *Gun Town* is mostly a background figure, one who is absent for most of the film. His biggest scene occurs near the beginning of the film, when a mob arrives and attempts to hang Kip for the stagecoach robbery. In the scene, Jane's brother Davy goes to the Sheriff for help to control the mob. However, the Sheriff goes back into his office to get the right hat. When Davy says he does not have time for the hat, the Sheriff argues that "it matters Davy" and that it is the same kind of hat worn by "Wild Bill Hickok himself . . . gives a man nerves of steel." This scene explains why this town's Sheriff looks exactly like Wild Bill, but also creates a discrepancy between his outward appearance, as western hero, and his actions. He is presented as an eccentric who is ineffectual at his own job, focused more on appearance based in myth than meaningful action.

Calamity Jane and Buckskin Jane in *Gun Town* present two different approaches to gender in western films. In *Badlands*, Jane is ridiculed for wearing men's clothing, and told the West is "no place for ladies," by Bob, whom she secretly loves. This creates tension between Anne and Jane, who in a later scene wears a dress in an attempt to appear more attractive to Bob. Interestingly, while Calamity is said to have helped Bob found the town, she does not appear in its leadership and is noticeably absent in discussions to find its next sheriff. In *Gun Town*, Jane may or may not have had a romantic relationship with Lucky, but by the events of the film it is entirely a business relationship. Unlike the way characters treat Calamity in *Badlands*, the clothing Buckskin Jane wears in *Gun Town* and her station in the community as the town's de facto leader are considered completely appropriate and natural.

ONE RAID, TWO FINALES

Gun Town borrows three main sequences from *Badlands*, and each occurs at times in which the plots arrive at similar points. The first is a scene in which Fuzzy Knight (who appears in both films) has his stagecoach robbed by men disguised as Indians, a fact we know at the time the action occurs in *Badlands* but do not know in *Gun Town*. For his film, Fox added the opening musical number to the beginning of this scene and cut out an extended gag in which the stagecoach, running out of control, seems to take on a life of its own, which takes the scene in *Badlands* into a far more comedic register. The second scene takes place at roughly the same point in each film (about two-thirds of the way in) and consists of a horse chase between Jim, Calamity Jane, and Wild Bill, and the robbers dressed as Indians. In both cases, a member of the gang drops an item that reveals their identity as members of the community. While both of these are important action set pieces that have important plot points, they are both relatively short. *Gun Town* reuses nearly the entire finale of *Badlands*, roughly 10 minutes (or a fifth of the film's runtime).

It is understandable that someone would want to reuse the footage from the climax of *Badlands*, as the sequence contains many impressive, potentially dangerous stunts and horsework. In one impressive stunt, a man is shot from the top of a building and falls into a hay-filled wagon that is set on fire and rolls wildly down Main Street. The amount of fire, and specifically the amount of set material set ablaze, also likely gave Universal incentive to reuse the expensive sequence. Fox even re-filmed several insert shots line-for-line from *Badlands*;

however, there are key differences that change the tone and provide vastly different endings to each film.

In both films, the villains up to this point have been members of the community carrying out raids dressed as Indians. In both sequences, actual Indians become part of the film for the first time in a violent attack. However, the justifications for this raid are different. Each sequence begins with Jane (Calamity and Buckskin) noticing signal fires in the hills, prompting Jim and Kip Lewis to call for the town to prepare to defend itself against an Indian attack. In *Badlands*, the explanation for the attack is given six scenes later when Bob and his gang, out on their horses and seeing the raid, decide they can use it as cover to rob Deadwood's bank. In *Gun Town*, the scene immediately following Lewis's instruction features Dorgan explaining to his gang that he told the Indians that the town was going to attack them because they blamed them for carrying out the stagecoach robberies. Dorgan reveals the treachery as part of his plan to rob the bank. In the first case, the Indian attack is part of the natural order of the frontier, one of the many dangers that Jim warns Anne about earlier in the film, a view supported by the observation of one of Bob's accomplices that "it's a wonder they haven't attacked yet, the town is wide open." This observation contrasts Buckskin and Kip's discussion early in *Gun Town* in which they note how out of character it is for the Sioux to attack the stagecoach line. In *Badlands*, the Indians act as a final obstacle for Jim to overcome as he sheds his Eastern sensibilities to become a capable town sheriff. In *Gun Town* the Indian attack is less of an antagonistic act; the Indians are justified and are attacking in self-defense, and given Dorgan's prominent place in the town's hierarchy, act as a source of justice destroying its civic corruption.

In the action that follows, *Gun Town* reuses nearly all of the major beats from *Badlands*' sequence, with one major exception. One of the sources of drama in *Badlands*' climax is drawn in form and content from D. W. Griffith. In both films, Jim/Kip instructs the town to collect the children for safety; however, the children only appear in *Badlands*, where we see roughly twenty of them brought into the saloon under the Anne's watch. The scene allows us to witness Anne's maternal capabilities as she comforts the children, but during the raid, the film cross-cuts from the violence back to the children as a source of suspense. The first such cut occurs as the raid begins, when an Indian rider carries away a woman on his horse. A war cry acts as sound bridge before we cut from this shot to one of Anne holding a child inside the saloon. This creates an entirely different context for a scene later in the sequence when, after the Indians break through the first barricade, one warrior attempts to enter the saloon. In *Badlands* we see Anne and Spearfish (Andy Devine, as one of several of the film's comic relief characters), fight off the would-be intruder and protect the children. In *Gun Town* the saloon feels empty and dark, with Ivory (Fuzzy Knight) the only visible occupant. The total absence of this subplot, other than a line in Kip's speech, suggests that it was intentionally removed. The set was reused for Ivory's scene, so it was clearly possible to reshoot these scenes as Fox did with other insert shots in this sequence. It could be that there is no counterpart for Anne's character in *Gun Town*, though, as there was in *Badlands* with Spearfish (a moment also not present in *Gun Town*), there could have been comedic interaction between the children and Ivory. Perhaps audience tastes had changed in the five years between the films, or audiences responded poorly to its original appearance. A last explanation is that, informed by his Native background, Fox decided against reshooting the scenes. He allowed the Indians in his film to commit a certain level of violence, but stopped at suggesting they were ready to attack and kidnap little children.

The greatest divergence between the two sequences is in how they end. The finale of *Badlands* concludes like a parody of a western film. Inside the bank, Jim confronts his brother, the two fight, and Jane saves Jim by fatally shooting Bob, only in one final act of redemption Bob shoots one of his henchmen before he can attack Jim, so saving his brother's life. As Jane mourns Bob, a bugle sounds and the film cuts to stock footage (the Monument Valley background seems out of place) of a cavalry ride. The Indians, hearing this, begin their retreat and are chased out of town as the soldiers retake the town. After Anne and Jim are reunited, the sequence fades out to the next morning as General Custer addresses the town from a pile of burned-out rubble. In the speech, Custer congratulates the townspeople for protecting themselves (recalling an earlier scene in which he tells them that the government cannot always protect them and they need to arm themselves) and notes that he and the Seventh Calvary are on their way to Little Big Horn to "have it out with Sitting Bull and the Sioux once and for all." Spearfish shouts "hooray for General Custer," Jim and Anne wish him luck, Jane goes into the saloon to get a drink, and the film ends.

In *Gun Town*, Kip and Jane see "the Indians" break into the bank and engage them in a shootout inside in which Jane shoots and kills who she later realizes is Lucky, who, unlike Bob, does not get to redeem himself. In contrast to *Badlands*, the Cavalry does not come. After burning much of the town, the Indians seem satisfied and ride away, and Kip and Jane walk out of the bank to survey the rubble and have the following encounter:

> Kip: We'll, they're gone
> Jane: So is Gun Town
> Kip: Only the rotten structure. The foundation is still here. You'll rebuild it.

As if this ending is not ambiguous enough, the two then note that Belle, Dorgan's co-conspirator, is still out there "somewhere in the hills." The film ends with Jane left to build a new town free from the corruption of men like Dorgan, but with the possibility of further difficulties.

Classical Hollywood images were and remain significant in Indigenous cinema as material for reworking narratively or materially, a tendency noted by several scholars. Carole Gerster has noted a "resistance" of vision in Native media as opposed to the persistence of vision related to Hollywood images of Native Americans[37] and focuses on that resistance at work in Native films, from Phil Lucas, Robert Hagopian, and Will Sampson's *Images of Indians* (1979) to Chris Eyre's *Smoke Signals* (1996), which she argues utilize a strategy of exposing and correcting existing misrepresentations of Native Americans in film. Gerster also suggests that educators, in teaching Native media, "can encourage students to find and to create other films and videos that reappropriate Indian images . . . and replace the images and change the thinking still encouraged by Hollywood."[38] Informed by their work studying Brazilian media, Shohat and Stam have labeled such practice of using the dominant media against itself and "turning tactical weakness into strategic strength" "Media Jujitsu,"[39] arguing that "texts perform media jujitsu by coercing Hollywood films and commercial TV into comedic self-indictment, deploying the power of the dominant media against their own Eurocentric premises." Enabled by new editing technologies, filmmakers can engage in this practice "by defamiliarizing and reaccentuating existing materials [such texts] rechannel energies in new directions, generating a space of negotiation outside of the binaries of domination and subordination, in ways that convey specific cultural and event autobiographical inflections."[40] Joanna Hearne adds another aspect to this approach. Noting the prevalence of recycled Western footage in contemporary Native media works, Hearne writes that,

> contemporary strategies of retrieval and reengagement demonstrate not only a tactical "raiding of the colonial archive" but also the ways that Indigenous media productions continue to be reflectively embedded in the wider field of national and international mediated images of Indians.[41]

For Hearne, "a crucial argument for revisiting these films is their renewed relevance for Native youth" and their place in "the reframing process in which artists and filmmakers continue to look back to an already-mediated past."[42] These works look forward while looking back, as Native media makers reclaim and often resist an archive of images as they negotiate their place in contemporary media. It is significant to reclaim Wallace Fox as part of Indigenous film history because looking back at Fox's B-westerns provides valuable insight into the work of an Indigenous filmmaker in the context of studio Hollywood. He suggests a longer tradition of approaches in Indigenous media as a filmmaker who, with the tools and relative opportunities he had in industrial practice, reused existing footage and generic motifs to subtly challenge the expectations of the genre in which he was working.

NOTES

1. Jim Kitses, *Horizons West: Anthony Mann, Budd Boetticher, Sam Peckinpah: Studies of Authorship within the Western* (London: Thames and Hudson, 1969), 11. Kitses was indebted to John Calweti's structuralist analysis in *The Sixgun Mystique*. Schatz repeats this formulation in "The Western" in *Hollywood Genres* (1981), but suggests the genre is more "flexible" and open to "cultural function" (45–6, 262).
2. Peter Stanfield, *Horse Opera: The Strange History of the 1930s Singing Cowboy* (Urbana: University of Illinois Press, 2002), 5, 7. As one example, The Rialto in Amarillo, TX gave *Gun Town* and its "renegades" top billing on a bill above a Donald Duck's short and *The Royal* Mounted Rides Again (1945). "Gun Town," Amarillo Daily News Friday Mar 22, 1946, 27. Available at <https://www.newspapers.com/image/16760059> (accessed December 4, 2021).
3. Thomas Schatz, *The Genius of the System: Hollywood Filmmaking in the Studio Era* (Minneapolis: University of Minnesota Press, 2010), 340–52.
4. "Universal Will Release 55 Features in New Season," *Motion Picture Herald*, September 1, 1945, 21. Available at <https://lantern.mediahist.org/catalog/motionpictureher1601unse_0029> (accessed December 3, 2021).
5. Ibid., 352.
6. Wheeler W. Dixon, *Lost in the Fifties: Recovering Phantom Hollywood* (Carbondale: Southern Illinois University Press, 2005), 36.
7. Robert Creighton Williams, who wrote *Lawless Breed* and *Trail to Vengeance*, Sherman L. Lowe who was co-credited for the story *Rustler's Round-Up* and *Gunman's Code*, and William Lively, who co-wrote *Gunman's Code* and wrote *Gun Town*, were the only recurring screenwriters in the series.
8. Richard Maltby, *Hollywood Cinema*, Second Edition (Malden, MA: Blackwell, 2003), 79–82.
9. Michael Rabiger, *Directing: Film Techniques and Aesthetics Third Edition* (New York: Focal Press, 2003), 10.
10. Jon Tuska, *The Filming of the West* (New York: Doubleday & Company, Inc., 1976), 421, 434, 437.
11. Harry T. Wachter, "*Gun Town*," *Motion Picture Herald*, November 9, 1946. Available at <https://lantern.mediahist.org/catalog/motionpictureher165unse_0131> (accessed December 4, 2021).
12. Stanfield, 134.
13. Laura Horak, "Landscape, Vitality, and Desire: Cross-Dressing Frontier Girls in Transitional-Era American Cinema," *Cinema Journal* 52:4 (Summer 2013), 74–98. Available at <https://doi.org/10.1353/cj.2013.0041>, 89–90 (accessed December 18, 2018).
14. Ibid.
15. Ibid.
16. Stanfield, 122.
17. Horak, 86.
18. Sue Brower, "'They'd Kill Us If They Knew': Transgression and the Western," *Journal of Film and Video* 62:4 (Winter 2010): 47–57. Available at <https://doi.org/10.1353/jfv.2010.0010>, 50 (accessed December 18, 2018).
19. Michael D. Butler, "Sons of Oliver Edwards: The Other American Hero," *Western American Literature* 12:1 (Spring 1977), 53–66. Available at <https://doi.org/10.1353/wal.1977.0051>, 62, 64 (accessed December 18, 2018).

20. Steve Neale, "Questions of Genre," in Robert Stam and Toby Miller (eds), *Film and Theory: An Anthology* (Malden, MA: Blackwell, 2000), 167.
21. Peter Stanfield, *Horse Opera: The Strange History of the 1930s Singing Cowboy* (Urbana: University of Illinois Press, 2002), 41.
22. Ibid., 4.
23. R. Philip Loy, "Soldiers in Stetsons: B-Westerns Go to War," *Journal of Popular Film and Television* 30:4 (2003), 197–205. Available at <https://doi.org/10.1080/01956050309602856> (accessed December 18, 2018).
24. Ibid., 198.
25. Ibid.
26. Lynette Tan, "The New Deal Cowboy: Gene Autry and the Antimodern Resolution," *Film History* 13 (2001), 89–101, 100.
27. Ibid.
28. For more on musicals as conservative reflexivity see Robert Stam, *Reflexivity in Film and Literature: From Don Quixote to Jean-Luc Godard* (New York: Columbia University Press, 1992).
29. Loy, 104.
30. Michelle H. Raheja, "Reading Nanook's Smile," in M. Elise Marubbio and Eric L. Buffalohead (eds), *Native Americans on Film: Conversations, Teaching, and Theory* (Lexington: University of Kentucky Press, 2013), 58–88, 66.
31. Ibid.
32. Mark Rifkin, *Beyond Settler Time: Temporal Sovereignty and Indigenous Self-Determination* (Durham, NC: Duke University Press, 2017), xi–x.
33. Rifkin, 29.
34. See Dudley Andrew, "The Roots of the Nomadic: Gilles Deleuze and the Cinema of West Africa," in Gregory Flaxman (ed.), *The Brain Is the Screen: Deleuze and the Philosophy of Cinema* (Minneapolis: University of Minnesota Press, 2000), 215–49. The affinities and potential connections between this concept and Indigenous cinema may be a fruitful one but are beyond the scope of this chapter.
35. A brief section of this sequence was used in the opening prologue montage of *Badlands of Dakota*, suggesting this was also stock footage that predates 1941. The IMDb entry says this was taken from *Riders of Death Valley* (1941). "Connections," *Badlands of Dakota*, IMDb. Available at https://www.imdb.com/title/tt0033370/movieconnections/?ref_=tt_trv_cnn (accessed December 6, 2021).
36. She is not called Calamity Jane in the film, but through the personal history she conveys in the film she is obviously Calamity Jane. That *Gun Town* does not also call her simply "Jane" but "Buckskin Jane" suggests that Fox wanted her to be a noticeably different character.
37. Carole Gerster, "Native Resistance to Hollywood's Persistence of Vision: Teaching Films about Contemporary American Indians," in M. Elise Marubbio and Eric L. Buffalohead (eds), *Native Americans on Film: Conversations, Teaching, and Theory* (Lexington: University Press of Kentucky, 2013), 141.
38. Gerster, 170.
39. Robert Stam and Ella Shohat, *Unthinking Eurocentrism: Multiculturalism and the Media*, Sightlines (New York: Routledge, 1994), 328.
40. Ibid., 331–2.
41. Joanna Hearne, *Native Recognition: Indigenous Cinema and the Western*, Horizons of Cinema (Albany, NY: SUNY Press, 2012), 302.
42. Ibid., 298.

CHAPTER 4

The Corpse Vanishes and the Case of the Missing Brides

Gary D. Rhodes

Monogram Pictures was not usually given to understatement, particularly when it came to Bela Lugosi. The title of Wallace Fox's *The Corpse Vanishes* is a fascinating exception. Released in May 1942, the film features Lugosi as Dr. Lorenz, a physician and scientist who abducts women in an effort to keep his aging wife, Countess Lorenz (Elizabeth Russell), alive and well. Three bodies disappear during its running time, along with the kidnapping of a journalist (Luana Walters). And that's to say nothing of at least three bodies Lorenz stole in the days, weeks, months, and perhaps years prior to the film's opening scene. To announce the vanishing of a single corpse in the film title hardly seems to be an adequate tabulation of Lorenz's crimes.

Shooting on *The Corpse Vanishes* began in early March 1942.[1] Sam Robins and Gerald Schnitzer received credit for the original story, which Harvey Gates adapted into a screenplay. When interviewed in 2012, Schnitzer mentioned that one of the producers had provided the idea for the tale: "I vaguely recall discussing the idea with Jack Dietz, who claimed he had read about a socialite bride being kidnapped, headlined in the tabloids."[2] Little else is known of the film's production.[3] *Daily Variety* joked that producer Sam Katzman had borrowed six coffins from an undertaker to use in the film, promising that they would be returned in perfect condition. Two were damaged, which meant an unhappy Katzman had to purchase them.[4]

The company moved through production and post-production rapidly, giving a preview screening on April 10, 1942.[5] The final cut was released on May 8, 1942, only two months after shooting had begun. Industry trade reviews were largely positive—somewhat surprising given that *The Corpse Vanishes* was just a B-movie, a "programmer" meant to complete the lower half of double features. *Motion Picture Daily* judged it to be "about as eerie an offering as has appeared on the screen," in spite of a merely "competent" production that featured some "inept" acting and dialogue.[6] *Film Daily* told readers:

> Bela Lugosi has made some horrifying horror films in his day, but this one tops them all for suspense and sheer, grim, mad frightfulness. It keeps just within the bounds of the Hays' Office ruling on the limits to which a producer can extend himself in his effort to scare audiences out of their skins.[7]

Daily Variety was equally enthusiastic, predicting "fans who like horror opuses will have a shrieking good time viewing *The Corpse Vanishes*." The trade added that Lugosi's "overplaying" actually constituted a "proper" approach to the story material, an opinion rarely voiced at the time, but widely held in the twenty-first century.[8]

What was that story material? At first, it might be seen as no more than the sum total of the aforementioned descriptions. Distilled further, it could be said that *The Corpse Vanishes* was just another low-budget mad doctor movie featuring a horror actor past his prime, a star no longer ascendant. As with so many other B-movies, however, a cursory viewing is not sufficient. Far more is here than meets the eye.

The Corpse Vanishes marks a few notable firsts, including Lugosi's initial pairing (of what became three films) with actress Minerva Urecal.[9] It was also his first mad scientist role for Monogram, at least if one views his plastic surgeon in *Black Dragons* (1942) as being murderously vengeful, but still very much sane. And unlike its predecessors, *The Corpse Vanishes* opens with urgent action, a bride saying "I do" before abruptly collapsing onto the church floor. Subsequent Monogram films, like Fox's *Bowery at Midnight* (1942), would also throw audiences immediately into the action, a plot device similar to that adopted by later Hollywood blockbusters.

Much more significant, though, is the extent to which *The Corpse Vanishes* activates the past in order to influence future horror movies. In its story, an intelligent "girl reporter" investigates the supernatural and exposes it with a scientific explanation. Those responsible form a monstrous family of the type that would plague American society and cinema in the late twentieth century.

TEN DAYS IN THE MAD-HOUSE

Ben Hecht and Charles MacArthur's play *The Front Page* took Broadway by storm when it opened in 1928, in no small measure because of Lee Tracy's portrayal of newspaperman Hildy Johnson. Its plot was simple: a police reporter attempts to capitalize on the pending execution of a condemned murderer while simultaneously trying to quit his job and marry his fiancée. Of the many journalists the play depicted, an article in the *New York Times* observed:

> The bored reporter, the bully, the nauseated esthete who finds his shiftless comrades revolting and sprays his desk with disinfectant, the nervous and merciless managing editor—all go through their paces. The skepticism, the callousness, the contempt, the vague dissatisfaction with their lot, the boorishness, the brutal jesting, and the omniscience are not invented.[10]

Hollywood quickly seized on the story, hardly surprising given the appeal that clever dialogue had for studios in the early years of the talkie. Lewis Milestone directed Pat O'Brien as Hildy Johnson in the 1931 film adaptation. Its opening text sets the scene, humorously remarking that *The Front Page* is "laid in a mythical kingdom."

Journalists proved enduring in Hollywood scripts, perhaps because many of them seemed as socially conscious as they were corrupt, as ingenious as they were conniving, as good as they were bad. Though he didn't get to reprise his Broadway role on film, Lee Tracy still found a home in Hollywood, playing Hildy Johnson-inspired reporters in *Doctor X* (1932), *Blessed Event* (1932), *The Strange Love of Molly Louvain* (1932), *Advice to the Lovelorn* (1933), *Behind the Headlines* (1937), *The Payoff* (1942), and—by way of a promotion to newspaper editor—*Power of the Press* (1943). But however much Tracy embodied the screen journalist, the most famous example remains Orson Welles's *Citizen Kane* (1941), whose title character (based on newspaper magnate William Randolph Hearst) famously remarks in 1898, "You provide the prose poems; I'll provide the war." Journalism was yellow, even in black-and-white.

While *The Front Page* encouraged Hollywood to produce sound films about the newspaper business, another, even older tradition is also crucial to consider, that of the woman journalist, the "girl stunt reporter," a role that originated with the real-life exploits of Nellie Bly (pen name of American journalist Elizabeth Cochrane Seaman). In 1887, the managing editor of the *New York World* suggested that Bly pretend to be insane so she could get remanded to an infamous asylum on Blackwell's Island. As Jean Marie Lutes notes, "Bly eagerly accepted the assignment."[11] Fooling the experts, who readily condemned her as crazy, she spent ten days inside the institution, where abuse of all kinds was ubiquitous. Bly later asked rhetorically, "Where could Dante have gotten a truer description of the tortures of Hell? Where could Doré have found a greater illustration?"[12] Her series of articles—collectively published in book form as *Ten Days in the Mad-House* (1887)—spurred a grand jury investigation. And her approach pioneered a new form of investigative journalism, one that placed a woman reporter in jeopardy.[13]

Bly's adventures continued in 1889, when she traveled around the globe with only one bag and a small amount of money. Just seventy-two days after her journey began, Bly successfully reappeared in New York.[14] Making reference to Jules Verne's novel *Around the World in Eighty Days* (1873), the *Chicago Tribune* announced, "Phineas [*sic*] Fogg of fiction has been outdone by the vigorous and sprightly young woman of fact."[15] Once again the famous journalist was triumphant. As Lutes explains, stunt reporters like Bly "boldly challenged the value of the experts' neutral pronouncements, insisting instead on the significance of their own bodies as sources of knowledge."[16] That knowledge came from gut instinct, as well as from hard-earned personal experience.

Girl reporters became popular, so much so that mystery fiction from the 1880s began to feature them. Sometimes they were assistant detectives, but by the early twentieth century, these women often became lead characters. LeRoy Lad Panek describes them as:

> independent, enterprising, intelligent, knowledgeable, capable, and successful women, women who, in spite of romantic distractions, succeeded in doing things conventionally associated with men. Not only do these women succeed in a traditionally male profession, but they also do so without significant outside help—particularly male help.[17]

Panek provides numerous examples of such novels, including Charles Carey's *The Van Suyden Sapphires* (1905), Reginald Kauffman's *Miss Frances Baird, Detective: A Passage from Her Memoirs* (1906), Leroy Scott's *Counsel for the Defense* (1912), Hugh C. Weir's *Miss Madeline Mack, Detective* (1914), and Anna Katharine Green's *The Golden Slipper and Other Problems for Violet Strange* (1915).[18]

Given their popularity, girl stunt reporters appeared onscreen during the early cinema period. "The Girl-Reporter saves the situation and makes a scoop at the same time," the *Moving Picture World* said of these characters in 1912.[19] In *The Insane Heiress* (1910), Nell—a character clearly inspired by Nellie Bly—solves the mystery of an abducted woman by pretending to be insane. Once incarcerated in an asylum, she chloroforms a nurse in order to change her disguise and uncover more clues.[20] Then, in 1914, Mary Fuller starred in Edison's serial *The Active Life of Dolly of the Dailies*, playing a "daring" journalist who makes her way up through the ranks of *The Comet*, a newspaper otherwise staffed by men.[21] Charles Ogle, notable for his work as the monster in Edison's *Frankenstein* (1910), played Fuller's editor.[22] Among the serial's twelve chapters were *A Tight Squeeze*, *A Terror of the Night*, and *Dolly Plays Detective*. In *The Chinese Fan*, the only surviving episode, an Asian villain kidnaps Dolly and holds her prisoner with another abducted woman. Dolly outwits and physically overpowers an opium-crazed guard, rescuing herself and her fellow inmate, as well providing *The Comet* with a major "scoop."[23]

After the success of *The Front Page*, the girl reporter assumed a new place of prominence in Hollywood, as can be seen in the horror film *Mystery of the Wax Museum* (1933). In it, Glenda Farrell plays Florence Dempsey, whom *Variety* described as follows:

> a hard-striding, hard drinking girl reporter, not so completely hard, however, that she doesn't find tears useful when the mean old managing editor doesn't like the way she's handling a story. Miss Farrell, talking and acting in the pretty darned tough manner Warner Brothers pictures admires in its femme players, does a generous bit of dashing about stalking clues and so on.[24]

Put another way, Farrell's gum-chewing, fast-talking character drew heavily on the role played by Lee Tracy in the horror movie *Doctor X*, produced by the same studio. To the extent that Farrell's character needed to be distinguished because of her gender, *Doctor X* drew upon the tradition of Nellie Bly. The character Florence Dempsey is a strong woman, her name evocative of Jack Dempsey, world heavyweight champion boxer from 1919 to 1926; the same year that Warner's released *Mystery of the Wax Museum*, Jack Dempsey appeared in MGM's film *The Prizefighter and the Lady*. As for Florence, she was a woman, but also one of the boys; at one point, she is even referred to as a "wise guy."

The girl reporter returned many times, including in a series of nine "Torchy Blane" movies produced at Warner Bros. between 1937 and 1939; seven of them featured Glenda Farrell as the intrepid title character. However, the most famous of these movies was Howard Hawks's *His Girl Friday* (1940), a remake of *The Front Page* and starring Rosalind Russell in what had previously been the male role of Hildy Johnson. Cary Grant's newspaper editor Walter Burns believes she is a great "newspaperman," a term that Russell's Hildy also uses to describe herself. The following year, Barbara Stanwyck starred as Ann Mitchell in Frank Capra's *Meet John Doe* (1941), a girl reporter who pulls a "circulation stunt," a "fake-a-roo" in which she concocts a letter to the editor that spurs mass public interest, so much so that she has to find someone to pretend to be its author, "John Doe" (Gary Cooper).

The lengthy history of the girl reporter of the screen also resulted in Patricia Hunter (Luana Walters), the hero of *The Corpse Vanishes* (Figure 4.1). She refers to herself using the non-gender-specific name "Pat"; Keenan (Kenneth Harlan), her editor at *The Chronicle*, and cameraman Sandy (Vince Barnett) do the same. On one occasion, she is called a "newspaperman." Like Ann Mitchell in *Meet John Doe* and Florence Dempsey in *Mystery of the Wax Museum*, Pat nearly finds herself out of a job, even though she is cleverer than the men around her. Nevertheless, Sandy derisively jokes that Pat wouldn't recognize a clue "if it bit her." She wants to do investigative journalism, but Keenan demands that she cover

Figure 4.1 Patricia Hunter (Luana Walters), the "girl reporter," meets Dr. Lorenz (Bela Lugosi, left).

society news like weddings, with an eye toward fashions worn by the guests. However, Pat's goal is to unravel the "Case of the Missing Brides," which she must do, not only for the sake of her career, but because the District Attorney's office clearly isn't up to the task. As her name suggests, she is a hunter.

Realizing that all of the kidnapped corpse brides wore the same type of mysterious *Stanhopea* orchid, Pat attempts to interview Dr. Lorenz, the man who originally hybridized the flower. She ignores the locals who fear him, to the extent that she hops on the back of a truck in order to sneak a nighttime ride to his home.[25] After being removed from the vehicle, Pat bravely takes a lift from another stranger, Dr. Foster (Tristram Coffin). When she finally meets Dr. Lorenz and his rude and abusive wife, Pat is undaunted. During the crazy night that follows, she is occasionally scared and even faints once, but none of that dissuades her from getting a "sensational" story. Her tenacity even leads Foster to ask if she is "one of those hard-boiled reporters that we read about or see in the movies."

To catch Dr. Lorenz, Pat convinces her editor to hold a "stunt" wedding, a "phony" ceremony with cigarette girl-turned-actress Peggy Woods (Gwen Kenyon) playing the bride. As expected, a *Stanhopea* orchid is delivered, but in a twist, Dr. Lorenz kidnaps Pat instead of the fake bride. She survives to tell the tale, in part because she physically overpowers the Countess. Then, in a conclusion not dissimilar to those seen in *Mystery of the Wax Museum* and *His Girl Friday*, Pat marries Dr. Foster. The film ends where it began, at a wedding. "Finally I make a newspaperman out of you and then you have to go and quit," Keenan complains. But Pat no longer has anything to prove: she is as tough and clever as Hildy Johnson and Nellie Bly.

IN THE WILDS OF TRANSYLVANIA

Many of the fictional characters in Bram Stoker's novel *Dracula* (1897) were deeply interested in, even dependent on, documenting the bizarre events that unfold. His novel unfolds through multiple perspectives, a variety of recorded observations, among them newspaper stories, diaries, and letters. Women write many of these, particularly Lucy Westenra and Mina Harker (née Murray), with the latter explicitly describing the role and even tools of authorship. As she notes in her journal, "I shall get my typewriter this very hour and begin transcribing. Then we shall be ready for other eyes if required." Mina later writes, "I took the cover off my typewriter, and said to Dr. Seward:—'Let me write this all out now.'" In his own diary, Seward recalls, "as I passed a while ago I heard the click of the typewriter. They are hard at it. Mrs. Harker says that they are knitting together in chronological order every scrap of evidence they have." Investigative reporting can solve crimes; compiling the research into narrative form can convince readers a crime has occurred.

Tod Browning's film version of *Dracula* (1931) does not rely on such reportage, but does not eschew it either. An onscreen newspaper article announces the arrival of the ship on which Dracula (Bela Lugosi) and Renfield (Dwight Frye) have traveled: "Crew of Corpses Found on Derelict Vessel." Later in the film, Martin (Charles Gerrard) reads aloud a newspaper article that records the tale of "two small girls" attacked by the undead Lucy (Frances Dade).

Without Browning's version of *Dracula*, there would not have been a star named "Bela Lugosi." The actor Bela Lugosi would probably have struggled onward in a variety of character roles in Hollywood and might even have achieved a degree of fame. However, Lugosi the horror icon would not have existed. By extension, it seems likely that, while Dracula would have remained an important literary and stage vampire, he would not have proven as enduring without Lugosi, whose appearance and voice have vastly overshadowed Stoker's own description. Of course, Browning's film was produced and it became a box-office success. Typecasting resulted, with Lugosi remembered decades after his death because of Dracula. Of all the many biographical details known about him, perhaps none resonates as strongly as his burial: Lugosi was interred in 1956 wearing one of his vampire capes.

With regard to Lugosi's career, it is possible to see the immediate effect Browning's *Dracula* had, not only on the horror film roles he was offered, but also in his billing. Publicity for a number of movies, among them Robert Florey's *Murders in the Rue Morgue* (1932) and Edgar G. Ulmer's *The Black Cat* (1934), headlined him as "Bela (Dracula) Lugosi," which reminded viewers of what they likely already knew. The actor and role had become synonymous, so much so that in the 1932 short subject *Hollywood on Parade No. A-8*, Lugosi plays a wax statue come to life. He does not portray Dracula in it, as some writers have mistakenly noted; rather, he plays "Bela Lugosi as Dracula." The two were separate, but forever linked in a kind of cinematic and cultural symbiosis.

Given how much the vampire consumed Lugosi, it's somewhat surprising that he did not actually play Dracula onscreen again until *Abbott and Costello Meet Frankenstein* (1948), seventeen years after the release of Browning's film. In fact, after 1931, he didn't play *any* vampires onscreen until Lew Landers' *The Return of the Vampire* in 1943. Horror film roles were plentiful, particularly mad doctors, but not vampires. The undead stayed dead, at least for many years (Figure 4.2).

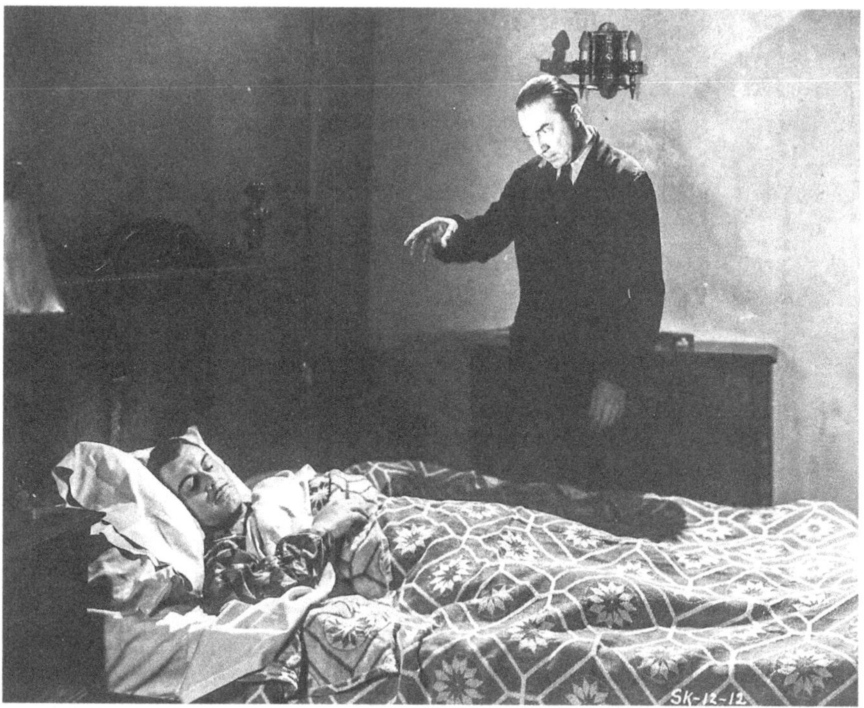

Figure 4.2 Dr. Lorenz (Bela Lugosi) in a scene that evokes the film *Dracula* (1931).

This is not to say that studios forgot about Dracula. From 1934 until the beginning of 1936, Universal hoped to cast Lugosi in *Dracula's Daughter* (1936). For a number of reasons, though, the Lambert Hillyer-directed sequel didn't feature any actor as Dracula, its narrative concentrating instead on his vampiric offspring. Lugosi did appear in Tod Browning's *Mark of the Vampire* (1935), an extremely atmospheric film that bears many similarities to the 1931 *Dracula*. Though Lugosi's costume resembles that of Dracula, his character Count Mora was not actually undead. Instead, Lugosi played an actor pretending to be a vampire.

Enter Sam Robins and Gerald "Jerry" Schnitzer. However much they were inspired by Dietz's memory of a kidnapped bride, their original story for *The Corpse Vanishes*—and Harvey Gates's screenplay based upon it—cited vampire lore repeatedly, more so than any film in which Lugosi had appeared since *Mark of the Vampire*. As *Motion Picture Daily* informed readers in 1942, *The Corpse Vanishes* attempted to "out-Dracula Dracula."[26] This is apparent from the opening credits, which feature artwork of a silhouetted figure wearing what appears to be a cloak or cape; he outstretches a claw-like hand toward a flower.

To be sure, Dr. Lorenz is a physician and scientist. It is quite possible that one of the film's writers appropriated Lorenz's name from Austrian surgeon Adolf Lorenz (1854–1946).[27] Famous for his work with bone deformities and orthopedics, Lorenz became known as the "Bloodless Surgeon of Vienna." His name had earlier appeared in *Dr. Lorenz Outdone*, Lubin's American retitling of Georges Méliès' *Up-to-Date Surgery/Une indigestion* (1902). In it, a surgeon saws off a patient's arms and legs before removing various objects from his stomach cavity. Once the operation is over, the doctor puts the man back together, but "a leg is placed where an arm should be, and vice versa."[28]

Lugosi's Lorenz is himself a man of science, a subject that interested Browning's Dracula, at least to a degree, as he announces that Professor Van Helsing's name is well known "even in the wilds of Transylvania." In *The Corpse Vanishes*, his wife is Countess Lorenz, whose title conjures the memory of Count Dracula's royal status, one that Dr. Lorenz may or may not share. Their accents suggest Eastern Europe or perhaps, at least in Russell's case, Germany. Dr. Lorenz is also a hypnotist, placing Dr. Foster into a "somnambulistic" state at one point; Dracula possessed the same skills. And to an extent, the kidnapped brides in Lorenz's basement echo Dracula's three Transylvanian wives.

Much like the carriage driver who does not want to take Renfield to Dracula's castle, a taxi driver is too scared to drive Pat to the Lorenz home, pretending to be "out of gas."[29] After all, Lorenz has the local reputation of being a "strange, spooky guy," one who has imported a special crate of moss, apparently from "somewhere in Europe," the location where he first hybridized the mysterious orchid. Here again the film recalls Dracula, who ships three boxes of earth from Transylvania to England. And like Dracula, who doesn't utter a single word in the Browning film for the first ten minutes, nearly fifteen minutes of *The Corpse Vanishes* pass before Dr. Lorenz speaks.

During the middle of the night, Lorenz wears all black as he hovers over the sleeping Pat and Dr. Fowler (Tristram Coffin), images reminiscent of the vampire approaching the beds of Lucy and Mina (Helen Chandler) in Browning's *Dracula*. Most visual of all is the fact that the Lorenzes sleep in coffins. Dr. Lorenz openly admits that he finds it "much more comfortable than a bed." During one of the kidnappings, Dr. Lorenz hides inside another coffin so as to fool police looking for a female corpse. No film had depicted Lugosi in a coffin since Browning's *Dracula*.[30] Here is one of the most memorable and visually arresting images of Lugosi, the Dracula actor inside a casket, and yet it is also one of the most rare in his film output.

None of this is to suggest that Dr. Lorenz is actually a vampire. In fact, he more closely resembles what Countess Zaleska (Gloria Holden) hopes Dr. Garth (Otto Kruger) will be in *Dracula's Daughter*: a "doctor of minds and souls," someone who "stands between [her] and destruction." Dr. Lorenz kidnaps brides in an effort to, as one character suggests, "sustain his wife in a youthful state." With his hypodermic needle, he extracts blood from his victims' necks and—after mixing it with some other chemical—injects the same into the Countess. "You're beautiful," he tells her, "and I shall always keep you that way." Without regular shots, she is wracked with pain, the effects of a rapid aging process. Even as he is dying, Dr. Lorenz attempts to give her a final injection. Failing to do so has immediate effect. As Dr. Foster has already realized, the Countess looks young, but is probably "seventy or eighty years old."

As much or more than Countess Zaleska, Countess Lorenz is reminiscent of Hungarian Countess Elizabeth Báthory de Ecsed (1560–1614, aka "Elizabeth Bathory" and "Elizabeth Bathori"), who tortured and killed dozens, if not hundreds, of young women between 1585 and 1609. After her death, writers claimed she had vampiric tendencies, bathing in the blood of virgins to maintain a youthful appearance. Dr. Lorenz's injections perform a similar function for his wife, to the extent that he kidnaps brides at the altar. "All of them must be [young]," he insists. Countess Lorenz requires virginal blood just as much as Countess Báthory allegedly did. And Dr. Lorenz acts at her domineering behest.

Accounts of Báthory appeared in the American press at least as early as 1827. In September of that year, the *North American* told readers:

> One day she struck [an "innocent" young woman] in a brutal manner, and the blood of the victim having flown into her face, she ran to a mirror to wipe it off. She fancied that her skin became whiter, more beautiful.[31]

In 1894, the *Chicago Tribune* published a similar story, telling readers that her "naturally cruel nature was spurred by the frenzied desire to retain her waning beauty at any price."[32] And in 1912, the *Cleveland Plain Dealer* maintained that the blood obtained for Báthory by her lackeys was "always saved, and in this life fluid the woman actually bathed."[33]

The *Plain Dealer* also published an illustration of the murderous Countess admiring herself in a mirror. *The Corpse Vanishes* created a similar image, the Countess admiring her reflection while Dr. Lorenz promises to "always keep [her] that way." In the *Plain Dealer* illustration, the Countess also holds a bloody cane over a defenseless maiden, a depiction of her sadism. Countess Lorenz shares this trait, as can be seen when she strikes Pat, as well as in the cruelty she displays toward members of her extended family.

THE LORENZ FAMILY

In the horror film, the American family can become twisted into a horrible inversion of itself. Nowhere is this more evident than in the 1960s and 1970s, beginning with Norman Bates (Anthony Perkins) and his mother in Alfred Hitchcock's *Psycho* (1960) and continuing through Roman Polanski's *Rosemary's Baby* (1968) and George Romero's *Night of the Living Dead* (1968). Depraved families then appeared in Wes Craven's *The Last House on the Left* (1972) and *The Hills Have Eyes* (1977), and—most infamously of all—in Tobe Hooper's *The Texas Chain Saw Massacre* (1974). In *Hearths of Darkness: The Family in the American Horror Film*, Tony Williams states that:

> typical American families [in these films] encounter their monstrous counterparts, undergo (or perpetuate) brutal violence, and eventually survive with full knowledge of their kinship to their monstrous counterparts. All these depictions contradict normal idealized family images in mainstream American film and television.[34]

Williams adds that these films belong to a "definable historical context," one that dates to the literature of authors like Nathaniel Hawthorne, Edgar Allan Poe, Ambrose Bierce, and H. P. Lovecraft.[35]

Horrifying families also appeared in the non-fiction press, whether in the case of the Manson Family in the late 1960s, or the exploits of the Bender Family in the 1870s. With the help of their two children, John and Elvira Bender murdered at least a dozen travelers who stopped at their hotel in Kansas. Usually daughter Kate distracted the victims while John or John, Jr. slit their throats. A trapdoor dropped the corpses into the basement, where the Benders looted them prior to burying them elsewhere on their property. By the time the authorities got involved, the Benders had disappeared, never to be apprehended. The press seized on their story, as did the fictionalized dime novel *The Five Fiends;*

or The Bender Hotel Horror in Kansas (1874), which overestimated the family's size by one member.[36]

Tony Williams traces the rise of horrifying families onscreen to Universal Pictures in the 1930s and 1940s.[37] In most cases, these relationships appeared thanks to sequels, the familial becoming the studio's key approach to continuing the narratives of monsters that had (apparently) been killed, as in films like Browning's *Dracula* and James Whale's *Frankenstein* (1931). Examples include *Dracula's Daughter* and Robert Siodmak's *Son of Dracula* (1943), as well as Whale's *Bride of Frankenstein* (1935), Rowland V. Lee's *Son of Frankenstein* (1939), and Erle C. Kenton's *The Ghost of Frankenstein* (1942). As Williams notes, these movies attempted to "externalize tensions emerging from the family."[38] They also represent a porous, even confused notion of what family means. Despite its title, *Son of Dracula* seems to feature the original Dracula, not his offspring. And the title of *Bride of Frankenstein*—as well as dialogue spoken in it—refers not to the betrothed of Dr. Frankenstein (Colin Clive), but instead to the mate he creates for his monster. By contrast, the title of *Son of Frankenstein* definitely refers to Baron Wolf von Frankenstein (Basil Rathbone), the doctor's son.

Despite reliance on the familial, it was actually rare for an individual film of the period to feature a horrifying family. James Whale's *The Old Dark House* (1932) supplies the key example of the 1930s. During a terrible storm, five travelers unexpectedly find themselves stuck at the Femm family home. Horace Femm (Ernest Thesiger) is an extremely nervous sort, one who might be wanted by the police. His gruff sister Rebecca (Eva Moore) is a religious fanatic. Their aged father Roderick (Elspeth Dudgeon, credited onscreen as "John Dudgeon") is allegedly "wicked" and "blasphemous." Butler Morgan is a "brute" when drunk, but the family must employ him to look after the maniacal Saul Femm (Brember Wills), who—during a brief moment of apparent sanity—accuses the others of murdering their own sister years earlier.

That same year, in Tod Browning's film *Freaks* (1932), the title characters represent a non-biological family, but a family nonetheless. "One of us! One of us!", the characters chant, their deep and loyal ties to one another bound by their physical challenges, as well as by their emotional connections. Indeed, their chant is heard when they admit Cleopatra (Olga Baclanova), a "normal" woman, into their family, the result of her marriage to a dwarf named Hans (Harry Earles).

However different *The Corpse Vanishes* is from *Freaks* and *The Old Dark House*, it also features a "family," some of the members related by blood, some not. And it is a family unknown to the authorities, who according to the press are searching for a lone "corpse thief." In his initial dialogue, Dr. Lorenz praises his "little family" for being "so very faithful." And yet the family members increase and decrease at the whims of Dr. Lorenz and the Countess. Perhaps the most unusual is Mike (George Eldredge, credited onscreen as "George Eldridge"). Physically and intellectually, he seems to be a healthy, middle-aged man. In his limited screen time, he is rude to Pat, but only because she wants to interview Dr. Lorenz without having an appointment. Whether he is transporting a newly arrived coffin from the train station or helping to kidnap women, Mike performs crucial tasks for Dr. Lorenz with complete loyalty. He is unusual because he lacks any narrative backstory. Why, in other words, is this man with no known blood ties to the family so deeply enmeshed in Lorenz's crimes?

Mike's limited footage results in part from the amount of attention devoted to Fagah (Minerva Urecal), a mysterious old woman, and her two sons, the mentally challenged Angel (Frank Moran), and the sadistic dwarf Toby (Angelo Rossito, credited onscreen as "Angelo"). The trio lives together in a single room inside the basement of the Lorenz home. Toby leaves the home on occasion with Mike and Lorenz. He also undertakes menial tasks like answering the front door and showing guests to their bedrooms. The Countess calls him a "gargoyle"; Pat calls him a "monstrosity." For his part, Toby takes joy in the suffering of others, gleefully telling Pat, "I guess you'll sleep very good . . . *maybe*," before laughing openly at what he knows will be a traumatic night (Figure 4.3).

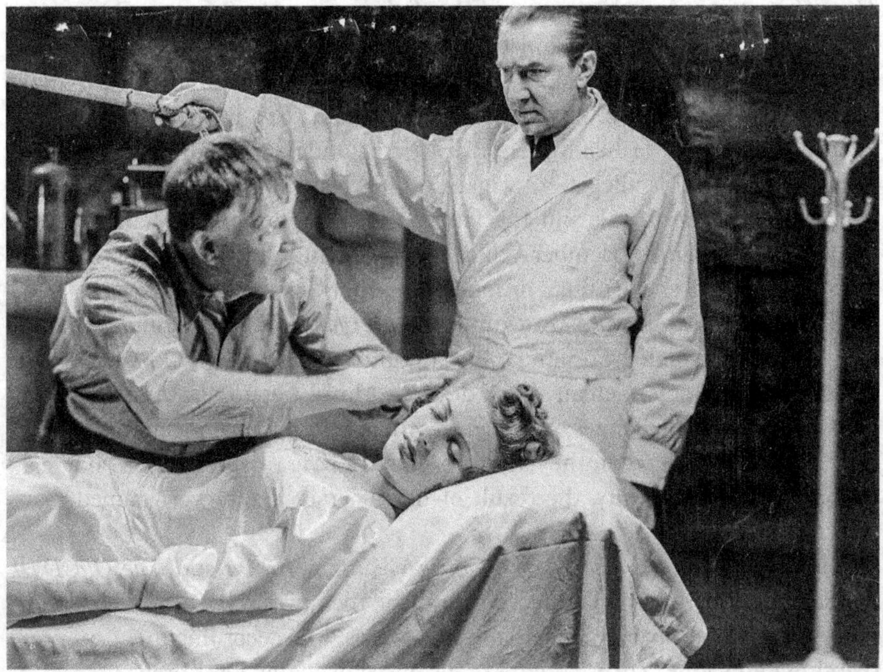

Figure 4.3 Dr. Lorenz (Bela Lugosi) with Angel (Frank Moran), one of the members of the Lorenz "family."

By contrast, Dr. Lorenz barks at Fagah when she appears on the ground floor of the home: she and Angel belong underground. That said, Lorenz gives Fagah the crucial task of assisting in the transfusions that keep the Countess alive and well. He also leaves the wellbeing of the kidnapped brides to Fagah, who obeys his commands unquestioningly. Like Toby, she refers to Lorenz as "Master"; this terminology (and the power relationships it denotes) recalls the language Renfield (Dwight Frye) uses to speak to the title character of Browning's *Dracula*.

Angel, on the other hand, seems to have limited duties, if any. He is allowed in the laboratory during one transfusion. But his penchant for admiring the kidnapped brides and caressing their hair has severe consequences. Catching him the first time, Dr. Lorenz whips Angel repeatedly while Toby watches, gloating and snickering in the most sadistic manner. "Why do you beat my son so hard?", Fagah asks. Lorenz replies, "Because he's a beast, an animal. And someday I shall have to destroy him."

Lorenz's threat soon becomes reality. During the night that Pat stays at the Lorenz home, Toby hears Angel getting out of bed. "I know where you're going," he says. "Someday the Master will catch you, then you'll be sorry." Grunting, Angel leaves, sneaking into Pat's bedroom. Later, he follows her in the basement, lasciviously chewing on a turkey leg with a smile on his face. By that time, the Countess has declared that Angel is a "menace" to the family's safety. Lorenz agrees and strangles Angel to death.

Trying to make their getaway at the final kidnapping, the Lorenz family again decreases in size. A policeman shoots Toby, who pleads with Lorenz not to leave him behind. Without hesitation, Lorenz literally kicks him to the curb. In retaliation, the grief-stricken Fagah stabs Lorenz, who in turn strangles her. Once Lorenz is dead, Fagah uses the last of her strength to stab the Countess, who has fallen to the floor after being overpowered by Pat. Disloyalty begets disloyalty, with Countess Lorenz's death not dissimilar to Countess Zaleska's in *Dracula's Daughter*; her jealous servant Sandor (Irving Pichel) shoots her with an arrow after she tries to give Dr. Garth eternal life.

The Lorenz clan also includes those women who have no opportunity to fight back, the kidnapped brides who are vaulted beneath the family home. They are alive, but trapped in a cataleptic state. It is clear that the doctor and the Countess consider them to be relatives, at least of a sort. When speaking excitedly about Peggy, the fake bride, Dr. Lorenz enthuses, "She'll make a charming addition to our family." And the brides are particularly precious in the eyes of the otherwise cruel Countess. When the Lorenzes decide to flee at the end of the film, she shows far more consideration to the kidnapped women than to anyone else. "The brides," she worries, "what will we do without them?"

At first, it seems the Countess's concern for the brides comes solely from their capacity to restore her health. While that is her key interest, the Countess does have another reason, one that Dr. Lorenz shares. Of one of the kidnapped women the Countess remarks, "She's pretty . . . very young." Later, given Lorenz's "very special reason" for asking Pat to spend the night, the Countess happily informs the reporter, "[s]ome time you too will be a bride." And when examining a photograph of the stunt bride, the Countess becomes particularly excited, perhaps more than at any other point in the film, lustfully exclaiming, "She's a most unusual type . . . such fascinating eyes." Dr. Lorenz and the Countess are infatuated with the brides, to the extent that their membership in the family seems sexualized. Along with shared attraction for the victims, the Lorenzes literally share in them physically thanks to the use of their blood.

CONCLUSION

The Corpse Vanishes remains a fascinating, if flawed film. For example, no single moment was meant to be more dramatic than Pat's discovery that the minister at the stunt wedding is actually Dr. Lorenz in disguise. His back is to her as she enters the minister's office; she learns the truth only after approaching him. But the camera angle and poor blocking greatly diminish its impact on the viewer, as it's obvious that the fake minister is Lorenz as soon as Pat enters the room.

Nevertheless, *The Corpse Vanishes* is a welter of ideas and influences, appropriating as it does the histories of girl stunt reporters and Hollywood vampires and placing them into an early example of the perverse kind of family that populated horror films of future decades. As with *The Texas Chain Saw Massacre*, for example, the Lorenz family seems to appear out of nowhere, and its storyline remains open-ended, at least to a degree. A policeman hits Mike, but his fate is never explained. The authorities might arrest him, or he might escape. We don't know.

Perhaps Monogram wasn't understated in its choice of title after all. No corpse vanishes, not even one. Instead, Dr. Lorenz kidnaps women who are actually still alive. But even more than with Mike, their fate forever hangs in the balance. The audience does not learn if all of them are rescued. Do they survive? And if so, have they been forever scarred by their temporary adoption into the Lorenz family?

In the end, *The Corpse Vanishes* is fascinating as much because of its questions as its answers—an unanticipated, enigmatic narrative, exemplifying as it does the fact that the efforts of directors like Fox to emulate the filmmaking style of major studios meant that the result inevitably became something else. Fox's film is thematically distinctive, genre-expansive, while marked by low budgets and rapid shooting schedules. Rather than being viewed merely as cheap imitations of high-end Hollywood product, B-movies, artistically complex and frequently the industrial narrative of aesthetic choice, should be understood as another genre of film, one that can be rightly lauded for playing by a different set of rules.

NOTES

1. "Eight More Features Get Starter's Gun This Week," *Film Daily*, March 10, 1942, 6.
2. Gary D. Rhodes, "Gerald Schnitzer," *Filmfax Plus: The Magazine of Unusual Film, Television & Retro Pop Culture* 129 (Winter 2012), 38. Unfortunately, it is difficult to find the news story Dietz read. Various brides were kidnapped in the 1920s and 1930s, one of them being an heiress named Helen Fisher Drill. See "Abducted Heiress Rescued in West," *New York Times*, April 20, 1931, 40. Other examples of such incidents include "Kidnapped, Swears Bride," *New York Times*, January 9, 1921, 2; "Abducted Bride Escapes," *New York Times*, March 14, 1923, 12; and "Jailed for Kidnapping, He Dodges Wrong Bride," *New York Times*, December 2, 1934, E2. A related story, one more similar to the plot of *The Corpse Vanishes* than the others, reported the kidnapping of a bridegroom who "had been kidnapped, chloroformed, and then left by the roadside" while his bride was waiting for several hours at a church in New York. After being rescued and revived, the bridegroom married "twenty four hours behind [the] scheduled time," with the "villain foiled" as in "all good melodramas." See "Villain Chloroforms and Kidnaps Bridegroom; Bride Weeps at Church, but Ending Is Happy," *New York Times*, October 26, 1925, 1.
3. Actor Tristram Coffin later claimed that Elizabeth Russell refused to get inside the coffin for a scene in *The Corpse Vanishes*, requiring the director to use a double. However, viewing the film makes clear that it is indeed Russell in the coffin. See Tom Weaver, *Poverty Row Horrors! Monogram, PRC, and Republic Horror Films of the Forties* (Jefferson, NC: McFarland, 1993), 72.
4. "Hollywood Inside," *Daily Variety*, March 18, 1942, 2.
5. "Chatter," *Daily Variety*, April 9, 1942, 2.
6. Vance King, "*The Corpse Vanishes*," *Motion Picture Daily*, April 15, 1942, 11.
7. "*The Corpse Vanishes*," *Film Daily*, April 16, 1942, 6.
8. "*The Corpse Vanishes*," *Daily Variety*, April 13, 1942, 3.
9. Lugosi would also co-star with Minerva Urecal in *The Ape Man* (1943) and *Ghosts on the Loose* (1943).
10. J. Brooks Atkinson, "*The Front Page*," *New York Times*, August 26, 1928, 95.
11. Jean Marie Lutes, "Into the Madhouse with Nellie Bly: Girl Stunt Reporting in Late Nineteenth-Century America," *American Quarterly* 54:2 (June 2002), 217.
12. Nellie Bly, "Among the Mad," *Godey's Lady's Book*, January 1889.
13. For more information on Nellie Bly, see Deborah Noyes, *Ten Days a Madwoman* (New York: Viking, 2016).
14. Ibid., 94.
15. "Nellie Bly's Trip Round the World," *Chicago Tribune*, January 26, 1890, 12.
16. Lutes, 245.
17. LeRoy Lad Panek, *The Origins of the American Detective Story* (Jefferson, NC: McFarland, 2006), 169.
18. Ibid., 169.
19. "Saved," *Moving Picture World*, October 19, 1912, 221.
20. "*The Insane Heiress*," *Moving Picture World*, December 24, 1910, 1492.

21. Other examples of girl reporters in early films appear in Vitagraph's *How Cissy Made Good* (1915) and Kulee's *How Molly Made Good* (1915).
22. "*A Terror of the Night*," *New York Dramatic Mirror*, May 27, 1914, 42.
23. A copy of *The Chinese Fan* is available on the DVD *Lost & Found American Treasures from the New Zealand Film Archive* (San Francisco, CA: National Film Preservation Foundation, 2013).
24. Cecilia Ager, "Going Places," *Variety*, February 21, 1933, 12.
25. Some of the outdoor shots of Pat at the train station were clearly shot in daylight, but the film suggests it is nighttime. Lanterns are lit at the depot, and Foster has his car headlights turned on. Through the windows of Foster's car (as well as Lorenz's home right after their arrival), it definitely appears to be dark outside.
26. King, 11.
27. The name was not the only allusion to a famous person that the script used. Their dialogue also references clairvoyant "Madame Zora." It also seems likely that the name of the film's "Forest Mortuary" was inspired by Forest Lawn Memorial-Parks & Mortuaries.
28. *Complete Catalogue of Genuine and Original "Star" Films (Moving Pictures), Manufactured by Geo. Méliès of Paris* (New York: Star Films, 1903), 26. Available in *A Guide to Motion Picture Catalogs by American Producers and Distributors, 1894–1908: A Microfilm Edition* (New Brunswick, NJ: Rutgers University Press, 1985), Reel 4.
29. Tom Weaver sees a parallel between the taxi driver in *The Corpse Vanishes* and the innkeeper in *Dracula*. See Weaver, 71.
30. At one point in *Mark of the Vampire*, the fake vampire Count Mora is at rest, but the shot does not clearly show him inside a coffin.
31. "The Castle of Cseisthe, in Hungary," *North American; Or, Weekly Journal of Politics, Science and Literature*, September 1, 1827, 123.
32. "One Woman's Secret of Beauty," *Chicago Tribune*, October 6, 1894, 16.
33. "The World's Greatest Murderers, XVI—Elizabeth of Transylvania," *Cleveland Plain Dealer* (Cleveland, OH), August 11, 1912, 3.
34. Tony Williams, *Hearths of Darkness: The Family in the American Horror Film* (Madison, NJ: Fairleigh Dickinson University Press, 1996), 13.
35. Ibid., 30, 27.
36. For more information on the Benders, see Phyllis de la Garza, *Death for Dinner: The Benders of (Old) Kansas* (Unionville, NY: Silk Label Books, 2014).
37. Williams, 30.
38. Ibid., 50.

CHAPTER 5

"Like a crazy nightmare": Noirish Vampirism and Deviance in *Bowery at Midnight*

Marlisa Santos

In 1942, the *L.A. Times* called Wallace Fox's *Bowery at Midnight* "maybe the most farthest fetched of the Bela Lugosi films."[1] Given Lugosi's filmography up to that point, that is indeed saying something significant. With such offerings as *Murder by Television* (1935), *The Phantom Creeps* serial (1939), and *Spooks Run Wild* (1941) in the intervening years after *Dracula*, one might well question that reviewer's assessment. *Bowery at Midnight* does indeed push the disbelief suspension quite far, but in fact, these very surrealistic, logic-stretched aspects of the film set it apart from conventional B-picture horror fare and place it squarely as a weirdly compelling proto-noir, in the same—albeit less polished—vein as Boris Ingster's *Stranger on the Third Floor* (1940) and Jacques Tourneur's *Cat People* (1942). Fox capitalizes on viewer associations with Lugosi's vampire roles, making the ensuing narrative about underground criminal networks, drug addiction, and class privilege much deeper than those of typical scare features and displaying the unapologetically violent, logic-averse, and morally ambiguous elements of film noir that would come to define the cycle.

As film noir developed, elements of post-WWII angst, including gender role shifts and global fears of communism and nuclear annihilation, became some of its significant themes. However, the roots of noir are solidly found in Depression-era economic and social crises, with 1930's pulp fiction depicting these crises and functioning as the source material for so many film noir narratives. At the core of these crises is the crushing sense of instability engendered by the Depression fallout. The depth of this instability is emphasized by Philip Hanson, who argues that "[i]ntensifying the collapse of prosperity was the sense that the reputations of society's pillars had been illusory; intensifying the dissolution of respected reputations was a fear that fundamental American values had themselves been an illusion.'"[2] It is these sensibilities that hover around the edges of *Bowery at Midnight*, centered on the ironically named "Friendly Mission"—soup kitchen on the outside, but criminal headquarters on the inside. Lugosi's apparently kindly Karl Wagner operates the establishment, offering "food for your body, as well as counsel for your troubled mind." The down-and-out clientele prefer Wagner's secular approach to social reform, as one comments approvingly, "Most places you go to, they want to save your soul." Despite the nourishing food and medical attention offered, soul-saving indeed seems to be the furthest mission of the Mission—especially since Wagner is actually a criminal mastermind who runs a nefarious gang of thieves. That the front for such crime is a charitable service that was so desperately needed and frequented in recent years before the film's release speaks volumes about the growing cynicism prior to World War II that would eventually pervade the mood of film noir.

It is hard to believe that the irony of Bela Lugosi playing a duplicitous feeder of men while all the time draining society of its wealth and even morality would have been lost on the viewing public of 1942. Lugosi himself mused,

Figure 5.1 "Fingers" Dolan (John Berkes), one of many expendable criminals in Wagner's ring, sees his "value" evaporate.

> Where once I had been the master of my professional destinies, with a repertoire embracing all kinds and types of men . . . I became Dracula's puppet . . . the shadowy figure of Dracula, more than any casting office, dictated the kind of parts I played.

Lugosi was likely referring to the many horror pictures that claimed his talents after 1931, but his recognizable name, visage, and accent would certainly have transferred vampiric associations to even the most human of characters. Karl Wagner is a different kind of monster, one who treats human life as cheaply as the meager fare he offers the underprivileged who frequent his mission. Fox seemed well aware of Lugosi's capital in these kinds of roles, even placing a poster from his foray with Lugosi earlier that year, *The Corpse Vanishes*, into a scene in the film. Also penned by Gerald Schnitzer, the writer of *Bowery*, *Corpse* similarly projects shadows of vampirism in its tale of a mad scientist draining virgins of glandular fluid to maintain the youth of his ancient wife. These associations likely led reviews like that of the BFI's *Monthly Film Bulletin* from January 1943 to conclude that the film was "[d]esigned merely for providing the audience with that particular brand of Bela Lugosi thrills," adding that "it is hardly more than that and far from original."[3] What is original about the production, actually, is its melding of horror and crime that projects in its cynicism noir's depiction of urban trials and its Depression-era roots.

Wagner is no ordinary criminal mastermind; his solipsistic disregard for human life beyond his own is striking by 1930's gangster film standards and even by eventual film noir standards. Wagner recruits experienced criminals with specific skills, such as the safecracking expertise of "Fingers" Dolan, in order to pull off jewel heists and other robberies. However, once "Fingers" has served his usefulness, he is killed by Stratton, Wagner's lieutenant. When Stratton protests, "But he's a valuable man," Wagner responds with the chilling, "WAS a valuable man." Moreover, this conversation unmercifully takes place right in front of "Fingers," as if he is not even there (Figure 5.1). And, for Wagner's purposes, he is not: once he has "done his job," his existence is irrelevant, except to send a message to the cops that they are not dealing with an ordinary criminal. Stratton himself is well aware that there is little to prevent Wagner from eliminating him as well, and this fear proves true when Wagner goads his newest recruit, career criminal Frankie Mills (Tom Neal), into killing Stratton to take his place. And Wagner, for the next job, easily tosses a recently recruited petty thief (who likely imagined his role in the job would be different) off a roof in order to create a distraction for Mills to slide into a jewelry store to rob it. Even the police realize, when they find Dolan's body in the jewelers' safe, that leaving the body of an accomplice on each job proves that the crimes are the work of a "homicidal maniac." Whereas most criminal organizations employ some sort of code that seeks to preserve the lives of those internal to them as well as their own existence, Wagner's operation runs on no such sentiment. It is the ultimate in parasitism, as it feeds off itself for sustenance, leaving countless human lives in its wake. Wagner's own wife—who knows nothing about his criminal activities—is treated as just another piece of collateral damage; he kills her and hides her body in a closet, rather than risk her divulging any information when the police come to question her. The frankly shocking disregard for any life outside his own posits Wagner as non-human—a machine or animal—in his pursuit of his own interests. This kind of characterization prefigures eventual sadistic lone wolf noir psychopaths, such as Richard Widmark's Tommy Udo in *Kiss of Death* (1947) and Lawrence Tierney's Sam in *Born to Kill* (1946).

A third aspect of Wagner's identity, and a further fragmentation of self that emphasizes his soullessness, is that of a criminal psychology professor at a local college (Figure 5.2). By day, he is an educator of youth; by evening, a feeder of the hungry; and by night, a robber and killer of the humanity that the first two enterprises are endeavoring to protect. How better to get close to this humanity, and thereby have deeper connections on which to prey? Wagner, also known as Professor Brenner, the alternate name a further bifurcation of identity, schools his students on such topics as paranoia, delusions of grandeur, superiority complexes, and persecution mania. He queries one of his students, Richard Dennison (John Archer), about why this kind of person is so dangerous, and Richard replies, "He acts logically. If you didn't study him, you wouldn't know he was maladjusted . . . he doesn't hesitate to use force to assert his personality . . . this leads to an antisocial conduct." Brenner/Wagner then adds that one could conclude that such an individual might even "enjoy a life of crime." Wagner's awareness of his own predilections seems clear and underscores his sociopathy. Michael A. Oliker, in his discussion of the depiction of educators on film, cites Lugosi's role as one that signifies the beginning of a decline of public confidence in education in an "age of paranoia" populated by film noir, in which "anyone—even your teacher—is a potential threat."[4] That Wagner's discipline is psychology is also telling, since popular fascination with—and suspicion of—psychoanalysis would flourish with the beginnings of film noir, as wartime use of psychoanalytic techniques to treat "combat neuroses" would filter down into popular magazine and film stories. Here, the suggestion that Wagner's knowledge of criminal psychological motivations would be used for the manipulative purposes of both enticing others and concealing his own wrongdoing point the film squarely in the direction of film noir's future path.

ASTOR PICTURES presents BELA LUGOSI in "BOWERY AT MIDNIGHT"

Figure 5.2 Wagner, in his alternate identity as Professor Brenner, debates with student Richard Dennison (John Archer) about the sociopathic enjoyment of crime.

Far from being troubled by his moral deviation, Wagner celebrates it, proclaiming that it makes him superior to others. He prides himself on his advanced organizational methods, keeping detailed files on local criminals and surveilling his current team with tele-video screens. His seemingly superhuman knowledge derives from these methods and is what makes him believe separates him from all other human beings. But interestingly, the only visible crack in this façade also derives from psychological roots: the fact that Wagner has terrible dreams. The viewer does not know the nature of these dreams, only that his wife implies he has had these "horrible nightmares" for some time. In one of the only scenes that displays any weakness in Wagner, the camera moves out from a close-up of his contorted, moaning face to reveal his wife, awake and watching him. Only his own tortured thoughts, allowed to surface in sleep, seem to have power over him, but these thoughts and any other possible motivations are a complete mystery to the viewer. This kind of scene anticipates noir's fascination with all things psychiatric; examples of dream psychology in disturbed characters are pervasive in noir, from Hitchcock's *Spellbound* (1947) to Rudolph Maté's *The Dark Past* (1948) to Lew Landers' *Man in the Dark* (1953).

The secrecy of Wagner's criminal operations, symbolized in the film by the succession of doors in the mission that lead to greater and greater mysteries, dovetails with the bizarre horror element of the film, the below-stairs realm of drug-addicted Doc Brooks (Lew Kelly). When Doc is not asking Wagner's employees to fill "small bottle" prescriptions for him, what Stratton calls "slow death," Doc does the dirtiest of Wagner's work: disposing of the bodies of the dead accomplices in a basement graveyard. Frankie Mills wonders if Doc is a real doctor, to which Wagner responds that he was actually once a great doctor, but is now just a "human derelict." Resentful of Wagner's dismissal of him, Doc secretly maintains his belief that he is still a great doctor by employing his talents on Wagner's victims: instead of burying them, he turns them into zombies who live yet another layer beneath the basement floor and are resurrected to do Doc's bidding (Figure 5.3). Doc himself might also be viewed as a zombie, a shell of a human being consumed by his addiction and relegated to the most disgusting of tasks. He tells the dead Stratton, "I'll save you from the dead; then you'll belong to me." Contrasted with this one-way conversation

Figure 5.3 The horrors of Doc's basement graveyard revealed.

is Wagner telling Mills, "Our place is not with the dead. Their work is done; ours is just beginning." In the same way that Doc values the dead for his own purposes, Wagner too has an odd fondness for his used-up accomplices, or at least their existence as confirmation of his superior criminal machinations, as he admonishes Doc for letting his cat "desecrate" the graves of the makeshift cellar cemetery. The fluidity between life and death is continually reinforced in the film, from Wagner's perpetual recycling of criminal talent, to Doc's revival of the dead for his own, unstated power-hungry motives, to the living dead specter of Lugosi himself permeating all.

As referenced above, Lugosi as actor almost provides a doppelganger image to Lugosi as character(s) in the film, and on a deeper level than simply as horror icon. According to Gary D. Rhodes,

> Lugosi's own image was a mask from which he could not escape. Lugosi's appearance and that of Dracula bore no distinction from one another. The slicked-back hair, tarantula-like hand movements, tall and trim physique, and mysterious and penetrating eyes became qualities forever associated with the vampire count; the same characteristics were Lugosi's own personal traits.[5]

Rhodes adds that that Lugosi's accent in particular, which Lugosi himself said that he struggled to overcome while continually cast in parts that demanded it, trapped him in such roles.[6] Ten years after *Dracula*, Lugosi's accent remains prominent in *Bowery*, rendering much of his dialogue, in combination with the substandard sound from its "less-than-a-week-and-it-shows" production values, hardly intelligible. Here again, as in his other films, whether overt horror or not, the "foreignness" of Lugosi's persona signifies the "fear of other" that intensifies the sinister role. Wagner's presence, both as he infiltrates one of the most fundamental and influential aspects of American society (education) and soils the most Christian of enterprises (charity), sends a message of profound anxiety in the film, looking back toward Depression-era economic fears and forward toward the threat of fascism and foreign powers threatening American freedoms. In his analysis of the evolution of horror films, Robin Wood argues that "in the 30's, horror is always foreign" and that in Lugosi films such as *Murders in the Rue Morgue*,

> the foreignness of the horror characters is strongly underlined, both by Lugosi's accent and by the fact that nobody knows where he comes from. The foreignness of horror in the 30s can be interpreted in two ways: simply, as a means of disavowal (horror exists, but it is un-American), and, more interestingly and unconsciously, as a means of locating horror as a "country of the mind," as a psychological state. . .[7]

Lugosi's presence in *Bowery* thus provides the kind of multifaceted menace that would have been impossible to convey with any other actor.

Amidst its interplay of crime and horror, *Bowery at Midnight* also provides compelling class commentary that further offers a bridge into film noir. The Bowery setting immediately provides a frame of economic want, but unlike popular '30s gangster pictures like *The Public Enemy* and *Little Caesar*, *Bowery at Midnight* does not display a hero-criminal who came from humble origins, and whose only real crime in the end is forgetting those origins.[8] Rather, Wagner is a genteel, upper-middle class figure whose gestures of charity only conceal parasitic greed and murder. The character of student Richard particularly highlights class issues in the film. Richard's girlfriend Judy volunteers at the Friendly Mission, a pursuit for which both he and her mother have contempt; their upper-class life is clearly portrayed in scenes of leisurely conversation and coffee from a silver set in an upscale apartment. Richard tries to convince Judy to stop working at the Bowery, scoffing at her wanting to help the "underprivileged . . . all this business about saving humanity; it's ridiculous." He even thinks that she is romantically involved with Wagner (not knowing that Wagner and Brenner are the same person) because he simply cannot believe she would spend her time on an entirely altruistic enterprise. It is telling that one of Judy's functions at the mission is first aid—to clean and bandage wounds and prevent them from becoming "infected," and that she wears nurse-like white at the mission, but a black, almost military-style dress when she arrives home. Though the mission is a sham, Judy believes in her service there, ministering to the poor, angel-like, while having to battle the more selfishly diseased forces of money and privilege in her private life.

Unwittingly, Richard becomes a catalyst for all three of Wagner's identities to converge when his search for research paper material brings him to the Bowery. Ironically, his original paper topic is "what a man thinks of right before he dies," but then switches to "the psychology of the underprivileged," telling Wagner, "I know very little about real people . . . you can't learn about life by cruising around on a yacht." Richard has a significant learning curve to overcome, however. Earlier, he dismissively tells Judy, "Go ahead and have all the fun you want . . . you and your social work." In contrast to Judy's "fun" at the Bowery, Richard finds the research process to be more difficult than he thought, as he prowls around the Bowery, eventually learning that he needs to buy some old clothes in order to assimilate better before the homeless men will interact with him at all; though he offers them cigarettes, they only sneer at his gentility and refuse to talk. His eventual arrival at the mission is the biggest threat for Wagner, as he will have to eliminate the only witness to his multiple, and criminal, identities. Wagner gleefully tells him that he will get his chance to learn about both of his proposed research topics, as Richard, masquerading as a tramp, will now be facing his own death. It is as if Wagner's ability to prey on victims depends on their transformation into poverty—whether it is Richard or his own crime associates. Who would care if such people were eliminated from society anyway, after serving his short-term purposes? Wagner's diet is ironically meager; he feeds the poor and then feeds on them. Right before Frankie kills him, Richard cannot comprehend what is happening to him, proclaiming "This is like a crazy nightmare!" This nightmare would have been intensified, had Richard known he would thereafter be transformed into a zombie. In fact, it may be that Richard fully realizes the powerless nightmare of the poor at this moment. Not only has he discovered that his professor is secretly the proprietor of the Friendly Mission, but also in short order, that this secret charity is a lie that reveals Brenner as a homicidal criminal mastermind.

Richard's experiences of this drastic turn of events heightens Lugosi's Brenner/Wagner as an eerie destructive presence, threatening to destroy the tenets of American society—both the privileged and the underprivileged alike. In his discussion of the link between the concepts of "un-American" and "uncanny" in film noir, Jonathan Auerbach argues that

> the uncanny in this regard is primarily a matter of trespassing or boundary crossing where inside and outside grow confused as (presumed) foreigners enter domestic space and, conversely, the home reveals dark secrets hidden within . . . Cinema scholars frequently link noir to existential alienation, abstractly or philosophically considered, but such alienation needs to be more precisely grounded in specific historical and cultural fears about enemy aliens lurking within.[9]

That Brenner/Wagner is so clearly presented as an immigrant creates an unveiled implication in this regard: that he has brought this uncanny instability to those supposedly safe [institutional] spaces of American culture—the classroom, the charity—and will destroy them, if not stopped. The "nightmare" is of course the converse of the American dream, shown for all its sad illusion in the noir cycle. It is for this reason that Wheeler Winston Dixon argues that *Bowery at Midnight* provides an especially bleak and noirish view of New York, "a locus of collapsed dreams rather than the zone of limitless possibility pictured in early twentieth century immigration narratives."[10] The idea of enemy alien infiltration shows its roots at this point, evolving into depictions of the threat of fascism in wartime noir (i.e. *The Fallen Sparrow*, 1943; *Ministry of Fear*, 1944) and the threat of communism in postwar noir (i.e. *I Was a Communist for the FBI*, 1951; *Pickup on South Street*, 1955).

It is ironic that police suspicion of Wagner's mission only comes about because of wealthy, upper-class Richard's disappearance. Because Wagner would often have his gang members masquerade as Bowery denizens—Frankie poses as a blind beggar, for instance, when he robs the jewelry store after the thief is thrown from the roof—the police crack down on Bowery activity, targeting the homeless there, rather than seeking a more complicated cause of the criminal activity. In a satisfying turn of events, Wagner's fate is that of his previous victims; Doc provides a "perfect" place for him to hide from police: opening a grave to reveal the basement full of zombies, who converge on Wagner and presumably eat him alive. Again, it is not a far stretch to imagine that Fox is making an intentional Lugosi connection with his audience, capitalizing on the portrayal of the appropriate place for Brenner/Wagner as an open grave revealing undead horrors. This resolution offers a more complex evolution from the gangster "crime doesn't pay" ending. Here, crime comes back from the dead to destroy the criminal. In this ouroboric climax, prey is consuming predator, for whom there will be no resurrection.

Elements that stop short of noir in *Bowery at Midnight* are also found in noir films during the full-blown period, including the final few minutes of screen time that offer a cheery conclusion antithetical to the hour plus of film that came before it. This resolution, as well as breakneck production choices like a singsong score that belongs more to a '30s caper film, make the film as a whole seem even more bizarre, leaving a multitude of questions unanswered and positing the film as even more of a "crazy nightmare." For instance, the final scene shows Richard in bed, presumably recovering (from being dead?) quite nicely. How does Richard come back to "real" life from his zombie state? Do the other zombies also come back to life, and if so, what becomes of them? As Richard is recuperating in the film's final scene, it is not merely a conveniently neat wrap-up that is supplied, but rather a weird, almost homespun ending, in which Richard waxes to Judy how they will have six kids, leaving her work at the Bowery behind. Her smiling response of "Yes, Richard" seems almost more zombie-like than Richard in his previous state. It is as if the foray into the Bowery were a dangerous interlude in their relationship that will never be repeated or revisited. It may be that this newly born Richard has amnesia or has seemingly learned nothing from his experiences, but regardless, he cannot stay dead, of course, if a rational universe is to be finally presented. It is one of the many peculiar shortcuts of the film, not unusual for Monogram and other Poverty Row studios' low-budget productions, even later when noir would come into its own. In fact, as Wheeler Winston Dixon also argues, this presentation is particularly fitting:

> What better way . . . to present a cheap and rotten urban universe than in an equally cheap and rotten film? *Bowery at Midnight* seeks no higher moral plane, and refuses to pass judgment on any of its protagonists, reveling in a New York where principle always lingers in the shadow of profit.[11]

And it is this defiance of the assumption of the benefits of the social contract, so ubiquitous in noir, that marks *Bowery* as a compelling precursor.

NOTES

1. "Novel Gang Film Opens," *Los Angeles Times*, November 13, 1942, 17.
2. Philip Hanson, "The Arc of National Confidence and the Birth of Film Noir, 1929–1941," *Journal of American Studies* 42:3 (December 2008), 392.
3. "Bowery at Midnight," *Monthly Film Bulletin*, British Film Institute, January 1, 1943, 50.
4. Michael A. Oliker, "On the Images of Education in Popular Film" *Educational Horizons* 71:2 (Winter 1993), 73.
5. Gary D. Rhodes, *Lugosi: His Life in Films, on Stage, and in the Hearts of Horror Lovers.* (Jefferson, NC: McFarland, 1997), 345.
6. Ibid.
7. Robin Wood, *Hollywood from Vietnam to Reagan. . .and Beyond* (New York: Columbia University Press, 2003), 77.
8. See Dennis Broe, *Film Noir, American Workers, and Postwar Hollywood* (Tallahassee: University Press of Florida, 2009), 10.
9. Jonathan Auerbach, *Dark Borders: Film Noir and American Citizenship* (Durham, NC: Duke University Press, 2011), 6.
10. Wheeler Winston Dixon, "Night World: New York as a Noir Universe," in Murray Pomerance (ed.), *City that Never Sleeps: New York and the Filmic Imagination*, (New Brunswick, NJ: Rutgers University Press, 2007), 247.
11. Dixon, 246.

CHAPTER 6

Voices and Vaults: *Pillow of Death*

Murray Leeder

During World War II, Universal Pictures licensed the name "Inner Sanctum Mystery" for a series of low-budget horror films. These were designed to borrow from the popularity of the eponymous radio show that aired from 1941–1952, which also had print and later television incarnations. The radio show was noted for its tongue-in-cheek format, with a succession of pun-happy hosts.[1] Somewhat more serious in tone were the six low-budget Inner Sanctum films: *Calling Dr. Death* (1943), *Weird Woman* (1944), *Dead Man's Eyes* (1944), *The Frozen Ghost* (1945), *Strange Confession* (1945), and *Pillow of Death* (1945).[2] Only the last was directed by Wallace Fox, whose horror credits in previous years included *The Corpse Vanishes* (1942) and *Bowery at Midnight* (1942) for Monogram.

The Inner Sanctum series mixes supernatural and crime/mystery elements. Dealing with topics like hypnotism (*Calling Dr. Death*, *The Frozen Ghost*), voodoo (*Weird Woman*), experimental surgery (*Dead Man's Eyes*) and spiritualism (*Pillow of Death*), they are largely what Tzvetan Todorov calls "fantastic-uncanny" narratives.[3] In such tales, the audience is obliged to hesitate between supernatural and naturalistic explanations, only for the naturalistic one to ultimately be affirmed narratively (in contrast to "fantastic-marvelous" narratives that resolve with the supernatural confirmed as "real" in the textual world and "pure fantastic" ones that never supply clear answers). Testing the generic lines between film noir, the murder mystery, the paranoid women's film, and horror, the Inner Sanctum style is reflective of the uncertain boundaries between these categories in the early 1940s.[4]

All of the Inner Sanctum series starred Lon Chaney Jr., the world's first second-generation horror star. Chaney vaulted to genre fame with Universal's *The Wolf Man* (1940) after a decade as a bit player. It has been complained, perhaps justly, that the series placed its "most exploitable asset . . . at a disadvantage by putting [Chaney] in roles unsuited to his working class persona";[5] doctors, scientists, and lawyers, much less artists, were hardly the most natural fit with Chaney's acting style. At best, something interesting comes from that disjuncture. Mark Jancovich notes that Chaney's characters are most often "tragic figures, men who were victims of forces beyond their control,"[6] and in the Inner Sanctum films those forces were often explicitly psychological.

The first five Inner Sanctum films maintain a link to the radio program through the host, a talking head in a crystal ball, laid out in the middle of a table in a wood-lined, bourgeois drawing room. The head speaks: "This is the Inner Sanctum, a strange, fantastic world, controlled by a mass of living, pulsating flesh: the mind. It destroys, distorts, creates monsters, commits murder. Yes, even you, without knowing it, can commit murder." However thinly, the conceit of the series rests on an uncanny blurring of mental spaces, the supernatural and the media that is consistent with a distinctly modern tradition dating back at least to the advent of Gothic literature in the late eighteenth century.[7] *Pillow of Death* is the only one of the six films that does not feature this intro, and yet it maybe suits it the best—in addition to involving a séance in a mansion's dining room, the film literally tells a story in which its protagonist commits murder without realizing it. Perhaps the introduction was excluded to avoid redundancy. Also holding over from radio incarnation of the Inner Sanctum is the prominence of voiceover. The first three are slathered with Chaney's voice, providing a regular stream of conscious expression of his characters' inner thoughts.[8] By *Pillow of Death*, there is no voiceover by Chaney's character himself, Wayne Fletcher, but instead he is haunted by the disembodied voice of his murdered wife (Figure 6.1).

Pillow of Death inverts many elements of the first Inner Sanctum film, *Calling Dr. Death*. In both, Chaney plays a professional (a doctor in *Calling Dr. Death*, an attorney in *Pillow of Death*) trapped in a loveless marriage to a demanding woman. In both cases he has a doting, younger female assistant who is in love with him but has demurred because of his marriage.[9] Both Chaney characters fall under suspicion when their wives die suddenly, but the two films resolve in strikingly different ways: in *Calling Dr. Death*, the young love interest turns out to be the killer, while *Pillow of Death* leads to the opposite revelation—Wayne Fletcher is himself the murderer.[10] Motivated by a desire to marry his secretary Donna (Brenda Joyce, also of *Strange Confession*) and claim her family's fortune, Fletcher has committed his crimes in a kind of dissociative state. Goaded to this realization by the spectral presence of his wife, he jumps to his death out of a window.

Despite being the lead, Fletcher is offstage for a solid portion of *Pillow of Death*, which instead focuses on the aristocratic Kinkaid family and their

Figure 6.1 Wayne Fletcher's perspective is drawn by the voice of his dead wife.

spooky old mansion (Figure 6.2). Donna shares the house with her uncle, the cantankerous patriarch Sam Kinkaid (George Cleveland), his sister Belle Kinkaid (Clara Blandick) and their poor, put-upon English relative Amelia (Rosalind Ivan), who acts as a maid. There is a trace of a haunted house film of *The Cat and the Canary* (1927) sort in the seriocomic perambulations through their mansion, which is replete with hidden rooms and secret panels, and in the theme of an "old money" family caught between tradition and modernization.[11]

Pillow of Death also involves dubious spiritualism, a popular theme at the time, although it interestingly holds just short of clearly confirming fakery. The portly spiritualist and "psychic investigator" Julian Julian (J. Edward Bromberg) was a spiritual advisor to the late Mrs. Fletcher. Though the characters and the audience periodically suspect Julian of being the real villain, he, fraud or not, is innocent of the murder. Julian is not the only other suspect, either; there is also Bruce Malone (Bernard Thomas), a next-door neighbor of the Kincaids and childhood friend of Donna, who carries a torch for her and goes to baffling lengths to implicate Wayne in the murder.

Pillow of Death uneasily grafts together three formulas: a serial killer whodunit, a fraudulent spiritualism story, and a drama of inheritance about a haunted house. In many ways it is a clumsy, overstuffed film replete with

Figure 6.2 A POV shot from the perspective of Wayne Fletcher (Lon Chaney, Jr.); he sees a ghost but we do not.

implausible storytelling, and yet it manages a certain fascination thanks to many visual and especially auditory choices made by Wallace Fox and his collaborators. The centerpieces to the film, I argue here, are three related sequences of "ghost following," where one or more character tracks a ghostly sound through film space. Though the film has been decried as "tediously paced and uninspired,"[12] *Pillow of Death*'s haunting sequences produce an almost surreal juxtaposition between their formal innovation and the banality of the film that surrounds them.

WOMEN, SPIRITUALISM AND FRAUD

Produced in the late stages of World War II but released after its end, *Pillow of Death* makes a few nods to the wartime context and particularly the changing roles of women. Belle is vitriolic about Donna working for Wayne and laments that no Kincaid woman before her niece has ever worked. She states, "In my day, no girl who thought anything of herself would think of going to a man's office to work at night," to which Donna answers, "But we aren't living your day . . . We're living in a new world." Tim Snelson describes the prominence of female monsters and murderers in horror films of the war era, including several of the Inner Sanctum series,[13] and shows the special relevance of wartime horror to the subject of women in the workplace; he interprets *Phantom Lady* (1944), for instance, as "attempt[ing] to actualize the temporary social and sexual liberations experienced by wartime women."[14] Though Snelson does not mention *Pillow of Death*, Fox's film does something similar. Its attitude towards women's changing roles is scarcely coherent, however, and it certainly should not be said to be unequivocally positive. Donna is full of wartime fortitude but barely survives her tragically misguided love for Wayne. The old spinster Belle is the strongest voice for bourgeois patriarchal norms and Amelia, though systematically degraded by her relatives, is also basically unsympathetic, eventually trying to gas Wayne and Donna to death out of cult-like devotion to Julian (in one of the film's most baffling moments, she is given no more than a mild rebuke for this attempted murder).

The common understanding of spiritualism as being practiced by women or feminized men goes back to its inception,[15] and in *Pillow of Death*, Wayne dismisses spiritualism in decidedly gendered terms: "those silly séances that women so often attend." Of *Pillow of Death*'s four female characters, all but Donna are devoted followers of Julian, who seems to have no male devotees (though Sam plays along while simultaneously scoffing); Julian also now lives in the Kincaid mansion, supported by Belle's largesse in return for help contacting the oft-mentioned "Kincaid ghosts." Despite *Pillow of Death*'s slight acknowledgments of the war, none of the women are bereaved mothers or wives attempting contact with the war dead; rather, the film constructs mediumship as a parlor game for the idle rich.

Suspicious psychics, spiritualists, and clairvoyants had been stock characters for decades, very often depicted as charismatic men with women in their thrall. Julian claims that the late Vivian Fletcher (Victoria Horne) was not only a follower but also "a natural medium for communication with the spirit world." Julian explains that he and Vivian had a pact that whoever died first would attempt to contact the other. This is likely a reference to the arrangement that Harry Houdini, a debunker of spiritualists who nonetheless entertained a hope that real proof of an afterlife might be found, had with his wife, Bess, who held regular séances after his death, awaiting a code known only to her. In the 1938 film *The Mystic Circle Murder*, Mme. Houdini plays herself, reflecting bittersweetly on the fact that ten years have passed and thus the absence of an afterlife was "proven." Fletcher claims that Vivian was "a changed woman from the day she met [Julian] . . . she lost interest in me, neglected our home and talked of nothing but death and life after death." Though *Pillow of Death* never overtly suggests a romantic or sexual relationship between Julian and Vivian, Wayne clearly regarded him as a rival influence on his wife.[16]

Exposures of fraudulent spiritualism regularly emphasized disastrous relationships between a wealthy woman and a man purporting supernatural knowledge and guidance. The anti-spiritualist writer F. Attfield Fawkes relates several examples, including a San Francisco woman who, "came in contact with a notorious occultist . . . She took his predictions and warnings so seriously that they produced a pitiable effect . . . acute hysteria and neurasthenia were the immediate result, followed by the most grotesque eccentricities." He also describes a British woman who "committed suicide by cutting her throat with a carving knife . . . At the inquest it was conclusively shown that she had been worried out of her mind by what a clairvoyant and spiritualist had told her."[17] In *Pillow of Death*, we are told that before her death Vivian had been obsessively reading about suicide.

Yet *Pillow of Death* both avoids conspicuous "fraudulent spiritualist" tropes and stops short of condemning Julian. Julian does not wear the customary turban, robes, and other Orientalists accoutrements, like Professor Fleece (George B. French) in *Shivering Spooks* (1926), the Great LeGagge (Robert Fiske) in *The Mystic Circle Murder*, the "Swami" (Russ Vincent) in *Heading to Heaven* (1947), Alexis (Turhan Bey) in *The Amazing Mr. X* (1947), and Drake (Robert Bice) in *Bunco Squad* (1950). Rather, he dresses in professional eveningwear, akin to the stock attire of a stage magician (he was once a professional ventriloquist). Julian is caught in no fakery, cooperates with the police, and in the end is credited with helping bring a murderer to justice; notably, the breakdown of the film prepared by the Production Code Administration (PCA) classifies Julian as a "Straight" rather than "Comic" type and as "Sympathetic."

Julian's veracity is kept ambiguous throughout *Pillow of Death*. Before the séance scene, he asks Amelia's permission to enter the dining room alone, "to attune myself to the surroundings," he says. He sits, ceremonially folds his hands and looks up at the ceiling, becoming blank as he enters an apparent trance. The camera tracking in on him and centering him in the frame adds to the ritualistic impression. Yet Julian is being discretely watched by the admiring Amelia and may be performing for her benefit. We are quickly shown that Donna is also observing him through a hidden panel. If we initially suspect that he might want time alone to set up some tricks, that seems not to be the case, though perhaps he is calculating to divert suspicion.

In any event, his control over the women around him, save for Donna, remains absolute. When the unglued Amelia attempts to murder Donna and Wayne, Julian rescues them by using his influence over Amelia to neutralize her threat. He remarks that, "Misguided loyalty is dangerous sometimes," yet does not further reflect on the implications of the power he wields over his followers. It seems significant that Donna is the lone Kincaid woman who does not buy into his power, yet her characterization as a rational and independent war-era woman is complicated by her misplaced loyalty in Wayne.

One might say that her entry into the working world only placed her under the sway of a masculine authority from that sphere (Wayne) instead of one from the domestic one (Julian).

WALKING AND HAUNTING

Pillow of Death has another substantial female *presence*, more monstrous and thus potentially subversive, in Vivian Fletcher herself. Perhaps it is better to call her the "Vivian Fletcher personality"—whether supernatural or psychological in character—that invisibly goads her husband to murder and suicide. Victoria Horne was cast in the role of Mrs. Fletcher but her in-the-flesh appearances were cut,[18] leaving Vivian only as a disembodied voice in the finished film, with the lone exception of a single shot of her purloined corpse. Vivian thus becomes an example of what Michel Chion termed the *acousmêtre*, a character constituted principally (or in this case, exclusively) through sound rather than image. Acousmêtre gain their effectiveness by inverting the usual hierarchies of image and sound, and are often explicitly or implicitly ghostly. They make effective villains because they seem to be beyond confrontation, since they are fundamentally *not there*.[19]

Mary Ann Doane also notes that when "the classical film allow[s] the representation of a voice whose source is not simultaneously represented . . . its potential work as a signifier is revealed. There is always something uncanny about a voice which emanates from a source outside the frame."[20] While Doane notes the temptation to claim sound as a feminine space outside the "phallic" image, she argues that this impulse overlooks the extent to which the voice is also an instrument of the patriarchal order; she goes on to note that "to mark the voice as an isolated haven within patriarchy . . . is to invoke the spectre of feminine specificity, always recuperable as another form of 'otherness.'"[21] *Pillow of Death* seems an ideal example, especially if we read the powerful, acousmêtric female voice of Vivian Fletcher as nothing but a figment of her husband's imagination—a male projection of the female voice, not the genuine article (rather like Mrs. Bates in *Psycho* [1960], one of Chion's exemplary acousmêtric characters).

The trappings of the conventional haunting house where *Pillow of Death* largely unfolds are principally aural. The reviewer for the *New York Herald Tribune* complained that *Pillow of Death* "is more like a radio script than a screen story. More of the so-called action depends on sound effects and mysterious voices than [it] does anything resembling acting or drama."[22] It is most certainly radio-mediated cinema, but of a more reflexive, interrogative kind than the reviewer allows. In the opening moments, Amelia complains of working in "this creepy old house, with its voices laughing and crying in the night, and footsteps, poundings, creaking doors . . ." The Kincaids claim to regularly hear laughing and chains (Sam claims that the place has gotten louder since Julian, Belle, and Amelia have been staging regular séances) and attribute the ghostly presence to either their deceased Uncle Joe or his wife. Julian takes the haunting seriously (or pretends to), asserting that he has yet to make contact with the specter. In an early incident, the no-nonsense police detective McCracken (Wilton Graff) leads them upstairs to investigate . . . only to find that the culprit is a raccoon.

The film suggests from early on that dispassionate investigation by a hard-bitten investigator like McCracken will answer all claims of the supernatural. In his treatise against spiritualism, Fawkes wrote that,

> No haunted house has ever yet produced a noise or a ghostly vision which, on investigation, could not be accounted for by some very ordinary cause, such as cats paddling about at night, rats scratching and scampering behind paneling, wind blowing articles about, air passing through empty water pipes, naughty persons who produce noises or sights for revenge or practical jokes . . .[23]

The priority Fawkes places on auditory phenomena reflects the special relationship of sound and the supernatural throughout Western culture. As Salomé Voegelin writes,

> Sounds are like ghosts. They slink around the visual object, moving in on it from all directions, forming its contours and content in a formless breeze. The spectre of sound unsettles the idea of visual stability and involves us as listeners in the production of an invisible world.[24]

The primacy of sound in *Pillow of Death* allows us to take the maligned "raccoon episode" seriously as an early, lighthearted articulation of the film's themes that also establishes the formal choices Fox uses to present haunting and investigation. As McCracken leads a small party through the halls of the house, they pause in a hallway. "I don't hear anything now," he says, and Sam Kincaid offers that perhaps the ghost of Uncle Joe heard them coming. Soon after, the characters' eyelines are drawn to the left of the frame and a cut soon shows us to what they are reacting: a POV shot shows a creaking door opening wider and then fully closing on its own. Says Sam: "That's my room. Uncle Joe's wife died in there. Maybe that's her spirit on the way to the attic to play with Uncle Joe's."

McCracken leads them through into Sam's bedroom, later the site of the film's climax. He searches the room, gun drawn; a curtain billows before an open window at the back of the frame. Finding the room empty, the characters decide to go to the attic, and hear odd noises as in the hallway. Sam attributes them to Uncle Joe. As the characters climb the stairs to the alley, we hear non-diegetic sound for the first time in the sequence. The score is heavy on tremolo, a stock method for producing suspense and often supernatural affinities. In 1947, in fact, Theodor Adorno and Hanns Eisler noted that the use of "tremolo on the bridge of the violin . . . to produce a feeling of uncanny suspense and to express an unreal atmosphere" had become a cliché.[25] Fox cuts between POV-coded tracking shots following the beam of McCracken's flashlight across the crowded, dark attic and low-key shots of the assembled onlookers. A shot closes on an open window, again foreshadowing the climax, and McCracken jokes, "Maybe your ghost left by that window."

Again, a sound cue draws the characters' attention, this time to the right of the frame. Searching for the source of a rattling noise, we again follow the beam of the flashlight as the music intensifies, before delivering the image of a raccoon sitting in a stuffed chair. The music turns whimsical to match the comedic image. "There's your ghost," declares McCracken; Sam jokes that the raccoon looks like Uncle Joe. It is a miniature version of the Todorovian fantastic-uncanny narrative, leading the characters through the paces of a lighthearted debunking narrative; simultaneously, it is a de-acousmatization sequence with a comical resolution. It plays as a dress rehearsal for the two more serious sequences of "ghost-following" later in the film (a sort of "first as farce, then as tragedy" structure), where we will see many of the same techniques, especially the prominence of POV shots and the ambiguous use of off-screen sound. But where unassigned sounds trigger the raccoon-hunt, opening wild speculations due to their lack of clear origin, it is a much more specific ghostly voice that drives the subsequent sequences: that of Vivian Fletcher.

We first hear Vivian's voice in the séance Julian holds in the Kincaid house's dining room, audible to all present (Figure 6.3). "In twentieth-century spiritualism," writes Steven Connor, "the voice became the most important form of embodiment and manifestation for non-embodied entities; it was at once the most powerful and the most versatile form of witness to the unseen." *Pillow of Death* depicts the séance's most powerful sonic manifestation: the "direct voice," which, unlike channeling, appears to bypass the medium's mouth altogether.[26] Vivian's voice says, "I want to accuse my husband, Wayne, of murdering me." Wayne immediately accuses Julian of faking her voice and staging the séance with the help of Bruce Malone, whom he discovers spying on the séance; the later revelation that Julian is a trained ventriloquist and voice imitator buoys the implication of fraud.[27]

But later that same night, Vivian's voice returns without such an explanation. We see Wayne nervously drinking and smoking alone in an armchair, when her voice intones, "Wayne." The tremolo returns on the soundtrack, and the camera tracks slightly right around him, as if suggesting the vantage of an

Figure 6.3 A séance led by medium Julian Julian (J. Edward Bromberg).

invisible character. Wayne reacts and looks to the right, and the film cuts to a POV shot of his view of the other half of the room. There is no one there, but we hear her voice asking, "Why are you drinking, Wayne? Do you think it will help you forget that you murdered me?" Despite the taunting tone, the voice is level and eerily calm. Vivian bids him follow her; he stands, walks to the right of the frame, ultimately walking out of the house "after" her. Outside he looks about confusedly (Chaney's forte) and scans the space until an offscreen voice says, "Here I am, Wayne," drawing his eyeline out of the frame. A POV shot of the exterior space follows, showing the location but no specter. Where the POV shots in the raccoon episode suggest the kind of objectivity associated with detective films, here they are radically subjective instead, anchoring us in Wayne's troubled mind. Now we hear her say, "This way," as if she is visibly indicating a direction but, as in a radio play, we can only infer as much from sound cues.

Wayne walks out of frame to the left and then there is a dissolve to a shot of him walking entranced, almost zombie-like, left to right, as the camera tracks horizontally with him. Then there is another dissolve to show him approaching the gates of a graveyard. Then we have another POV shot of a set of tombstones while Vivian's voice says, "Come in, Wayne. Don't be frightened." He silently opens the gate and walks, again guided by her voice, to a crypt labeled "FLETCHER." Over a POV shot of the crypt, her voice says, "Why do you stop? Come inside with me." As he approaches, the drone increases in pitch as a more conventional suspense score sets up, along with a faster editing rhythm. Wayne struggles with the locked gate and begins to shout. Now the film reveals another character on the scene, Malone, watching Wayne; soon Wayne seems to come out of his daze as the graveyard's sexton (J. Farrell MacDonald) confronts him. Though Malone's role is only clarified later (he stole Vivian's corpse in a baffling plan to shock a confession out of Wayne), at this point the revelation of his presence works to complicate the interplay of gazes in the scene: Wayne looks at Vivian, seen by him but not by us, while himself being watched by Malone, seen by us but not by him.

Fox's choices in the eerie graveyard sequence, which even *Pillow of Death*'s critics call its highlight,[28] suggest that Wayne is both seeing and hearing Vivian, yet we are not seeing what he sees. For whatever reason, the film withholds the visual component of his experience. In the subsequent scene, Wayne's account of his experience stresses the visual: "I *saw* my wife . . . She said she wanted to *show* me something . . . Then she *disappeared* . . . I tell you I *saw*, spoke to her.'" Yet even though the film uses a familiar shot-reverse-shot editing pattern, we only see empty spaces where Wayne sees Vivian's form. But we *do* hear her voice, situating her presence at the level of soundtrack.[29] Chion describes "the filmic acousmêtre [as] 'offscreen,' outside the image, and at the same time *in* the image."[30] It is such with Vivian.

The final of the three "ghost-following" scenes constitutes the film's climax. We again find Wayne nervous and smoking in an armchair, this time in the Kincaid house. Vivian's voice's intones, "Wayne, I'm waiting," and once again he rises and walks to the right. "This way, Wayne," she says, and the camera tracks after him, but this time she leads him to a staircase and bids him, "Upstairs." The voice leads him once more into the late Sam Kincaid's room, where the door seems to open on its own for the second time.[31] At this point Wayne and the voice engage in a dialogue about how he murdered Sam by sneaking into his room and smothering him with a pillow. When Donna comes in to confront him, he casually confesses, "I was just telling Vivian how I killed her." This exchange follows:

Donna: But Vivian isn't here.
Wayne: Oh, yes she is.
Vivian: Wayne . . .
Wayne: There she is now. Can't you hear her?
Donna: No. I don't hear anything.
Vivian: Donna can't hear me but she knows. At last she realizes that you are a psychopathic killer.

The blandly earnest delivery style that sometimes weakens Chaney's performances is chillingly effective in his final scene, his guileless confessions of murder contrasting with the flatly sinister vocalizations of Vivian. Vivian's voice then goes on to command Wayne to kill Donna to keep her from telling the police. He forces her onto the bed and tries to smother her with the titular pillow, as Vivian commands him, "Hold the pillow very tight, Wayne." But he is quickly interrupted by the police and Bruce. Captive at gunpoint, he implores, "What'll I do, Vivian?" She replies, "I'll take you away with me. Here I am, at the window." He turns and the film cuts to a POV shot of the open window, through which we now know that he climbed to kill Sam Kincaid, and where he is purportedly seeing Vivian. "Hurry, Wayne, there's no time to lose," she says. Wayne lunges out the window. Too slow to stop him, the policeman melodramatically lowers the shade, leaving his corpse, like Vivian's, as a thing unrepresentable.

Joseph Breen of the PCA, while disapproving of the film's pillow smotherings, specifically endorsed Wayne Fletcher's fate. At the time, the Code insists that: "Suicide, as a solution of problems occurring in the development of screen drama, is to be discouraged as morally questionable and as bad theatre—unless absolutely necessary for the development of the plot."[32] However, Breen specified that the final suicide was fine since clearly "his act is that of an insane man." The PCA was, it seems, convinced that the voice of Vivian Fletcher was a hallucination of Wayne Fletcher or, to use Todorovian language, that any fantastic ambiguity has resolved in the mode of the uncanny. No doubt the choice not to visualize Vivian's specter helped encourage that judgment. Yet the audience may not be as certain.

THE END?

Pillow of Death's final scene finds Julian preparing to leave the Kincaid house, loading his effects into a car. He addresses Bruce and Donna, saying, "I had a psychic presentiment that things would turn out like this. I hope you're very happy . . . with the Kincaid ghosts." He then speaks to McCracken, who thanks him for his help in exposing Wayne Fletcher, noting, "That psychic abracadabra of yours is quite a thing." Julian mildly rebukes him, stating that, "the word 'abracadabra' is anathema to the true believer in the occult." He waves his fingers theatrically, the music swells briefly and the image dissolves to a "THE END" card. It is just the kind of unnaturally happy, pat ending to which admirers of classical horror films are very much accustomed, but it bears some examination.

David Bordwell argues that closure, the target to which classical narratives drive, is more properly seen as a "closure effect" or "pseudo-closure";[33] this distinction is relevant to *Pillow of Death*, where the apparent closure and the restoration of order it implies is distinctly anxious and rushed (a mere 40 seconds). The last-minute unification of the heterosexual couple is especially forced, since Bruce is a schemer, stalker, and literal grave-robber who merely happened to be right in his suspicions. What has he done to earn Donna's love, beyond being the last man standing? Julian is leaving, presumably because his financial support network of wealthy women is now devastated by the murders of Vivian and Belle; what's more, the house's new owner, Donna, has no interest in contacting its ghosts. In a period when screen depictions of spiritualists are almost uniformly negative, *Pillow of Death* takes the unusual step of giving Julian the final word, defending his profession/faith against McCracken's skepticism.

But this scene conspicuously—especially in a film so much about women's voices—give no words whatsoever to Donna. Her ascension to the head of the household is simultaneously subjugation, marked by her sudden muteness. Her wordlessness in the final scene leaves her last vocalization as a scream when attacked by Wayne. She is now the inheritor of the "Kincaid ghosts" (presumably now including Sam and Belle) and with them the Kincaid fortune. Belle's initial complaints about Donna working for Wayne Fletcher are now resolved by both Wayne's death and Belle's own, which leave Donna both without an employer and with independent wealth. One might take the message as being that the wartime working woman will eventually stand down and become an angel of the hearth . . . except that here, she owns this hearth, and it is haunted. Pseudo-closure, indeed.

In a sense, the lack of closure or definition extends to the lack of ultimate clarification of whether Vivian's voice was a hallucination or a real ghost. If we return to Todorov's terminology, *Pillow of Death* does seem to be a rare "pure fantastic" narrative, in which neither a naturalistic nor a supernatural explanation is clearly supplied. This ambiguity is broadly consistent with the non-separation between the supernatural and the psychological implied by the Inner Sanctum format, but *Pillow of Death* "feels" more fantastical than the rest of its series. This is particularly because of Fox's use of subjective POV shots and acousmêtric voices, combining to produce a spectral threat, whether from beyond the grave or from an insane mind, which threatens to upend the hierarchy of image and sound upon which narrative film depends.

NOTES

1. For an overview of the Inner Sanctum series, see Charlie Ellbé, "Making Visible the Sonic Theatre: *The Inner Sanctum Mysteries* Radio Series and Its Universal Studios Film Adaptations," in Mario DeGiglio-Bellemare, Charlie Ellbé, and Kristopher Woofter (eds), *Recovering 1940s Horror Cinema: Traces of a Lost Decade* (Lanham, MD: Lexington Books, 2015), 129–46.

2. The name would be licensed once again for a film called simply *Inner Sanctum* (1948), a detective story directed by Lew Landers.
3. Tzvetan Todorov, *The Fantastic: A Structural Approach to a Literary Genre* (Ithaca, NY: Cornell University Press, 1975).
4. Mark Jancovich, "Thrills and Chills: Horror, the Woman's Film and the Origins of Film Noir," *The New Review of Film and Television* 7:2 (2009), 157–71.
5. Tom Weaver, Michael Brunas, and John Brunas, *Universal Horrors: The Studio's Classic Films, 1931–1946* (Jefferson, NC: McFarland, 2007), 512.
6. Mark Jancovich, "'The Theme of Psychological Destruction': Horror Stars, the Crisis of Identity and 1940s Horror," *Horror Studies* 6:2 (2015), 166.
7. For one important study of the supernaturalization of thought in modern culture, see Terry Castle's *The Female Thermometer: 18-Century Culture and the Invention of the Uncanny* (New York: Oxford University Press, 1995).
8. Some have claimed that these voiceovers were motivated by Chaney's limited faculty for technical language (Weaver, Brunas, and Brunas, 382).
9. The PCA requested several script changes to lessen the implication that Wayne and Donna are involved romantically as the film begins. This and several later notes come from the author's examination of files contained the Margaret Herrick Library in Beverly Hills, California.
10. *Pillow of Death* somewhat anticipates the "amnesiac killer" narrative that came in vogue with *Fight Club* (1999) and *Memento* (2000).
11. The relationship of ghosts, money, and inheritance has been treated extensively in scholarship on the Gothic (for example, see Andrew Smith's *The Ghost Story 1840–1920: A Cultural History*, Manchester: Manchester University Press, 2010).
12. Weaver, Brunas, and Brunas, 512.
13. Tim Snelson, *Phantom Ladies: Hollywood Horror and the Home Front* (New Brunswick, NJ: Rutgers University Press, 2015), 75–8.
14. Ibid., 111.
15. Key examples of the extensive scholarship into women's role in spiritualism include Alex Owen's *The Darkened Room: Women, Power, and Spiritualism in Late Victorian England* (London: Virago Press, 1989); Ann Braude's *Radical Spirits: Spiritualism and Women Writers in Nineteenth-Century America* (Bloomington: Indiana University Press, 2001); and Amy Lehman's *Victorian Women and the Theatre of Trance: Mediums, Spiritualists and Mesmerists in Performance* (Jefferson, NC: McFarland, 2009).
16. It seems possible to read Julian as gay, as many male mediums were reputed to be (Jenny Hazelgrove, *Spiritualism and British Society between the Wars*, Manchester: Manchester University Press, 2000, 5–6).
17. F. Attfield Fawkes, *Spiritualism Exposed* (Bristol: J. W. Arrowsmith Ltd., 1920), 137–8.
18. Weaver, Brunas, and Brunas, 512. She did apparently film at least one full day as the living Mrs. Fletcher.
19. Michel Chion, *The Voice in Cinema* (New York: Columbia University Press, 1999), 24–5.
20. Mary Ann Doane, "The Voice in the Cinema: The Articulation of Body and Space," *Yale French Studies* 60 (1980), 40.
21. Ibid., 49.
22. "'Pillow of Death,'" *New York Herald Tribune*, January 26, 1946, 8.
23. Fawkes, 56.
24. Salomé Voegelin, *Sonic Possible Worlds: Hearing the Continuum of Sound* (New York: Bloomsbury, 2014), 12. Other sources on the uncanny properties of sound include Robert Spadoni's *Uncanny Bodies: The Coming of the Sound Film and the Origins of the Horror*

Genre (Berkeley: University of California Press, 2007), and Isabella Van Elferen's *Gothic Music: The Sounds of the Uncanny* (Cardiff: University of Wales Press, 2012).

25. Theodor Adorno and Hanns Eisler, *Composing for the Films* (New York: Oxford University Press, 2005), 17.
26. Steven Connor, "The Machine in the Ghost: Spiritualism, Technology and the 'Direct Voice,'" in Peter Buse and Andrew Stott (eds), *Ghosts: Deconstruction, Psychoanalysis, History* (Houndmills, Basingstoke: Palgrave Macmillan,1999), 222.
27. There is another, briefer séance scene later in the film, where Donna spies on Julian, Belle, and Amelia. Perhaps to test their gullibility, she poses as her ancestor Deborah Kincaid, saying to "Tell [Belle] never to stop believing in the spirit world. Never." Julian intones, "I shall tell her." Fox briefly treats Donna as an acousmêtre like Vivian, since she only does her impersonation when out of frame.
28. Weaver, Brunas, and Brunas, 512.
29. *Ghost* (1990), an example of a supernatural film squarely located in Todorov's marvelous mode, does the opposite, visualizing Sam Wheat (Patrick Swayze) for us even though the medium Oda Mae Brown (Whoopi Goldberg) can only hear him.
30. Chion, 23.
31. This might seem one of the more unequivocally supernatural events in the film, except that the perpetually open window inside the room leaves open the possibility of a breeze.
32. Thomas Doherty, *Hollywood's Censor: Joseph I. Breen and the Production Code Administration* (New York: Columbia University Press, 2007), 355.
33. David Bordwell, *Narration in the Fiction Film* (London: Routledge, 1985), 159.

CHAPTER 7

Wallace Fox and America's "Career Girls"

David J. Hogan

Between 1930 and 1940, 11 to 13 million American women aged sixteen and older were pushed into the workforce by the Great Depression. Figures in the 1940 U.S. census show that 13 million, the high end of the estimate, amounted to 27 percent of all women in the country.[1] After the U.S. entered World War II in December 1941, millions more women went to work. By the time the war neared its finish during 1944–1945, 35 to 36 percent of all American women—19.2 million people—were employed in the civilian sector. Another 350,000 women served in the U.S. armed forces, at home and abroad.[2] The greater proportion of these civilian and military jobs were in manufacturing, service, or support rather than in positions oriented to careers. And yet as these currents of short-term or dead-end new employment manifested themselves, Hollywood, devoted to a fantasist's notion of glamour and escape from the everyday, celebrated the plucky "career girl"—the unmarried young woman who aspires to not just a paycheck but fulfillment. If she served food or labored in a steno pool, the work was an interlude and not a destination. For the liveliest of Hollywood's fictional career girls, the goal was stardom—a rarefied status assumed by Hollywood to affirm the woman's value via the reductive quality of fame, and useful also as a signpost to romantic love.

During the 1930–1940 period mentioned above, thirteen features and ten shorts[3] directed by B-movie workhorse Wallace Fox saw release across America. Engaged during that time mainly by Poverty Row stalwarts PRC and Monogram, Fox was in a professional rhythm that placed him at the center of Hollywood's B-movie segment.

ASSEMBLING A PRODUCT

Formed as Producers Distributing Company by Ben Judell (a film-exchange manager) in 1939, and built on the physical plant of the failed Grand National Pictures,[4] PRC endured a wobbly first year before dumping Judell, handing production responsibilities to Sigmund Neufeld, and changing its name to Producers Releasing Corporation. Mid-war, as women's employment rolls swelled, the tiny studio assigned Wallace Fox three light film projects designed to perpetuate the "career girl" convention. *The Girl from Monterrey* (1943) concerns a vivacious Mexican warbler who develops her nightclub career while her brother and boyfriend pursue careers as boxers. The central figure of *Career Girl* (1944) is a struggling young vocalist torn between her desire to sing and her fiancé's wish that she stop all the nonsense, come home, and marry him. And in *Men on Her Mind* (1944), a successful but troubled singer weighs her career against the charms and failings of various men who want to marry her.

The Girl from Monterrey is just 58 minutes long, and *Career Girl* and *Men on Her Mind* run a few minutes more than an hour each. Not simply low-budget, all three pictures have the brisk running times of programs intended for the bottom of double bills at larger theaters, usually in support of more prestigious films from other, bigger studios. Alternatively, urban grindhouses or small neighborhood theaters ("nabes") might combine two or even three such films on single bills intended for quick playoff in two- or three-day frames. Drive-in theaters (which dated to 1933) often ran similar programs. Whatever the particulars of exhibition, movies such as these existed mainly to fill time, and to keep audiences strolling back and forth to the concession stand until the scheduled main feature. Poverty Row films were *devices* every bit as much as they were entertainment.

All Poverty Row studio-era films were conceived as "product." But even MGM and the other majors thought similarly, cranking out films like sausages in order to justify the overhead required to keep the plant running. However, the majors understood the importance of craft, and manipulated budgets and shooting schedules to encourage it. Big money bought top-flight producers, screenwriters, directors, and cinematographers; art directors, makeup artists, musical directors, and choreographers; costumers, stunt coordinators, carpenters, painters—the full range of salaried professionals who were encouraged to work with care, and assemble sleek and glossy entertainments. Unable to match the financial or human resources of the majors, PRC fashioned its product on short money, employing on- and off-screen personnel that could only yearn for the luxuries provided by MGM, Twentieth Century-Fox, Warner, and the other dominant players. (Even the relatively modest advantages of the slickest Poverty Row studio, Republic, were beyond PRC's reach.)

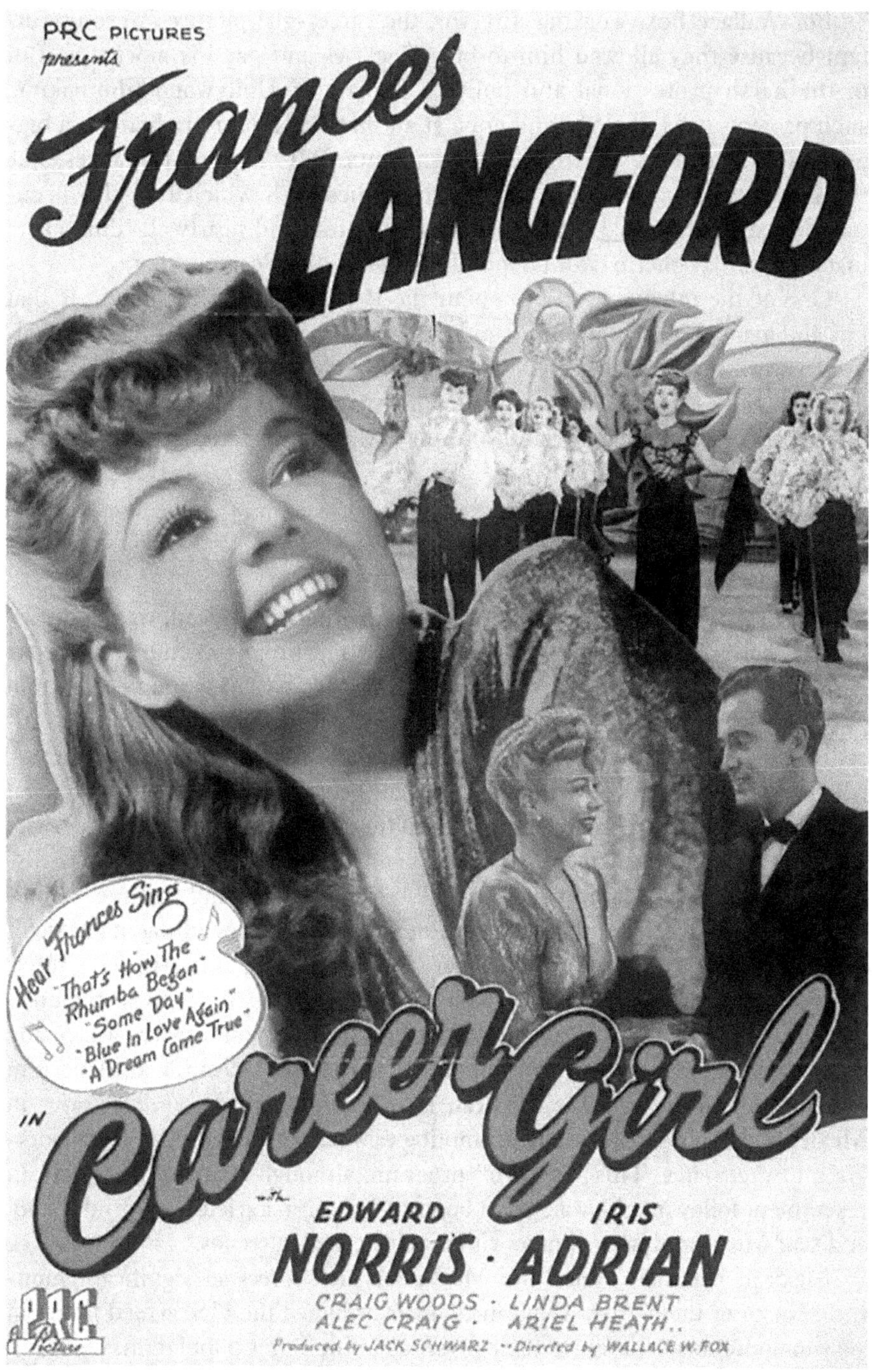

Figure 7.1 The one-sheet poster for *Career Girl* (1944).

For Wallace Fox, working director, the career-girl pictures were important because they allowed him to buy groceries and pay his mortgage. But in the harsh professional and political climate of Hollywood filmmaking, such projects offered almost no hope at all that Fox might graduate to a bigger studio and more prestigious assignments. PRC musical romances, like the B-westerns, serials, and two-reel comedies with which Fox also occupied himself, amounted to a professional ghetto—and nearly all filmmakers installed in that ghetto could depend on ending their careers there.[5]

One of the intriguing things about the B-movie sinkhole, though, is that Fox and many directors like him—although seldom inspired—did professional-caliber work. At moments, limitations of time and budget forced Fox to be perfunctory. But as we'll see in this chapter, he was not a lazy filmmaker. Stifled by limited resources, perhaps even as a result of them, he created value.

THE GIRL FROM MONTERREY (1943)

The Girl from Monterrey,[6] which is about many things Mexican, was shot during mid-summer 1943, for an October release.[7] The project's summertime start date came very close to the first anniversary of Mexico's May 1942 declaration of war on Germany and the other Axis powers. Although that declaration officially allied Mexico with the United States and the world's other free powers, Mexico's earlier relations with the U.S. had been fractious. America's illegal 1845 annexation of Texas, for instance, and the subsequent Mexican–American War of 1846–1848, stung Mexican leaders and everyday citizens, who were disinclined, generations later, to reward the U.S. with a trusting attitude. Immediately prior to World War II, Washington's considerable meddling in Mexico's industrial affairs, and grabs of her natural resources, caused Mexico's intelligentsia and many of her politicians to gaze northward with deep suspicion.

Despite lingering Mexican antipathy, the nation was on board as a U.S. ally in the fight against fascism and military adventurism. Encouraged, American industry seized on available Mexican labor, building plants and factories in Mexico and in border areas, and promoting easy passage of Mexican farm workers into the States. This "bracero" program, although a source of American resentment following the war, was a boon to American agricultural production, and sent Mexican workers home with much-needed currency.

Mexican nationals joined the Mexican armed forces in significant numbers. North of the border, Mexican-Americans joined the U.S. armed forces in very high numbers relative to their presence in the larger population; Dennis J. Bixler-Márquez of the University of Texas at El Paso has estimated that out of a wartime U.S. population of about 2.7 million Mexican-Americans, between

Figure 7.2 The one-sheet poster for *The Girl from Monterrey* (1943).

375,000 and 500,000 became G.I.s.[8] This clear display of patriotism, as well as economic cooperation between the two nations, helped bring a modest "hands across the Americas" glow to the U.S. and Mexico alike. It was in this cultural-political context that PRC and Wallace Fox put together *The Girl from Monterrey*, and looked for star power in a Mexican-born singer named Armida.[9]

PUNCHING AND SINGING

In this boxing-melodrama songfest—or light songfest with plenty of boxing—the kindness and sparkle of Mexican-born New York nightclub singer Lita Vance (Armida) is in inverse proportion to her 4′11″ stature: she pays the law school tuition of her "baby brother," Alberto; sings patriotic tunes with enormous gusto; and gets up early to prod pugilist-boyfriend Jerry O'Leary through his roadwork and other fight prep. True to Hollywood's conception of Mexicans, Lita has a big voice, a big laugh, and a big presence bursting with assertiveness and self-confidence. When, for instance, a smooth would-be suitor refuses to take the hint and stop pursuing her, she tells him off in the middle of the nightclub, and then smashes a wine glass onto the floor, for emphasis. She's a real *petardo*.

Contrary to early mid-century American films' usual depiction of Irish-Americans, Lita's boyfriend O'Leary (Terry Frost) is thoughtful, articulate, and gentle. A skilled boxer, he lacks knockout power but exhausts opponents with his sterling defense and relentless jabs. Because Lita approves of O'Leary, she assumes that everyone in the fight game is honest and clean.

So consumed with fondness is Lita for her brother, "Baby" Alberto (Italian-American actor Anthony Caruso),[10] that she barely blinks when he returns home from college to drop this bombshell: "I'm quittin' law school so I can box!" Because *The Girl from Monterrey* is a frothy confection with a weak grasp of boxing and an even more tenuous understanding of the Mexican-American struggle for respect, Lita expresses brief concern that Alberto will end up with "a push-up face," but quickly grows excited about his eagerness to abandon the law to get his brains scrambled. Never mind that he has traveled from New Haven (that is, Yale Law) to announce the decision that tosses away his place in an old-money Anglo-establishment school that, we may surmise, had not been thrilled to enroll him in the first place.

A succession of newspaper headlines and snippets of fights suggest Jerry O'Leary's journey as he bobs and weaves his way to the championship. In a twist that's not much of a surprise at all, hard-hitting Alberto is tapped to be O'Leary's first challenger. After some hand-wringing, Lita comes around to the prospect of her fiancé and her brother going toe to toe in the squared circle. Rather than be concerned about physical hazards or boxing's institutionalized corruption, Lita struggles mainly with the thought of O'Leary and Alberto not liking each other. When the two men in her life vow that the fight will not affect their friendship, Lita relaxes.

The latter portion of the story is driven by a cliché of fight melodramas—manipulated bettors and a duped boxer—as Alberto's manager, Al Johnson (Jack La Rue), loudly hails his boy while betting heavily on O'Leary; he's depending on a singer named Flossie (Veda Ann Borg) to romance Alberto and then deliver him to the arena in such shape that he has no chance of victory.

After growing suspicious, Lita confronts the much taller Flossie and knocks her to the floor. Flat on her back beneath Lita and straddled like a saddle, Flossie confesses that she stands to make a thousand dollars from bets placed for her by Al.

Flossie shortly explains the scheme to Alberto, who inexplicably expresses his love for her. When Alberto defeats O'Leary in the ring, Flossie is delighted, Al is angry, and Lita is left alone in the empty gallery, unsure of how to react. Her singing career now seems quite forgotten.

Following a confusing fade-in to a moment some months after the fight (nothing in the transition suggests the passing of time), Lita is surprised at her club by the contrite Flossie, and by Jerry and Alberto, still pals, and kitted out in the uniforms of the U.S. Army and the Mexican Army, respectively. Reenergized by the return of her emotional equilibrium, Lita dashes to the bandstand and belts a patriotic tune called "Jive, Brother, Jive."[11]

TIME IS MONEY

Wallace Fox functioned prolifically in the hurry-up-and-shoot milieu of Poverty Row. In the three years prior to *The Girl from Monterrey*, he directed a half-dozen *East Side Kids* comedies at Monogram, a couple of Bill Elliott–Tex Ritter westerns at Columbia, and a pair of deliriously entertaining Bela Lugosi horror thrillers for Monogram (including the resolutely wonky *Bowery at Midnight*, 1942). Fox had even directed a three-quarter-hour industrial film, *Blame it on Love* (1940), produced by General Electric's Hotpoint division, to showcase a new line of electric ranges. During the full span of his career, 1927–1954, Fox amassed ninety-one directorial credits.[12]

For all of its plot machinations and ostensible action, *The Girl from Monterrey* is not visually stimulating. Wallace Fox knew that close-ups and especially trucking shots are difficult to set up and light, and they take time—focus must be pulled properly, blocking must ensure that the player remains in the key light, and care must be taken so that complex movement will match other angles of the same scene. Rehearsal takes time, too, and although rehearsal is useful in ensuring that a setup can be shot in just one or two takes, time at PRC was at a premium. Fox likely rehearsed his static masters and two-shots so the actors could practice their dialogue, but, generally speaking, budget precluded anything but the barest movement. If Wallace Fox had ever held hopes of breaking through to a major studio in a meaningful way, he had surely abandoned that hope by 1943. He had been a director since 1927, and had picked up numerous jobs at PRC, and even secured a dependable berth at Monogram. He would continue to labor at that busy but déclassé studio into 1951, after which he devoted himself exclusively to television, an upstart medium that gave jobs to many under-employed filmmakers who could shoot fast and cheaply.

KEEP YOUR RIGHT UP!

Today, with professional boxing in disarray and pushed into remission by the more kinetic mixed martial arts offered by the Ultimate Fighting Championship, it is not easy to recall that, beginning in the 1920s and continuing for some fifty years, boxing was one of America's most popular sports. Public interest during the pre-war years wasn't just national but a reflection of forces that germinated and flourished at many lower levels—regional, state, municipal, and even neighborhood-by-neighborhood. Everybody had a "favorite son," and boxing became a lingua franca capable of uniting strangers. As *The Girl from Monterrey* suggests, Irish and Hispanics were particularly well represented. In those years when the dominant informational media were newspapers, magazines, radio, and newsreels, boxing was an Everyman diversion. The sport's only challenger was baseball.

Hollywood studios eagerly brought boxing into scripts, not merely because of the sport's enormous popularity, but because boxing matches were visually lively, easy-to-grasp interludes that emphasized plot points about ambition, courage, and redemption. Boxing action provided screenwriters with a kind of shorthand in which a story's morass of emotions and motivations could be conveyed via flurries of punches, and by the climactic display of one man standing, the other prone.

Unfortunately, Wallace Fox seems to have had little understanding of boxing technique. He certainly had no significant time to stage bouts believably, and if PRC had an available boxing consultant, then that person was elsewhere when the matches of *The Girl from Monterrey* were choreographed. Anthony Caruso, Terry Frost, and others cast as fighters dance about the ring almost perfectly upright, heads bobbing high atop stretched necks rather than safely tucked into the shoulders, and with chins thrust into the air, as accessible and vulnerable as marshmallows on a stick, begging to be tagged. The fighters hold their elbows away from their sides (as if to prod bothersome commuters on the subway), instead of protectively pulled in, and when someone lets loose with a right or left cross, the move is invariably executed in the potentially disastrous and undisciplined "windmill" style that throws the aggressor awkwardly off balance and leaves his head and torso unprotected. Despite the enthusiasm of a ring announcer (possibly, the real thing) who calls some of Alberto's bouts and makes favorable comparisons to Georges Carpentier and other polished, real-life boxers, the movie's fight sequences are to boxing what a child's pedal car of 1943 is to a Cadillac Sixteen.

The film's lack of boxing credibility is amusingly obvious during one of Jerry O'Leary's sparring matches with a pug played (without credit) by Noble "Kid" Chissell, who boxed professionally, as a lightweight, during 1924–1931. Although dialogue establishes that Jerry "wins" the spar, actor Terry Frost clumsily lunges at Chissell again and again, opening himself up for counter-blows (that never arrive) and looking perfectly awful. Chissell, in contrast, maintains a compact stance and whips ruler-straight jabs that suggest a "real boxer"; Frost's O'Leary looks like an outclassed amateur.

Still (and so that wartime audiences might enjoy sequences suggestive of "high living"), O'Leary and Alfredo are never left spent, bloodied, or even bruised; to the contrary, when both fighters win bouts on the same night, an unblemished O'Leary quickly locates a tuxedo and takes Lita dancing in a swanky nightclub. The romance between these two seems to be in bud, but—once again—the twin PRC bugaboos of time and budget militated against intimate close-ups on the two as they share their first post-fight dance. The moment is photographed as a medium two-shot—sufficient so that we are able to see the two smile at each other, but too far removed to generate real sparks.

RIOTS IN THE STREETS

After *The Girl from Monterrey*'s various schemes and misunderstandings have been ironed out, Mexican-American Lita pronounces herself ready to marry the Irish-American Jerry O'Leary. If that doesn't seem radical, it's only because we have forgotten the disposition of American culture in 1943. *Abie's Irish Rose*, a Broadway hit of 1922–1927, brought sympathetic attention to American urban culture's slow acceptance of "intermarriage" (in that instance, marriage of a young Jewish man to an Irish-American woman); nevertheless, even two decades later the notion of an Irishman marrying a Mexican woman provoked frowns from a society that cast Mexicans as amoral, promiscuous, shiftless, or criminal. The U.S.–Mexican tensions mentioned earlier helped provoke the familiar (and fallacious) "They're stealing our jobs" complaints. Then, too, there was a sexual element, by which young Hispanic men were viewed by some Anglos as threats to the presumed purity of Anglo women.

In Los Angeles during June 3–13, 1943, just four months before the release of *The Girl from Monterrey*, scuffles later dubbed the Zoot Suit Riots were touched off by Anglo soldiers and sailors who objected to the unique Chicano (Mexican-American) culture, particularly the fondness of some young Chicanos for suits distinguished by high-waisted trousers with cinched ankles; and heroically shoulder-padded suit coats with cinched waists and fabric that reached the wearer's fingertips. Wide-brimmed hats and long gold watch chains were popular accessories. What was, to the zoot suiters, a badge of pride and cultural cohesiveness ("We exist, we are here") was interpreted by some Anglo servicemen as an aggressive insult that mocked U.S. military uniforms and military commitment, and, somehow, encapsulated all of the imagined crimes perpetrated by Hispanics against Anglos.

The physical effects of the Zoot Suit Riots are less dramatic than myth suggests. Nobody died. Anglo and Hispanic men were injured, but none seriously. Riots historian Mauricio Mazón points out that even property damage was limited, and carried out mainly by servicemen who carefully targeted cars, businesses, and other property owned by Mexican-Americans.[13] Chief among this property were the zoot suits themselves, which were torn from the bodies of scores, perhaps hundreds, of Mexican-American youths and then slashed or burned.

Establishment Los Angeles (including the *Los Angeles Times*), already fielding a violent and corrupt police force, and eager to protect the interests of old-money Angelinos and the new money of war production and the film industry, gave loud approval to the lawless servicemen, claiming that a cleansing sort of justice had been achieved.[14]

Mazón interprets the zoot suits as visible symbols of male Hispanic culture, and Anglo aggression against them as a metaphoric castration intended to demean and make powerless young Mexican-American men. Because many establishment newspapers outside Los Angeles agreed with the *Los Angeles Times*, the victims' embarrassment (and fabricated culpability) spread from coast to coast.

Given that PRC, like the other denizens of Hollywood's Poverty Row, operated on astonishingly slim margins, it is intriguing to consider that the studio went ahead with production of *The Girl from Monterrey* in spite of (or perhaps because of) the well-publicized riots. In the contemporaneous business model of low-budget indie filmmaking, profit or loss of discrete movies was measured in mere thousands of dollars.[15] And yet PRC made use of the July 30, 1943 edition of *The Hollywood Reporter* (published six weeks after the end of the Zoot Suit imbroglios) to announce *The Girl from Monterrey* as one component of the tiny studio's upcoming slate. Instead of trite, darkly menacing stereotypes that would have been embraced by some Anglo audiences in America's West and Southwest, *The Girl from Monterrey* traffics in another kind of stereotype:

unthreatening, lighthearted Mexican-Americans, personified by Armida and Anthony Caruso.

CUTTING IN THE CAMERA

The culture-clash element of *The Girl from Monterrey* is both diminished and heightened by the presence of Armida's Lita. On the one hand, her bright spirit, talent, and kindness mark her as a desirable addition to America. But during a significant interlude inside a promoter's office—and one that defies Wallace Fox's generally static visual approach—Lita is introduced to the boxing commissioner (Bryant Washburn), a tall and distinguished-looking middle-aged fellow who personifies Anglo privilege and establishment power. Pleasantries fall by the wayside when the commissioner flatly tells Lita that a bout between Alberto and Jerry *will* take place. Lita loudly objects. Fox designed this critical moment with power and visual flair, as the camera follows Lita (initially seen screen right in a two-shot that favors her over Washburn) as she strides to screen left, the camera trucking leftward with her, allowing the back of Washburn's head to pass across the frame. As Lita continues to stride away, the camera keeps focus on her as she leaves close-up territory and moves into a medium shot, the camera trucking across two more men in the shot as Lita walks, maintaining a dense and dynamic composition and giving us ample elements to look at—even as Lita remains the focus of our attention.

Lita reaches a window and stops, and then turns back toward the camera, to look screen right and continue her verbal objections. Although Fox and his director of photography, Marcel Le Picard (like Fox, a Monogram mainstay), had the small technical problem of ensuring that Armida remained in focus as she moved from close-up to medium shot, the beauty of the sequence is that Fox effectively cut in the camera, carrying on with Armida's dialogue and physically moving her from here to there without need for an edit. At this economy-minded level of filmmaking, time spent in post-production is as precious as time spent on set. By shooting reasonably complex action in a single cut, Fox ensured that the picture's editor (Robert O. Crandall) had one less sequence to analyze and physically cut and paste. And into the bargain, Fox ensured that the moment would end up on screen *his* way—a real triumph in the indie-studio arena, where virtually no directors had the luxury of final cut.

THE LIFE OF THE ACTOR

When *The Girl from Monterrey* was released, Armida Vendrell was a thirty-two-year-old, Mexican-born veteran of vaudeville. She was young, certainly, but not youthful by the standards of the film industry. Blessed with a big smile and dark, appealingly wide-set eyes, Armida had been in Hollywood since 1929, occupying herself for nearly fifteen years with musical shorts (*See, See Senorita*, 1935, is one); with leads and second leads in Poverty Row features produced by Tiffany, Republic, and Mascot; and with leads and supporting parts in second features from the B-units at RKO, Fox Film, and Warner Bros.[16] By 1943 Armida was well known around town, and pegged—still—as a specialty act with no potential for bigger things. Although talented and vivacious, she followed a career path that grew narrower with time; subsequent to *The Girl from Monterrey*, between 1944 and her retirement in 1951, Armida appeared in just seven features and one serial (Republic's *Congo Bill*, 1948).[17] A mere eight Hollywood jobs over a seven-year span would have been insufficient to pay for a daily sandwich, let alone rent, groceries, a car, and the other accoutrements of modern life.

Despite Fox's experience as a director of broad comedy (see *Bowery Blitzkrieg* and his other *East Side Kids* movies), the director made only modest use of the comic gifts of second-billed Edgar Kennedy, cast as Doc Hogan, a fight promoter. Hogan is a large and appealing presence in *The Girl from Monterrey*, running a stable of boxers with unusual honesty, and babying the prized geraniums that festoon his office. Early in his career, Kennedy was one of Mack Sennett's silent-era Keystone Kops, and he later excelled as pompous types and frustrated, "slow burn" cops and irascible neighbors at Roach and elsewhere. But the familiar Kennedy bits of business, which were happily anticipated by audiences that saw *The Girl from Monterrey*, are in short supply; the film revolves, after all, around Armida, a personality with enough charisma so that expansive contributions from the likes of Kennedy were unnecessary.

CLICHÉS AND HAPPINESS

Because of the animated performances of Armida, Veda Ann Borg (just four years after a grinding car crash that nearly finished her career), and Anthony Caruso (touching later as the doomed safecracker in John Huston's *The Asphalt Jungle*), *The Girl from Monterrey* is a better-than-average PRC release. It probably did not disappoint audiences but it could not have surprised them, either. The boxing-tale clichés had been well imprinted on the American mind by 1943, and characters that burst into patriotic song were becoming ho-hum (partly because the tide of war had unmistakably turned to favor the Allies when the picture was released).

Although career girl Lita's path to a career is defined by men, she at least loves those men freely and joyously. With lover and brother soon to go to war, Lita will pursue singing with more concentration and fewer day-to-day distractions. She'll make her own way, and will be her own woman once again. After the war, when she becomes Lita O'Leary, that will change—but that's another story for another day.

CAREER GIRL (1944)

Although appealing, Armida never made a strong impression on the movie-going public. Her greatest successes came as a singer in live venues. Even PRC would not bend over backward to showcase her. But singer Frances Langford, star of Wallace Fox and PRC's follow-up "working girl" fancy, *Career Girl* (1944), came from a higher stratum of show business. A radio veteran since 1931 (when she was just eighteen years old), Langford gained a following not just for her continuing work over the airwaves, but for a high-profile slot as the featured vocalist with the Glenn Miller big band. Langford was a force in the recording industry as well, established since 1936 as a Decca and Brunswick (American Record Corporation) recording artist, and scoring hits with "Harbor Lights" and "So Many Memories" (both 1937).[18] Even more popularly, she brought her talents to wartime USO shows (frequently partnered with Bob Hope) that delighted American G.I.s, who raved about Langford in letters they sent home. By the time of *Career Girl*, then, Langford was on her way to becoming a show-business institution. Little wonder that PRC billed her as "Miss Frances Langford."

Regarded as a singer who incidentally acted, Langford nevertheless had the natural equipment to command the screen. Slender, blonde, and about five feet tall, she had a gamine face suited for the movies. Her singer's contralto was reflected in a smoothly expressive speaking voice. (Very soon after *Career Girl*, and continuing well into the 1960s, Langford displayed her skill as a tart comic actress in the much-loved "Bickersons" radio, record, and TV domestic-comedy sketches that co-starred Don Ameche.) She began her film career in 1935, with featured parts in musicals produced by Paramount and MGM.[19] Given Langford's talent and pedigree, she deserved as sleek a product as PRC could muster, and the studio took care to showcase her appropriately.[20]

Practical limitations, though, were ever present at PRC. In the course of a 1970 magazine interview, PRC mainstay director Edgar G. Ulmer explained to Peter Bogdanovich that the company's pictures—typically about sixty minutes long—had six-day shooting schedules, which amounts to an astonishing ten minutes of usable footage secured in the can every day. Per feature, PRC directors were expected to expose only about 15,000 feet of raw film, which works out to a meager 2:1 ratio of exposed film to the approximate running times of the finished product.[21] *Career Girl* runs to the PRC standard: sixty-seven minutes. Not just better scripted than *The Girl from Monterrey*, *Career Girl* also is noticeably better as a piece of craft. Some PRC pictures

Figure 7.3 Lobby card for *Career Girl* (1944).

look dreadfully threadbare, but *Career Girl* is nearly as handsome as what came from the B-units of Columbia and Universal.

A HOUSEFUL OF AMBITION

In *Career Girl*, talented young singer Joan Terry (Langford) has reached a crisis point in her search for Broadway stardom: with her money running low, she leaves a handsome mid-level hotel and takes a room at a lively boardinghouse—a "girls' hotel," as dialogue expresses it—that caters to hopeful ingénues. As at New York's real-life Barbizon Hotel for Women and the west coast's Hollywood Studio Club, the energy in Joan's new residence is generated by a variety of show-business dreamers. Thelma (Linda Brent) is a mean and conniving schemer; Louise (Marion [Marcy] McGuire) holds a day job as a legal secretary. Painfully naive Sue (Ariel Heath) seems headed for emotional disaster, and may be a chronic depressive. A key resident is Glenda (Iris Adrian), a clever and comically shrewd blonde who lightens the mood with retorts and jibes that amuse the other hopefuls and help steer them in the right direction. These and nearly a dozen other starry-eyed residents alternately confound and amuse the elderly landlord (Alec Craig).

After mis-delivered flowers bring Joan into the orbit of a likeable Broadway playboy, Steve Dexter (Edward Norris), a few breaks begin to come her way. Except for the ill-tempered Thelma, who actually steals a role right from under Joan's nose, the other women support Joan's ambitions and believe in her chances. In an unlikely turn, they incorporate themselves on Joan's behalf as Talent, Inc., offering a weekly stipend so that Joan can have photos made and continue to make the rounds of theatrical agencies. When Joan lands the lead in a promising new musical, wealthy James Blake (Craig Woods), the stuffy boy she left back home in Kansas City, comes to New York—not to offer encouragement but because he thinks Joan's ambitions are absurd. Convinced that he can make her return home and marry him, James *buys* the show and plans to close it before opening night. Backed by Steve and her girlfriends, Joan appeals to James's better nature. Finally grasping the importance Joan puts on her career, James relents. The show is saved and Joan will, presumably, allow James to leave her life so that she can be with Steve.

The central set, the boardinghouse's common area, is reasonably large, and within the space, Fox and cinematographer Gus Peterson (a two-reel and B-western specialist) found room enough to avoid unsightly clots of bodies. Thoughtful blocking of players helps. When legal secretary Louise dictates the Talent, Inc. contract, Fox directed actress Marcy McGuire to slowly move back and forth across the group of women seated behind and around her—bringing movement to what could have been a visually dead assembly of players.

Fox and Peterson effectively utilized the common-room set front-to-back, as well, turning to deep-focus setups to follow figures as they enter the room from the background and then stride forward to join players seated or standing in the foreground.

THIS IS STRANGELY FAMILIAR . . .

Fox and Peterson's visual competence is satisfying, but *Career Girl* succeeds most brilliantly in its display of the reductive genius of PRC. Like other very small, essentially powerless production companies, PRC had to either eschew innovation or innovate differently to major studios, so that prospective audiences could be tantalized by pre-digested entertainment—films that were similar to successful pictures from other, larger studios. Moviegoers who had been paying attention over the years would have recognized *Career Girl* as PRC's bald theft of RKO's *Stage Door* (1937), based on a successful play written by Edna Ferber and George S. Kaufman.[22] The film adaptation directed by Gregory la Cava is headed by Katharine Hepburn and Ginger Rogers, playing women who are tumbled together with other hopeful actresses in a spacious New York boardinghouse. *Career Girl* story men Dave Silverstein and Stanley Rauh, plus scripter Sam Neuman, looked to *Stage Door* to find audience-pleasing "types" that they might purloin: a lively, wisecracking type (Rogers, plus the similarly voluble Eve Arden and Lucille Ball); a beautiful and mean-spirited sneak (Gail Patrick); a dangerously sensitive striver (Andrea Leeds); and an aging, overstressed landlord (Elizabeth Dunne). And *Career Girl*'s stuffy boyfriend exists in *Stage Door*, too, as the Hepburn character's father (Samuel S. Hinds), who puts money into his daughter's show, hoping it will flop.

RKO was one of the "minor majors," and had only sporadic interest in matching the glossy splendor of top-tier Twentieth Century-Fox, Paramount, or MGM. Still, the RKO lot held estimable contract players, writers, and directors, as well as skilled cinematographers, set designers, costumers, and other craft professionals. Further, RKO's Culver City back lot (known around town as the "Forty Acres") gave convenient and money-saving access to standing sets, false-front buildings, and various styles of urban streets.[23] For these reasons, *Stage Door* was an "A" production with enough name- and star appeal to show a profit of $81,000.[24] Although that sum was less than what RKO had hoped for, the great success of the original Broadway play, the film adaptation's profit status, and the fact that PRC could produce a knockoff for far less than the $150,000 combined salaries RKO gave to Katharine Hepburn and Ginger Rogers alone,[25] encouraged the tiny studio to go ahead with *Career Girl*.

Much of what is appealing about *Career Girl* comes from Frances Langford. Essentially carrying the film due to the story construction and her own celebrity, the singer-actress is relaxed and congenial. She moves with natural ease, makes appropriate eye contact with others in the cast (she shows a nice spontaneity in two-shots), and appears to *listen* to the lines that are fed to her. To use jargon that became fashionable later, Langford *inhabits* the role.

The successes of *Stage Door*, *Little Women* (1933), *The Women* (1939), and some other big-studio hits aside, movies dominated by large female casts (though far more common three generations ago than in the twenty-first century) remained faintly novel in 1944. The *Career Girl* script called for more than a dozen boardinghouse residents, and of that number, ten have speaking roles—quite a lot by the standards of PRC. The climactic production number (about which more later) features Langford and some thirty dancers. None of that largesse was typical of the PRC product.

Because so many of the boardinghouse women are "types," shorthand characterizations are the norm for characters other than those played by Langford and Iris Adrian. The naive girl is sweet but weak. The schemer is consistently awful. The legal secretary who dictates the Talent, Inc. contract wears glasses to indicate a gawky intelligence. Adrian's Glenda is at least as dimensional as Langford's Joan, though that may be due as much to Adrian's considerable experience and talent as to anything in the script. By 1944, she had long experience as the sexy, worldly wiseacre, playing waitresses, chorus girls, and girlfriends called Jinx, Dixie, Sugar, Toots, and Goldie.[26] Frances Langford provided *Career Girl* with a big talent and pleasant appeal, but what texture the film has comes mostly from Adrian. Although the honest ambitions and various upsets of Joan dominate the film, and while we arrive at an appreciation of what drives the character, Joan is fundamentally no different from dozens of other protagonists in dozens of other career-girl movies.[27]

Male characters are stock creations, as well, though sixty-year-old Alec Craig appears to have had some fun playing the flummoxed landlord. Handsome Edward Norris, cast as the kindhearted but diffident-seeming playboy, Steve, is a stock figure, too, but as with Iris Adrian, Norris was a good enough actor to pull more from Steve than the script gave him. Norris broke into films in 1933 as a contract player with MGM, and eventually freelanced, working for Universal, Republic, Monogram, and PRC.[28]

Norris's Steve initially strikes us as a little too slick for comfort, and we are meant to understand that he's a player—and a mildly capricious one, at that. Male society swells can turn out to be good or bad in movies like *Career Girl*;

Figure 7.4 Advertisements for *Career Girl* (1944).

here, Steve reveals himself as a straight-up fellow whose romantic interest in Joan is sincere and deep, and whose apparent diffidence is actually his gentlemanly nature.

WHAT THE CAMERA SEES

That Joan finds romance as well as a career in *Career Girl* suggests that marriage is at least as desirable as an ability to work and support oneself. (*Stage Door* takes a different tack: when the character played by Lucille Ball abandons acting for marriage, the implication is that she's made a mistake.) Joan's fiancé James is the scion of a wealthy Kansas family, so marriage to him would bring material comfort. (The central character in *Stage Door*, played by Katharine Hepburn, is wealthy at the outset, so her ambition cannot be derailed in favor of "security.") The "get married" message is a regressive one today, and limiting even in 1944, when many American women were gaining financial independence by doing "men's work" in defense factories.

At least *Career Girl* focuses on women who aspire to work they will find meaningful. But even in this, *Career Girl*, like most other aspiring-actress tales, assumes that audiences will share characters' belief that performance careers are realistically possible. Acting, singing, and dancing are legitimate ways to make a living, and to express oneself. But even the barest entrée into the professional ranks is achieved by just a few, and jobs for women can be demeaning, and keyed to male voyeurism. Even in her off hours, the aspiring actress may feel compelled to "sell" sex in order to get something she wants—as when boardinghouse resident Polly (Renee White) undertakes a cynical seduction of a foolish, middle-aged dress buyer.

HAS ANYONE LOOKED AT THE COSTUMES?

Frances Langford, cast for her looks as well as her talent, is the natural highlight of the big, dance-filled production number (supposedly a dress rehearsal) that closes the film. She is as polished and engaging as one could hope, and although she doesn't belt out her final number, she is sufficiently assertive so that the uniqueness of her voice can be appreciated. Trouble arises because of budget realities that prevented Wallace Fox from giving the sequence life, and from Fox's own misjudgments. Too much of what appears on screen during the final set piece is a series of master shots: long-distance views of the stage, as if the camera were a viewer watching a live show while seated in row L. Cut-ins to Langford are medium shots, with the actress at center frame, occasionally drifting a bit left and right, and a bit forward and back, while dancers behind her bring additional movement.

Not until the last line of the song's final stanza (". . .thaat's how the rhumba bee-gaan. . .") does Fox move in closer on Langford. Good idea—but the camera halts too soon and too far away, framing Langford from the waist up, when a more aggressive dolly-in, culminating with Langford's face filling the screen for the prolonged final note, is what the musical and dramatic situations demand. That this doesn't happen is more than just a lapse—it's a dreadful lost opportunity. The damage is compounded because Langford's gaze is slightly off-center as she sings; she's making eye contact with Steve and two other friends seated in the audience (whose presence is established via medium-shot cut-ins), but not with us. Far better if Fox had moved in for a tight close-up, *and* asked Langford to cut her gaze to the camera eye at the same time, to achieve a desirable exchange of intimacy between performer and movie audience.

The production number has other problems. The sequence is a two-part piece that begins with a locked-camera view of female dancers who fill the proscenium from one side to the other. Most of this 72-second prelude looks as if it were shot from row Q; the women appear minuscule on screen, and the only visual relief comes from two reaction cuts to Steve and others in the theater seats, and a five-second cut to the dancers in medium shot, filmed from the stage so that the women move in a lively diagonal.[29]

And then there are the costumes. About half of the thirty dancers seen in the number's first segment wear light-colored satin short-shorts adorned at the crotch with a dark, V-shaped assemblage of feathers. From the great camera distance chosen by Fox, the women appear to sport bushy pubic hair—good for a chuckle (or a grimace of surprise), but almost certainly not the effect the uncredited costumer intended. (Original *Career Girl* title cards display the requisite Motion Picture Production Code seal, which suggests that industry censors didn't blink when the faux-bottomless dancers emerge.)

When Langford strides onto the stage from screen left, the oddly feathered dancers exit behind her and Fox shifts to a medium shot. Now we're closer to Langford, and to a line of female chorines, assembled behind Langford and wearing showy Afro Cuban garb. The number exhibits some movement, with the dancers taking each other's arms and gracefully swirling in the middle ground while Langford executes understated glides left and right, and forward and back.[30] The camera movement is overdue, but the sequence's overall lack of energy is only partly the fault of Fox; mostly, the flaccidness reflects the plain reality of no-budget filmmaking. A more expansive schedule (that is, more money) would have allowed a substantial length of track to be laid parallel to the dance stage, so the camera could move dynamically with the lateral moves of the dancers and a more active Langford. A larger budget would also have permitted overhead shots accomplished with a boom or a crane. But the logistics of dealing with thirty dancers are daunting even on generously budgeted films; although PRC raised the ante for *Career Girl*, opening its pocketbook wider than usual and creating a nice showcase for Langford, the budget was nevertheless short of what the project really required.

By shooting most of the first dance segment in a long-duration master, Fox saved considerable time and avoided giving the editor the headache of trying to match footage. By directing Langford to move only slightly as she sings, Fox sidestepped time-consuming issues of pulling focus, and the need for repeated rehearsals of dance numbers aggressively shot from multiple angles and points of view.

From the perspectives of PRC executives, Fox's ability to edit in the camera was a boon. And indeed, during some moments this concession to budget develops sequences *more* dynamically than if they had been shot from multiple angles. For example, when a couple of boardinghouse women stride along a wide hallway, they walk toward the camera, which trucks backwards as the women move forward. The necessary dialogue is delivered, and the moving camera effectively involves the viewer with the characters, the dramatic situation, and the physical environment. Similarly, when Langford's Joan explores her room for the first time, the camera subtly trucks forward and back as she moves, allowing us to examine the room with her and once again giving the cutter footage that is pre-edited.[31] In other moments, the camera moves dramatically closer to Joan's unhappy fiancé when he's on the phone with her, and again inside the theater near the end, when the defeated fiancé finally tells playboy Steve to acknowledge that Joan loves him (Steve), and that Steve must continue to pursue her. Yes, the latter moment allows the fiancé to *give* Joan to Steve—a hugely arrogant conceit that produces winces today. But the dolly-in emphasizes the fiancé's seriousness of intent, and brings us close enough to enjoy Steve's pleased reaction.

Langford is an enormous asset to *Career Girl*, and her presence gives the climactic production number a lot of lift. Still, a very modest budget and schedule prevented Fox from effectively underscoring the picture's whole *raison d'être*: the richly deserved triumph of a struggling singer.

MEN ON HER MIND (1944)

Like any film director, Wallace Fox depended on competent scripts. But unlike contract directors at major studios, who were typically attached to projects only after screenplays had been routinely rewritten, and then tweaked and perhaps rewritten all over again, Fox toiled for PRC, which hadn't the means (or inclination) to massage a script until it was as good as it could be. Budget and the quality of available writers often meant that Fox and other Poverty Row directors were obliged to shoot flawed scripts that other, larger studios would never consider for production. This is the bifurcated, money-driven nature of classic-era Hollywood, and it brings us to the last of Fox's mid-1940s "career girl" dramas, *Men on Her Mind* (1944, Figure 7.5). Like the other two pictures discussed in this chapter, *Men on Her Mind* is propelled by an attractive young

Figure 7.5 The one-sheet poster for *Men on Her Mind* (1944).

woman who is determined to succeed as a singer, and who finds romantic love along the way. If that sounds familiar, it is—to a point. The real wonder of *Men on Her Mind* is that even as the film explores the familiar dreams of an aspiring vocalist, it also—and quite unintentionally—chronicles the peripatetic life of a sociopath.

Raymond L. Schrock's screenplay is only ostensibly concerned with careerism; what it most distinctly explores is a beautiful young woman's ability to switch off her emotions and literally run away from conflict, abandoning people that care about her, over and over again. *Men on Her Mind* is a literal journey, and a peculiar one.

Lily Durrell (Mary Beth Hughes) works at an Oregon orphanage, brightly shepherding happy little girls through their daily routines. Her charges adore her, but because Lily has already confided to the headmistress that "a singing career is all I want in this world," we are not surprised when she decides to leave her job and head south to Los Angeles. Talented people should be ambitious—but why does Lily pack her bag and suddenly depart without a word to the children?

Subsequent interludes in Lily's life amount to mere way stations: while hitchhiking from the orphanage late at night, Lily meets Joe (Lyle Latell), a kind but dim truck driver. Lily allows herself to fall into a quasi-romantic relationship with him, but is put off by Joe's overbearing mother and bratty nephews. Lily is uncomfortable with Joe's guileless working-class manner. ("Darn these hiccups," he confides after one supper, "I get them every time I eat cabbage.") Lily also fancies that Joe's wit is beneath her, and she may be right: one of Joe's jokes concludes, "So the moron walked through the screen door and strained himself!"

When Joe finally proposes, Lily awkwardly puts him off, and then secretly packs her bag and flees.

Finally in Los Angeles, Lily has a successful audition at a night club, only to be horrified when the owner's jealous wife shoots him dead in the next room. Rather than call (or even simply wait for) the police, Lily hops on the first train out of town, and spends the next few months working as a waitress at a drive-in and attending secretarial school.

A helpful older man, Roland Palmer (Alan Edwards), hires Lily as his secretary, befriends her, and pays for her vocal lessons. He falls in love with her, as well, and even though she's diffident and puts him off—as she put off truck driver Joe—Palmer's catty sister (Kay Linaker) erroneously pegs Lily as a gold digger, and threatens to have her "investigated." Thoroughly cowed, Lily packs an enormous bag and rushes into the street, where she has a "meet cute" in a cab with a handsome young rich fellow named Jeffry Wingate (Edward Norris). A perceptive guy, Wingate asks, "What are you running away from?"

Although Lily's plan is to take the first bus out of town, Wingate persuades her to stay. Soon, they fall in love, but when Wingate stops with Lily at his own home to retrieve something from a safe, Lily assumes her new beau is a jewel thief. (The house is empty and without electricity because Wingate has not been living in it.)

The next sequence opens with Lily at a bus station, gripping that giant suitcase again.

HER ON HER MIND

Audiences may have grown weary of all this furious running but Lily, well, Lily has a seemingly inexhaustible supply of energy (and travel money). The eventful incidents continue. At the station she is mistaken for "Miss Andrews," the "physical culture" teacher newly hired by the nearby Van Rensaleer School for Girls. As passive-aggressive as ever, Lily "becomes" Miss Andrews and allows her bag to be loaded onto the school's station wagon. Already a serial heartbreaker, a determined avoider of conflict, an uncooperative ear-witness to murder, and an eyewitness to what she believes is safecracking grand larceny, Lily now becomes an impersonator. In a particularly unnerving moment, she passes a mirror in the privacy of her school quarters and says, "Well, how do you do, Miss Andrews?" After a half-beat, she smiles coldly and laughs.

Lily settles in at the school, charming students, faculty, and the headmistress. But finally worried (perhaps) about the imminent arrival of the real Miss Andrews, Lily packs the suitcase *again*, only to ditch it when she's intercepted on the school grounds by a young music teacher and aspiring songwriter named Jim Lacey (Ted North).[32] Like every other man in Lily's orbit, Jim falls in love with her, lost in idle reverie like a smitten schoolboy.

Jim is a sweet soul—too sweet to suit Lily, who sits with him in a romantic, night-shadowed glade and blurts,

> I can't help wondering why a strapping big six-footer like you would've chosen to be a music teacher when there's so many more important things in the world for a man to do . . . I've always associated big men with big jobs. Being leaders in their chosen fields. Now how far do you ever expect to get by just being a music teacher? If you're interested in music, why don't you, why don't you become an orchestra leader or a composer?

Instead of being rightfully insulted by Lily's tactless stupidity, Jim perks up and smiles! "You know," he answers, "it was *awfully* nice of you to give me such constructive criticism."

Lily looks at her watch. "Well, I could tell you a lot more, but it's getting late." If scripter Raymond L. Schrock had ever met any real human beings, he hides it well here.

By this time, the real Miss Andrews has written to the school, saying she cannot accept the appointment. Jim has somehow managed to intercept the letter before it can reach the headmistress, and he leaves it for Lily with this reassuring scribble: "Mum's the word!" Later, Jim assures Lily that her criminal impersonation is simply an act of "self-preservation" (the foremost preoccupation of a sociopath); Lily is inclined to agree. And true to his dog-like nature, Jim composes a song, just for Lily, and calls it "Heaven on Earth."

Lily's wealthy older suitor, Roland Palmer, has somehow traced her to the school, to offer her a solo radio spot underwritten by a national advertiser. Although Lily had been falling in love with Jim, she abruptly cools to him; her "self-preservation" instinct is again taking hold. Jim tells Lily he wants to marry her. Lily answers, "You don't think I'd give up a career for just love, and a cottage with a music professor?"

Lily grabs that suitcase again and follows Palmer back to the city. But we're not quite done yet.

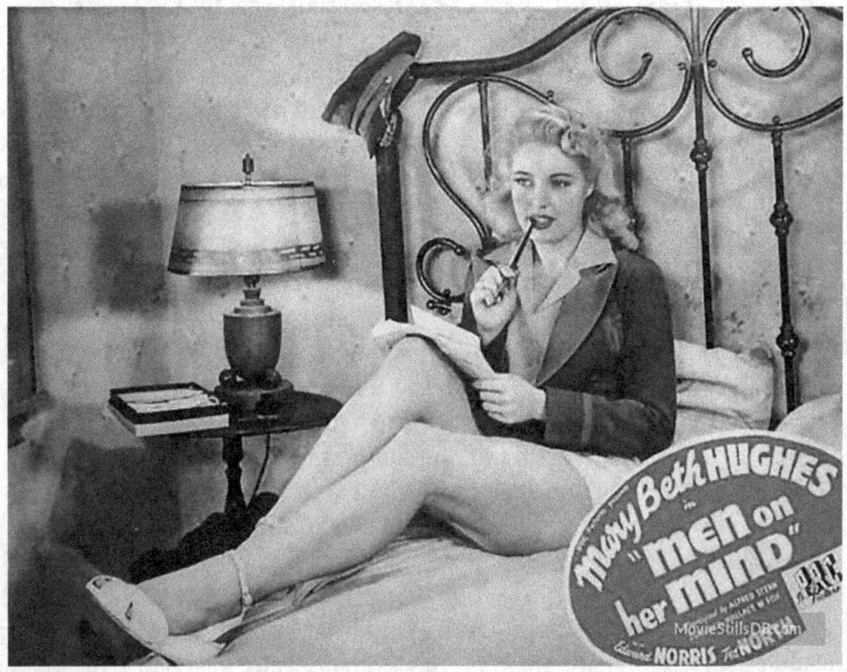

Figure 7.6 Lobby card for *Men on Her Mind* (1944).

BAD BEHAVIOR HAS ITS REWARDS

As in PRC's most celebrated film, *Detour*, the events of *Men on Her Mind* unfold within a framing device; all but a few minutes of the story are recalled by Lily in flashback, as she sits alone in her dressing room, by now a radio star with a tangled skein of men and tumult behind her. Framing devices purposely manipulate the false reality of movies to suggest 1) determinism (the protagonist's struggles lead to an unavoidable conclusion); 2) an epiphany (the main character "learns" something important and is the better for it); or 3) ultimate vindication or other victory (as in Don Siegel's 1956 thriller, *Invasion of the Body Snatchers*).

When the framing device heralds a deterministic point of view, the protagonist may end up in an existentially bad place, but may also have achieved some level of self-awareness (recall the miserable acceptance of *Detour*'s Al Roberts). As utilized in *Men on Her Mind*, the device is clearly meant to be of the second and third types, a triumph, because Lily suddenly resolves to return to her last and most modest suitor, Jim Lacey. She's still running, but this time she runs straight into his arms. The pair kiss and embrace for the fadeout, but what, really, has Lily learned? Avoidance brings happiness? Cowardice leads to success? Meanness guarantees love? It pays to be pathologically self-absorbed? Lacey has no self-respect?

Lily has almost certainly learned nothing about herself. Why should she have? Events have worked out to what she momentarily feels is her satisfaction, but we've seen her in action often enough to give her marriage to Jim about a month—particularly because the film goes out of its way to display marriage's negative consequences (such as irritating mothers-in-law, stale jokes, boredom, infidelity, and murder) and the horrors of family (bratty children, noisy meals, too many bills to pay). All of that negativity is staged not for the audience, but for Lily.

HITS AND MISSES

Late in the framing section, Palmer takes Lily to meet the radio-show sponsor, who is curious to learn which song Lily wishes to perform for her debut. A reasonable question, which led Schrock to create this absurd and ridiculously concise exchange:

LILY
It's a song called "Heaven on Earth."
SPONSOR
Mmm. Sounds intriguing.
LILY
But it's an unpublished number by an unknown composer.

SPONSOR
That makes no difference if it's good.
VOCAL COACH
It has the earmarks of a popular song hit!
SPONSOR
It's just the kind of a song I want!

Mary Beth Hughes[33] had not risen to the level of fame of Fox's earlier collaborator, Frances Langford, but just prior to *Men on Her Mind* she had been under contract to Twentieth Century-Fox, where she had enjoyed showy second leads in B- and B-plus pictures since 1940. Not strictly a leading lady, Hughes was a young character actress whose name and image had been prominently featured on one-sheet posters and other promotional material from Twentieth, as well as from studios that bracketed her tenure there.

Hughes photographed well from any angle and under a variety of approaches to lighting. During a song sequence set at the Van Rensaleer School, Fox shot Hughes's face in crisply lit close-up, from a low angle that brings some visual energy. And when Hughes and Norris interact at Jeffry Wingate's enormous empty house, they are wrapped in heavy, evocative shadows that bring out the contours of their faces, generate some visual texture, and build audience apprehension.

A few key moments fall flat, notably the murder that sends Lily fleeing the nightclub audition. When the angry wife confronts the husband, Fox framed the moment as a standard two-shot, with the man standing far left and the woman screen right, facing him. To depict the killing itself, Fox and editor Charles Henkel cut to a slightly closer vantage point (same angle) that shows the husband only; the homicidal wife and the gun are out of frame, somewhere beyond screen right, when the trigger is pulled.[34] The moment unfolds perfunctorily and much too quickly, a flaw that could have been leavened by keeping both players in the frame, with close-up cutaways to reaction shots of the wife (an instant before the gun is fired), followed by the husband (immediately after the fatal shot).

There are no such cutaways.

Lily's discovery of the body is handled even more disappointingly, via a plain medium shot of our heroine, who doesn't move because the camera has no intention of moving. We see alarm on Lily's face but no horror. Even a simple cut to her reaction in close-up is lacking, which suggests that Fox neglected to shoot one, or had no time to do so. Neither is there a subjective shot of the corpse from Lily's POV, which would have ginned up the audience a little and encouraged a cut back to a close-up on Lily, to add weight to her reaction. These lacks are critical miscalculations that burden what should have been an emotionally charged moment with an unfortunate remoteness.

Too many of the film's sets are small and claustrophobic, another mandate of budget that has the side effect of preventing viewers from properly orienting the characters. A song sequence inside Palmer's club is much better, with an expansive, nicely dressed set occupied by dozens of extras. The interiors of the Van Rensaleer School, too, are sizable enough to effectively suggest *place*; about thirty extras playing students give the set the feel of a real institution. School exteriors are effective, too, showcasing a good-looking building surrounded by well-manicured grounds.

Most satisfying of all is Palmer's house, a spacious and smartly dressed space that indicates wealth and taste. It is during the Palmer-house sequences that *Men on Her Mind* comes closest to big-studio B-level work.

THE WORKING LIFE

Wallace Fox's working-girl assignments define parts of his professional life, but more pointedly reveal the hopes and challenges faced by the real-world women who paid to see his movies—that is, when those women were free of shop or factory work, relieved of child care, had caught up on housework, and were inclined to spend time with spouses or friends. To varying degrees, *The Girl from Monterrey*, *Career Girl*, and *Men on Her Mind* suggest that satisfaction and even glory are possible for men who follow well-defined paths to sport, education, or lives in uniform; and that men can thoughtlessly enjoy romance as well as careers. At the same time, the films suggest that women's quests for fame require a willingness to compromise or sacrifice altogether the concept of choice, and to nurture a dedication that, if not properly managed, can bring deep disappointment. Sometimes, female ambition can shade to callousness and even madness.

Because Fox's working-girl protagonists, even the quite mad Lily, emerge fulfilled, their lives are implicitly trivialized. They've struggled, yes, but covertly conditioned audiences understood that the struggles have been "female," and thus of importance only to the women and a few people in their immediate orbits. In other films, in films with male protagonists, ambition, professional disappointment, and troubled minds are "big" stories, heavy with dark emotion, existential crises, and, sometimes, violence. The consequences of these male-centric stories extend beyond a small circle of characters into the larger world, via consequential business deals, hardball politics, or art that (unlike simple singing) might change the world.

Following *Men on Her Mind*, Wallace Fox worked in the industry for another ten years, directing an additional thirty-five features and more than twenty-five installments of episodic television.[35] He passed away in 1958, just four years after his retirement.[36]

Fox probably had no illusions about doing work capable of changing the world. He pursued his assignments not in the eternally hopeful manner of one of his career girls, and not in the manner of a filmic or real-world "big shot," but as an industrious journeyman who functioned efficiently to create value from the materials at hand. Fox was a professional, working on one job and probably already thinking about the next, pursuing his plain but eventful career, and thus well suited to direct this trilogy of career-girl adventures.

NOTES

1. United States Census Bureau, 1930 Census, National Archives and Records Administration publication T626. Available at <www.census.gov/history/pdf/t626.pdf> (accessed December 12, 2021). United States Census Bureau, 1940 Census (www.census.gov).
2. Emily Yellin, *Our Mothers' War: American Women at Home and at the Front during World War II* (New York: Free Press, 2004).
3. Les Adams and Buck Rainey, *Shoot-Em-Ups: The Complete Guide to Westerns of the Sound Era* (New Rochelle, NY: Arlington House, 1978); Wheeler Dixon (ed.), *Producers Releasing Corporation: A Comprehensive Filmography and History* (Jefferson, NC: McFarland, 1986); Ephraim Katz, *The Film Encyclopedia* (New York: HarperPerennial, 1994); Leonard Maltin, *The Great Movie Shorts* (New York: Crown, 1972); Ted Okuda, *The Monogram Checklist: The Films of Monogram Pictures Corporation* (Jefferson, NC: McFarland, 1987).
4. Dixon, *Producers Releasing Corporation*.
5. There were exceptions during Hollywood's classic era: for example, directors Anthony Mann (a PRC alum), Robert Wise, Edward Dmytryk, Budd Boetticher, and Fred Zinnemann forged significant careers after toiling in Bs. PRC's best-known director, the prolific Edgar G. Ulmer, never escaped Hollywood's B-ranks (he did his most prestigious pictures for European producers), but left a legacy that marks him as an important, if quirky, talent. For Wallace Fox and numerous others directing at PRC and Monogram, career salvation came postwar, when television began to dominate American entertainment, and experienced directors who could shoot quickly became highly valued. Along with Fox, Joseph H. Lewis, Sam Newfield, Lambert Hillyer, Reginald Le Borg, William Beaudine, Lew Landers, and Jean Yarbrough were some who prolonged their careers on the small screen during the 1950s and '60s.
6. *The Girl from Monterrey* is available as an Alpha Video DVD. *Career Girl* is available as a Synergy Entertainment DVD; at the time of writing, it also is available for streaming via Amazon Video. *Men on Her Mind* is available as an Alpha Video DVD, and as one component of Sinister Cinema's DVD series, *Poverty Row Studio Collections: PRC Volume 2*.
7. *Billboard*, December 18, 1943.
8. Dennis J. Bixler-Márquez and Carlos F. Ortega (eds), *Chicana/o Studies: Survey and Analysis, 4th edition* (Dubuque, IA: Kendall Hunt Publishing, 2014).
9. The singer-actress's full name was Armida Vendrell.
10. Others involved in the film's anomalous casting are Native-American actor Jay Silverheels (famous later as television's best-liked Native American, Tonto) in a bit-part as a fighter named Tito Flores; and German-born Alphonse Martell, as Juanito, Lita's boss at the club.
11. In the film's opening credits, the song's title is shown without commas, as "Jive Brother Jive."

12. Adams and Rainey, *Shoot-Em-Ups*; Dixon, *Producers Releasing Corporation*; Katz, *The Film Encyclopedia*; Maltin, *The Great Movie Shorts*; Okuda, *The Monogram Checklist*.
13. Mauricio Mazón, *The Zoot-Suit Riots: The Psychology of Symbolic Annihilation* (Austin: University of Texas Press, 1989).
14. Ibid.
15. A chief PRC competitor, Monogram, reported net income of $99,144 for the year ending June 26, 1943. PRC cut into its own profits when it spent $305,000 to purchase the physical plant of Fine Arts Studio in September 1943. Both items noted in *Motion Picture Herald*, September 25, 1943, 34, 41.
16. William A. Ewing and Todd Brandow, *Edward Steichen: In High Fashion, the Condé Nast Years* (Minneapolis, MN: Foundation for the Exhibition of Photography, 2008); Gary D. Keller, *Hispanics and United States Film: An Overview and Handbook, Vol. 10* (Tempe, AZ: Bilingual Press, 1994); Miles Kreuger (ed.), *The Movie Musical from Vitaphone to 42nd Street* (New York: Dover, 1975); Roy Liebman, *Vitaphone Films: A Catalogue of the Features and Shorts* (Jefferson, NC: McFarland, 2003); Emilio Garcia Riera, *Mexican Americans in Motion Pictures* (Mexico City: Ediciones Era, 1987).
17. Ibid.
18. In her first film, Paramount's *Every Night at Eight* (1935), Langford introduced the Jimmy McHugh-Dorothy Fields song, "I'm in the Mood for Love." The Brunswick Records release was a smash (*Billboard* chart #15), and became Langford's signature tune.
19. Jeanine Basinger, *The Movie Musical!* (New York: Knopf, 2019). Ben Ohmart, *Frances Langford: Armed Forces Sweetheart* (Albany, GA: BearManor, 2017).
20. PRC licensed three of Langford's four *Career Girl* numbers for 1945 release as discrete Soundies seen and heard on Panoram 16mm movie jukeboxes owned by Soundies Distributing Corporation of America. Panorams were installed in bars and restaurants, bus stations, bowling alleys, military bases, and other high-traffic areas. The Langford–*Career Girl* Soundies are *Tropical Moon* (the *Career Girl* finale, released as a Soundie on February 5, 1945); *A Dream Came True* (April 2, 1945); and *Someday When the Clouds Roll By* (April 30, 1945).
21. Bogdanovich–Ulmer interview first published in *Film Culture* nos. 58–60, 1974; reprinted in Todd McCarthy and Charles Flynn (eds), *Kings of the Bs: Working within the Hollywood System* (New York: Dutton, 1975).
22. The title is also similar to *Cover Girl* (1944), Columbia's extravagant A-level musical starring Rita Hayworth and Gene Kelly. Although released later in the same year as *Career Girl*, *Cover Girl*—title and all—was widely discussed in the trades well before PRC began production of *Career Girl*.
23. The most famous structure on RKO's Forty Acres was Tara, the mansion erected for use in independent producer David O. Selznick's *Gone With the Wind* (1939). A generation later, television viewers saw Forty Acres buildings and streets in episodes of *Adventures of Superman*, *The Untouchables*, *The Andy Griffith Show*, and the original *Star Trek*. Most of Forty Acres was razed by developers in the 1970s.
24. Tino Balio, *Grand Design: Hollywood as a Modern Business Enterprise, 1930–1939* (New York: Charles Scribner's Sons, 1993); Charles Higham, *Kate: The Life of Katharine Hepburn* (New York: W.W. Norton, 1981); Alvin H. Marill, *Katharine Hepburn* (New York: Pyramid, 1973).
25. Ibid.
26. Michael Pitts, *Poverty Row Studios, 1929–1940* (Jefferson, NC: McFarland, 1997); David Quinlan, *Quinlan's Illustrated Directory of Film Comedy Stars* (London: Batsford, 1992); Jordan R. Young, *Reel Characters: Great Movie Character Actors* (Beverly Hills: CA, Moonstone Press, 2008).

27. In a welcome turnabout, career girls in some earlier, Depression-era films are cunning, cynical, self-centered, and materially ambitious. Two startling examples are Glenda Farrell's fast-talking gold digger in *Girl Missing* (1933) and, most famously, Barbara Stanwyck's ruthless, emotionally numbed bank employee in *Baby Face* (1933).
28. Dixon, *Producers Releasing Corporation*; Kaitz, *The Film Encyclopedia*.
29. When material shifted them out of their element, even the slickest and most talented Hollywood directors could struggle to achieve appropriate screen treatment of musical numbers. Curtis Bernhardt, for example, had won acclaim for his handling of *Devotion*, *A Stolen Life*, and *Beau Brummell*, but when he directed *Interrupted Melody*, a 1955 MGM biopic about Australian opera diva Marjorie Lawrence, he realized that he had no clue about how to bring life and dynamism to the simulated opera performances. Biographer Peter Ford (whose father, Glenn Ford, played Lawrence's husband in the film) quotes star Eleanor Parker as recalling, "[Bernhardt] didn't know where to put the camera or where to have us stand. They shut down [production] for a few days and found an actual opera director who knew how to stage those scenes properly"—Peter Ford, *Glenn Ford: A Life* (Madison: The University of Wisconsin Press, 2011).
30. Although Rudy Schrager is credited with "musical direction," no choreographer is noted.
31. The showiest bit of business Fox devised for *Career Girl* illustrates neither in-camera editing nor the need for a conventional edit. Rather, it demands an optical effect: when the focal character moves screen right to screen left, the camera pans left to follow, "pulling" behind it a leftward wipe that duplicates the character's movement *and* carries us into the next scene.
32. Mary Beth Hughes and Ted North were married during 1943–1946. Besides *Men on Her Mind*, they both can be seen in *Charlie Chan in Rio* (1941) and *The Ox-Bow Incident* (1943).
33. Latter-day interest in Mary Beth Hughes developed into a minor cult because of her role in *I Accuse My Parents* (1944), a proto-juvenile delinquency melodrama from PRC that was sent up by the satiric *Mystery Science Theater 3000* television series in 1993. But Hughes is seen to best advantage (and earned third billing) in William Wellman's *The Ox-Bow Incident* (1943), as Henry Fonda's former flame (a three-minute appearance that throws off sexual heat); and in *Highway Dragnet* (1954), the first movie produced by Roger Corman. Although the character played by Hughes features throughout the story, as a murder victim, the actress is on screen only in the opening sequence, as a slightly tipsy barfly who encounters co-star Richard Conte, and who progresses from passivity to curiosity to flirtatiousness to anger and finally to naked lust in a mere two-and-a-half minutes. It is a remarkable cameo.
34. Hollywood's Production Code frowned upon shootings in which the victim and the firing gun are captured in the same frame. Regardless, the murder sequence in *Men on Her Mind* could have been presented more forcefully.
35. Monogram's *Montana Desperado* (1951) is the last feature directed by Fox. From 1951 to 1954, the veteran filmmaker helmed nearly thirty episodes of various children's television series: *The Gene Autry Show*, *The Range Rider*, *Annie Oakley*, and *Ramar of the Jungle*. *White Goddess*, a seventy-minute compilation of *Ramar* episodes directed by Fox and released to theaters in 1953 by Lippert Pictures, is sometimes erroneously identified as one of Fox's standalone features.
36. Eugene Michael Vazzana, *Silent Film Necrology* (Jefferson, NC: McFarland, 2001).

CHAPTER 8

She Made Her Own Deadline: Fox's *Brenda Starr, Reporter*

Sara Rutkowski

When movie theater audiences in 1945 sat down for the first installment of the film serial *Brenda Starr, Reporter* (Fox 1945), entitled *Hot News*, they no doubt felt in familiar territory. There was Brenda, the daring crime reporter they knew well from Dale Messick's syndicated comic strip of the same name (which ran for 71 years, from 1940 until 2011). Played by B-movie starlet Joan Woodbury, Brenda was now a blonde instead of a redhead, her clothes more modest and less form fitting, yet she promised the same pluck and courage as her comic book original (Figure 8.1).

But Brenda was not only recognizable from her life on the printed page; she also fit the big-screen archetype of the "girl reporter"—a formula character who by the mid-1940s had been replicated in hundreds of Hollywood movies, among the most famous of which were the "Torchy Blane" series (1937–1939), *His Girl Friday* (1940) and *Woman of the Year* (1942). The opening scene of *Brenda Starr, Reporter* is the hallmark setup for the "girl reporter" genre: we see Brenda at the wheel, her sidekick photographer, Chuck (Syd Saylor), beside her, on their way to the hiding place of a burglary suspect (Figure 8.2). "Step on it Brenda," he says, "we want to beat that police friend of yours Lt. Farrell and that dumb *[unintelligible]* of his."

The shot soon shifts to Lt.—Larry—Farrell himself (Kane Richmond) in a car alongside his sidekick cop partner Tim (Joe Devlin). And there you have it: the attractive female reporter chasing a scoop and the handsome police lieutenant chasing a suspect, the two locked in a professional rivalry whose contours vibrate with romantic tension. The girl reporter offered audiences a tough but always beautiful heroine who was part fantasy—for both men and women—and part reality, as she emerged out of the Depression era when newspaper reporting began to open up as viable professional path for women in search of

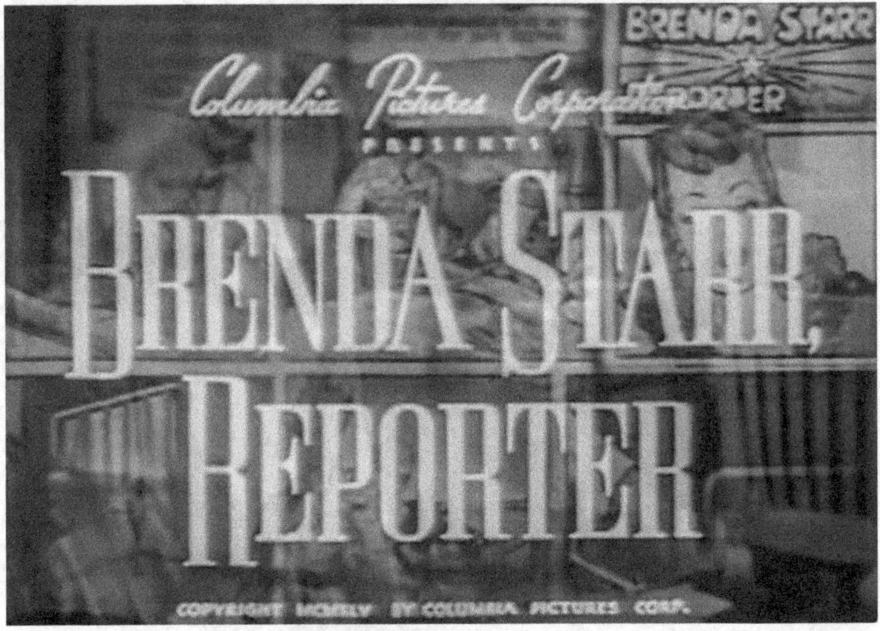

Figure 8.1 Original still from opening credits of *Brenda Starr, Reporter* (1945).

Figure 8.2 Original still from *Brenda Starr, Reporter* (1945): Brenda and Chuck exchange banter while on assignment.

a paycheck. Indeed, she was birthed by the paradox of the ages: the clashing desires to buck traditional gender roles and to cleave to them.

Given the popularity of both the Brenda Starr comic strip and the girl reporter genre, a film serial surely must have seemed a safe bet for Sam Katzman who produced it for Columbia Pictures. Katzman brought with him director Wallace Fox, who by then had directed dozens of films since the late 1920s, and screenwriters Ande Lamb and George Plympton, both of whom had impressive careers in television and film serials (Plympton had perhaps written the most serials of anyone in the business). Indeed, in 1945, serials were still lucrative for the big studios that had begun producing these low-budget, short episodic films during the silent era; their value faded quickly by the late 1940s and early 1950s as television shows took their place. Popular serials, such *The Green Hornet* (Beebe and Taylor 1940), *Batman* (Hillyer 1943), and *Captain America* (Clifton and English 1944) all featured melodramatic good guy-bad guy plots that ended in suspenseful cliffhangers, and lured audiences back to their neighborhood theaters each week to be treated to the next gripping installment in advance of the feature film.

And like all serials, Fox's *Brenda Starr* featured non-stop action and unlikely death-defying scenarios that kept the hero alive another week, each episode ending with a voiceover narration along the lines of: "Has Brenda been lured into sure death?" or "Are all of Brenda's sacrifices and escapes from death been in vain?" The thirteen episodes, or "chapters" as they were called, follow Brenda as she tries to track down a missing payroll cache of $250,000, whose disappearance is the suspected mastermind of gangsters, headquartered in a secret backroom at a local nightclub. Always hungry for a scoop, Brenda zig-zags across Chicago and beyond with Chuck at her side, trying to outrun Lt. Farrell, and under pressure from her editor, a paternal full-bodied newspaperman, Mr. Walters, at *The Daily Flash*.

All thirteen chapters were shot in only 21 days, a schedule that Woodbury later indicated in an interview was grueling, especially given that the script was, as she put it, the size of a telephone book. But that was not unusual for serial productions, which operated on low budgets and required cast members to perform long hours with little rehearsal time and tight shooting schedules. According to Woodbury, she got the role only because "I could learn dialogue fast enough to do everything in one take." She recalled doing the last scene alone with nineteen pages of dialogue on the telephone and a full bar behind her on set, awaiting the wrap-up party: "I shot all 19 sequences in one take, because they were going to kill me if I didn't, with all that booze waiting; and I proceeded to get bombed after that."[1]

After its short life on the screen in 1945, the serial essentially vanished. Stored in the Library of Congress, the negatives suffered decades of nitrate damage and the soundtrack from the third and fourth chapters was lost (according to Leonard Maltin, a self-professed serial buff). It was not until 2011, the same year that the *Brenda Starr* comic strip was retired, that Bob Blair of VCI Entertainment released what he was able restore of the serial. In his review of the newly refurbished and long forgotten footage, Maltin praises Blair for releasing *Brenda* "warts and all." Serials, he maintains, are worth watching for their "utter simplicity of storytelling."[2]

There are other good reasons to watch *Brenda*. For one, because it disappeared for so many years, it has only very recently even begun to be considered within film scholarship—and specifically within the girl reporter genre and the now historical medium of the film serial, which frequently recycled material from the comic strips and books from era. A great deal has been written about both the girl reporter genre and the film serial over the last seventy-some years, much of it terrific criticism that leaves Brenda out except in the most cursory way.

But *Brenda Starr, Reporter* is also worth a fresh appraisal for how it deviates from such scholarship. Although it would seem easy to slot it into the mix of girl reporter films—the character was, after all, a copy of a celebrated girl reporter—upon closer examination, it turns out to pose a bit of a quandary. Brenda actually bears little resemblance to the comic strip heroine either in appearance or personality, or even in action; yes, she is a reporter, but despite the opening scene that seems to foretell a romance, Brenda of the screen has virtually no love life and no apparent sexual appeal—the lynchpin of Messick's strip. As film historian Geoff Mayer notes, the serial transformed comic strip Brenda from a "glamorous reporter into a workhorse."[3]

But nor does Brenda quite harken back to the parade of girl reporters before her who were typically portrayed as hardboiled—or, at the very least, fast-talking—women who had to fight back the chauvinism that surrounded them in order to make it in their male-dominated trade. Brenda is decidedly *not* hardboiled; but she also never has to defend her position as a crime reporter, since everyone throughout the serial seems to treat it as acceptable. Moreover, Brenda Starr was not typical material for film serials, which in the 1940s tended to rely more on superheroes and cowboys for their weekly thrilling installments.

It is Brenda's anomaly—her inability to fit comfortably into the norms of any of her categories: as a comic book character, a girl reporter, or a film serial—that is the subject of this chapter. Coming on the heels of the era of the girl reporter in film, she embodies its enigmas like no other. But before I can show how, we need to examine her influences, i.e. what exactly it was that she was supposedly imitating.

BRENDA STARR THE COMIC STRIP

First and foremost, *Brenda Starr, Reporter* the serial was supposed to be *Brenda Starr, Reporter* the comic; or at least the promotional poster seemed to suggest it would bring to life the sexy scoop-hunting redhead from the funny pages. We see an illustrated approximation of Joan Woodbury with fiery red hair against a red backdrop (as noted earlier, Woodbury was actually a blonde); she is pointing a gun, and her arm just covers the end of her blouse's plunging neckline. Next to her is the handsome Kane Richmond, who, curiously, is holding a camera, though in the serial he plays the police lieutenant and not her photographer sidekick. Together they evoke a crime-fighting team that promises sexual intrigue (Figure 8.3).

The comic strip debuted in June of 1940 in the Sunday supplement of the *Chicago Tribune*. Its creator Dale Messick, who worked as a greeting card illustrator for the Chicago Tribune Syndicate, had originally pitched a comic strip about a female pirate, which was rejected. But she managed to sell the Brenda idea, no doubt capitalizing on the girl reporter formula that had been popular in films throughout the 1930s. It was signed for national distribution the following year, but it was not until 1945—the same year that the serial was produced—that it made its national Sunday debut. The daily strip went national about six months later.

Messick based Brenda's looks on the movie star Rita Hayworth, known for her lush red hair, and her name on the 1930s debutante Brenda Frazier, a young woman whose abundant wealth and glamorous social life became a cultural fixation during the Depression. In the early years Brenda Starr was less curvy than she would later become; the navels and cleavages that Messick drew in were routinely erased by prudish editors. But she was nonetheless distinctive for the glamour and sex appeal she exuded through fashionable clothes and her signature twinkling eyes. The strip's plotline played on her allure; throughout her 71-year life of eternal youth, Brenda was forever entertaining and deflecting many suitors, the most famous of whom was Basil St. John, a mysterious man with an eye patch who raised black orchids.

But also central to the strip's storyline was the conflict that these romances—and men in general—posed to Brenda's work as an adventurous and gutsy reporter. Especially in the early years, the comic strip made much of Brenda's efforts to navigate the chauvinistic obstacles routinely placed before her. In the very first frame we see Brenda protesting her role as a "sob sister," the pejorative nickname for female reporters tasked with the society pages or other "lifestyle" news.

Over the years, this theme would become less prevalent in the strip, particularly as American culture itself changed and Brenda's profession appeared less exceptional. But it is telling that Messick's *Brenda Starr* was most popular throughout the 1950s—featured in some 250 newspapers nationwide—when the culture promoted marriage and the domestic realm as the ideal place for women. Brenda surely must have offered a counter-cultural vision of women as empowered and daring professionals, while her curves and sex appeal were a draw to male readers. Indeed, her dual role as fantasy for both sexes was perhaps the key to her longevity.

Figure 8.3 Original promotional poster for "Chapter 9" of *Brenda Starr, Reporter* (1945).

Messick retired for good in 1985, and other illustrators and writers took over until the strip finally folded in 2011. Apart from the 1945 Brenda serial, though, the only filmed adaptations were produced in the 1970s and 1980s, beginning with a made-for-TV movie starring Jill St. John (1976), which took place in a 1970s newsroom, and television pilot that was never sold starring Sherry Jackson (1979). But the most famous—and certainly most disparaged—was the 1986 feature film starring Brooke Shields. After a long dispute over distribution rights, the film was not shown in the United States until 1992—around the same time as the blockbusters *Batman* and *Dick Tracy*. Alongside those blockbusters, *Brenda Starr* seemed weak and outdated. Although it lavishly characterized the comic book world of the 1940s, the movie was widely criticized for its retrograde treatment of Brenda. Film critic Janet Maslin argued that Shields's Brenda seemed more concerned with "running her stockings or breaking her high heels" than with covering the news.[4]

Perhaps ironically, you could say no such thing about Woodbury's Brenda of 1945. In fact, all of the screen adaptations of *Brenda Starr* seem to play off the comic strip's themes and aesthetic (Brooke Shields's eyes twinkle like comic strip Brenda's) in ways that the serial simply doesn't. It might be that, despite its name, *Brenda Starr* the serial was less influenced by Dale Messick's version than by the girl reporter of the movies—a generic creature, though not without complexity.

GIRL + REPORTER + MOVIES = MIXED MESSAGES

The girl reporter's emergence as a cinematic type in the early 1930s was no accident; she was pulled from real-life Depression culture in which women were increasingly turning to journalism as a viable source of income. In fact, the ranks of female journalists more than doubled from the previous decade, although as a number of cultural historians have pointed out, there were far fewer in real life than in the movies, and many of them were so-called "sob sisters" who covered the social beat or gave the feminine—i.e. emotional—angle to the guys' stories. But not so on the big screen where throughout the Depression era and beyond, a lot of women were doing the tough job, the detective work, on the hunt for murder suspects and gangsters.

Of course, the girl reporter genre is actually a subgenre (though I continue to call it a genre here) to the genre of journalism films, which had also taken off in the 1930s in part because the new "talkies" required more complex storylines developed through dialogue. The newspaper genre, with its promise of suspense and excitement through a narrative that was strung together largely through speech, was ideal. Many of the studio writers were themselves former "newsies," with knowledge of the industry and a keen sense of audience interest in the hard-edged, unsentimental world of the press. *The Front Page* (Milestone 1931), starring Adolphe Menjou and Pat O'Brien, is typically considered the first major newspaper film, though other less famous ones preceded it. As Matthew Ehrlich explains in *Journalism in the Movies*, from the beginning nearly all of these films feature four key elements: a reporter (often with a sidekick); a story that needs cracking; a paternalistic editor; and a love interest. The girl reporter uniquely satisfied the needs of this genre; for one, she could do double duty, acting as both the lead character *and* the love interest. Instead of an underling or minor player, she was at the center of the action just as she was the object of affection. Moreover, by 1934, the Hays Production Code was being enforced, which meant, as Verna Kale points out, that you couldn't just have female characters lounging about seductively; they had to *do* something. She writes, "The girl reporter—who challenged male authority, exposed corruption, solved crimes, and did so with every hair in place—offered limitless possibilities for celluloid adventures."[5]

The girl reporter thus became a staple figure throughout the decade, a tough broad who could not only make it in a man's world, but beat the men at their own game. Torchy Blane, whom Philippa Gates calls the "quintessential fast-talking dame of the 1930s," was the main character in nine films between 1937 and 1939, beginning with *Smart Blonde* and ending with *Torchy Blane. . .Playing with Dynamite*.[6] Actress Glenda Farrell played her in seven of these films, making her name synonymous with the hardboiled women of action. Torchy's popularity helped breed more female reporters who were challenging traditional gender roles with their rough-around-the-edges personae and willingness to face danger, and even their bordering-on-masculine fashion sense (Torchy was known for her tailored suits, Figure 8.4).

At the same time, however, virtually all of these films build their plotlines around the growing attraction between the girl reporter and the leading man, often a police chief or fellow reporter, sometimes an editor with whom our leading lady initially butts heads. Thus it is essential that the girl reporter was young and single. The story she was covering often wasn't the main story of the film, but the backdrop against which the romance could play out. And because romance at that time signaled marriage—which was generally seen for a woman as inherently incompatible with chasing gangsters—these films had to deal with, often explicitly, the push and pull between being a journalist and being a wife. As Howard Good argues, in all of these films "journalism functions as a vehicle for exploring certain gender-based conflicts—career versus marriage, workplace versus home, co-workers versus family, freedom of the night versus middle-class domesticity."[7] Even Torchy at one point considers babies over stories.

So while these feisty dames get to occupy a man's world, they do so with a near-constant reminder that they are moving against society's grain. Their

Figure 8.4 Still from *Torchy Blane in Chinatown* (1939): Torchy (Glenda Farrell) lights up.

fight to keep going might indeed be a losing one, and the other side—marriage and stability and an escape from this dangerous man's world—is always calling them over.

Indeed, the girl reporter formula rests on a friction caused by two cultural desires bumping against one another: the need to keep women in—and reward them for—their position as mothers and wives, and the craving for women who exist outside of this role in a world where their femininity is redefined by courage and grit. The latter was more fantasy than reality, which is why it offered viewers such an exciting escape. But just as important as the girl reporter's bold evasion of gender separation is her temptation, even deep longing, to conform to that social order whereby she is eventually "freed" from the masculine realm in which she only temporarily played.

Not surprisingly, much scholarship on the girl reporter focuses on the inherent paradox in this character, what Verna Kale describes as an "irreconcilable tension between the independent, cosmopolitan, activist reporter and the glamour girl looking for a man to rescue her from her latest scrape—and, perhaps, from the profession entirely."[8] But critics debate the extent to which the films convey feminist versus conventional messages about gender.

Philip Hanson, for example, maintained that girl reporter films were typically "unwilling to pursue the questions they had uncovered."[9] Howard Good argues that Torchy Blane's "rapid fire repartee and man-tailored suits" belie her capitulation to male authority:

> Torchy herself isn't important, just a stereotypical brash blonde in a series of low-budget films. What Torchy represents, however, *is* important, and what she represents is ideology in motley, patriarchy in drag, oppression disguised as humor. She demonstrates the amazing (appalling?) ability of popular culture to ideologize and mystify even while it entertains.[10]

However, others point out that these kinds of criticisms tend to overemphasize the predictable aspects of the narratives at the expense of the groundbreaking qualities embodied in the girl reporter. As Kale writes, "Even if the heroine ultimately capitulates to male authority, the importance of the gesture is that she challenged it at all and that this challenge is a recognizable trope within its genre."[11] Indeed, that the girl reporter even resists marriage at all represents an irreversible signal of rebellion. Although she relents, the damage, as it were, is done. Philippa Gates notes that although Torchy Blane is at times tempted by marriage and domesticity, and perpetually deferring both in favor of her career, she is never shown to need rescuing by her male counterpart. Moreover, when the girl reporter does in the end choose marriage, Gates argues that such a conclusion is often "tacked on" and does not automatically represent a restoration of the social order: "the addition of a socially prescribed conclusion need not necessarily devalue the independence of the heroine in the rest of the narrative."[12] Overall, the Depression-era girl reporter, Gates writes, "can be seen to offer a decidedly feminist hero in that she defies the stereotype of the masculine (i.e. unnatural) woman; she is presented as a successful detective—catching the criminal—and a successful woman—attracting her investigative competition."[13]

But if the girl reporter of the 1930s revealed (and reflected) an emergent crack in women's primary role as wife and mother, then the girl reporter of the 1940s provided a sealant. While praising the pioneering features of her earlier character, Gates detects a thematic shift in the girl reporter, who by 1940, seemed less a heroine and more a warning to young women, becoming, as Gates writes, "a potential disruption to dominant masculinity."[14]

And it's true that *His Girl Friday* (Hawks 1940), which was an instant success at the box office, takes on a much darker tone than the earlier girl reporter films. It was essentially *The Front Page* rewritten to replace Hildy the man with Hildy a woman, played by Rosalind Russell. Early on Hildy declares to her editor and ex-husband Walter: "I wanna go where I can be a woman"—which is as far away as possible from the newspaper business. The film is in fact a rather cynical portrayal of journalism, which it shows to be as corrupt as the criminal world it covers. And so too is its treatment of the marriage plot. Although Hildy is the best reporter Walter has, she is desperate to live a "normal" life but proves utterly unable to do so. She can't help but be lured back into the world she rejects, and ultimately she leaves her well-meaning insurance-selling fiancé to remarry Walter. But it's not the happy ending we envisioned, because we know they are incapable of having a "normal" marriage. Their union is itself corrupt, and the ultimate message is: being a journalist means sacrificing your womanhood.

Though not nearly so ominous, *Woman of the Year* (Stevens 1942) similarly attempts to caution its viewers that bucking the status quo with gender-bending professions can have dire consequences. We are forever told that Tess Harding, an award-winning foreign correspondent played by Katharine Hepburn, is failing at being a wife to her more traditional sports writer husband Sam, played by Spencer Tracy. In fact, a great deal of the film is dedicated to these failings—directly caused by Tess's dedication to her job—culminating in the final scene when we see her miserably fail at cooking a simple breakfast as her husband looks on. Eventually he reassures her that she can meet him halfway, by being a loving wife *and* retaining some of her independence. But though it might have seemed like a generous compromise, what lingers in our minds is the disharmony that womanhood and career invariably creates.

Another stream of films from the era tried a different angle: to re-feminize the girl reporter. As men were being shipped abroad and women were needed to fill their shoes in the workplace, Hollywood was helping the war effort with positive portrayals showing women who didn't actually have to sacrifice their femininity when they temporarily entered the working arena. And so, this new girl reporter softened her edges. In many of the films of the early 1940s, we see a very watered-down version of women in the newspaper business, often playing more minor, certainly less dangerous, roles, and rarely fighting for the tough stories. Gates writes, "Suddenly, being brash, fast-talking, and masculine seemed out of style for a woman, and Hollywood's female detectives became more feminine in appearance, less ambitious in their careers, more desirous of marriage, less prominent in terms of screen time, and less respected by the male law enforcers."[15]

GIRL + REPORTER + BRENDA STARR + JOAN WOODBURY + 1945 = VERY MIXED MESSAGES

It is perhaps no surprise that *Brenda Starr* embodies the culminated contradictions inherent in both the girl reporter subgenre and the wider culture at the dawn of postwar American society. By the time Brenda hit the screen in 1945, audiences knew her type well, and Hollywood, with its allergy to risk, promised the same mixed messages about femininity to which everyone had become accustomed.

But Fox's *Brenda Starr, Reporter* is especially ambiguous, and its messages acutely mixed. As noted earlier, Woodbury's Brenda is different from most of her famous predecessors, like Torchy, Hildy, and Tess, and certainly from her comic strip original. And her difference is notable in one particular way: she is wholesome. She lacks their glamour and sexual edge. She is not curvy, or sassy, or cynical. She wears sensible clothes, a ruffled blouse and a bright smile (Figure 8.5). She can be witty but never cutting, and remains unfailingly lovely throughout every chapter. She is utterly dedicated to her job, which has no apparent downside, and you never get the sense that she'd bend morality for a scoop. She'd also never light a cigarette, and routinely practices that female trick whereby frustration is turned into a sweet smile.

It might be tempting to locate Brenda in that last group of the 1940s girl reporters who presented a feminine palliative to the fast-talking tough figures of the 1930s. But that wouldn't be quite fair. Because Brenda is ambitious and is the center of the story. And if her demeanor and wardrobe don't read "tough reporter," the script goes to great lengths to spell it out for us.

Figure 8.5 Original still from *Brenda Starr, Reporter* (1945): Brenda's hot on the trail of the missing payroll.

We are constantly hearing how "smart" and "daring" Brenda is, and how difficult it is to outdo her. One gangster says to another: "I gotta feeling that girl is going to bring us a lot of bad luck." He replies, "That Starr girl—she's dynamite." Pesky the office boy (William Benedict) tells the newspaper editor and Lt. Farrell: "Miss Brenda ain't scared. She told me many times she knows it's dangerous but she's gotta get the news!"

We can't be sure if it's a love of adventure or her fervent work ethic that keeps her on the hot pursuit of a story. Sometimes it's her survival instinct. We see Brenda ingeniously get out of dangerous situations, like when she slices open the exhaust pipe to let air into the backseat of a car where the bad guys are attempting to asphyxiate her.

Or we see her cheating death, as she does when she is lured alone into a deserted warehouse where gun-toting gangsters lurk. A gun fight ensues, at which Brenda proves competent, her photographer Chuck noting ironically, "This is the first time I've ever had a woman do my shooting for me."

Blindfolded in the front seat of a car driven by the most wanted gangster, Joe Heller—who is also assumed to be dead—Brenda is the vision of composure. And she only appears moderately discomposed as she attempts to flee the mobsters on her trail by hiding in a rock mine. Despite a sign that reads "DANGER, KEEP AWAY, EXPLOSIVES" *and* a man's voice calling out to her, "Get away from the tunnel! That tunnel is full of explosives and ready to go!" Brenda disappears into the cave. At the end of the episode, the voiceover asks viewers: "Can Brenda escape the horrible death of being buried alive in the tunnel?"

The following week, they see that the answer was yes. But only because Lt. Farrell went in to retrieve her. Draped over his arms is her unconscious body: the vision of the fair lady and her savior. Incidentally, it's also an image that Brenda mocks in an earlier scene when the police lieutenant tries to help her up after an explosion causes her to fall. "The gallant Lt. Farrell, all ready to help the fair lady," Brenda tells him sarcastically.

Brenda puts Lt. Farrell in his place at other times as well. For example, when she tells him that she has witnessed the supposedly dead Joe Heller, Lt. Farrell accuses of her of lying: "Now be sensible, Brenda. Now tell me the truth." To which she replies, "Look, Larry, I'm a newspaper woman. I deal in realities because I haven't got time for anything else."

And it's true: with all of this death-defying action, Brenda has little time for anything, including romance. While the standard girl reporter formula hinges on romantic tension—usually overtly pitting marriage against career—*Brenda Starr* nearly avoids that narrative altogether, as if the brevity of the serial form forced the writers to skip over the storyline that we anticipate with each episode but never manage to see. Brenda and Larry are forever locked in the professional rivalry that we expect in this genre—they have run-ins throughout, and seem perpetually perturbed by one another—but the serial is remarkably lacking in any romantic intrigue or allusions. In fact romance, never mind marriage, is never mentioned. Not once.

Nevertheless, Fox's *Brenda Starr* does manage to address the conflict between the domestic realm and the workplace that is at the heart of the girl reporter genre, but it does so from a slightly different angle. Unlike many films that portray the girl reporter's incompetence around the home as an ugly consequence of her devotion to career, Brenda's decidedly *anti*-domesticity is portrayed as a strength rather than a weakness. Amidst all the action are scenes in her apartment where she lives with her cousin, Abretha (Lottie Harrison), who is chubby and ditzy, and indeed very domestic. Through Abretha, domesticity seems rather unattractive and even unnecessary. She is the "housewife"—always doting on Brenda and scolding her maternally for putting herself in danger; the script seems to pokes fun at Abretha for being a little overweight and housebound, while Brenda appears sharp and self-possessed. In one scene, as Brenda reluctantly recovers on the couch from one of her recent escapades, her cousin enters carrying food:

ABRETHA: Here's something to delight your tummy, Cousin Brenda.
BRENDA: Thank you . . . two plates?
ABRETHA: (*sheepishly*) I thought I'd join you for just a little snack.
BRENDA: That's right—I forgot about your diet. Just a little snack.
Phone rings
ABRETHA: If that's the newspaper office, you're sick and you're staying here.
BRENDA: (*firmly, reaching for the phone*) Give it to me please.

Brenda, of course, gets her way, and Abretha is quieted. It's as if these women, with similar sounding names, are two halves of one female portrait—Abretha is the homely domestic spinster while Brenda is the comely career gal. In a sense, Abretha is Brenda's worst fear—an alter ego that she needs to beat down lest it takes over. She asserts herself as the man of the house, at one point telling her cousin, "You be a good girl and get us some coffee." Later, as she climbs in through her apartment window in an attempt to flee the bad guys, she admonishes Abretha for her hysteria: "Stop screaming!" she yells. We get the sense that Brenda might not only be yelling at her cousin, but at the female race in general (and perhaps her own repressed impulses?) for its inability to hold it together—and stay cool like the guys—in the face of danger.

It's a twist on the genre that this overt sexism comes directly from the heroine. Whereas other films often openly display the girl reporter's domestic ineptitude for us to gaze uncomfortably upon—think Katherine Hepburn struggling to make scrambled eggs in *Woman of the Year*—here the gaze is shifted from the girl reporter herself and directed at another (less attractive) woman—*not* because of her incompetence but for her very domesticity. The effect is to align the audience with Brenda in a conspiratorial scorn for the feminine domain and its unappealing effects. Either way, though—whether the woman is mocked for being too domestic or not domestic enough—the primacy of the masculine is preserved.

That the short chapters of the Brenda serial take on domestic life at all underscores Howard Good's point that journalism films are ultimately a means for "exploring certain gender-based conflicts." Loyal to the genre, Fox's serial manages to squeeze in scenes with the cousin (unfortunately, one extended scene still lacks audio) as if to remind the audience that Brenda's role as a crime reporter cannot be taken for granted; rather, it is fulfilled against the backdrop of women behaving like, well, women.

But if the cousin is a parody, an amplified stereotype whose bubbleheaded fussiness and need to diet make her the butt of a sexist joke, Brenda represents a type of parody—one of the "new women" who runs around acting like a man at work and at home. They are, in effect, two sides of the same coin.

Then again, these films do not treat the cousin's scatterbrained ways as uniquely feminine. In fact, Brenda's two male colleagues, Chuck the photographer and Pesky the office boy, are even flakier than Abretha; their dopey antics offer most of the serial's comic relief and a foil to Brenda, who is always asserting her control. At one point, as Brenda and Chuck approach a house where they believe the gangsters are hiding, Brenda sternly instructs him, "Be quiet and follow me." But once inside the house, Chuck manages to cause an explosion when he lights a match after they smell gas. Brenda later reprimands him like a child. Pesky, too, is childlike, especially in his inability to keep anything straight. When Brenda sends him to fetch her lunch—"vanilla ice cream with chocolate syrup and a hamburger with nothing on it but tomato ketchup"—Pesky returns with the order all mixed up—a hamburger with chocolate syrup and ice cream with tomato ketchup. It's a comical scene, of course, but one that also reinforces Brenda's masculine authority. If she plays "the man" to Abretha in the home, she also does so to these two man-children at work.

And yet the same time that Brenda is out there acting like a man, she is perpetually called a "good girl" (just as she told her cousin). The police sergeant Tim, frustrated by what he sees as Brenda's meddling in the case, tells her, "You stay right out here like a good little girl." Larry also tells her to be "a good girl." We know that Brenda will do no such thing, and nor do we want to chasten her. In the very final scene, when Brenda has cracked the case and recovered the payroll money, Larry leans over and kisses her on the head, and then says, "That's for being a good girl." It's the final line of the entire serial, after which Brenda is shown beaming at her desk. But it doesn't make a lot of sense, because Larry has continually fought and undermined Brenda's efforts to solve the case. She, not he, managed to recover the missing payroll, and to do so, she has acted in his eyes like anything but a "good girl."

Actually, more than anything else, this final scene—the kiss and the good girl remark—encapsulates the swirling contradictions of the Brenda Starr serial. One could argue that it is what Gates described as a "tacked-on" scene—not so much a necessary resolution to the plot as a gesture to the genre, as if Wallace Fox decided at last to quickly adhere to narrative conventions and throw in some romance. Within the plotline, the kiss doesn't logically follow what we have witnessed between Brenda and Larry. In fact, its inspiration is ambiguous. Is it even romantic at all? Perhaps it is simply a paternalistic kiss, which of course in the culture of the 1940s, could itself be a romantic expression. In any case, it provides no assurance that any liaison between the two is imminent, and nor does it signal the restoration of traditional gender roles. After all, Brenda is rewarded for her professional achievement—she proves she can outdo the police department. There is no indication that she will give up her role as a stellar reporter; if anything, it seems more secure.

Then again, sitting there at her desk smiling proudly after Lt. Farrell has kissed her, Brenda does look very much like a "good little girl." Void of the sex appeal, glamour, and grit possessed by her girl reporter forerunners, she is incapable of appearing cunning, much less naughty. Instead, she looks earnest and feminine, her glowing face framed by soft blonde curls. Brenda might be a daring reporter, but this final image of her as the innocent just-been-kissed girl could have the last word.

THEN AGAIN, IT'S JUST A SERIAL . . .

Theoretical approaches to film genre tend to focus on variations within genres—what makes individual films both normal to their genre *and* weird within it. Such variations, many have argued, reflect both the changing societal contexts in which films are produced over time, *and* the filmmakers' interest in feeding audiences' expectations while keeping them on their toes. Steve Neale's paradigm of repetition and difference, for example, posits that a genre becomes so both by repeating narrative tropes so as to be recognizable and predictable and at the same time subverting those conventions to be unique and continue to attract viewers. So, in order to remain commercially and aesthetically viable, *Brenda Starr*, for example, must be repetitive within the girl reporter genre, which it is, but also offer noticeable differences from that genre, which it does.[16]

Christian Metz saw variation within the lifespan of a genre whereby the various changes the genre undergoes in its evolution mark a series of "stages." The early stage, as the genre is establishing itself, is "experimental," the next stage, when the genre is in full swing, is "classical", and the third stage, as the genre is winding down, is "parody." The final stage, "deconstruction," is when the genre picks and chooses from other genres, forming a fusion variety. According to Metz's evolutionary model, *Brenda Starr* falls into the parodic stage, as it emerged in 1945 toward the end of the girl reporter genre.[17] As I pointed out earlier, there are plenty of evidently self-conscious elements of the serial that can be read as parody. Brenda's doting roommate-cousin constitutes a spoof of the genre's obsession with the girl reporter's domestic shortcomings; Pesky and Chuck and their airheaded antics seem to parody the formula of the sidekick in journalism—not only girl reporter films—who often provides some comic relief and highlights the main character's competence. Parody is of course only possible when an audience knows a genre well enough to be "in on the joke."

But the quirkiness of Fox's *Brenda Starr* might be accounted for as much by the fact that it was a serial production as by theories around genre. For one, Columbia Pictures, which produced it, was known for its playful content that tended to not take itself too seriously. As Roy Kinnard writes in his 1983 book *Fifty Years of Serial Thrills*, "Columbia's serial formula involved lighthearted gentle spoofing of the subject matter." Kinnard points to the *Batman and Robin* 15-episode serial (1949) which, like *Brenda*, was produced by Sam Katzman, for the way it playfully transforms—perhaps dumbs down?—the original material from the Batman comic book.[18]

Indeed, among Katzman's strategies was to mine successful material from other media, like comic strips, radio, and pulp fiction. *Brenda Starr, Reporter* was in fact his first such exploit, to be followed by *Hop Harrigan* (1946), *Congo Bill* (1948), and *Superman* (1948). Bottom line: on Katzman's watch, Columbia's serials contained few original heroes.

But though it proved profitable for a period—at least until serials were made obsolete by television—such a strategy has not earned critical praise. As Raymond Williams Stedman notes, "What Columbia was trying to do in the mid-1940s was trade upon—some would say tarnish—the reputations of heroes of other media," precisely because Katzman played so fast and loose with the original content.[19] Katzman seems to be now widely held as a prolific and tight-fisted producer who often compromised quality for output.

But such compromise is often seen in serials across the board, regardless of who produced them. Though treasured by some critics and film enthusiasts, serials were and still are often regarded as a lower film form, a now antique vehicle for discounted thrills. Kinnard's Introduction is a notably negative preamble for a book devoted to the subject:

> Cheaply and hastily produced, with their ludicrous plots, wooden heroes and cardboard sets, the serials were held in contempt by nearly everyone. They were the dumping ground for has-beens, the last refuge of the hack, the lowest common denominator in the studio equation.[20]

At the same time, however, Kinnard points out that serials were able to kick off careers of young actors, like John Wayne, and take on "subjects considered too outlandish for features."[21] Indeed, like other art forms deemed marginal and inferior, the serial had a certain freedom to bend the rules, to play with material that might be too risky for the more established (higher budget) forms. So, one could approach the serial, at least in theory, as a kind of scrappy, outlaw form.

On the other hand, when budgets are miniscule and profits essential, bending rules is usually not a result of creative expression. The economy of the serial form often necessitated the content. In the case of Katzman's productions that recycled well-known material and tropes, this meant offering a shorthand version of the original that could safely squeeze into thirty-minute installments with effective cliffhangers. In other words, the serials could abbreviate and simplify their stories because the audience could fill in the gaps.

So if we consider Fox's serial as a streamlined narrative within the girl reporter genre—missing key elements from the feature films like the marriage plot and explicit conflicts around gender roles—then the serial form may have made it so. The marriage plot is abridged—so abridged that it is practically non-existent—because the serial assumed that audiences knew the genre so well that the narrative motions of courtship would be redundant. A few key signals would suffice not only to satisfy expectations, but also to poke fun at those same expectations. Beautiful girl reporter, handsome police lieutenant, blah blah blah, the rest is history, let's focus on the action, shall we?

Serials were by their very nature all about action because the cliffhangers are so critical to their economic model. To get the audience to come back the following week you have to build suspense, and suspense and action go hand in hand. Of course you can create suspense with the stuff of soap operas—romance and betrayal—but serials needed to cater to wider audiences, often the younger audiences of Saturday afternoon matinees. Action casts a wider net; it is a universal language that everyone can understand and become emotionally invested in.

And perhaps therein lies the key to the full picture of *Brenda*'s strangeness. As a serial—as opposed to a comic or a feature film—*Brenda Starr, Reporter* needed to reach across age and gender demographics. It could do so first by exploiting the Brenda Starr name specifically and the girl reporter genre more generally, both of which were well known and bound to attract audiences. But in execution, it needed to deviate from both of those sources—for the simple reason that they were too grown-up—and instead adapt to the serial form with a more modest, i.e. kid-friendly, girl reporter who was less brash, wisecracking or sexual than many of her predecessors. This was also convenient in 1945, when the girl reporter as a Hollywood fixture was being re-feminized to suit the postwar cultural shift to more traditional gender roles. But within the serial model, the girl reporter also needed to partake in all of the thrilling and daring escapades as the superheroes and cowboys who were frequently portrayed in this form. In essence, Brenda was everything at once, and being so, was not quite anything in particular. She was, at heart, a copy that turned out to be rather original. And today, she can serve as a historical artifact that embodies all of the incongruity and resourcefulness of mid-twentieth century American popular culture. After all these years, it's good to have her back.

NOTES

1. Quoted in Boyd Magers, "Serial Report, Chapter Eight: Sam Katzman," *Western Clippings*, n.d. Available at <http://www.westernclippings.com/sr/serialreport_2009_08.shtml> (accessed April 9, 2018).
2. Leonard Maltin, "Brenda Starr, Reporter—Rescued!" *IndieWire*, March 16, 2011. Available at <http://www.indiewire.com/2011/03/brenda-starr-reporter-rescued-179116> (accessed April 9, 2018).
3. Geoff Mayer, *Encyclopedia of American Film Serials* (Jefferson, NC: McFarland, 2017), 56.
4. Janet Maslin, "Shields as Intrepid Reporter." Review of *Brenda Starr, Reporter*, directed by Wallace Fox. *New York Times*, April 19, 1992.
5. Verna Kale, "The Girl Reporter Gets Her Man: The Threat and Promise of Marriage in *His Girl Friday* and *Brenda Starr: Reporter*," *Journal of Popular Culture* 4:2 (2014), 343.
6. Philippa Gates, *Detecting Women: Gender and the Hollywood Detective Film* (Albany, NY: SUNY Press, 2011), 114.
7. Howard Good, *Girl Reporter: Gender, Journalism, and the Movies* (Lanham MD: Scarecrow Press, 1998), 30.
8. Kale, 343.
9. Philip Hanson, "The Feminine Image in Films of the Great Depression." *The Cambridge Quarterly* 32:2 (2003), 131.
10. Good, 115.
11. Kale, 341.
12. Gates, 131.
13. Ibid., 96.
14. Ibid., 136.
15. Ibid., 138.
16. For a full discussion on the repetition and difference paradigm, see Steve Neale, *Genre and Hollywood* (New York: Routledge, 2000).
17. See Christian Metz, *Language and Cinema*, trans. Donna Jean Umiker-Sebeok (The Hague: Mouton, 1974). English version of *Langage et cinema* (Paris: Larousse, 1971).
18. Roy Kinnard, *Fifty Years of Serial Thrills* (Lanham MD: Scarecrow Press, 1983), 101.
19. Raymond William Stedman, *The Serials: Suspense and Drama by Installment* (Norman: University of Oklahoma Press, 1977), 138.
20. Kinnard, 4.
21. Ibid., 4.

CHAPTER 9

Bathos in the Bowery

Phillip Sipiora

Wallace Fox was a prolific film director, having made eighty-four films in the space of only twenty-six years (1927–1953). Fox directed a wide range of B-movies, as this volume explores, but one of his most distinctive achievements was the *East Side Kids* (*ESK*) series, which I believe is a more complex accomplishment than is sometimes acknowledged.[1] It depicts Fox's representation of the boys of the bowery as somewhat charming depictions of juvenile delinquents and their daily encounters with the community, the police (who are dominant across the *ESK* series in maintaining social and cultural order) and, of course, their interactions with one another, which lead to interconnected, symbiotic narratives of social critique and entertainment value. As I. C. Jarvie argues, "The cinema is both a social and an aesthetic occasion, and these two aspects are intertwined since its social character may (affect) art; and its artistic effects may (affect) society."[2] Hence the essential bond between social structure(s) and aesthetic effects in creative film, especially cinema that explicitly examines popular culture as its subject matter. Entertainment is clearly a dominant purpose of these films, yet not all of them derive from an exact generic formula and, I would suggest, there are a range of social issues woven into the fabric of the films. Is social and legal reconciliation at film's end a goal or an inevitable by-product in the adjudication of these comedies? I do not believe that there is a simple assessment at hand, but I do think that there are strategic social purposes in play in these fine films. What holds the films together, individually and collectively, is the systematic integration of *bathos* and *pathos* as alternating, pulsating forces of energy that nourish narratives and serve as integral principles informing the *ESK* enterprise.

ESK was one of many films series to come out of Poverty Row, all of which worked with tiny budgets and very short shooting schedules, sometimes less than a week from beginning to end. It should be no surprise that plots are relatively simple with little explicit nuance.[3] My goal is to briefly explore four *ESK* films: *Bowery Blitzkrieg* (1941, hereafter *BB*), *Let's Get Tough!* (1942, hereafter *LGT*), *Smart Alecks* (1942, hereafter *SA*), and *'Neath Brooklyn Bridge* (1942, hereafter *NBB*). My focus is to identify the elements in these films that identify them as more than lightweight drama/comedy, revealing the challenges, humor, sadness, and social struggle(s) in the daily confrontation of urban characters in the early 1940s, many of them relatively young males. *Bathos*, colloquially described as "quirky chaos" or "daffy dizziness," is a hallmark of *BB* and other Fox films in the *ESK* series. Many scenes can be described as cascading parades of encounters that are superficial or serious (or a combination of both), which lead to the formulation of plots that, arguably, are more complicated than they may superficially appear to be. In terms of discourse, the *ESK* series is rampant with bursts of staccato dialogue, as well as copious conversations that are sober and, occasionally, semi-serious. Like all earnest comedy, the dialogue reveals an ebb and flow of relationships, intensity of language, and emotional outbursts that are critical to attract and maintain viewer interest. The effect(s) of *bathos* (hyperbole) are to ameliorate the significance and seriousness of the underlying issues: crime, social unrest, family relations, and other issues. *Bathos*, as a strategic *modus operandi*, allows Fox to be deftly aggressive in representing cultural and social values in conflict.

A CITY WITHIN A CITY

I believe that it is revealing for viewers to enter the lives and narratives of the characters in order to experience a deeper, empathetic understanding of motifs informing this cinematic world, which becomes our world, even if only for an hour. This connection between us and them is strategically important, according to Penelope Gilliatt: "The experience of the film *is* the experience of being this character."[4] Other commentators have suggested that viewers often surrender emotionally to characters and their circumstances as we enter a film as participants in order to fully identify with characters at a primal level. As James Linton has noted, actuated cinematic participation becomes a matter of *compulsion*: "The object of the filmmaker, then, becomes one of persuading us to cross the distance that separates us from the screen and to imaginatively enter the space of the screen world, experiencing vicariously the events that occur within that world. This is where the emotional aspect of film becomes important."[5] Film and sociology have an essential, natural connection, according to Sutherland and Feltey: "The core of any sociological curriculum examines film around four interrelated themes: 1) identity, 2) interaction, 3) inequality, and 4) institutions."[6] Oftentimes this experience of viewer empathy is considered "identification," as we relate to characters in ways unique to our own intellectual and emotional frame(s) of reference. This concept of "fore-having" (*Vorstruktur*) is an important part of the analytical architecture by which we interpret all experience.[7] However, identification further requires an active involvement that transcends mere sympathy and compassion and compels a level of self-analysis. As Edward Branigan argues,

> Identification . . . is not an attitude but a process of forming and reforming one's identity in comparison with or against something else . . . Identification deals with our emotional response, involvement, appreciation, empathy, catharsis (Aristotle), or feeling toward the film. Identification relates to our active participation with a text.[8]

I would add to this perspective the concept of *eunoia*, or the bonding between and among individuals based upon a shared attitude of "good will."[9] In terms of the *ESK* series, I think that it is important for viewers to desire positive outcomes for the characters with whom they identify, even though identification will vary, of course, from scene to scene and character to character. For example, Muggs McGinnis (Leo Gorcey) is not a particularly positive character in the early scenes as he bullies nearly everyone, but it is not uncommon for Muggs to grow on viewers as we see deeper into his character, particularly into the ways in which causes and effects begin to shape a pattern that explains, more or less, why he is, what he is, and what he does, which often is in service to his tenement boys and the larger community. Consequently, his developing portrait becomes an increasingly sympathetic depiction as we become more familiar with Muggs's point of view. I believe that it is important to recognize changing qualities of characters. As Branigan points out, interpretation can be limited if we tend to too quickly stabilize character, and reject their mutability and evolution: "Character is no longer a stable unity . . . but a function in the text which is constantly being split, shifted and reformed elsewhere."[10] There are, of course, many possible explanations for fluctuating characterization, yet the ethnic grounding of *BB* plays a role in character identification, since the series is set in America's most diverse city and the first half of the twentieth century was an especially vibrant period of immigration, especially from Western Europe. New York City, in particular, was teeming with migrants from the Emerald Isle and most of the boys of the bowery have Irish roots and surnames. There is an explicit representation of Irish-American characters, with only a very small number of characters, beyond the boys of the bowery and the police, who do not share this ethnic background.

Ethnicity therefore plays a role in the *ESK* films, although the nine *ESK* films that Fox directed do not feature, in a major way, foreign-born characters speaking a language other than English (with some limited exceptions, as in *LGT*). In speaking of ethnicity in the B-movies, Brian Taves notes,

> Unlike mainstream quickies, with their use of repetitious, formulaic genre stories, such as Westerns, ethnic films typically emphasized the group's traditional stories. Frequently the performers were not experienced movie players but non-professionals or stage actors identified with ethnic theater; the novelty of their film appearance served as a principal box-office draw.[11]

This reference is to Yiddish, Black, and Cantonese films, but I would suggest that there is strategic social understanding to be gained by exploring characterization in films like *BB* that is rich in Irish-American identification and values, as well as representative of lower middle-class and middle-class stratification in New York City in the early 1940s. Further, ethnic perspectives are intensified by spatial configurations, such as housing patterns. It is no coincidence that the four major characters in *BB*—Muggs, Danny, Tom, and Mary—live in the immediate area, close enough to intensify their evolving tensions and relationships. They form a non-blood family with a range of nuances and implications. In *LGT* Pops Stevens and his daughter Nora are separated from Danny and his family by a single floor and Glimpy and his mother also live in the same building. However, what binds together so many of the characters, beyond their proximity to one another, is their shared idioculture, which can be defined as "a system of knowledge, beliefs, behaviors, and customs shared by members of an interacting group to which members can refer and employ as the basis of further interaction."[12] This shared experience provides a level of cultural homogeneity and common values that reinforce group behavior and strengthen the resolve of its members. An idioculture can be small in size: for example, a narrow group of individuals (as in a juvenile gang), but it is an important configuration for reinforcing values and holding together a group. The tenement boys are an idioculture with its own sociolect of speech, a major distinguishing characteristic of the group. The group clearly does not speak like other adults, such as the police and shopkeepers. Each member of the group, of course, has their unique idiolect, which is one of the ways in which the East Side Kids endear themselves to audiences, whether it is the staccato (and bizarre) speech rhythms of Muggs or the mangled syntax and illogic in the idiolect of Glimpy (Huntz Hall).

BATHOS AND *PATHOS*

BB was Fox's first entry into the *ESK* arena and it is a powerful film as it delineates a series of challenging social and developmental issues in the heart of tenement New York City and its modest residents, who collectively grapple with the emerging war and a plethora of tensions, anxieties, and dimensions growing out of social distress. *Bowery Blitzkreig*, an apt title that captures connotations of "surprise" and "attack," offers a microcosm of New York's East Side as representative of a larger macrocosm of a threatening, dangerous environment. Not unlike the screwball comedies of the 1930s,[13] which offered comedic respite from the economic struggles of the nation, so, too, do Fox's *ESK* films provide distractions from stressful circumstances and challenges of daily living, especially in wartime. Similar to the social comedies of the 1930s, *ESK* films appeal to heterogenous audiences and the tenor of the films is farcical and buffoonish, with simple, linear plots. Yet some of Fox's *ESK* films are somewhat more serious (for example, *LGT*, which includes two deaths, international intrigue, and a complex narrative structure). I believe that a powerful thread of incongruity is woven into specific scenes and the overall narrative of Fox's films. More specifically, the use of incongruity infuses pulsating currents of solemnity and buffoonery which, arguably, make the films more compelling because they induce a dynamic rhythm from scene to scene, and sometimes within scenes. On one level, it may appear that these contrapuntal representations conflict with and undermine the rhythm and cadence of the story line. However, the interconnection of the comic with the serious facilitates deeper layers of interpretative penetration into critical social configurations and salient ethical values that undergird and inform the films. Underlying the conjunction of *bathos* and *pathos* is the principle of incongruity—things are not always quite what they seem. Incongruity has long been recognized as a normative principle of comedy, but it also plays a role in contouring grave issues in the films. Sometimes one focus dominates the other, but the two forces are co-important—they modulate and contextualize one another. Put simply, you cannot have *bathos* without *pathos* in *ESK* cinema. One recurring example is the complicated relationship between the tenement boys and the police. Although, theoretically, it is an adversarial relationship, there are indications from the very beginning that there are bonds between the boys and the police that transcend the explicit friendship of Officer Tom Brady (Warren Hull), a former Golden Gloves boxer. When Muggs agrees to represent the police department in the Golden Glove tournament, every officer in attendance visibly cheers for him. Muggs represents the police and they represent him, in kinship, as a member of their community, which transcends the boundaries of juvenile delinquency and law enforcement.

The work of Wallace Fox is a reminder that film, at all levels, can reveal strategic insights into contemporary cultures and subcultures with a plethora of social meaning exuding from popular cinema. Popular art, especially cinema, is laden with social significance, both lurking on the surface and embedded within deep structures, reflecting values, meanings, and interpretations that often are accessible only through the media of popular culture(s). As James Linton observes, "[O]ne central myth [that] dominates the world of fabricated fantasy [is] the idea that entertainment and recreation are value-free, have no point of view, and exist outside, so to speak, the social process."[14] *Bowery Blitzkreig*, an exemplar of popular culture, teems with "values" in a co-mixture of the silly and the serious, as illustrated by individual and collective responses to everyday disturbances in social and personal order. For example, when Muggs is sent to the reformatory, he abhors the decision and insults everyone with whom he comes into contact, including the matron of the reform school, whom Muggs nicknames "Pickle Puss," revealing his natural disrespect for authority. Yet, not surprisingly, the matron and Muggs reconcile later in the film, when "Pickle Puss" cheers him on with a wink and a smile when he is discharged from the reformatory. The inference to be drawn is that adversarial relations are often fleeting and ephemeral, lasing but for a moment and signifying little beyond the drift of the present. Antagonism is often instinctive and reactionary, neither logical nor based on any firmly established value system. Relationships are temporary, expedient, and evolving. Survival is the name of the game in the bowery. Juvenile delinquents and others need to be more than comic characters in their quest for endurance, as Wallace Fox demonstrates with probing insight and nuance. Indeed, characters need humanization, which Fox achieves with subtlety and precision. It was no coincidence that there are eleven *ESK* films (nine directed by Fox) and more than three-dozen movies from the 1930s well into the 1950s featuring many of the same characters.

Bowery Blitzkreig begins with a panoramic overview of New York City's architectural and transportation infrastructure, juxtaposed with dense scenes of citizens milling about on crowded streets. Plot and setting in the early scenes are carefully woven together in a generic urban perspective. Subsequent scenes become more personal—Danny Breslin (Bobby Jordan) boxes while "studying" from an economics textbook, revealing his complicated character. Danny is a "good kid" and his schoolteacher sister, Mary (Charlotte Henry), is engaged to Officer Tom Brady. Initially, Danny is depicted as temperamental, as revealed in his mercurial attitude toward Tom in early scenes, especially at dinner in the Breslin home with Mary and Tom. Danny is furious that Tom is investigating the reasons behind Danny's fight with Muggs and Danny tells his mother and sister that he "hates coppers." Mary blames Muggs for her subsequent fallout with Tom, yet this subplot is not developed, as is often the case in B-movie narratives. However, the main plot does focus, explicitly, on the personalities of the leading tenement boys. Danny, like the rest of his crew, often reverts to his instinctive role as a loyal member of the gang, which reveals the melodramatic and complicated nature of the boys.

LAW AND ORDER IN THE BOWERY

The opening panoramic city shots of *Bowery Blitzkreig* suggest urban tranquility (regardless of how congested the city actually is), while subsequent scenes personalize the narrative and introduce a major focus of interaction in the Bowery: the boys and the police. The relationship is sometimes friendly, however, and there are jovial officers, especially Tom. One of the other officers, early on, is disdainful of the bowery kids, taunting "They'll all wind up in jail." However, Tom, an unrelenting optimist, quickly responds, "What all kids need is to be taught . . . reform school is not the answer." This exchange calls attention to the eclectic attitudes of the police officers: some are instinctively antipathetic and others are more sympathetic to the street boys. This difference in attitude is a highly charged motif running through the film and leads to a series of encounters that can be viewed as pathetic (emotional attachment of compassion, pity) or bathetic (sentimentality, mawkishness, buffoonery, exaggeration). There are villains in *BB*, of course, including Monk (who later reveals his "good side" in confessing his wrongdoing). It is Monk who triggers the arrest of Muggs by calling the police to inform them of the fight between Muggs and Danny (Monk had lied to Danny about Muggs making salacious comments about Danny's sister). Officer Tom, in contrast to low-level punk and fixer Monk, is a softhearted, yet complicated character, but he truly cares for his tenement boys. For example, when the fight between Danny and Muggs is being investigated, Tom works as a peacemaker when the boys are brought to the precinct for questioning. The gang boys arrive with a swaggering air of authority—their default defensive posture—as they search for Muggs. This lighthearted (yet also semi-serious) scene reveals an air of playful social familiarity that subverts the motif that the police and the boys are steadfast antagonists. The boys call the officers by their first names, not necessarily to show disrespect, but rather to imply familiarity. Even though Muggs is considered to be the aggressor because Monk has instigated the fight between Danny and Muggs, Tom instinctively intervenes to seek a dismissal of the charges. And it is Tom who gives Muggs the Golden Gloves announcement in the jail and strongly encourages him to compete. Tom is an exemplary illustration of the merging of social and ethical forces into the tapestry of the tenement, where unrestrained juvenile impulses and desires so powerfully influence antisocial behavior and necessarily facilitate police reaction(s).

The *ESK* films of Wallace Fox, I would suggest, illustrate not only the complexity of the characters and their environment(s), but also explore how "city life" itself is, inherently, an entangled mixture of the farcical and the solemn. Troublesome situations oftentimes have an underside of humor, and comic representations embedded within them often trigger consequential reactions, for example, Slats Morrison (Eddie Foster) hiding a bribe of $1,000 in Muggs's possessions to throw the boxing match, which allows Slats the opportunity to frame Muggs. There are, of course, numerous examples of vaudevillian *bathos*, such as the boxing trainer fainting at the sight of blood, another example of the oxymoronic as an integral part of bowery humor.

One of the effects of *bathos*, as hyperbole, is to ameliorate the significance and seriousness of the underlying issues: crime, social unrest, family relations. Thus *bathos*, as excess, allows Fox to be aggressive and tensile in representing cultural and social values. Conversely *pathos*, as sympathetic identification, allows Fox to tell his story as a rich conundrum of incongruity—the comic and the serious melded together in the cauldron of the Bowery where, sometimes, the effects are neither predictable nor stable. Yet the manifest characteristic of *ESK* films that is worth exploring is the intertwining of *bathos* and *pathos*, which is the warp and woof of the series. Bathetic scenes call attention to the boring mediocrity of daily life in the bowery yet, simultaneously, allow viewers to distance themselves from the frightening underside of life in wartime 1940s. Pathetic motifs, scenes, and characters are uplifting in presenting a vista that rises above the tonality of living from day to day in dealing with life's challenges and frustrations. Examples abound in clubhouse scenes and elsewhere where displays of verbal theatrics are a mainstay of daily rituals in the bowery. The first order of business of the boys of the bowery is survival and street reputation, which are always conditioned and configured by the pragmatic contexts of circumstances.

Figure 9.1 Survival and street reputation.

ETHICS, *ETHOS*, AND VALUES

Ethics is a major motif in *BB* and "toughness," ethics, and *ethos* are closely interrelated too, in particular because *ethos* has long meant character and the values that are explicitly represented by character. In Antiquity, ethics was commonly conjoined with *ethos*: characters literally wear their ethics as a turtle wears a shell. In drawing upon Martin Heidegger, William McNeill elaborates on the symbiotic relationship between *ethos* and ethics in summarizing Heidegger's drawing upon the historian Herodotus (c. 484–c. 425 BCE): *Ethos* is a "fundamentally historical abode, whose beginning is already a stretching forth."[17] The metaphor of "stretching" is critical here because it invokes a dynamic, pliant scope in the art and act of living ethically, which is not an inert action but rather a performative configuration that necessarily depends upon contexts, connections, and various exigencies of particular places and times. *Ethos* and ethics are more than abstractions and nowhere is this more apparent that in the *ESK* series, where daily ethical decisions are determined by circumstances and the evolving values of characters. According to Heidegger,

> *Ethos* means a . . . dwelling place. The word names the open region in which man dwells. The open region of his abode allows what pertains to man's essence, and what in thus arriving resides in nearness to him, to appear. The abode of man contains and preserves the advent of what belongs to man in his essence.[18]

Thus the very essence of the boys of the bowery is defined by their actions, which is their determinative dwelling place. Every scene dramatizes encounters in which the boys illustrate their ethics through their *ethoi.*[19] As the boys function in their daily lives, especially in their clubhouse, and then take to the streets in their misadventures, their individual (and collective) "essences" become manifest in their roles as tough guys, buffoons, and social commentators. Muggs's donating a pint of blood to save Danny's life and his subsequent performance in the climactic Golden Gloves tournament is reflective of Muggs's abode—it defines what and who he is and reveals a rife expression of his character by his acts.

Muggs is an exemplar of an enchanting punk-thug, who carries his *ethos* on his sleeve as a well-known street brawler whose reputation precedes him wherever he goes. He is tough, as revealed in the opening scene when he throttles Monk Martin (Bobby Stone). Muggs's introduction to viewers begins with him throwing Monk into the street, landing punches to Monk's head, much to the approbation of Muggs's devoted delinquents. What is ironic, however—and illustrates the underlying structural principle of dual conflict in *BB*—is what Muggs does after beating his victim: He immediately attends to Monk's facial injuries. So, first brutality and then compassion, revealing an ethical vein running deep within Muggs's bully exterior. This introductory scene is a synecdoche for many of the scenes in the film as it demonstrates not only the bifurcated nature of characters, especially Muggs, but also reveals a double-layered, social network in place. Nothing is quite what it seems to be, at least initially, and relationships and attitudes vacillate from minute to minute. The "abode of man" contains and preserves the advent of what belongs to individuals in their essence. The turtle and the shell are one.

Cinema is a potent medium and the *ESK* tales provide penetrating insight into a vibrant, resonant sociological infrastructure—but the viewer must earn the meaning. An emphasis on the microcosm of the East Side is representative of a larger, expanding macrocosm, especially the unfettered and oftentimes displaced energy of young males of the 1940s (and earlier, going back to the "Dead End Kids" of the late 1930s). The full cycle of films dramatizes the impulsivity of raw youth in which self-control is often absent. Their behavior is usually reactive, impetuous, and instinctive, which characterizes many, but not all, of the juvenile delinquents. Exceptions are Clancy (Keye Luke), an Asian-American, and Scruno (Sunshine Sammy Morrison), an African-American, who are both full-fledged members of the gang but fit into a softer category of juvenile delinquency. By contrast, Muggs is a leading illustration of the prototype boy-thug; however, even Muggs has a soft, flexible inner lining in his psychological inscape. For example, he is reactively hostile to the police, yet he readily embraces them when they show their support for his amateur boxing career, supporting him in the local Golden Gloves tournament. Muggs beams with pride when he is announced as sponsored by the Policeman's Athletic Club. This change of perspective is not meant to suggest that Muggs and his crowd are inherently intractable without interest larger than themselves and their group. However, it does suggest that their collective mercurial nature illustrates an inherent instability as they often respond reflexively to circumstances without much thought given to immediate consequences.

SOCIAL CONTEXT

In film there would seem to be an overall social structure of the community and the communal relationships between and among its constituent elements. As Don D. Smith argues,

> In its social accuracy . . . film carries cogent lessons, even if unintentional, on social stratification, interpersonal relationships, the exercise of power in small group, communication in formal and informal settings, social organization and personality–social structure, to say nothing of marriage and family.[20]

The complex relationships within the tenement boys' social networks offer a range of cogent lessons that tell us much about how their community functions. Arguably, the sociology of the bowery offers an analytical method that grows out of other disciplinary approaches to cultural interpretation. In speaking of the emergence of sociology in interpreting art, Hauser observes that sociology plays a significant role in interpretation that was previously restricted to other disciplines, particularly philosophy and religion: "Art has this new orientation (sociology) to thank for the growing consciousness that it enjoys a unity with the rest of the cultural structures."[21] Muggs is a wisecracking social predator who sometimes, but not always, takes advantage of others in a variety of encounters. For example, when Muggs becomes thirsty he sees Clancy selling beverages and steals a nickel from Clancy, then uses it to pay for a bottle of soda pop (already opened by Muggs). This scene is playful, yet also reveals a serious, metaphorical portrait. In *LGT*, Scruno (Sunshine Sammy Morrison) is a highly visible minority member of the gang, who participates in most scenes, and one of his major functions is to serve as a lookout at the espionage meeting place. Scruno is not portrayed as being as aggressive or as delinquent as the more hardened members of the gang. The presence of Clancy and Scruno provides a more balanced view of the East Side Street for reasons beyond ethnicity. A group that is not exclusively homogenous adds humor (Clancy is amazingly glib, speaking like a poet at times), and Scruno is accepted by Muggs as a senior advisor (for example, in his advocacy for prayer when Danny is shot in *Smart Alecks*, which convinces tough guy Muggs to break down in prayer, a rare scene indeed.)

"President" Muggs, however, is the unchallenged bossman of the gang as well as a headstrong juvenile delinquent, even if the stakes are low and only a nickel is at stake; his theft of Clancy's money illustrates Muggs's *ethos* in small, yet revealing ways. The puny theft, like so many incidents in the film, is treated comically as "Muggs being Muggs," but it reveals his natural predatory instincts and, most important, the acceptance of them in his cultural circle, including the victim's acquiescence. What de-emphasizes the act of theft is that everyone, especially Clancy, shrugs off the pilfering as a familiar (and acceptable) part of bowery living. The social scales tilt the ethical scales. It is not unreasonable to dismiss these types of juvenile pranks as the quirky chaos of tenement living, but they do reveal salient codes of the community, which illustrates a complexity that may not be superficially observable. Another example of more serious bowery thievery involves Monk's robbery, in which Danny participates as the getaway driver in *BB*. Danny has been mesmerized by Monk's flashy car, flush wallet, and grand style of living. None of the other boys appears to own a car, much less a very expensive convertible. The most significant example of public social corruption in the community, however, is when mobster Dorgan (Dennis Moore) pays Slats to throw the Golden Gloves bout by bribing Muggs with a thousand dollars, hidden by Slats among Muggs's personal belongings. Muggs refuses to throw the bout, of course, and fights so hard that he knocks out Ryan (Bill Cartledge) for the TKO, after which Muggs collapses from exhaustion. Hence the ethical scale has been preserved and the film ends on the "right side" of things as Dorgan is arrested and Muggs and Danny are adjudicated as "good boys" after all. Even Monk proves his *ethos* by penning a confession of his troublemaking, right before he is killed by Tom in the shootout.

CODES AND VALUES

All art obviously reflects life as artists subjectively perceive it, and cinematic art is reliably aggressive in the interrogation and exposition of values, whether individual attitudes and beliefs or community-held standards of values, which tell viewers what is "normal" and within the bounds of the acceptable as behavior conforms (or not) to the local mores of the community. As Hauser observes:

> Art forms the substratum of normative aesthetic behavior just as long as it remains related to the *totality* of concrete, practical, and undivided life, as long as it is the vehicle of expression and the medium of empathy for the "whole person," and as long as it can embrace the sum of experience, which results from existential practice and remains capable of including all these in the homogenous forms of its statements. The true aesthetic phenomenon is the whole experience of the *totality of life* [my emphasis].[22]

This emphasis on lived experience can be seen in the ways in which Fox meshes multiple spheres of community interaction: the boy-to-boy social structure, the relationship(s) between the delinquents and the police, and the connections between and among individuals and families. Officer Tom is a compassionate man by nature. In speaking of all the tenement boys, Tom says to his fiancée, Mary: "Every one of those kids deserves a break." Tom proves himself to be a serious and warmhearted man as he makes the decision to take Muggs into the home that he shares with his mother, Ma Brady (Martha Wentworth). Tom's avuncular, kind gesture is a significant act of social and ethical commitment. Tom and his mother both strongly believe that: 1) Muggs is essentially a "good boy"; and 2) all that Muggs needs to straighten out his life is a stable home. This explicit demonstration of compassion does not come without a price, however, as Tom's relationship with Mary suffers, at least temporarily, because of Muggs's arrival to live in their tiny apartment. Tom's generosity, therefore, reveals an important value in his personal code of living: help others when it is within your means to do so. Thus *pathos*, intertwined with ethics, is once again demonstrated to be an integral part of the infrastructure of *BB*, so very important in the depiction of bowery characters in their struggle for survival: "What is of primary importance is . . . their common participation in the human endeavor to come to terms with reality and survive in the struggle for existence," writes Hauser.[23] The dialogue throughout *BB* also reveals the flow of the social dynamic. When Muggs is brought to the police station to be questioned about his fight with Danny, he responds to the precinct officer: "Hold your sermon, Copper. I'm Thirsty." This brief encounter shows a playful kind of disrespect, certainly a deep-seated familiarity, and there is similar banter throughout the film. The boys of the bowery are the "wiseguys" of the 1940s and there is much evidence that *BB* goes far beyond a struggle for survival. Indeed, the film concludes in a manner not unlike a Shakespearean comedy: Muggs's opponent, Johnny Ryan, is conquered in the ring as Muggs wins the Golden Gloves championship event, even though Muggs risks his life by fighting with less than a full tank of blood (he has provided a transfusion right before the big bout, in order to save Danny's life). Muggs knows that he is endangering himself but he does not care—friendship and loyalty transcend all else. In true Shakespearean style, Muggs holds the championship trophy, Danny is recovering from his shooting, and Tom and Mary will marry—with Muggs wearing silk as the best man! Like all resounding, serious cinema, there is an ebb and flow in *BB*, perhaps best represented at the film's end by Muggs's epiphanic conversion to save a loyal friend. A happy ending on all counts.

TOUGH TIMES: THE SOLEMN AND THE ZANY

Let's Get Tough! was made in 1942. *In BB*, farce and buffoonery drive the plot. In *LGT*, the solemn narrative drives the burlesque staging. So, in the sense of tone and balance, the two films are different. *LGT* is, arguably, a more sobering film as it chronicles the early days of World War II. Yet, the comic behavior that explicitly characterizes *BB* is also in force in *LGT*, although a little more subdued in natural deference to the seriousness of the story. The film opens with a military parade, evoking patriotism at a time when the nation was obviously suffering extreme anxiety following the attack on Pearl Harbor. Wallace Fox adroitly addresses these circumstances head on, with a constant stream of buffoonery that we have seen in *BB*. The plot is relatively simple. After Pearl Harbor is attacked, the tenement boys desperately try to enlist in the military, but no branch of the service will take them, principally because they appear to be too young and do not have identification. So, they attempt to enlist in the Army, Navy, and Marines, with no success. Their interviews with recruiters are rife with the verbal buffoonery and typical farcical antics that viewers are accustomed to. The recruiters are receptive to the boys (they accept them as members of the community, not unlike the attitude of some of the police in *BB*) and as soon as they realize that the boys are too young to be taken seriously, the desk officers join in the verbal theatrics, participating in the lighthearted give-and-take of the moment because they know that the boys are well-intentioned patriots. Yet soon the plot complicates when Phil Connors (Tom Brown), who is Danny's brother and a naval soldier, enters the scene. And, expectedly, there is a beautiful young woman, Nora Stevens (Florence Rice), stunning in her military uniform and deeply in love with Phil. This love story is, of course, a staple subplot in bowery episodes, similar to Mary and Tom in *BB*. Romance, as portrayed in *ESK* films, often exemplifies mid-century American melodrama.

The main plot is not without complication as the boys attempt to infiltrate the sabotage ring, the Black Dragon Society, led by Japanese spies Joe Matsui Sr. and Jr. (Philip Ahn playing both), and a German accomplice, Fritz Heinbach (Gabriel Dell). The story is a crime drama—yet there is a critical inversion in the plot resolution. In this international criminal tale, the boys of the bowery prove to be the masters of detection in the bowery, far superior to their professional counterparts in the NYPD. For example, Glimpy steals the pen with the all-important sabotage message from Joe Matsui Jr., which opens the door for the resolution of the case, and Danny shrewdly calculates that the unseen message can be decoded with a light source beneath it, which proves to be true. Yet the police continue to fumble and stumble in their bumbling investigation. Before the film is at the halfway mark, Muggs tells Officer Pops Stevens about the spy ring, but the officer doubts that Muggs has anything serious to offer police investigators. The boys, however, are sharp-eyed and they accuse conspirator shopkeeper Heinbach of hiding a Japanese saboteur in the back room of his second-hand store. And they are right. The boys are relentless in pursuing every angle to investigate the sabotage ring, including surveilling the headquarters of the conspiracy, the Matsui Tea Shop. The conspirators are revealed to be a considerable number; more than a dozen hooded members attend the meeting infiltrated by the boys. The young spy hunters are led by Muggs, of course, and the police are far behind the boys in figuring out exactly what is going on with the saboteurs in their own neighborhood. This film serves many purposes but is clearly a propaganda vehicle, as was common throughout World War II.

There is a layering of subplots in *LGT*, including the up-and-down relationship between Phil and Nora, reminiscent of the on-and-off relationship between Tom and Mary in *BB*. However, it is the comic schemes and scenes that steal the day in this film, as they often do across the *ESK* series. For example, one

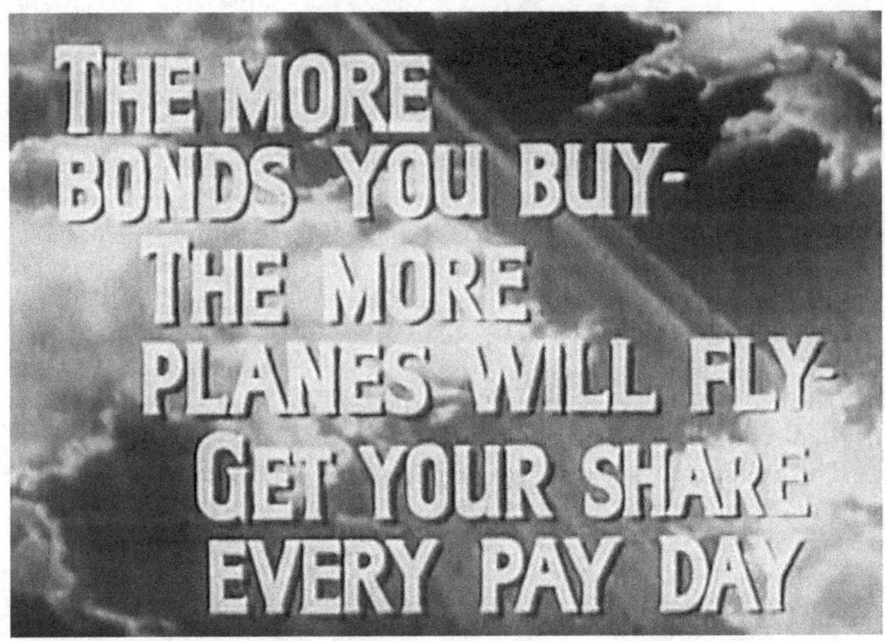

Figure 9.2 Popular art and nationalism.

of the most farcical scenes in *LGT* occurs when Glimpy is given an extensive violin lesson by a music master (Jerry Bergen) who bears a striking similarity to Moe Howard (Moses Harry Horwitz) of *The Three Stooges*, complete with ridiculous wig accompanied by absurd antics and facial expressions (Figure 9.3). The musical burlesque scene runs nearly four minutes, a significant allotment of time in a sixty-one minute film. This elongated scene provides a respite from the very serious plot of espionage and national crisis. Following Glimpy's buffoonery, in an act of compassion the boys pawn the violin to buy flowers for Mrs. Keno, the wife of a Chinese store owner who is found dead in his store. So, mistaken identity—confusing a Chinese shopkeeper with a Japanese store owner—adds to the complication of the plot and is reminiscent of a common motif of mistaken identity in Shakespeare's comedies, such as Falstaff of the chronicle plays, *A Midsummer Night's Dream*, and *The Merchant of Venice*. Shakespeare and Fox, to a certain extent, achieve a common effect: influencing the perspective and emotions of the audience. In the case of Mr. Keno, his Chinese identity cost him his life, thus sensitizing the audience to the serious and pernicious realities of ethnic conflicts embedded within a nation at war. Fox and Shakespeare are very interested in the complications of love and Phil's mistaken identity as a Japanese spy creates the dynamics of abandonment that turn into ideal love once Nora recognizes Phil's true identity as a patriot. Similarly,

Figure 9.3 Maestro Glimpy.

Nora Stevens has something in common with Portia in *The Merchant of Venice*. Such complications of identity in drama and film surely intensify and enrich their respective narratives.

The narrative is an entanglement of intertwined plot segments. The violin case, for example, contains magnesium (an explosive compound often used in sabotage). The magnesium becomes prima facie evidence of subversive war materials, which is discovered quite by accident in a comic scene in which the magnesium ignites on the stove of Glimpy's mother, initiating a fire farce. More buffoonery ensues as "Ma Glimpy" (Patsy Moran) is frightened by the explosion and chases away the boys, using her mop as a farcical weapon.

The plot thickens as Phil is now believed to be a Japanese agent and Nora is taken hostage by the saboteurs in the Tea Shop. The gang's entry to the building is comical and complicated, as they attempt various means to ascend to the upper story, first using their bodies as a climbing platform, which cannot support the weight of each boy. They then use boxes and Muggs successfully reaches the upper floor. The street boys reveal, once again, their readiness to adapt to changing citrumstances.[24] It is essential to Fox's comedic plan to continue to use farce throughout the film and there are no scenes without comic elements. The ongoing burlesque infrastructure reminds viewers that *ESK* films should be considered in totality—lighthearted yet always with serious undertones—in order to create a composite portrait of tenement life in its rich intellectual, emotional, and physical diversity. Clownishness is often coupled with a weighty plot as a complex amalgamation of *bathos* and *pathos* to tell a fulsome story.

The main plot segment that controls the outcome of the narrative involves the substantial scenes in which the boys enter Matsui's building and hide upstairs above where the secret meeting is being held. The infiltration scenes are especially long, taking up nearly ten minutes of the film. Once safely ensconced upstairs, the boys engage in comic bowing to two conspirators and descend to the master meeting room wearing robes and facial hoods in order to blend in with the saboteurs. Stereotypical (and propagandistic) gestures take place, such as rubbing the statue of an iconic figure upon entering the conspiracy setting, as well as the use of conspiratorial phrases in conjunction with an Axis speech condemning democracy and calling for all saboteurs to "strangle democracy." Serious language, indeed, for a film heavily informed by travesty, yet there is an important dialectic in play.

"A LANGUAGE IS A DIALECT WITH AN ARMY AND NAVY"—MAX WEINREICH[25]

Dialogue, as a form of dialectic, catalyzes the air of tension that envelopes physical encounters and conversations across the spectrum in all *ESK* films. In speaking of dialectic, Hauser has observed, "We have to understand sociology from the beginning as a dialectical doctrine pure and simple," since "[h]istorically conditioned attitudes are at the most more unmistakably involved in dialectical antinomies, their conflict and their reconciliation, than thinking, which is related to practice and critically established action in general."[26] One colloquial illustration of the role dialogue plays in representing social values and conflict is the scene early in *BB* at the clubhouse when Muggs and Tom discuss Freddy Flynn, a local boxer, scheduled to be executed that evening. The point of the discussion is that the office is trying to use dialogue to convince Muggs that crime catches up with criminals. Muggs rejects the advice and prefers to listen to Slats Morrison (Eddie Foster), a career criminal with a golden tongue. Slats proudly brags to Muggs that he only completed the third grade, a testimony to his intellectual and cultural acumen.

International espionage is, of course, more serious character mettle than clubhouse discussions of local criminals, and dialogic exposition becomes very serious in *LGT* at the Tea Shop when the saboteurs take an oath of fidelity and their wrists are cut to draw sacred blood, proof of their commitment to the cause. Soon after, the saboteurs are confronted by Phil, and the leader of the conspirators commits suicide by stabbing himself, precipitating the beginning of the end of this morality play. Good has essentially won over evil, even though Heinbach attempts to rouse his remaining Japanese allies one last time with German invective, an impassioned *cri de couer*—and a scene not without consequential, slapstick *bathos*. Nora is rescued and the police soon arrive to find that the tenement boys have rendered unconscious (or worse) the saboteurs, all neatly piled together in the meeting room, with Muggs presiding over the scene as Glimpy dutifully bangs the royal gong announcing "Emperor Muggs" in his regal robes. Once again, Fox produces a closing scene bathed in *bathos*—and the boys of the bowery demonstrate a general system of logic and reason underlying their spontaneous and (often) illogical words and actions. There is a guidance system, a collective matrix of thinking that influences what they say and do. One aspect of their collective sensibility is an instinctive tendency to respond aggressively to any situation that confronts them. In the streets and crevices of the tenement, to live passively is to open oneself to aggression from the outside. Far better, according to bowery mores, to confront trouble with trouble, whether the means are fists or fighting words or, as is common, comic responses that oftentimes defuse threatening situations. Each boy is an army of metaphors that comes together with the rest of the gang to form a giant organism that provides a cogent peek into the mindset and behavioral orientation of disciplined street boys as they defeat the Axis saboteurs. The film ends with Nora and Phil getting married. However, Phil is ordered to report back to his base as soon as possible, thus deferring their honeymoon. At this point, however, the marital announcement is more important than its consummation, signifying, once again, a happy (and appropriate) ending.

WISEGUY CULTURE

Smart Alecks makes its mark on the series by featuring a shift in perspective that is not emphasized in many other *ESK* films. *LGT*, as we have seen, begins with the boys witnessing a military parade, which motivates them to enlist immediately. *SA* begins with the soundtrack, "Take Me Out Ball Game," set against a giant mural of a baseball team on the field—an explicit tribute (and reminder) of American culture, as the film is intended as an example of propaganda, like so many movies made in the early 1940s. The opening scene features Scruno tap dancing to Glimpy's harmonica as the boys attempt to raise money from passers-by. This scene is relatively long (more than a full minute) and it serves at least two purposes: 1) It features Scruno in a solo performance (the shot begins with the camera directed at his feet), who is deeply admired by his yellow gang members (Glimpy's harmonica playing is necessary but he is merely a sideshow performer); and 2) It foreshadows Scruno's enhanced role.

The other boys, especially Muggs, now actively seek Scruno's participation in the gang's conversations and decisions. In *SA*, Scruno has more "airtime" than in other films now he has achieved senior status in the gang's hierarchy. For example, when the boys are held in the city jail, Muggs speaks directly to Scruno about their incarceration and ways of dealing with it. Muggs then asks Glimpy to play a few chords on his harmonica, wherein Scruno proceeds to lift the boys' spirits with ten seconds of tap dancing, of which only he is capable. It is explicit in *SA* that Scruno is now one of the four prominent characters, along with Muggs, Glimpy, and Danny.

The plot of *SA* is rife with violence, not uncommon in *ESK* narratives (there are three deaths in *LGT* and in *BB* Monk Martin is shot and killed by Tom after Monk shoots Danny at close range). Morley the mobster is killed in *SA*, and this sequence of actions precipitates the savage beating that Danny receives. The plot of *SA* is less complicated than that of *BB* or *LGT*. Ruth Jordan (Gale Storm) is Danny's sister, a nurse, and girlfriend of Joe Reagan.[27] One of the older, more experienced tenement boys, Hank Salko (Gabriel Dell), is a lookout for two hardened criminals, Butch Brocalli (Maxie Rosenbloom) and his unnamed enforcer when they rob a bank. Hank is caught by policeman Joe Reagan (Roger Pryor) and is taken to jail awaiting adjudication. Meanwhile, Butch and his henchman are hiding in Ruth's apartment awaiting her return and they imprison her when she comes home. Joe hears the noise in the hall and draws his weapon. The boys show up and come to the rescue through the upstairs window, subduing both criminals. Hank then knocks out Butch's henchman on the rooftop. In saving his sister, Danny catches Butch, who is arrested, and Danny is awarded two hundred dollars for his valor, which is where the trouble begins for the gang, since the boys expect Danny to share his money with them. Danny refuses, so the boys steal the money from Danny's apartment. Ruth calls Joe, who then arrests the gang. The theft is easy for the tenement boys since the clubhouse is near Ruth's apartment, reinforcing the social configuration of major characters living very close together. However, once the criminals are released, they viciously beat Danny, who requires immediate surgery to keep him alive. A benevolent brain surgeon, Dr. Ormsby, comes to the rescue and not only saves Danny's life but helps him recovers so well that he will now join the gang's baseball team, whose new uniforms are provided by Dr. Ormsby. A simple plot but not without valuable nuance.

This narrative summary contains manifold illustrations of the kind of *bathos* and *pathos* that we have seen in *BB* and *LGT*. However, stakes of the narrative are intensified by the bizarre cake scene near the beginning of the film (Figure 9.4). Butch forces his way into Ruth's apartment after she has baked a cake for the boys. Butch sees the cake and begins stuffing it into his mouth, giving viewers a face full of farce. The boys appear in the middle of the clown scene and they quickly seize advantage of Butch's gluttony by offering

Figure 9.4 Cake farce.

to add frosting to the remaining cake, since he complains that it is insufficient. Out of sight, the boys proceed to creating a frosting made out of soap and other chemicals. Butch greedily devours the rest of the cake and becomes sickened, so the boys throw him into the hall. What this comic scene accomplishes is to reduce the seriousness of the main criminal in the film and, simultaneously, create empathy for Danny and Hank. The counterforce of serious criminality has been diminished, at least momentarily, by playful farce. Butch is a buffoon underneath a rough exterior. Danny's fate, however, is the crux of the film as nearly everyone is intertwined in his struggle for survival: the police, medical community, the boys, and, of course, Ruth.

The viewer's vicarious connection with Danny's fate has an effect, both physiologically and emotionally: most viewers are predisposed to positive outcomes for empathetic characters and this natural reaction is *pathos*. However, the pathetic environment is in place prior to Danny's medical recovery. As Muggs prattles on about the gang's plight and what to do about Danny, Scruno attempts to bolster social reconciliation when he mildly rebukes Muggs, "You talk a whole lot just to hear yourself talk." Scruno, in scenes like this one, illustrates his elevation to a leader, a wise member of the gang. His words have gravity and the other boys respectfully listen to him. Earlier, when the boys worry about Danny's chances of recovery, Scruno remarks: "I believe that this business of praying pays dividends." However, when the boys speculate about Danny's situation turning dire, Scruno plants a more persuasive seed in Muggs's mind: "Maybe we oughta do what Danny does, pray." Muggs is quite moved by Scruno's suggestion and he does something that is very out of character. He stands in the darkened clubhouse, takes off his hat, looks at the light coming in through the window, and then bows and prays:

> Listen Lord, dear Lord, I don't want to ask you no favors because you don't owe me nothing. I never did nothing for you . . . I just want you to do this little thing for a friend of mine, Danny. He's pretty sick now, maybe too sick to pray for himself. You gotta pull him through, Lord. That's all.

Muggs is weeping profusely as Joe then walks into the room to bring the boys to the hospital. Such a display of emotional support from Muggs is a groundbreaking moment in the film as it dramatizes the intense social and emotional bonds among the boys.

As we have seen, identification becomes an integral part of the sociology of *ESK* films. Ruth is sympathetic to the boys and she tells the precinct captain that they should not have been arrested. One of the more explicit illustrations of Joe's emerging identification with the boys is his increasing sympathy for their struggles. Joe is not unlike Officer Tom in *BB*, except that Tom displays natural empathy for the tenement boys from the very beginning. Joe, on the contrary, is initially stern in his demeanor as he enforces the law, as he is trained to do, but then his attitude evolves as he comes to know the boys, coupled, of course, with his growing relationship with Ruth. In a moving scene late in the film, Joe proudly announces to the team that Hank has been cleared of all charges and is now free to play on their baseball team. The hospital scene is a good example of different idiocultures and idiolects coming together, from the surgeon to the nurse to the police to the boys, and they all gather in a spirit of unity in celebrating Danny's survival. Further, the interactions in the hospital reveal how concentric circles of idioculture interact with one another in synergistic ways to create an interpretive whole that is greater than the sum of its parts. Fox's directorial prowess comes through extraordinarily well in these scenes.

However, the film does not close with resurrection and exoneration, but rather with sensual farce. An over-sexualized (unnamed) nurse enters Danny's room and flirts with one of the boys, kissing him on the cheek.[28] Muggs takes command of the situation and kisses the nurse full on the mouth, in a passionate embrace as he bends her body under him, and the sensual scene dramatically ends the film as Muggs joyfully douses his head with a jug of ice water to cool himself down while everyone celebrates. Muggs is no Lothario and this finishing touch reveals Fox's wry sense of humor. And, most important, social order in the community has been restored.

MURDER AND *BATHOS* UNDER THE BRIDGE

'Neath Brooklyn Bridge, like *Bowery Blitzkrieg*, begins with a panoramic overview of the Brooklyn Bridge as it towers over a teeming swarm of Lilliputian people in diurnal commercial activities, a beehive of activity in the first year of World War II. Muggs and his gang are chaotically unloading household furniture from a cart, helping Glimpy's mother (Patsy Moran). Muggs barks orders at the other boys, as usual. Skid (Gabriel Dell) appears in a suit, flush with cash. The boys all know that Skid is doing crime and there is clear resentment on their part. An officer comes along and refers to Skid as a "cheap crook, . . . who works for McGaffey," so the interconnected idiocultures of the boys and the local police conflict early on, which is not always the case, as we have seen in other *ESK* films. This movie, as much as any other *ESK* production, is rich in slapstick from the first scene (particularly the boy's buffoonery as they move Mrs. Glimpy's belongings) to the last scene (grown men in a crib performing as gurgling babies).

There is considerable serious action in the early scenes. Morley (Bud Osborne), another gangster, steals money from McGaffey (Marc Lawrence), who is not someone to be trifled with. Morley runs to his apartment, shared with his stepdaughter Sylvia (Anne Gillis), who is attractive and cares for her invalid grandfather "Bright Eyes" (J. Arthur Young). Morley tries to force Sylvia to abandon the apartment, but the tenement boys come to the rescue when they hear the commotion in the building. The fight is part farce, part serious, yet the struggle becomes complicated when McGaffey and Skid arrive, both armed and ready for violence in an adjoining room. ("Bright Eyes," who is paralyzed, watches the fracas, tethered to his wheelchair, Figure 9.5) Muggs finishes off the fight by knocking out Morley with a chair leg. Muggs questions "Bright Eyes" about the whereabouts of Sylvia but the paralyzed invalid cannot speak. "Bright Eyes" can communicate only by blinking his eyes (which the boys cannot interpret), so they leave, looking for Sylvia. Meanwhile, McGaffey and Skid return to take the money that Morley had stolen from them. McGaffey kills Morley with the club and takes it with him in order to frame Muggs for the murder since Muggs's fingerprints are on the murder weapon.

These early scenes are complicated and reveal a complex of social dynamics in play: 1) The camaraderie of the boys, who have excluded Skid from their social group because of his criminal activities; 2) The presence of serious criminals in the immediate environment, principally McGaffey, Skid, and Morley; 3) The identity of a young attractive woman in distress, Sylvia; 4) The role of

Figure 9.5 "Bright Eyes" sees all.

the mute invalid, who is the only uninvolved witness to the homicide. The seriousness of the film is foreshadowed by the introduction of these social interactions very early on and the tenor of the narrative is enriched by the gathering of multiple idiocultures in the first handful of scenes. We are introduced to hardened criminals, police officers, the gang boys in their usual community of spirit, Mrs. Glimpy with her many idiosyncrasies, and the strange spectacle of Sylvia and her incapacitated grandfather.

The complexity of the introductory scenes foreshadow a convoluted narrative in which the murder involves a strange series of twists of social interaction(s) with knotted nuances. Yet the salient codes of the community (justice, due process, accountability) are made problematic by the presentations of radically different interpretations of events. Even the tenement boys, successful sleuths as we see in *LGT*, are at a loss to explain how events have unfolded until fate steps in with the arrival of Sailor Butch (Noah Beery Jr.), who understands Morse code and can interpret the blinking grandfather, thus moving the conflict toward a resolution that addresses the needs and values of the law-abiding community—except, of course, for the criminal community, who are menacing outsiders. Individual community attitudes and beliefs each contribute to social confusion, in one way or another, as they represent acceptable community standards of value, which are intensified during wartime. It is not incidental that Butch, an active duty sailor, is the key to delivering the probative evidence of McGaffey's guilt and he is an excellent exemplar of ethics in action, guided by a rigid code of *ethos*. Butch's "abode," symbolically illustrated by his uniform, is dedication to his country and his people and it is important to note that Butch is a former gang member, so he is in very familiar company.

Officer Phil Lyons (Dave O'Brien) is convinced that McGaffey is directly involved in Morley's murder and Phil convinces the precinct captain to allow him to talk to Danny. Phil, of course, wants Danny to tell him the truth about what happened at Sylvia's apartment but Danny is resistant to talk about events, even with his brother, Phil. Their broken communication gives Wallace Fox an opportunity to inject a meta-cinematic moment as Phil admonishes his brother: "You know, Danny, I'm afraid that you've been seeing too many movies lately. Cut out the act and give me the whole thing." So, a fictitious "movie version" of events won't satisfy Phil—he wants the truth, the straight story. Phil is equally tough with McGaffey when he confronts him at his bar and dance club, The Bridge Café, and the policeman tells him "Lay off of the East Side Kids. They're good boys. They're not like those cheap gutter snipes that usually hang around you." These scenes show us the inner nature of Phil, who is not only a good cop but a man devoted to serving his family and community. Phil's comments about the essential goodness of the boys is reminiscent of Joe in *BB*, and both policemen serve as synecdoches for motifs of interaction and inequality.

The boys locate Sylvia on the waterfront and they suspect, with good reason, that she is in serious danger. The stage is now set for serious detective work and murder is involved. Muggs makes an executive decision to take Sylvia to their clubhouse, where she will hide under the protection of the boys. Muggs decides to dress Sylvia as a boy in order to ensure her safety. We see the motif of mistaken identity, as in *LGT*, and it plays a role in the plot development of *NBB* as Danny is mistaken as Morley's murderer because he is identified as having been seen at the murder scene, although he had returned there only to retrieve Sylvia's clothes. So, once again, *ESK* films often rely on confusion and misinformation—and problematic identity enriches Fox's narratives, just as they do in Shakespeare's comedies, where mistaken identity is accepted as a norm in the turmoil of stories that build upon the cornerstones of sexual attraction, love, and marriage.

Social context is complicated in *NBB* because there are, roughly, four distinct yet intermingled groups: boys, police, hoodlums, and the Sylvia/Butch romantic subplot. However, there is another idioculture in play and that is "Bright Eyes." He is *sui generis*, and turns out to be the pivotal character in the film, saving Danny's life with his unique talent of blinking letters in Morse code, therefore testifying that McGaffey killed Morley. Three words dramatically change the outcome of the film: "McGAFFEY KILLED MORLEY," as Butch slowly pronounces each of the letters as they pour forth from the eyes of the witness.

The ending of the film? There are no surprises. In Wallace Fox fashion, justice has been done and the film concludes with slapstick absurdity as the boys wheel a baby crib to greet lovers Butch and Sylvia, who are planning their marriage. The crib, however, contains two adult males, gurgling and slurping milk—ridiculously silly as adult babies. Thus, gross *bathos* ends the film on the heels of a solemn story of Fox's poignant commentary about the integral, inseparability of *bathos* and *pathos*. Yet *NNB*, like Fox's other *ESK* films, ends with emphatic camaraderie and fellowship. And Shakespeare poignantly anticipated Wallace Fox's cinematic art in *All's Well That Ends well*.[29]

NOTES

1. The names of some of the characters change over episodes. In *Bowery Blitzkrieg*, Huntz Hall's character is Limpy, who becomes Glimpy in later episodes. Leo Gorcey's character is spelled Muggs McGinnis in *Bowery Blitzkrieg* and *Let's Get Tough!*, but then the spelling changes to Mugs McGinnis in *Smart Alecks* and *'Neath Brooklyn Bridge*. Scruno's actual name is credited as Sunshine Sammy Morrison in *Bowery Blitzkrieg* but he is listed as Sunshine Sammy Morrison in *Let's Get Tough!* There are other inconsistencies in spelling, such as with Gabriel Dell's name listed as Fritz Heinbach, although the name on the family store is Hienbach's Second Hand Store.
2. I. C. Jarvie, "Introduction: The Relevance of Cinema and Sociology in General to the Sociology of the Medium-at-Large," in *Towards a Sociology of the Cinema: A Comparative Essay on the Structure and Functioning of a Major Entertainment Industry* (London and New York: Routledge, 1970), 1–17.
3. Poverty Row was a loosely associated groups of filmmakers who produced some quite impressive B-movies, including Joseph H. Lewis's *That Gang of Mine* (1940), which was the third film in the *East Side Kids* series. Lewis relies on the complex intertwining of *bathos* and *pathos* in this film as well as in other B-movies he directed, including *Detour* (1945), a low-rent film which told the tale of an impoverished musician who hitchhikes across the county, motivated by love, and who during his misadventures subsequently becomes entangled in two deaths. *Detour* (1945) is a powerful noir, rich in exploring the surreal underside of greed, love, and life in the 1940s. See Phillip Sipiora, "All Wrong Turns: Tracking Subjectivity in Edgar Ulmer's *Detour*," in Gary D. Rhodes (ed.), *Edgar G. Ulmer: Detour on Poverty Row* (Lanham, MD: Lexington Books, 2008), 145–63.
4. Penelope Gilliatt, Review, "The Current Cinema," *The New Yorker* (44) 26 (August 17, 1968), 74–7.
5. James Linton, "But it's only a movie." *Jump Cut*, 17 (April 1978), 16–19. Available at <https://www.ejumpcut.org/archive/onlinessays/JC17folder/OnlyAmovieLinton.html> (accessed April 17, 2020).
6. Jean-Anne Sutherland and Kathryn Feltey, "Chapter One: Introduction," in Sutherland and Feltey, *Cinematic Sociology: Social Life in Film*, Second Edition (London: Sage, 2013), 1–23.

7. Martin Heidegger connects our interpretation of the "world" with our capacity to interrelate common experiences to ourselves and those whom we encounter: "[O]ur ordinary prereflective agency when we are caught up in the midst of practice affairs. The 'phenomenology of everydayness' is supposed to lead us to see the totality of human existence." Charles B. Guignon in "Heidegger," *The Cambridge Dictionary of Philosophy*, Second Edition, Robert Audi, General Editor (Cambridge: Cambridge University Press, 1995), "Martin Heidegger," 371. Heidegger also explores the importance of anticipatory, pre-interpretations of persons and experiences in his treatment of Forestructure (*Vorstruktur*) and the cycle of interpretation in Martin Heidegger, *Being and Time*, trans. John Macquarrie and Edward Robinson (London: SCH Press, 1962), 150–3, 157, 232–4, 327.
8. Edward Branigan, "The Problem of Point of View," in *Point of View in the Cinema: A Theory of Narration and Subjectivity in Classical Film* (Berlin, New York: Mouton Publishers, 1984), 10.
9. *Eunoia* (good will) is an important quality of public discourse that traces back to Greek Antiquity and relates to Branigan's reference to an emotional component to identity, sympathy, and empathy in understanding point of view. In small group association and differentiation, as well as discernment with individuals, there is an element of bonding in play. The *ethos* of individuals or of a group (collective *ethoi*) must resonate, to a certain degree, with that of the viewer. Otherwise, bonding cannot take place.
10. Branigan, 16–19.
11. Brian Taves, "The B Film: Hollywood's Other," in Tino Balio (ed.), *Grand Design: Hollywood as a Modern Business Enterprise, 1930–1939* (New York: Charles Scribner's Sons, 1993), 343.
12. Gary Alan Fine, "Small Groups and Culture Creation: The Idioculture of Little League Baseball Team," *American Sociological Review* 44 (October 1979), 734.
13. Screwball comedy was a powerful genre in addressing socio-economic conditions of daily life in the 1930s. Such films often focused on the foibles and footfalls of upscale families, their love and courtship functions and malfunctions. *My Man Godfrey* (1936) is illustrative of the buffoonery that was commonplace in this genre. Like the *ESK* series, these films allowed viewers to escape the dreariness of their lives.
14. Linton, 16–19.
15. Part of the *bathos* across all the *ESK* films involves verbal playfulness, and perhaps the most prominent example of verbal humor is the display of malapropisms, most often expressed by Muggs and Glimpy, for example "I depreciate that" for "I appreciate that" and "I'll give you (kissing) lessons in oscillation" for "I'll give you (kissing) lessons in isolation." When Muggs and the boys are speaking gibberish to brain surgeon Dr. Ormsby, he fails to understand their wacky syntax and vocabulary. Muggs asks him, "Don't you understand English?" The surgeon sharply retorts, "Not that kind of English." There are literally hundreds of malapropisms spread across the dozens of films depicting the boys of the bowery. Another common linguistic device in the series is epenthesis: the non-standard pronunciation of a word ("filém" for film, for example).
16. Arnold Hauser, *The Sociology of Art*, trans. Kenneth J. Northcott (London: Routledge & Kegan Paul Ltd., 1982), 10.
17. William McNeill, *The Time of Life: Heidegger and Ethos* (Albany, NY: SUNY Press, 1992), xi.
18. Martin Heidegger, Letter on Humanism (GRV, July 2000, 1:1), 103.
19. Julie Kuhlken elaborates on the nuances between ethos and ethics in a rich examination of Heidegger's penetration into the area of pragmatics, which is helpful in exploring ethics and *ethos* in both theory and practice in popular art. See Julie Kuhlken, "Heidegger and

Aristotle: Action, Production, and Ethos," *Journal of Speculative Philosophy* 28:3 (2014), 371–9.

20. Don D. Smith, "Teaching Introductory Sociology by Film," *Teaching Sociology* 1:1 (October 1973), 48–61.
21. Hauser, 15.
22. Ibid., 4.
23. Ibid., 11.
24. "The readiness is all" (Hamlet Act 5, Scene 2) is good advice for the boys in their daily encounters with the complications of life, particularly in matters of life and death, as is the case with the espionage scenes. They continually strive to learn to anticipate circumstances and events—to be "ready" to address any and all challenges.
25. This comment is attributed to Max Weinreich. The earliest known published source is Weinreich's article, "The YIVO and the problems of our time", originally presented as a speech on January 5, 1945 at the annual YIVO (*Yidisher Visnshaftlekher Institut*) conference. It points out the influence that social and political conditions can have over a community's perception of the status of a language or dialect.
26. Hauser, xxi.
27. In the *ESK* series, the policemen/boyfriends of young women (who are often related to Danny) are usually age-balanced with their police paramours. However, in *SA* Roger Pryor is twenty-one years older than Gale Storm and the age difference is obvious, which makes him appear more appropriate as her father than her boyfriend. Further, he is nicknamed "Pops."
28. The steamy scene with Muggs is foreshadowed by the nurse's flirting with Glimpy in an earlier scene. One of the effects of these scenes is to show that the hospital is not a safe refuge from the humor and buffoonery that characterizes all other settings.
29. William Shakespeare's *All's Well That Ends Well* was published in the First Folio in 1623, where it is listed among the comedies. There is a debate regarding the dating of the composition of the play, with possible dates ranging from 1598 to 1608.

CHAPTER 10

Infernal Devices: Wallace Fox's Aeroglobe, Cosmic Beam Annihilator, and the Pit of Everlasting Fire

Michael L. Shuman

Movie theaters in 1947 offered audiences significant films by directors generally considered auteurs, filmmakers who exercised authority in a collaborative artistic enterprise with the intent of expressing a unique personal vision. Alfred Hitchcock's *The Paradine Case*, Fritz Lang's *Secret Beyond the Door*, and Charles Chaplin's *Monsieur Verdoux* deal with the complexities of adult relationships and, while adding the lobby-card attraction of familial homicide, deliver the unique stylistic techniques and visual preoccupations of the director. For Hitchcock, distinctive camera angles create a nearly oppressive emotional atmosphere and sense of the audience as voyeur; Lang, relying upon his early Expressionism to explore film noir, uses light and shadow to illuminate his perception of an oppressive social order; and Chaplin contorts the audience's notion of good and evil as the protagonist, a bigamist who routinely marries and murders his ancillary brides in Bluebeard-fashion, is just suave enough to seduce the audience as well. These are provocative motion pictures intended for a mature, reflective audience: big themes for big people.

Wallace Fox, whose 1947 film *Jack Armstrong: The All-American Boy* appeared in a weekly series of short video bites of twenty minutes or so, had a different goal and audience for his films. In over eighty movies directed between 1927 and 1953, Fox characteristically delivered Westerns, mysteries, and tough-talking Bowery Boys vehicles with the rock 'em sock 'em content intended to keep viewers in their seats and cash flowing to the theaters and studios. Fox was adept at directing B-movies, films appreciably shorter than top-of-the bill A-releases, as well as serials, movies shown weekly at theaters in short chapters over an extended period. Tino Balio, in his study of the commercial aspects of film during the 1930s, notes that the audience for both B-movies and serials, also known as chapter plays, generally was the same: school-age kids seeking pulp magazine and comic strip thrills at their neighborhood theaters. "[T]he narrative traits of B films echoed not only the pulps but also movie serials," Balio writes, "emphasizing thrills, pace, and low budgets over mood, coherence, and characterization. B's and serials have similar action-oriented heroes, displaying fisticuffs, athleticism, and cheery youthfulness. B's move rapidly, often at the expense of probability, loading the narrative with action-filled incidents and twists of plot and character."[1] Ed Hulse provides a more fan-based assessment specifically of movie serials and their audiences in *Cliffhanger Classics*, a two-volume examination of the format compiled from his columns in a niche magazine devoted to chapter plays, by noting that serials were

> a staple of Saturday-afternoon matinees, where hordes of screaming children—and, in some cases, undiscriminating adults—could be found rooting for an endless procession of intrepid heroes struggling to foil an equally endless procession of diabolical villains bent on acquiring large fortunes, revenging themselves against society, or conquering the world.[2]

Roy Kinnard, in his book-length critical filmography of science fiction serials, emphasizes that chapter plays were economically justified by attracting movie ticket-buyers to theaters where they also would enjoy higher-budget main features produced by the studio.[3] The outlier influences for serials, he notes, often gave producers and directors freedom to deal with subjects untouched by major productions. As Kinnard writes,

> [d]rawing their inspiration from fringe cultural sources like pulp magazines and comic books, [serials] were often free—by their very lack of acclaim and respectability—to exploit subjects that the producers of more "distinguished" movies considered too outlandish and too much of a risk to bother with.[4]

Success directing a B-movie or serial was therefore predicated upon different criteria, and often demanded a different set of creative assumptions to higher-budget A-pictures.

Serials such as Fox's *Jack Armstrong* represent an even more marginalized form of film, both creatively and economically, compared with both the big screen standard-bearer A-movies and the minimalist Bs, and studios routinely devoted limited resources to their production. "Most chapter plays were made on minuscule budgets," Hulse writes, "and shooting schedules charitably described as breakneck."[5] This miserly approach to serial production, common to all studios in the chapter-play market, was even more pronounced at Columbia when, in 1945, Sam Katzman became the new serial producer and tightened the budgets even further. Katzman was "one of the best-known and most stereotypical low-budget producers from Hollywood's golden age," writes one critic in "Handing Off the Torch: Columbia Pictures' Sound Serials (1937–1956)," on a website devoted to movie serial reviews. "Notoriously tight-fisted, blithely unconcerned about film-making quality, and certain that his audiences consisted of undiscriminating kids and adult 'morons,' [Katzman] cared only about making cheap product that could be ballyhooed effectively enough to turn a profit."[6] Columbia's practice of requiring exactly fifteen chapters for every serial, relaxed only once with the thirteen-chapter, Fox-directed *Brenda Starr, Reporter* in 1945, perhaps unintentionally cut production costs even further as writers padded lean scripts with excessive talking and humorless bickering, long walks with obscure intent, and the reuse of footage, bookending each episode, reminding viewers of earlier action and providing a peek at upcoming thrills. One review of *Jack Armstrong* maintains that Fox's serial presented "a strong cast and a good basic storyline," but suggests that the narrative structure sags under the weight of the studio's finicky requirements. Columbia's fifteen-chapter directive, writes the reviewer, "forces writers Leslie Swabacker, Royal Cole, George Plympton, Arthur Hoerl, and Lewis Clay to spin their narrative wheels at too many points throughout the serial."[7]

Fox, who Katzman brought to Columbia along with *Jack Armstrong* cinematographer Ira Morgan, similarly would have been creatively constrained by Katzman's penny-pinching approach and studio guidelines, aiming for pedestrian efficiency rather than communicating any personal artistic vision of his own. These were rough-hewn productions, after all, with a short production schedule requiring directorial talents more akin to those of an efficient carpenter rather than a creative architect. When shooting for *Jack Armstrong* wrapped and film was sent to post-production, the editor, Earl Turner, would have created fifteen chapters, each around twenty minutes long, with the same methodical approach that constricted Fox's directorial efforts. Although Columbia was the last studio to produce and distribute a chapter play, with *Blazing the Overland Trail* in 1956, *Jack Armstrong* was decidedly a one-off attempt to capitalize on the familiarity of the heroic teen's adventures before both the radio drama—already in decline—and the chapter-play format would evaporate from audience attention forever.[8]

Jack Armstrong, lensed late in Fox's career, was an ideal vehicle both for Columbia Pictures' bottom line and for the director's talents. The film, in serial format, is based upon the immensely popular radio series tracking the adventures of an athletic teenage hero as he deals with cutting-edge mid-century technology, mostly created at Uncle Jim's Fairfield Aviation Company, as well as occasional mystical marvels. "Jack Armstrong was a pinnacle of juvenile American radio serials," writes John Dunning in *On the Air: The Encyclopedia of Old-Time Radio*, "heard for the same sponsor across a two-decade run that touched all four networks."[9] The sponsor was General Mills, at that time a relatively new company, and a fifteen-minute radio adventure airing every weekday at 5:30 p.m., right after school, provided the ideal environment for selling Wheaties to hungry kids. Dunning cites 1933 through 1940 as the "golden years" of the broadcast, when Jack and his high-school friends, Billy and Betty Fairfield and their Uncle Jim, breezed through thrills in exotic locations such as Africa, the Arctic, Shanghai, Zanzibar, and the Philippines, in Fairfield Aviation hydroplanes and dirigibles, all in pursuit of sophisticated evildoers.[10]

Jack Armstrong, the character, had long represented an aspirational model for school-age audiences in a variety of media, and his All-American qualities of idealized intellect and ability are important components in the construction of Fox's serial landscape. An astonishingly wide variety of tie-in promotional toys, games, and souvenirs offered by Wheaties added to the young audience's adoration for the character and perpetuated the radio drama's success. "The goodness of the cereal was secondary," Dunning writes.

> [w]hat the kids wanted was the boxtop, which could be used to obtain a Jack Armstrong ring, medallion, bombsight, or pedometer . . . The earliest known premium was a shooting plane, offered in 1933 for two boxtops and drawing 424,441 orders. Almost any tangible object mentioned in a storyline could be expected to turn up as a premium.[11]

These mail-order goodies, perhaps first documented by Fred L. King in a self-published "scrapbook" and now more generously available for inspection on eBay, helped fashion the Jack Armstrong mythos and contributed to the character's appeal to an excitable audience. Visual documentation of Jack's prowess and adventures—in comic books, newspaper comics, or film—appeared only when ratings for the radio program began to fade and rights to the franchise became cheap enough for Columbia to finance Fox's serial. "Jack Armstrong had a long run in radio," King notes, "before he became a comic character. In fact, the radio program was fourteen years old before the comic appeared."[12] The *Jack Armstrong* comic book series, published by Parents' Institute almost concurrently with the run of Fox's serial in theaters, lasted thirteen issues between 1947 and 1949 and maintains the notion of Jack as an admirable guy with a fine intellect and an interest in science.[13] The inside front cover lists most of the main characters from the film and describes Jack as "A clean-cut American boy who exemplifies the motto, 'A sound mind in a sound body.' He is athletic, alert, and always on the side of the underdog. Meeting him for the first time you'd say, 'There's a regular fellow!'"[14] Daily and Sunday comic strips written and drawn by Bob Schoenke appeared in newspapers during the same period and presumably helped Columbia attract even more interest in the ongoing chapter play. These toys and games, along with books, comics, and other consumables offered to radio audiences, effectively become ancillary devices helping Fox construct an onscreen alternate universe by providing his audiences with expectations about Jack and his indomitable spirit and abilities.

Fox therefore had the essential elements of a storyline, along with its characters and their not-so-complex motivations, imposed upon him before production began, and his goal was to conform to the melodramatic conventions of the movie serial, or chapter play, format and provide the thrills of action and adventure for a pre-defined audience of youngsters. "There is no more representative form of sensational melodrama than the film serial," writes Geoff Mayer in his encyclopedia of the genre, continuing:

> It is the extreme manifestation [of] an "externalized" drama, a key attribute of any form of melodrama. Everything happens on the outside. There is little, if any, character development, psychological anguish or internal division between conflicting impulses. The threat is always externalized—from villains of various forms. There is little or no introspection or debate.[15]

The director's intent, then, was to present predominately juvenile audience members with enough chases, fistfights, and close-shave escapes to keep them in their seats before the next animated cartoon, newsreel, or feature film in a jam-packed afternoon schedule. Fox appropriated the conventions of the serial format and, with an extensive career of producing thrills and suspense on a low-budget, directed a chapter play that met the stated goals of the format admirably and, perhaps, more consistently than Hitchcock, Lang, or Chaplin fulfilled their own ambitions.

The gadget-filled exploits of Jack Armstrong's radio broadcasts, while not quite saturated enough with interstellar travel and high-collar space wear to qualify as science fiction when translated to the theater screen, nevertheless gave Columbia Pictures one giant leap toward matching the success of the earlier Universal Pictures outings *Flash Gordon's Trip to Mars* (1938) and its sequel, *Flash Gordon Conquers the Universe* (1940). Kinnard relegates Fox's contribution to an appendix of thirty-seven serials with incidental science fiction elements, while the main text deals with such out-there chapter plays as *Buck Rogers* (1939), *King of the Rocket Men* (1949), and *Captain Video* (1951).[16] Audiences nevertheless may marvel at an atomic automobile, complete with fashionable DeLorean doors, constructed by Jack (John Hart) and his friend Billy (Joe Brown, Jr.) (Figure 10.1); an "Electronic Deactivator" that freezes the controls of airplane engines; a "Cosmic Beam Annihilator" developed for world domination by the evil Jason Grood (Charles Middleton) and powered by "Solarium," a laser-like material derived, somehow, from the sun; and the "Pit of Everlasting Fire," a sacramental abyss used by island natives to execute

Figure 10.1 Jack's atomic car.

transgressors but actually a mechanical contraption installed by Grood and controlled manually by levers. Perhaps the most kid-catching invention, however, is Grood's "aeroglobe," a manned, sub-space rocket intended to hover in the stratosphere and terrorize nations.

Indeed, the fantastic mechanics of the gadgets, used by heroes and villains alike, indicates a mid-century appreciation of scientific advancement and mirrors the mechanical nature of the serial plot, with takeout followed by action followed by cliffhanger, that the audience expected. These technological wonders, mostly infernal devices constructed by an evil mastermind to implement his all-too nefarious plans, provide Fox's serial narrative with the context and structure necessary to keep the action going, melodramatically, without the A-movie elements of character development, nuance, or thoughtful dialogue. The storyline moves from one invention to the next, chapter after weekly chapter, leaving audiences speculating about the scientific marvels Jack and his pals might encounter next. Postwar kids in the audience may have seen early forms of computers or fantastic rockets in their science schoolbooks or on the covers of *Mechanix Illustrated* or *Popular Electronics*, each a constant presence on late-1940s newsstands and in garage workshops. *Collier's* magazine, amplifying the mid-century public's fascination with science, soon would launch their influential space symposium featuring the innovative ideas of the famous rocket scientist Werner von Braun and artist Chesley Bonestell's otherworldly paintings of doughnut-shaped space stations and planetary landscapes.[17] *Planet Comics*, published by Fiction House from 1940 to 1953, routinely cover-featured complex, pseudoscience gizmos in far-out contexts, usually with brave young heroines or space-suited heroes dauntlessly confronting otherworldly technological challenges.

Kids certainly were attracted to such imaginative images, even if they paid no attention to other, more adult, magazines with science-oriented covers. But here, in the theater in 1947, new gadgets and scientific spectacles seemed to appear from week to week, repetitive marvels designed by savvy studio executives to keep quarters flowing into the box office. You didn't *see* such wonderment in the real world, but here it was, right in front of you, and larger than life. Going to the Saturday matinee was routine business for many young serial fans, an automatic act of its own very nearly emulating the mechanical wonders there on the screen. Serials such as *Jack Armstrong* were a window into a heroic future, and enjoying repeated content, after all, provided the comfort of consistency while satisfying youthful expectations.

Fox also appropriates other conventions of the chapter-play format to propel the narrative and, just as importantly, satisfy audience expectations. Grood's secret radio room behind a revolving bookcase, for example, joins the countless other representations of pirouetting library shelves and hidey-hole rooms in other serials and B-films. Mad scientists in isolated areas, especially islands with an extensive system of tunnels, pits, and caves to frustrate the hero's escape, are especially welcome to audiences of these movies and, later on, Grood's choice of location would influence the big-budget plots of the James Bond thrillers as well as the other, more derivative, spy movies to follow. Yes, Fox deals with the inevitable genre peril of quicksand appearing to swallow a clumsy Billy, rapidly and unrealistically, into its endless vortex, only to be saved by a well-placed rope. Never mind that quicksand is denser than water, allowing an alert person to float rather than sink; quicksand is a trope of B-movies, don't you know, so the audience no doubt anticipated the impending hazard and cheered louder at the salvation.[18] The narrative devices of the serial, whether natural locales or man-made gadgets, exist solely through expectation and convention rather than realism and logic.

Fox's art director on *Jack Armstrong*, Paul Palmentola, had previously designed production visuals for a wide variety of B-movies in the 1930s and 1940s, including *Bluebeard* (1944), complete with puppet shows and a sinisterly named strangler who murders women after painting their portraits, and *Fog Island* (1945), a mystery-bordering-on-horror film with a crazed inventor luring guests to his booby-trapped island home to exact revenge. As a chapter play on the periphery of the science fiction genre, *Jack Armstrong* presented significant visual challenges for the budget-conscious production designer.

Jim Harmon and Donald F. Glut, in *The Great Movie Serials*, note that science fiction was an important aspect of the chapter play, with elements of the genre occurring even in Westerns, where odd devices might portent imminent destruction of the white-hatted cowboys. "But the number of straight space opera chapterplays," they write, "due to the costliness of constructing other worldly sets and costumes to outfit entire alien races, are relatively few."[19] Palmentola's background in the Bs allows him to interpret the visual culture of the chapter play with journeyman efficiency, establishing a design language that is at once characteristic of the serial form, evocative of science fiction tropes, and inexpensive to produce. The offices of Uncle Jim's Fairfield Aviation Company, for instance, suggest the rough comfort expected for working engineers of the era, Grood's island provides an exotic film foray into bleak and rocky desert landscapes, while the set design for the Pit of Everlasting Fire is gratifyingly spooky. One reviewer, identifying the shooting locations as the Monogram Ranch and Kernville in the southern Sierra Nevada, notes that the scenery is "certainly well worth looking at, even if it doesn't really resemble a tropical or even semi-tropical island."[20] While that is true during wide-angle shots of buildings and landscape, Palmentola successfully translates more intimate locations, such as Princess Alura's secret grotto, into a tropical oasis attractive to any kid anxious for an alluring locale. The rugged jungle explorer costumes of the heroes and the clothing of the island natives—primitive sulus and paisley shirts for tribal members and loud print sarongs and halter tops for the princess and her cohorts—also adds to the visual appeal and faux-glamorous attraction of Fox's serial production. Palmentola's work, at times, seems to effectively approximate, or at least evoke, the spaceship-and-captured-heroine covers of comic books and pulp magazines on mid-century newsstands while complimenting the revolutionary gadgets, a testament to his steady, workmanlike visual instincts despite the low budget of the production.

The pulp magazine, as Balio implies, is an influential cultural influence on both movie serials and their audience, but Fox's reliance upon gadgets and austere art direction to provide narrative structure—a practice in the subgenre of science fiction chapter plays—aligns the serial closer to the earlier "scientification" pulp publications of Hugo Gernsback rather than the more sophisticated science fiction magazines lining the newsstands while Fox was filming *Jack Armstrong*. Fiction in the 1926 inaugural issues of Gernsback's *Amazing Stories*, successor to his fact-based hobbyist publication *The Electrical Experimenter*, generally fulfill science fiction writer and editor Frederick Pohl's description as "a sort of animated catalogue of gadgets," fiction relying upon flashy inventions rather than carefully constructed plots, themes, and characterizations.[21] J. Harvey Haggard's story "An Adventure on Eros," for example, appeared in the September 1931 issue of *Wonder Stories*, another Gernsback venture, and deals with a "Telepadion Instructor," a device using "a long celluloid strip record" moving under a needle to train entry-level space pilots.[22] Mike Ashley, in his study of Gernsback's influence on the science fiction genre, cites this story as "an ideal Gernsback gadget story," relating the Telepadion Instructor to the "Hypnobioscope," a similar contraption described in one of Gernsback's own seminal stories.

Despite the clumsy prose and cardboard characterizations, Haggard's story manages to predict both video games and virtual reality through early 1930s technology.[23] In this respect Haggard additionally adheres to Gernsback's editorial requirement that authors follow accurate accounts of scientific and technological knowledge in their speculative fiction. "As an exposition of a scientific theme," Gernsback writes in a two-page "Suggestions for Authors," "it must be reasonable and logical and must be based upon known scientific principles. You have the perfect right to use your imagination as you will in developing the principles, but the fundamental scientific theory must be correct." Gernsback additionally insisted that stories maintain the reader's interest even when "making a description of some dry scientific apparatus, invention or principle," although this dictate often exceeded the abilities of many members of his authorial cohort.[24]

The contrast between the pulp-infused science fiction of Fox's work and the comparative sophistication of the stories beginning to appear in adult-oriented, mid-century science fiction magazines reveal not only the target audiences of the two imaginative entertainment media but the emerging cultural context that Fox's serial, appearing in theaters after the heyday of chapter plays, seemed to resist. Ed Hulse's definition of pulp fiction as relying on "narrative drive and dynamic action more than character or atmosphere" very neatly describes *Jack Armstrong* and every other specimen of chapter-play film entertainment. "The pulps didn't waste time on nuance or abstraction," Hulse writes, extending Mayer's observations about the externalized nature of the chapter-play narrative and illuminating the relationship between serials and the pulps. "[S]tories were built around the immediate objectives of their protagonists, who went about achieving said objectives with a minimum of deliberation."[25] Hulse further emphasizes the cultural import of pulp fiction and maintains that appreciation of that cultural import may be obscure to most modern moviegoers or readers. "Only by reading a lot of pulp fiction can one appreciate the extent to which it shaped our popular culture," he continues, even mentioning that the prominent pulp writer Talbot Mundy wrote scripts for Jack Armstrong's radio adventures for six years prior to Mundy's death in 1940.[26] "Eventually, the very predictability of serials began to work against them," writes Roy Kinnard, "even for their juvenile audience. After World War II even that formerly loyal core audience began to dissipate, lured away by similar fare shown for free on the new medium of television."[27] Although Kinnard does not mention the similarly new medium of *Astounding* and, a bit later in the 1950s, other science fiction publications emphasizing more adult themes, plots, and characterizations, serial audiences no doubt might grow up to look for more complex and engaging entertainment in the pages of those publications to supplement their television viewing excitement.

The February 1947 issue of *Astounding Science Fiction*, in fact, could have been purchased by audience members on their way to a showing of *Jack Armstrong*—an extension-on-film of Gernsback's gizmo-oriented narratives—but the short stories and novellas therein represent a more mature sensibility by emulating the conventions, if not the content, of literary fiction. Edited by John W. Campbell, a prolific writer and generally considered, along with Gernsback, as one of the most influential figures in early science fiction, *Astounding* published stories which not only relied upon scientific accuracy but also realistically developed theme and character.[28] "[T]he type of science fiction that was appearing in *Astounding*," writes Ashley in his examination of early 1940s issues of the magazine, "stands out so much in quality that one might wonder why at the time so many were prepared to read other magazines and why so many authors wrote for them."[29] Theodore Sturgeon's short story "Maturity," published in that February 1947 issue, is a remarkable example as much for its subject matter, character development, and themes as for its title, a signifier of adulthood in a genre once embraced mostly by children and scientific boffins. Sturgeon's protagonist, Robin English, is a brilliant young man who cannot succeed due to chronic immaturity, and who undergoes treatment with an experimental drug which gives him the adult skills necessary to succeed. Ultimately, he perceives that human beings are not intended to be fully mature before they die, and thus he exists as an unnatural hybrid of animal and impossibly mature *homo sapiens*, bored beyond endurance.[30] Sturgeon's theme of the human conundrum of consciousness provides a revealing metaphor for the growing pains of science fiction as a genre, whether printed in magazines or projected on theater screens, with literary intent constricted by the popular dismissal of the form as inept monster cartoons in prose.

If the contents of pulp magazines were represented in film terminology, that issue of *Astounding* would top the bill as an A-list entry, while the issue of *Amazing*, over two decades earlier, would appear on lobby cards as a B. The motion picture industry during Fox's directorial career, however, had no concept of an A-list science fiction film, the subject generally relegated in the public mind to tentacled aliens and wild imagination not suitable for serious-minded adults. Both gadget films such as *Jack Armstrong* and the elemental science fiction of *Flash Gordon* were relegated to the kid-pleasing chapter play, influenced by the contents of pulp magazines published primarily for far-out thrills.

In the gadget-filled universe of Jack Armstrong's cinematic adventures, a total of four hours and thirty-nine minutes of runtime exhibited in theaters over a fifteen-week period, scientific accuracy and logic thus gives way to the chapter-play standard of jiggery-pokery. Grood's primary instrument of evil, the Cosmic Beam Annihilator, is "several steps above an atom bomb" in the verbalized specs, yet when turned on Jack and his pals during a dust-up in Chapter 10, the Armageddon machine does little more damage than a flame-thrower and perhaps is less accurate at hitting its target (Figure 10.2). Professor Hobart Zorn (Wheeler Oakman), Grood's main man, mad scientist, and head of the cavern lab, proclaims that "just two micrograms of Solarium is needed to destroy an entire continent," yet when the Cosmic Beam Annihilator is captured by the treacherous Gregory Pierce (John Merton), Zorn discovers that burning a few circles in the ground while shooting at our heroes apparently has exhausted the supply.[31] The most revealing instance of hokum science, however, occurs early on when Professor Zorn lectures captured good guy Vic Hardy (Hugh Prosser) on the celestial mechanics of a space platform (Figure 10.3). After contacting Dr. Albuor (Robert Barron) and the other aeroglobe pilots, in flight, using "supersonic waves," Zorn reveals a concealed chart of Earth's upper atmosphere and takes pointer in fist: "You have heard me speak with outer space," he explains, slowly and precisely, accenting important words,

Figure 10.2 Professor Zorn demonstrates the Cosmic Beam Annihilator.

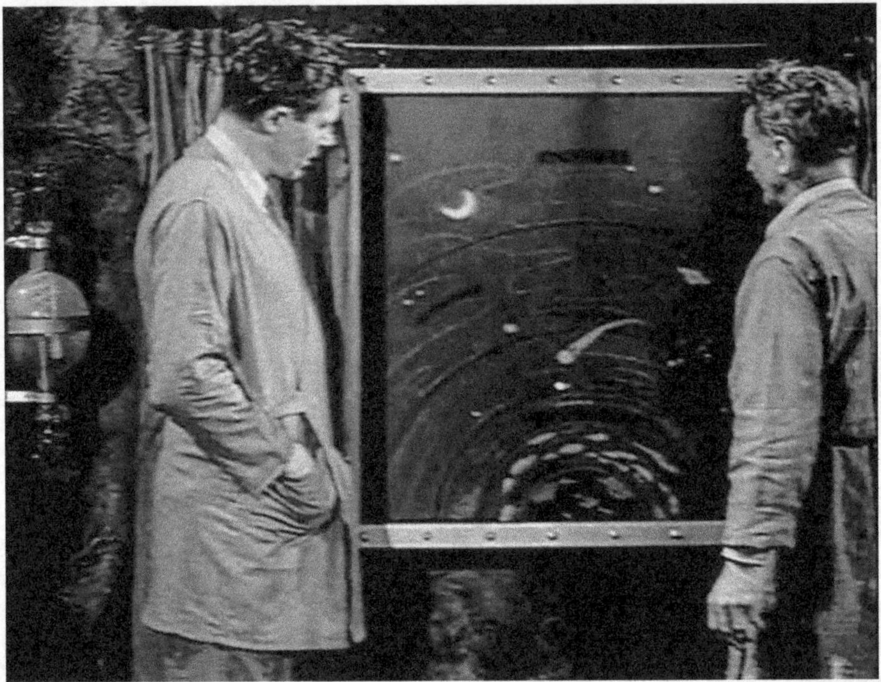

Figure 10.3 Professor Zorn lectures Vic Hardy.

"at a point there of zero gravity. Where the pull of gravity from the sun and outer solar planets equalizes the pull of earth gravity, there you have *zero gravity*, creating a space platform. On this our aeroglobe rests, remains stationary, floating like a cork on the sea." The matinee audience may have assumed that the professor's measured speech and frequent pauses, mid-sentence, were the affectation of a wise scientist preoccupied with other matters, or perhaps the sluggish pontification is indicative of an underpaid actor struggling to remember his lines. Ultimately it matters very little: this lesson approaches gilded gobbledygook, skirting around important factual details to produce an illusion of scientific insight and take up screen time, perhaps flummoxing an audience of twelve-year-olds in the process. The actual physics behind the Lagrangian point, the three-body problem in celestial mechanics dependent upon position, mass, and velocity, that Zorn attempts to describe, was available with just a bit of research, even in those pre-Internet times.[32] And why use waves that are merely supersonic to communicate with outer space, when common radio waves travel at the speed of light?

Professor Zorn's lecture, while too superficial as a factual description for a story in either *Amazing* or *Astounding* from nearly any period of publication, nevertheless has a whacky logic of its own and one that admirably fulfills the expectations of the chapter-play formula. Fuzzy logic, in fact, effectively serves as one of narrative devices supporting the serial and provides an otherworldly atmosphere for the high-strung action and adventure. The serial audience, for a short twenty minutes in a long Saturday afternoon, is transported to a wonderland where consistency and logic have no bearing, motivation resolves into an imposed credo, and dialogue conforms to an imaginary language of tough guys and erudite sophisticates. "Dialogue in melodrama is inadequate to convey its full meaning," Mayer writes in his discussion of the high-strung nature of serials. "It is a world of explosions, torture, fights, chases, last minute rescues and the constant threat of violation."[33] Highbrow speech intended to convey scientific meaning, in particular, appears truncated to the barest form of utterance, with known words in physics or chemistry interspaced with mumbo jumbo to present a semblance of meaning. The actor-scientist delivers these lines with a sense of authority, privilege, and condescension, giving direction to assistants in a tone suggesting rigorous planning, even though chaos may be descending all around the secret lab. The language of ruffians and henchmen resolves into tough-guy grunts, or at times the alibi-invoking "I don't know what you're talking about," an utterance apparently mandated by the scriptwriter's union to appear, at least once, in every action film project yet rarely heard in daily life. For the juvenile audience members just beginning to comprehend the puzzle of the adult world and its complexities, serials may have provided an alternative, and simpler, solution to the mechanics of living. For Hulse's "undiscriminating adults," the supersonic waves, cosmic beams, and effects of solarium may confirm that human lives are affected as much by unknown invisible forces as by fistfights and chases, especially in that post-atomic bomb culture. The haphazard production values of the serial, as much the responsibility of audience expectation and convention as the scant studio budget, finally serves as one of the director's building blocks for a strange new world.

Jack's adventures in this extraordinary serial landscape generally conform to the conventions of the typical chapter-play outline, with heroic captures and escapes punctuated by furious action in each short weekly segment. The first installment introduces the audience to Jack and his pal Billy as they inspect Jack's invention, a rather battered but futuristic-looking atomic-powered car they soon use to catch the hit-and-run driver who callously mows down a blind pedestrian. Jack's heroic credentials thus are established immediately in a melodramatic incident unrelated to the remainder of the film. The audience also meets the other members of Jack's band of adventurers, including Betty (Rosemary La Planche) and Uncle Jim (Pierre Watkin), as they congratulate Jack on his good deed in the offices of Fairfield Aviation (Figure 10.4). A greater challenge is presented in successive chapters, however, when Vic Hardy (Hugh Prosser), Uncle Jim's lead scientist on a project to develop atomic-powered aircraft, is kidnapped by Grood's thugs and taken to a remote volcanic island,

Figure 10.4 Jack, Billy, Uncle Jim, and Betty.

Point X, where he is forced to work on Grood's own nefarious Cosmic Beam Annihilator project. Jack and Uncle Jim track Hardy's location by triangulating strange impulses registered on their radiation indicator, and the adventurers fly to Point X, where Grood's Electronic Deactivator freezes the controls of their airplane, causing it to crash. Jack and Betty are falsely accused of murdering one of the indigenous island natives, and Princess Alura (Claire James) orders the Panther Woman (Carmen D'Antonio) to perform a ceremonial dance to invoke Xalta, the tribe's deity, for judgment and sentencing. Xalta, actually the voice of Grood transmitted to radio receivers hidden in the sacred grotto, condemns the pair to the Pit of Everlasting Fire. Jack and Betty find that the pit really is a mechanical contraption with gas-jet fixtures, while Umala (Russ Vincent), an exiled member of Princess Alura's tribe, rescues them by slugging one of Grood's minions and turning off the pit's controls. Naga (Frank Merlo), Princess Alura's advisor, condemns her as a heretic when she becomes suspicious of Xalta's reanimation after centuries of silence, and Alura and Jack are tied to a tree while a not-so-masterful tribal knife-thrower uses them as target practice (Figure 10.5). Gregory Pierce, who covertly purchased scientific supplies from Fairfield Aviation to supply Grood's project, finds an opportunity to steal the Cosmic Beam Annihilator and convinces a trio of Grood's henchmen to

Figure 10.5 Human targets.

join him in his treacherous conspiracy against Grood. Jack subdues Pierce and forces him to reveal the location of the secret laboratory, and when the two men approach the underground facility, Pierce is killed by Zorn's security contraption, a maze of "Tanilic light," ostensibly another "new element" discovered as a by-product of the cosmic ray experimentation. Jack takes Vic's place on the aeroglobe launch, subdues Zorn and the other members of the aeroglobe crew, and parachutes, gloriously, to safety. The aeroglobe explodes, thus depriving Grood of success in world domination, and in the final chapters, Uncle Jim blows up the cavern lab and Grood is dispatched when his own explosive device detonates following a dramatic fistfight with Jack. The island tribe is once again united as a cargo ship, our heroes' transportation home, propitiously arrives with the loud blast of a steam whistle, a decidedly low-tech conclusion to a faux-tech serial.

Here is one immediate testament to the success of Fox's serial: reading even a long plot summary like this one fails to communicate the peculiar logic of the film in nearly every way. A recap of the characters, action, and fiendish devices is very like holding a map of Alice's looking-glass world, upside down, and trying to find your way home. The narrative structure of a serial normally is circular, Mayer points out, and his description of the back-and-forth movement of the typical plot is enough, almost, to produce vertigo on its own. Chapter plays, he continues,

> placed little emphasis on narrative causality, a key element of the classical feature film. Causality occurs when action is clearly motivated and each sequence knits neatly into the overall story. Causality, logic and motivation were often neglected in the serial in favor of spectacle and graphic action.[34]

Events propelling *Jack Armstrong* from one week's chapter to the next are one step beyond logic and causality; simply keeping the narrative going and the film reels spinning is the major concern. In Fox's serial, rough-and-tumble scuffles and fistfights, much as you would find on a middle school playground, provide a sense of narrative progress and generally break out two or three times in a short chapter. *Something's really happening now*, the audience might think, collectively, as the story soon resolves to another scientific device or serial convention intended to start the cycle all over again. Characters running through the Alabama Hills landscape, a stand-in for Grood's volcanic island, also give a gratifying feeling of urgency to the messy situation unfolding on the screen at any moment. Umala deserves special mention for his distinctive gait, with erect posture and short steps, while Betty earns top honors for her anxious sprint, gun in hand, simply because she participates in the action at all.

Chapter plays, with their incessant action, thus are self-perpetuating and isolated worlds powered by devices found in no other universe, and with a contorted causality all their own. Why, the viewer may ask, does Billy believe he must hide in a box on the bed of an evildoer's truck in order to discover the hideout when Jack and the gang, in their car, follow along behind? And why does he repeat the stunt, eagerly, later in the film? Why does Grood decide to land the aeroglobe in the Pit of Everlasting Fire just to kill our trapped heroes when the pit's gas jets are there, waiting to be re-activated? Why would one of Grood's henchmen toss a cigarette into a bin of dynamite on the speeding truck that he is driving simply to dispatch Jack, with no regard to his own safety? And how, in that wind, is his aim so good? The reasons, of course, all involve sustaining the action and preparing for yet another improbable event, or adhering to standard chapter-play conventions, such as hero-in-a-box.[35]

While persistent action managed to keep audience members in their seats for each short chapter, another device, the cliffhanger ending, became the standard method of ensuring those seats were filled, too, the following week. "The truly distinctive ingredient that positively identified the serial as a separate storytelling form," writes William C. Cline in his examination of the conventions of serials, "was the open-end climax to each chapter." Cline continues:

> As a means of provoking the moviegoer to return the following week, it was discovered early in the silent days that nothing worked quite so well as having the main player involved in a seemingly futile situation—staring into the jaws of death or teetering on the brink of destruction—at the end of each episode.[36]

The next chapter, one week later, provided viewers with a "takeout" or recap of the events leading up to the catastrophic ending, a refresher not only allowing viewers to become terrified all over again, but also saving the studio money in production costs by using a few minutes of footage a second time. Cline also notes elsewhere, a bit more enthusiastically, that theaters "actually devised a trick to keep viewers coming back at the end of a chapter film: they would play the first chapter of the next one!"[37] Each week, then, young moviegoers would leave the theater in packs, yammering excitedly about the hero's latest predicament, only to continue the animated discussion in playgrounds, on back porches, and in trees, until the next matinee offered short-lived catharsis. Jeffrey Klenotic, in his case study of movie audiences at the Franklin Theater in Springfield, Massachusetts during the heyday of serial matinees, cites the memories of one theatergoer, Richard McBride, as testimony to the week-long, continuing enthusiasm of neighborhood kids enthralled by the serials. After the Saturday matinee, McBride recounts, "you'd go back home, and then that night, or during the week, you'd sit on the stoops at night after supper and talk about the movies." Kids would argue, too, and speculate about next week's electrifying installment. "[We'd say] 'this is what's going to happen,' 'no it ain't, your're wrong,' and everybody had their ideas, because they knew they were going to get another 15 episodes, and they'd always start another one, about 8 or 10 episodes into this one, so you always got two going, one almost finished and a new one starting."[38] The serial's singular narrative structure thus breaks through to the real world, imposing its circular form on the desires and expectations of everyone who spends lunch money or allowances on a ticket. Cline suggests that successful cliffhangers, as serial chapter endings, had to be "diabolically conceived, insidiously perpetrated, destructively fatal, and seemingly inescapable."[39]

Fox made effective use of the cliffhanger to maintain audience interest in the *Jack Armstrong* serial, generally keeping within the accepted chapter-play conventions and not obsessing about originality or hand-wringing about repetition. Young fans, after all, were "in effect paying to see the same movie fifteen times," as Kinnard observes, so originality effectively is a non-starter while repetition is part of the continuing game.[40] Audiences therefore were thrilled to see, in cliffhanger events, Jack, Billy, and sometimes Uncle Jim trapped together in a burning storeroom three times. The same team of heroes also falls into a deep pit once, prefiguring the very next cliffhanger showing

Billy sinking in that ubiquitous pool of quicksand. Princess Alura tied to a tree with Jack must have been a marginally exciting oddity hinting, as it does, at covers on magazines hidden away by adults. And the crash landing leaving our heroes on Point X, thus beginning the island adventure, would have been nothing if not expected. A few surprising incidents, however, punctuate the more traditional use of the cliffhanger device in Fox's film. The confluence of events leading up to the end of Chapter 10 allows Pierce's gang to turn their stolen Cosmic Beam Annihilator on a group of charging natives rather than one of the serial's heroes, and the audience would have exited the theater that day without speculation over the fate of Jack or his allies. Most puzzling is the end of Chapter 12, with Professor Zorn's maze of Tanilic light zapping the evil Pierce while Jack looks on. ("*Wait,*" the audience gasps, "*our hero isn't in a fix this time!*") As the chapter play approaches the final episode, each week's cliffhanger appears to stray further from the conventional norm.

Regardless of these outlier cliffhanging incidents, Fox rarely resorts to narrative cheats intended to deceive audiences one week, leaving the hero in peril, only to demonstrate the following week that the danger, really, was not so bad. "The cliffhanger as a technique," Cline maintains,

> suffered the most damage when it was treated dishonestly, tongue in cheek, or cynically. For it to work, the audience had to believe that there was a real threat to the hero's life and whatever happened to save him from that threat had to be credible. When a solution was not credible or was too farfetched, then the whole thing became suspect. It may sound high blown, but between the serial makers and the serial watchers, there was a substantial element of trust.[41]

Only one cliffhanger in Fox's segmented narrative approaches a violation of this director-audience trust, and that perhaps predictably occurs late in the serial. At the end of Chapter 13, while Jack and one of Grood's strongmen grapple on a speeding truck hauling dynamite, the truck careens over a cliff, exploding just before the dissolve to next week's previews. This may have caused considerable chatter among theater patrons until the following week, when the takeout included a shot of the dynamite tumbling off the truck just before the crash. One probable cheat, however, diminishes Fox's accomplishments only marginally, and I'll bet most young viewers would double-dare anyone to complain, especially when Jack rolls off the truck, unharmed, and vanquishes the bad guy.

The emotional effects of serial cliffhangers and takeouts were suitably enhanced by rousing music, and Fox made good use of the talents of Lee Zahler, Musical Director at Columbia Pictures and Fox's uncredited musical collaborator on the *Jack Armstrong* project. "A favorite device of Zahler's to create a feeling of haunting mystery," writes Cline, "was the use of a sustained violin tremolo passage similar to the fatality theme in Georges Bizet's operatic masterpiece 'Carmen,' but backed by a rumbling, threatening orchestral vibrato that smacked of Richard Wagner."[42] The opening title sequence for each week's episode of Fox's serial, an action shot of the ascending aeroglobe followed by a painted still of Jack's atomic automobile and Grood's spaceship, indeed evokes a feeling of Wagnerian expanse tempered with the tones of a patriotic All-American march (Figure 10.6). The special effects of the aeroglobe are relatively convincing, while the narrator (Knox Manning) enthusiastically shouts "Jack Armstrong" three times, apparently imitating, with a single voice, the crowd of sports fans cheering Jack's athletic accomplishments in the radio serial. The result somehow asserts the hero's power and presence rather than provides encouragement for yet another touchdown. The subsequent card illustrating the title of the specific episode, usually a noun and modifier suggesting danger or menace, elicits a short musical passage with more ominous implications. The sense of dread and expectation for "Tunnels of Treachery," "The Secret Room," and "Wheels of Fate" is effectively accentuated by one long chord descending into silence.

Figure 10.6 The Aeroglobe ascends.

In addition to establishing an emotional tone for the action, music often reflects the two main characters in the serial, protagonist and antagonist, by a theme representing manner, intent, and agency. Jack's theme is the full-throated high-school march of the opening credits, a heroic accompaniment indicating a valiant young man. John Hart may have stretched the boundaries of the high-school hotshot's age bracket, approaching thirty at the time of *Jack Armstrong*'s production, but he somehow manages to wear the sweater vest, wide-collared shirt, and oxfords well. The added decade or so imparts a sense of authority necessary for the role, and the undercut hairstyle encourages an age-related suspension of disbelief. The menacing Grood, however, walks the island set as a superior and condescending force on legs, constantly lighting a cigar to punctuate the casualness of his confident evil. Grood's scenes generally are highlighted with quiet, foreboding music, an accompaniment more indicative of impending menace or disaster than immediate threat. Charles Middleton also portrayed the domineering and mad ruler Ming the Merciless in the earlier Flash Gordon serials, and his lanky presence, while unrecognizable from the bald, mustachioed planetary maniac, gives the serial a welcomed sense of legitimacy (Figure 10.7).

Figure 10.7 Grood deceives Naga.

Other, more minor characters appear to symbiotically attach themselves to the major characters' themes, demonstrating their allegiance through associated musical treatments. Pierre Watkin plays the role of scientist and explorer Uncle Jim with the calm and assurance of Marlin Perkins, ready to lead his band of daredevils into another Wild Kingdom adventure. The music accompanying Uncle Jim's screen time lets the audience know that as a youth he, too, was a regular fellow. Hugh Prosser as Vic Hardy is more difficult to pin down, musically, as he works at various times for both Uncle Jim and Jason Grood and therefore earns musical hand-me-downs from both sides. Princess Alura benefits from the elegance of Claire James's presence if not from her acting skills, and a quiet lushness of oboe and flute is especially appropriate as she combs her hair in a hut bedroom before a suspiciously Western-looking wicker dresser. Perhaps most notable among characters at the periphery of Jack's musical influence is the mysterious Panther Woman, danced rather than portrayed by Carmen D'Antonio with a remarkable 1940s Sunset Strip tiki bar appeal. Tribal drums thunder compellingly as the exotic, sarong-clad figure dances with broad gestures, finally invoking Xalta. D'Antonio enjoyed a reasonably extensive film career prior to her *Jack Armstrong* appearance, usually in roles requiring dance moves. Her performance in the 1944 B-movie *Cobra Woman*, rumored to be edgy filmmaker Kenneth Anger's favorite movie, was no doubt good preparation for Fox's serial. A variation on the Panther Woman's drum-based theme supports the other island natives collectively, although when the time comes for fast-paced action and running, the music is indistinguishable from the standard Western movie American Indian melody. As for John Merton's Pierce and the other heavies: evil is all the same, of course, regardless of form, so Grood's one theme guides them all.

Fox brought his *Jack Armstrong* heroes and villains to the screen not only near the end of his career but also perilously close to the time when the motion picture serial, as both Kinnard and Hulse note, would be superseded by other media. By 1950, Hulse writes, "the serial was already an endangered species. Television had just reared its ugly head, and the half-hour adventure series being made for the video screen bore more than passing resemblance to serial episodes—and were free to watch, besides."[43] Blair Davis explains that the exotic locales and frugal production values of B-movies and, by implication, the chapter plays actually encouraged TV show production by establishing easily achievable audience expectations. Davis writes:

> This is particularly true of half-hour programs, which regularly featured those genres which the B's had specialized in, such as the western or jungle adventure films. Since each of these genres is mythic or exotic in nature, producers could allow for a more neutral approach in their set design. Rather than be recreated in precise detail, settings such as "the

> savage jungle" and "the old west" merely had to be suggested, allowing the (typically juvenile) audience's preconceptions and imagination to fill in the rest.[44]

Shows dealing with outer space adventures were particularly popular during the early days of television, and at least ten heroes, including *Captain Video & His Video Rangers* (1949–1955), *Rod Brown of the Rocket Rangers* (1953–1954), *Rocky Jones, Space Ranger* (1952–1954), and the wonderfully named *Captain Z-Ro* (1951–1956), all invaded cathode tubes around the nation during kid-friendly hours. Realizing the marketing potential of character-related premium toys, television producers adapted the radio series model of mail-away gizmos and even amped-up their success by featuring premiums in on-air storylines, an early portent of product placement. As Lawrence R. Samuel points out,

> Show-related merchandise was an essential element of sponsorships, an almost sure way to keep young viewers tuned in and to make sure mom bought the right product at the grocery store . . . In 1949, for example, sponsor PowerHouse candy bars offered a Captain Video secret identifying ring free with a purchase of the product and a dime for postage and handling, precisely the kind of "space-age pizzazz" that added value to ordinary consumer production.[45]

The release of Fox's *Jack Armstrong* serial coincided with other significant cultural events that indicated a change in kid-oriented popular entertainment. RCA began advertising the first commercial television, the 630-TS, in November of 1946, and the 10-inch model was widely available in five major cities during 1947, selling around 250,000 units that year alone.[46] Jack's radio adventures began to decline, too, relying upon situations and events ever more implausible. "The beginning of the end came in 1947," writes Dunning, "when ABC vice president Ed Boroff canceled the quarter-hour format. Boroff had been critical of juvenile cliffhangers for some time, and one particular *Armstrong* episode contained all the elements he had long disdained."[47] Just as one radio broadcast of the teenage hero's adventures exposed the frayed fabric of an exhausted format, ending the broadcast series with a whimper, so did Jack Armstrong's movie career end after one episodic run. The final chapter of Fox's film concludes with Jack tentatively speculating that more adventures would follow, but instead these fifteen chapters represent the hero's only excursion into serial territory, a signpost leading the way toward space exploits on television. Alva Rogers, in his history of *Astounding Science Fiction*, also points to 1947 as the beginning of the magazine's "Silver Age," when published stories began to develop even further as impressive literary creations.[48] Young adult fiction started speculating about space travel as well, giving science fiction new legitimacy, beyond the pulp-and-paperback newsstand, in hard cover bookstore format. "In all likelihood," writes Francis Molson in her article on The Winston Science Fiction Series, one of the first and most popular juvenile fiction series of the early 1950s, "such a market was virtually created in 1947 by Robert Heinlein's *Rocket Ship Galileo* and then sustained by his subsequent successes, *Space Cadet* (1948), *Red Planet* (1949), *Farmer in the Sky* (1950), and *Between Planets* (1951), all published by Scribner's."[49]

Just as the Jack Armstrong radio broadcast provided Fox with the basic elements of plot, character, and intended audience for his chapter play, the new hardbound novel format derived inspiration from radio plays and the serials. Karen Sands and Marietta Frank, in their study of juvenile science fiction publications, also cite Heinlein's work as the beginning of a new trend, and the characters and subject matter are curiously familiar.

> These models for the [novel] series of the late 1940s and early 1950s depict a teenage (or slightly older) boy, often with a male sidekick, who uses his own inventions and intelligence in order to avert a danger that threatens not just himself but others as well—frequently the entire planet![50]

Citing several different heroes from young adult science fiction novels, the authors note that the young protagonists all "demonstrate an unusual amount of independence, intelligence, and ingenuity."[51] This description would work well on the inside front cover of a *Jack Armstrong* comic book or printed on a radio show Secret Whistling Ring premium toy, but instead serves as the outline for stories in a radically more respected format.

Heinlein's 1947 juvenile novel also inspired *Destination Moon* (1950), generally acknowledged as the first big-budget science fiction film and yet another disruptive element in popular children's entertainment. "Except for Fritz Lang's *Frau im Mond* twenty years before," Bill Warren writes in his mammoth account of science fiction movies in the 1950s, "no other film had treated space travel as a practical reality. None had even dealt with it; space travel had been confined to lurid serials. But *Destination Moon* approached the subject with vividness and believability, and permanently changed the average moviegoer's mind about space travel."[52] Warren's verbal swipe at the chapter play format is a good interpretation, over thirty years later, of the cultural trends ultimately ending the serial format's saturation of movie screens in small towns and major cities across the nation. Fox conformed to the new media and began working on television productions, directing five episodes of *The Gene Autry Show* between 1951 and 1953, as well as episodes of *The Range Rider* (1951–1952), *Ramar of the Jungle* (1953–1954), and *Annie Oakley* (1954), his last directorial work. Jack Armstrong, the character, the serial, and the All-American mystique, finally was defeated by a rogue scientist's infernal device, but that scientist was Philo Taylor Farnsworth, and the device was television.

Hitchcock, Lang, and Chaplin may have succeeded, mostly, in achieving auteur status with complex films dealing with mature subjects, but Fox's intent was perhaps equally satisfying to his intended audience and no less difficult to accomplish. Working within the conventions of the chapter-play format, Fox succeeds in providing the low-budget thrills demanded of the genre and delivers the workmanlike direction expected in cliffhanger movies. *Jack Armstrong*'s success was predicated upon integrating gadget and adventure, devices and heroics, to keep the action going, melodramatically and without the narrative assistance of characterization, nuance, or natural dialogue, until the next B-movie or feature reel was threaded into the projector. Ultimately, gadgets providing narrative structure to *Jack Armstrong* and other serials of the day demonstrate the era's optimistic appreciation of scientific wonders, celebrated in the science fiction pulps, while reflecting the mechanical tradition of plot development that restricted Fox's artistic latitude but, at the same time, provided him with the conventional dramatic elements allowing him to succeed in a restricted directorial environment. Twenty-first century viewers, inundated by the computer-enhanced special effects, hip acting, and uber-cool directing of films released to theaters or streaming to pocket-sized screens, might find the postwar serials impossibly inept and even downright dismal. But the aging population that attended these serials in their youth, or viewers appreciative of the serials' cultural representations, know that the significance of chapter plays extends beyond nostalgia or artifact.

Michael Chabon, an imaginative contemporary novelist and short story writer, is among the younger cohort appreciating the value of movie serials and their continued relevancy. In an engaging essay about career choice and the perplexing influence of his father, Chabon relates an important conversation between the two, during Chabon's youth, in a throwback Mexican restaurant lined with dark wood and Naugahyde:

> He told me about the Elevated trains of Brooklyn, about the all-day programs at his local movie theater: a newsreel, a cartoon, a serial, a comedy short, the B picture, and, finally, the A picture, all for a dime. He talked about comic books, radio dramas, *Astounding* magazine, and the stories they'd all told: of rocket-powered heroes, bug-eyed monsters, mad scientists bent on ruling the world. He described to me how he had saved box tops from cold cereals like Post Toasties, and redeemed them by mail for Junior G-Man badges or cardboard Flying Fortresses that carried payloads of black marbles . . . He described having spent weeks in the cellar of his Flatbush apartment building as a young teen-ager, with some mail-order chemicals, five pounds of kosher salt, and a lantern battery, trying to re-create 'the original recipe for life on earth,' as detailed in the pages of *Astounding*.[53]

Fox's work with chapter plays may have ended in 1947 with that one Jack Armstrong adventure into the ionosphere, and serials as a form may not have survived much longer. But by mixing serial conventions with gadgets, the infernal devices of heroes and madmen, into a ray of light projected on a screen, Fox may have succeeded in finding that recipe for life on earth, at least for a band of excited children or a Brooklyn boy named Chabon, on a long Saturday afternoon when school was out and time seemed endless.

NOTES

1. Tino Balio, *Grand Design: Hollywood as a Modern Business Enterprise, 1930–1939*, History of the American Cinema, Volume 5, 1930–1939 (Berkeley: University of California Press, 1995), 334.
2. Ed Hulse (ed.), *Blood 'n' Thunder's Cliffhanger Classics* (Morris Plains, NJ: Murania Press, 2012), 14.
3. Film studies scholar Guy Barefoot makes a persuasive case that studio executives in the 1930s intended serials for adults as well as children, and that the survival of the serial format through the 1930s and beyond was not entirely due to Saturday children's matinees. "Serials were made with children in mind and attracted a sizeable child audience," Barefoot writes, "but that audience was not limited to screenings marked as exclusively for children, nor were serials only made with children in mind or only watched by children." Columbia, in fact, briefly marketed its early serials to adults as well as children, but ended that policy after their first two serial releases in 1937. Barefoot concludes that the word "children" can be interpreted as anyone lacking cultural capital, regardless of age. In fact, Barefoot's research supports the notion that, as the postwar population gained intellectual sophistication and entertainment media became more complex in subject matter and presentation, chapter plays would fade as a big-screen attraction. See Guy Barefoot, "Who Watched that Masked Man? Hollywood's Serial Audiences in the 1930s," *Historical Journal of Film, Radio and Television*, 31:2 (June 2011), 183.
4. Roy Kinnard, *Science Fiction Serials: A Critical Filmography of the 31 Hard SF Cliffhangers; with an Appendix of the 37 Serials with Slight SF Content* (Jefferson, NC: McFarland, 1998), 1.
5. Hulse, *Cliffhanger Classics*, 15.
6. "Handing Off the Torch (The Serials of Columbia)," The Files of Jerry Blake: Movie Serial Reviews and Other Cliffhanging Material, last modified January 12, 2018. Available at <https://filesofjerryblake.com/2018/01/12/handing-off-the-torch-the-serials-of-columbia>
7. Ibid.
8. Clive Hirschhorn's coffee-table book, *The Columbia Story*, briefly charts the decline of the studio cliffhanger in a side note to the volume's index of Columbia productions. "Universal shut down its serial unit as early as 1946, and Republic followed suit in 1955. Columbia held out until 1956, and then brought the curtain down on an era with *Blazing the Overland Trail*" (382). The marginalized nature of film serials continues to this day, as critical discussion of chapter plays generally is confined to fan publications or niche-market publications intended for readers anxious to relive old serial thrills. Fewer than two pages of Hirschhorn's oversized, 456-page overview of Columbia is devoted to the serial format, and even that meager treatment is restricted to a perfunctory list of the fifty-seven

chapter plays produced by the studio, along with the names of the principal actors for each film and a short, one-sentence plot summary. Hirschhorn's chronologically organized introduction makes no mention of serials at all. Bernard F. Dick's *Columbia Pictures: Portrait of a Studio*, aside from noting the first Columbia serial in a studio chronology, confines attention to the form in one short, early paragraph. Such skimpy resources make niche books by Ed Hulse, Roy Kinnard, and William C. Cline invaluable, and websites such as "The Files of Jerry Blake" indispensable for continuing the critical discussion of a form nearly forgotten by serious film scholarship. See Clive Hirschhorn, *The Columbia Story* (London: Hamlyn, 1999), 382–3, and Bernard. F. Dick (ed.), *Columbia Pictures: Portrait of a Studio* (Lexington: The University of Kentucky Press, 2010), 12.

9. John Dunning, *On the Air: The Encyclopedia of Old-Time Radio* (New York: Oxford University Press, 1998), 352.
10. Dunning, 352–5, provides an insightful overview of the radio series. The broadcast script from September 30, 1940 is available online: Generic Radio Workshop Script Library, Jack Armstrong, All American Boy, A Typical Episode, <http://www.genericradio.com/show.php?id=5e80b8e759ba461a> (accessed February 2, 2018). Full episodes are available for streaming or download as public domain files: Jack Armstrong, <https://archive.org/details/JackArmstrong> (accessed February 2, 2018).
11. Dunning, 355.
12. Fred L. King, *Jack Armstrong Scrapbook: A Study in Premium Advertising* (Greentop, MO: Fred L. King, 1979), 65.
13. Robert M. Overstreet, *The Overstreet Comic Book Price Guide*, 46th ed. (Timonium MD: Gemstone Publishing, 2016), 749.
14. *Jack Armstrong: The All-American Boy of Radio Fame*, 1 (November 1947), inside front cover. Seven of the thirteen issues are available in digital format as public domain files: Jack Armstrong. Available at <https://archive.org/search.php?query=jack%20armstrong%20comics> (accessed February 6, 2018).
15. Geoff Mayer, *Encyclopedia of American Film Serials* (Jefferson, NC: McFarland, 2017), 1–2.
16. Kinnard, 203.
17. *Collier's*, a major, high-circulation magazine during the 1940s and 1950s, published the influential space symposium in a series of eight installments between March 22, 1952 and October 30, 1954. This series of futuristic articles capitalized upon the postwar interest in science and technology, and Bonestell's design of space hardware and off-world landscapes influenced later science fiction films, most notably *Conquest of Space* (1955).
18. Daniel Engber offers an amusing and often astonishing overview of quicksand misconceptions and the motif's appearance in recent films. The slyly pedantic nature of the article is as surprising, almost, as the film statistics he documents. Daniel Engber, "The Rise and Fall of Quicksand," Slate. Available at <http://www.slate.com/articles/health_and_science/science/2010/08/terra_infirma.html> (accessed February 3, 2018).
19. Jim Harmon and Donald F. Glut, *The Great Movie Serials: Their Sound and Fury* (1972; repr., London: Routledge, 2005), 45.
20. "Jack Armstrong," The Files of Jerry Blake.
21. Frederick Pohl, "The Day After Tomorrow," *Galaxy Magazine*, 24:1 (October 1965), 4.
22. J. Harvey Haggard, "An Adventure on Eros," *Wonder Stories: The Magazine of Prophetic Fiction*, 3:4 (September 1931), 550–1.
23. Mike Ashley and Robert A. W. Lowndes, *The Gernsback Days: A Study of the Evolution of Modern Science Fiction from 1911 to 1936* (Holicong, PA: Wildside Press, 2004), 326.
24. Ashley and Lowndes, *Gernsback*, 150.
25. Ed Hulse, *The Blood 'n' Thunder Guide to Pulp Fiction* (n.p: Murania Press), 18.
26. Ibid., 19.

27. Kinnard, *Science Fiction Serials*, 6.
28. Campbell frequently would assemble scientific information from various sources and suggest story ideas to his writers based upon that research. Cleve Cartmill's story, "Deadline," published in the March 1944 issue of *Astounding*, detailed the development of an atomic bomb with such accuracy that agents of the FBI, charged with enforcing Manhattan Project secrecy, visited both author and editor for extensive interviews. The anecdote is perhaps the best indication of Campbell's editorial policy concerning factual science and technology descriptions. The most detailed account of this incident, derived from government documents, is Albert I. Berger, "The *Astounding* Investigation: The Manhattan Project's Confrontation with Science Fiction," *Analog Science Fiction/Science Fact*, 54:9 (September 1984): 125–37. Fandom lore holds that Campbell, aware of *Astounding*'s extensive subscription base of scientists and engineers, claims to have known something was up when the magazine began receiving multiple change of address forms to a post office in New Mexico. I hope that legend is true.
29. Mike Ashley, *The Time Machines: The Story of the Science-Fiction Pulp Magazines from the Beginning to 1950*, The History of the Science-Fiction Magazine, Volume 1 (Liverpool: Liverpool University Press, 2000), 157.
30. Theodore Sturgeon, "Maturity," *Astounding Science Fiction*, 38:6 (February 1947), 50. As Paul Williams documents in his "Story Notes" for a volume of Sturgeon's collected fiction, the author later demonstrated artistic ambition by significantly revising the novella prior re-publication in an early edited collection, an act of creative dedication perhaps not seen before in the genre. Paul Williams, "Story Notes," in Theodore Sturgeon, *Thunder and Roses: Volume IV: The Complete Stories of Theodore Sturgeon*, ed. Paul Williams (Berkeley, CA: North Atlantic Books, 1997), 339.
31. *Jack Armstrong: The All-American Boy*, DVD, directed by Wallace Fox (1947; Tulsa, OK: VCI Entertainment, 2004).
32. Hal Clement's short story "Trojan Fall," for example, appeared in an issue of *Astounding* not quite three years before Columbia released the first chapter of *Jack Armstrong*. Clement traces, in impressive detail, the efforts of La Roque, a runaway criminal with rudimentary mathematical skills, to avoid capture by parking his spaceship in a Lagrangian point of a binary star. He ultimately fails disastrously, and the navigator of the pursing outer space paddy wagon provides a technically satisfying explanation concerning the fallacy of three-body calculations involving double stars. Hal Clement, "Trojan Fall," *Astounding Science Fiction*, 33:4 (June 1944), 57–69.
33. Mayer, 6.
34. Ibid., 15.
35. Both *Mysterious Doctor Satan* (1940) and *Batman* (1943) involve calculated self-boxing. See William C. Cline, *Serials-ly Speaking: Essays on Cliffhangers* (Jefferson, NC: McFarland, 1994), 210.
36. William C. Cline, *In the Nick of Time: Motion Picture Sound Serials* (Jefferson, NC: McFarland, 1984),: 6.
37. Ibid., 19.
38. Jeffrey Klenotic, "'Four Hours of Hootin' and Hollerin': Moviegoing and Everyday Life Outside the Movie Palace," in Richard Maltby, Melvyn Stokes, and Robert C. Allen (eds), *Going to the Movies: Hollywood and the Social Experience of Cinema* (Exeter: University of Exeter Press, 2007), 150. Cline shares a similar recollection of youthful serial-goer excitement early on in his book, *In the Nick of Time*. As an eight-year-old, Cline was allowed to tag along with a pack of excited older kids on their Saturday afternoon trip to the local theater, with everyone in hot anticipation of seeing a new episode of a serial starring the costumed hero named the "Eagle." Part of the journey to the theater, Cline

recalls, was to speculate about how they would handle the bad guy if they wore the Eagle's suit, and later, in the theater, he learned how to properly "cheer the hero and hiss the villain." Then, at the cliffhanger conclusion, Cline had a revelatory experience. "I suddenly realized," he writes, "that I was perched on the very edge of my seat, holding on for dear life to the back of the seat in the next row. I could hardly believe what I had just gone through. It was truly incredible to me that any such excitement as that could exist." (viii–ix)

39. Klenotic, 6.
40. Kinnard, 6.
41. Cline, *Serials-ly*, 207.
42. Cline, *Nick*, 174.
43. Hulse, 30.
44. Blair Davis, "Small Screen, Smaller Pictures: Television Broadcasting and B-Movies in the Early 1950s," *Historical Journal of Film, Radio and Television*, 28: 2 (June 2008), 229.
45. Lawrence R. Samuel, "The Sky is the Limit: Advertising and Consumer Culture" in Cynthia J. Miller and A. Bowdoin Van Riper (eds), *1950s "Rocketman" Television Series and Their Fans: Cadets, Rangers, and Junior Space Men* (New York: Palgrave, 2012), 137.
46. Gary Edgerton, *The Columbia History of American Television* (New York: Columbia University Press, 2007), 77. See also Early Television Museum, Postwar American Television, RCA 630-TS. Available at <http://www.earlytelevision.org/rca_630.html> (accessed February 9, 2018).
47. Dunning, 355.
48. Alva Rogers, *A Requiem for Astounding* (Chicago: Advent: Publishers, 1964), 142.
49. Francis Molson, "The Winston Science Fiction Series and the Development of Children's Science Fiction," *Extrapolation*, 25:1 (1984), 34.
50. Karen Sands and Marietta Frank, *Back in the Spaceship Again: Juvenile Science Fiction Series Since 1945*, Contributions to the Study of Science Fiction and Fantasy, Number 84 (Westport, CT: Greenwood Press, 1999): 35–6.
51. Sands and Frank, 36.
52. Bill Warren, *Keep Watching the Skies!: American Science Fiction Movies of the Fifties* (Jefferson, NC: McFarland, 1982), 2.
53. Michael Chabon, "The Recipe for Life," *The New Yorker*, 93:47 (February 5, 2018), 23.

CHAPTER 11

A Fox in the Wild: *Ramar of the Jungle* and the Crisis of Representation

Robert Singer

"You get the lion, or the lion gets you"

Robert Ruark

When it comes to representing minority cultures, whether expressed in linguistically challenged utterances of fragmented English or in moments of stereotypically déclassé behavior, the postwar media frequently displayed a qualified perspective, an ontological image of race, class, and gender; various representations were calculated, affective factors sustaining the plot and overall continuity of illusion in countless comedic or dramatic narratives, and many were recurrent images of sociological others as entertainment spectacles. Those productions, in particular, director Wallace Fox's episodes of television's jungle-fantasy, *Ramar of the Jungle* (1953–1954), are potentially classified as ideologically circumscribed narratives. It is my contention that Fox's *Ramar* episodes are not markedly racist and merit reassessment. National and international media productions from the postwar era invite intergeneric, alternative readings of the socio-political matter, while acknowledging obvious controversies. These are *problematic*, not superficial, narratives. The postwar media was ripe with such illustrative material, and this chapter examines, in an intertextual capacity, the eleven episodes of *Ramar of the Jungle* directed by Wallace Fox, especially as they recall and renew Western narratives in the sustained imaginative framing of Africa-African images.

One notably transgressive practice involves the recycled racial images and representative patterns of social alterity produced as entertainment spectacles in the postwar American and European media, especially in film and television productions which depict Africa, Africans, and related Western cultural myths associated with progress and civilization. Despite the preponderant number of

Figure 11.1 Dr. Tom "Ramar" Reynolds (Jon Hall) and Prof. Howard Ogden (Ray Montgomery).

these media spectacles, many significant exceptions to the culture of misrepresentation did exist, albeit on the edges of industrial marketing, as "B" productions. Multiple literary and film productions, produced during the rise of the postwar, nuclear era, reveal substantial issues associated with the eroticized, demeaned, or ignored sociological other; these racially charged images saturate popular national and international cultures as signifying spectacles, in notable dialogue with a controlling ideology.

Commenting on this postwar trend in media narrative, and specifically referring to *Ramar of the Jungle*, Wheeler Winston Dixon has concluded that, "The world of *Ramar of the Jungle* is a dark and complicated social terrain, marked on the one side by the dying inequities of colonialism and on the other, by the rule of violence and reprisal."[1] In a somewhat conspiratorial tone, Dixon concludes that, "[Series creator and star] Hall aligned himself with those already operating on the margins of Hollywood to create a series that would further marginalize the citizens of Africa . . . and racist stereotypes could be reinforced in the name of 'entertainment.'"[2] *Perhaps*, but I would suggest a re-reading of the racial themes and general content in Fox's *Ramar* episodes as part of a distinctive, critical experience.

These imperfect postwar narratives merit rediscovery, but this admittedly raises complicated questions. One illustrative and relevant historical example of the problematic racial narrative involves a critical transitional text in American film culture, the blackface "talkie" spectacle *The Jazz Singer* (1927). In his article, "Why Did Negroes Love Al Jolson and The Jazz Singer?", Charles Musser notes that despite the contemporary critical opposition concerning Al Jolson's performance in blackface makeup and the film's overall identity politics involving assimilation and race, there exists a fascinating, ironic historical counterpoint: "In the late 1920s, African American newspapers and moviegoers warmly embraced the actor-singer Al Jolson and *The Jazz Singer*."[3] Musser deliberates on this conundrum:

> The taking-on of other ethnic identities evident in the production of *The Jazz Singer* (and many other Hollywood films) has its counterpart in the process of spectatorship. Indeed one could argue that the publicized nature of these disjunctive performances encouraged audiences to follow suit, allaying guilt or anxiety as they are sutured into the fictive world of the film. Perhaps the movie theater was, in this respect, the great melting pot for America.[4]

Not all audiences saw the same film. Classic film or racist narrative: which/whose *The Jazz Singer* is it? Nearly thirty years later, Wallace Fox directed an episode of the *Ramar of the Jungle* series entitled "Drums of the Jungle." Fox's episode featured broken English spoken by the African population, witch doctor and natives, ivory as fetish object, and stock footage of the aroused wild jungle, complemented by a soundtrack comprised of diegetic and non-diegetic background sounds, noise, and musical leitmotifs. This B television show, like *The Jazz Singer*, retrospectively reveals layered narrative substance involving race and representation. While not attaining a level of artistic or historical profundity, *Ramar*, like other popular, postwar media productions to be discussed, may be categorized as a co-presence, another representative narrative, revealing the ideological ambiguities of a specific socio-historical milieu. The entertainment narratives of the 1950s contain corresponding levels of A and B industrial classificatory status but are not newsreels or documentaries which allege to record and reveal the imperfect world as it concerns race and racism. However much these episodes reflect the value systems and ideological norms of the 1950s, each may be read retrospectively to demonstrate subtle, critical distinctions, "problematics," when representing race and racism, and like *The Jazz Singer* and other, later media productions, these episodes resist the "either/or" critical imperative associated with race narratives. *Ramar* is classifiable in the historical space of the popular imagination.

While deep in the foreboding environment depicted in "Drums of the Jungle," Jabba, the local chief's son, saves Dr. Ramar, a nearly mythic symbol of cultural exchange and progress, from a rampaging lion. Jabba, also a progressive figure, was an African who desired to learn the white man's ways and to serve as a bridge between both cultures. Jabba is falsely accused of ivory theft and is dishonored before the tribe. The real Conradian villain is a white man who corrupts several of the susceptible natives, especially the witch doctor, to obtain ivory for illegal trade with the world outside of the jungle. This Anglo interloper and his native cohorts are detected and caught as a result of two events: a hidden camera snaps a photo of the crime in progress, and Jabba testifies that he is innocent and willingly undergoes a ceremonial act to confirm his status. Since there are no witnesses, Jabba must prove his innocence by accepting the sanctioned, ritual act of swallowing a magical liquid that establishes or refutes one's guilt. Although he imbibes the poisoned fluid, Jabba is saved by Ramar, for modern medical technology provides the antidote for this auto-da-fé.

In this episode, a series of oppositional strategies function within the narrative that arguably exceed the effects of the questionable racial images perceived by the audience. These binaries incorporate: tribalism—progressivism; witchcraft—technology; unethical black and white—honest black and white; basically, the primitive—the new world. Yet it is more frequently corrupt and corrupting white people who are the real others in several *Ramar* narratives. Ramar, like Superman, his postwar media contemporary, is a positive symbol of male virtue in the act of "doing"; specifically, Ramar represents the positive presence of a foreign culture—another other—in the midst of imaginary others.

These repetitive, interrelated, and controversial representational strategies are endemic to Fox's *Ramar* episodes. To sustain its B production sensibility, *Ramar of the Jungle* features Dr. Tom "Ramar" Reynolds, and his sidekick, Prof. Howard Ogden, with a supporting cast of good and bad natives, who collectively provide an entry point into the fictitious Africa of the burgeoning postwar imagination. These episodes reveal compositional tropes endemic to the overall African narrative of the 1950s: quasi-anthropological, antiquated magical-tribal customs versus Western medicine and technology, corrupt versus enlightened men and women (of both colors), and in imaginings of requisite closure, reassuring, albeit compressed, resolutions associated with progressive power and race relations. This episode instigates multiple possibilities for generic applications and regenerations of the familiar, in opposition to the other, in narrative culture. For example, several postwar film and television narratives representing Africa and the African involve an informing, compromised ideological schema. These images involving race and racism are not isolated phenomena; Africa is one such site, and Africans, one example of the problematic image.

These eleven *Ramar* episodes establish that the Africans are "not us," and like indexical, pointing fingers, shots of natives and settlers in crises repeatedly direct the viewer's gaze, and this representational strategy includes Ramar, negotiating alterity: the other in the midst of others. This reception experience, the "less than real effect," involves suspending the totalizing capacity of the audience and media critic to affix absolute values and meaning, and instead, to review these perplexing images as signifying spectacles negotiating existence. The audience neither accepts nor refutes the ideological other, but newly reflects upon its historical context and intertextual linkage.

This counter-reading of Fox's *Ramar of the Jungle* episodes demonstrably challenges the critical preoccupation with immediate plot points involving Africa, Africans, race, racism, and a suspect white culture. While acknowledging the necessity of critical, judgmental perspectives, I contest the assessment that *Ramar of the Jungle* dismissively depicts Africa and Africans as "a savage, backward, cultureless continent,"[5] which includes several other protracted, censorious decrees:

> *Ramar of the Jungle* combined the anti-Communist hysteria of the McCarthy era with the lingering ghost of the Victorian colonialist instinct, and an almost overwhelming dose of cultural imperialism and blatant racism, to create a hothouse hybrid of violence, sadism, sexism, and lurid spectacle that was unrivaled in its sheer excess and brutality by any of its Saturday morning competitors.[6]

These are the last rites pronouncements of a compelling critical positioning, yet Ramar, along with the eponymously named figure in *Jungle Jim* (1955–1956), was not the only controversial character on the postwar small screen. There is a discernable intergeneric blending of thematic tropes in western television productions, like *The Lone Ranger*, and the Jungle/Africa narratives in Fox's *Ramar* episodes. Fox, the director of westerns such as *Bullets for Bandits* (1942), *Riders of the Santa Fe* (1944), *Gunman's Code* (1946), *Arizona Territory* (1950), and multiple television episodes of *The Gene Autry Show* (1951–1953), was a director whose movement amongst industrial production templates was notable. Along with his extensive career directing B films and serials, Wallace Fox, like André De Toth, directed multiple television dramas.

During the 1950s, American film culture specifically experienced multiple productions of the African jungle narrative. In these films, frequently set in an earlier decade of the century, the pre-nuclear era for dramatic and historical distancing, Africa and Africans were cast as backdrops to examine white populations, especially colonists, in states of socio-political and occasionally, romantic crisis.[7] While critics have documented numerous examples of these historical narratives, such as *The Snows of Kilimanjaro* (dir. Henry King, Twentieth Century-Fox, 1952), *Bwana Devil* (dir. Arch Oboler, Oboler-United Artists Productions, 1952), and *Watusi* (dir. Kurt Neumann, MGM, 1959), among others, two examples relevant to this study are Henry Hathaway's *White Witch Doctor* (Twentieth Century-Fox, 1953) and André De Toth's *Tanganyika* (Universal

Studios, 1954). These two films expose an exploitive colonial past for the 1950s audience's consumption via tropes of racial and gender discourse and merit a comparative analysis with several episodes from the *Ramar* series.

Set in the colonized Belgian Congo in 1907, during the infamously abusive reign of King Leopold II, the man who "owned" the Congo, Hathaway's *White Witch Doctor* is a redemption melodrama that utilizes Africa and the Africans as background to refresh familiar film generic parameters. Ellen Burton (Susan Hayward), a nurse, called "little mama" by the natives, newly arrived in the jungle to leave behind her unsettling guilt after her husband's death, assists with the progressive medical practices of an elderly hermit-like, ailing woman doctor. In order to get into this remote and dangerous bush area, a journey into a Technicolor "heart of darkness," nurse Burton must persuade hunter-businessman John Douglas (Robert Mitchum), introduced in the film as callously crating wild animals for shipment to zoos in foreign ports of call, to take her along on his safari, in which he secretly intends to locate and steal for himself and his partner the gold located in the vicinity of a dangerous indigenous tribe: the Bakuba. Like Fox, Hathaway utilizes stock footage of animals and dancing natives, complemented by diegetic sounds of jungle birds and signifying drums, to establish a familiar setting for the audience. This is the Africa of the imagination.[8]

Ostensibly, director de Toth's *Tanganyika* is a film set in Kenya in 1903 and, borrowing freely from the "wagon train/family of settlers into dangerous territory" trope of the western film, a group of collated white people, traveling together for disparate reasons, and accompanied by servile natives, set out to locate another Kurtz-like, deranged figure who has instigated violent civil insurrection against cooperative natives and European interlopers. These are traditional gender and racially specific good/evil and uncivilized/progressive tropes of narrative fabulation. The dangerous Nukumbi tribe, functioning in the collective imagination of the audience like prototypical, nationalist Mau-Mau warriors, seeks respite and revenge against the perceived trespassers into their country, and a white man shall lead them. The leader of the trek into the remote region of the jungle to ensnare these seditious criminals is the gun-toting colonist and capitalist (sheriff) John Gale (Van Heflin), who collects four survivors along the way: a schoolteacher Peggy Marion (Ruth Roman), a mysterious counterpoint male, Dan McCracken (Howard Duff), whose brother is the deranged killer-insurrectionist they seek, and two adorable, needy minors. This family-in-the-making could only exist in Hollywood's Africa.

John Gale, businessman and hunter, also performs restorative medical-magical procedures in which he uses flashing gunpowder to cauterize a wound, skillfully shoots his rifle (like a god hurling lightening) before the natives, and detonates dynamite in several places to confound the natives and the escaped white transgressor: these technologically driven spectacles of magical balms, afflictions, loud unnatural sounds, and rising smoke, created by a commanding white witch doctor, are images signifying power to the intimidated natives. Magic enables the trek. André De Toth, director of such films as the noir narrative, *Pitfall* (Regal-United Artists, 1948), the western, *Carson City* (Warner Bros., 1952), and the 3-D horror *House of Wax* (Warner Bros., 1953), utilizes the recurring trope of white magic in this film, as opposed to black magic, with its curses, poisons, and destabilizing violence associated with native witch doctors, to impress upon the ignorant tribe and the audience that technology—whether to cure the ill or to kill the evil—is the overpowering, near-supernatural, and alien means to control. In *Tanganyika*, any measure of realism—the studio setting, like Ramar's set design—is obviously constructed, and character development is essentially void. De Toth deploys multiple close-up, shot-reaction (affect) shots indicating suspicion, anger, and yearning, which then frequently cut to medium shots of stock footage of the jungle, full of eruptive noise and creatures lurking in bushes. This compositional strategy, however facile it may appear, creates a symbolic, postwar family. Illusory romantic experiences allow personal and social misdeeds and scores to be settled and enable the colonial empire to be maintained, over a landscape littered with African bodies and a few corrupt white men.

Throughout De Toth's film, the African natives either menace each other and the white colonial presence, or the Africans support the safari as exploited labor; they are backdrop: part of the functional plot and setting, exhibiting scant personal identity. One recalls Nigerian novelist Chinua Achebe's negative evaluation of Conrad's novella, *Heart Of Darkness* (1899), and how the narrative centers on the criminal dissolution of one European's moral consciousness, set against the African continent, which is portrayed "as a foil to Europe,"[9] to which Achebe adds: "*Heart of Darkness* projects the image of Africa as 'the other world,' the antithesis of Europe and therefore of civilization, a place where man's vaunted intelligence and refinement are finally mocked by triumphant beastiality [*sic*]."[10] Achebe's point, however condemnatory, raises very significant issues to the contemporary audience involving who represents whom. Fox's eleven *Ramar* episodes, as well as other television productions from the postwar era—*The New Adventures of Charlie Chan* (1957–1958), *The Goldbergs* (1949–1957), and especially, *The Lone Ranger* (1949–1957)—illustrate the recurring ethical conundrum involving racial (mis) representation, whether set in the illusory African jungle or the old west of nineteenth-century America.

According to Chadwick Allen, *The Lone Ranger* was an immensely popular American television production:

> The popular Lone Ranger television series, which for Americans and for increasing numbers of international television viewers immortalized

> Clayton Moore [The Lone Ranger] and Jay Silverheels [Tonto] as the quintessential Lone Ranger and Tonto pair, first aired in 1949. In the mid-1950s its viewing audience was estimated at over 33 million . . . Following the success of the television series, in 1956 and 1958 Moore and Silverheels starred in two financially successful Lone Ranger feature films.[11]

In *The Lone Ranger* episode entitled "Ghost Canyon," director Earl Bellamy, whose career extended into film as well as television productions, freely mixes stereotypes of Native Americans, especially those involving language acquisition skills, with subject matter involving Native American rituals and culture.[12] In "Ghost Canyon," a man pretending to be the lost nephew of a Native American chief violently aids in the rustling of cattle from the indigenous tribe. The audience learns that the imposter nephew was a fellow inmate of the two rustler-murderers who had killed the chief's son. Eventually, the fabled Lone Ranger and his sidekick Tonto arrive in time to thwart the theft, but other matters remain unresolved. Tension builds as the nephew attempts to turn the chief against the untrustworthy white settlers. Ironically, the true outlaws are white men, rapidly identifiable to the audience as corrupting agencies, for it is they who kill and steal. After some negotiation with the tribe, the Lone Ranger and Tonto conceive of a way to catch the criminals as the chief's surviving son goes off to experience the sacred ritual of entering manhood prior to leaving in order to protect the remaining cattle. Unbeknownst to the thieves, Tonto substitutes himself for the son and fakes undergoing the ritual. Although the thieves are caught, they do manage to escape along with the now exposed imposter; these thieves take the surviving son hostage and threaten to kill him unless they are given the remaining cattle.

As the outlaws negotiate a deal with the chief and the tribe, the Lone Ranger works his way up to the top of the mountain range where the criminals are positioned. While the Lone Ranger subdues the two white thieves, the imposter falls off the mountain to his death. With order restored, the Lone Ranger and Tonto ride off into the network sunset, and, according to Michael Ray Fitzgerald: "the Ranger's Anglo-Saxon-Protestant values say a lot about the culture as well as the program's ideological aims. Tonto's presence raises the question of whether, and if so, how, a minority figure or nonwhite can fit into this project."[13] Order is restored by the masked, but not hooded, white man and companion, and Western values are maintained. As Fitzgerald notes: "This series contains several specific tropes that identify the Ranger as godlike,"[14] and god was assuredly pale-skinned.

How does the constructed, *racialized* image of the socio-political other signify, while simultaneously comprise, a real-fictional person? Fitzgerald notes that: "Tonto replies in his pidgin English"[15] and throughout the episode, Tonto follows this pattern of linguistic irregularities as he exclaims to the Lone Ranger and others: "Where you find him" and "him make trouble for his tribe," among other choice utterances. This suggests the repetitive role of "broken" language in signifying otherness as a contributory factor in the postwar popular culture.

The Lone Ranger, produced in postwar California, composed mostly of wide and medium one and two shots, with a frequently inserted reaction close-up, often features the rugged terrain, the western landscape in a framing, posterior perspective, to resemble the painter's conception of action-order imposed on a setting. According to Fitzgerald,

> The land and how it is portrayed is a crucial issue in *The Lone Ranger*, as it is in most Westerns. After all, the land is the prize: who controls it and how it is to be used is generally the primary issue. Like any Western, this series features lots of panoramic, wide shots that emphasize the landscape.[16]

In *The Lone Ranger*, as in the case of the exotic jungle environment in *Ramar*, setting is a functional presence, effectively engaging and revealing character traits. In this *Ranger* episode, the isolation of the mountains and stark plains are essentially spaces in which characters' strength and intrigues are revealed: the "passage into manhood" ritual takes place in a sequestered area, and to prove his mettle as he "faces the spirit of evil," the young Native American lets the smoke of "strong powder" make the "magic open his ears, eyes, and spirit." Magic consistently functions as an edifying trope of transformative power.

In the *Ramar* episode entitled "The Sacred Monkey," Ramar's colleague, Howard, also notes the medicinal value and potential, the dormant magic, to be discovered in the African wildlife and natural environment. Amidst the cut-away, stock footage shots of lions and panthers, Howard and some natives go on a trek, but he is wounded and taken to the local witch doctor who treats him as the locals pray to the sacred monkey in which dwell the redeeming spirits of their ancestors. This raises a question of simian magic; how do these monkeys apparently live so long? In the name of progressive science, a raid on the natives to obtain some specimens and information is planned. On the other side of the village reside the monkeys, in a colony forbidden to outsiders which recalls the primitive, near-stone age abandoned settlement of tribes past. One old monkey is taken by the white interlopers back to civilization for further study, but the witch doctor secures the monkey and they return to the village. Although the white settlers once again act to retrieve the critical specimen, they fail and are nearly caught, promising to return. The mystery remains an unresolved clinical concern, but the indigenous belief system is not derided or ignored.

Hidden amongst a dense expansion of overgrown bushes and trees, amidst the Ed Wood-like cut-away stock shots of playful or rampaging wildlife in

Ramar of the Jungle's set design of an imaginary Africa, we find a collection of clichés, characters, and plot points which exemplify the postwar, revelatory ideological gamut, including white invaders' manipulation of natives, jungle "magic," and theft of natural resources. The *Ramar* episodes directed by Wallace Fox, himself a citizen of the Chickasaw Nation, characteristically employ slated, worn gender and racially based individual and group behavioral patterns.[17]

Fox's *Ramar* episodes, saturated with suturing stock footage and familiar plot intrigues, reveal an Africa of the postwar American imagination, in which two principled and educated white males consistently "set things right" for the local inhabitants. This is set against a recognizably artificial studio setting, with frequent cut-away stock shots of life in Africa. In *Ramar* episodes, the African landscape shots facilitate the audiences' sense of imaginative space and time and link to survival narratives, suggesting both natural beauty and encroaching violence (Figure 11.2).

These landscape and stock footage cut-away shots function as painterly backdrops to the foreground action: consider how Frederic Remington's *The Parley* (1903), and Henri Rousseau's *Le lion ayant faim se jette sur l'antilope* [*The Hungry Lion Throws Itself on the Antelope*] (1905)[18] capture moments of communication, peril, and generally, moments of life in the wild environ. These

Figure 11.2 Fox's *Ramar of the Jungle*: a moment of violence.

paintings suggest a dynamic, direct relationship with *imaginings* of the early twentieth-century idea of the uncivilized world, the space and time of others. *Ramar* exists in the world of the 1950s middle-class television audiences' collective imagination of an unknown-known place: Africa. In Fox's *Ramar* episode "The Blue Treasure," the (unseen) color blue functions as a vivid marker of painted African faces and a hidden reserve of cobalt in this setting full of spiders and angry natives. Deep in the shrouded, wild, Rousseau-like brush, a reserve of unmined cobalt, a sign of familiar nuclear coding for the 1950s audience, is more desirable than even gold beyond the jungle setting. According to postwar American congresswoman Frances P. Bolton, these resources were a relevant concern for Africa as well as for abroad:

> Africa is a country of great extremes and many emotions . . . Those of you who have been to Africa know something of its vastness, its insensibility. You have felt its mystery, you have been stirred by its almost incredible possibilities . . . I have spoken of the fabulous wealth of Africa, her cobalt, copper, gold, diamonds, rubber, cocoa, coffee—all the raw materials of inestimable value to us.[19]

The emphasis is on "us." One never sees but could almost grasp the forbidden, colorful substance, but it remains sealed off from colonial machinations in a mine. Scrutinizing these western and jungle paintings, one intuits a model, an interpretive vision of reality while not experiencing it as a fact, for these images are to be looked at, absorbed as perceptions. Likewise, the viewer of Fox's *Ramar* episodes has been positioned to consume images of processed others passing as types—markers—serving a dramatic function, in a postwar experiential context. In his *Ramar* episodes, Fox consistently composes shot sequences in a series of medium one and two shots, close-ups, and a cut-away to stock footage. There is the occasional pan to follow the action, with shot-reverse shots to cue the audience on what to anticipate. Consistent with his B film directing experiences, Fox notably adds stock footage into the *Ramar* narrative in critical, establishing sequences to provide a sense of the imagined authentic. Dixon precisely notes that, "*Ramar*'s production schedule was helped along with liberal inclusions of stock footage . . . the Vertovian abandon with which stock footage was utilized remained one of *Ramar*'s most distinguishable traits."[20]

In addition to analogous settings, jungle genre narratives routinely share other tropes which are evident in *Ramar* episodes: the western frequently has an out-of-the-way home or fort, scattered settlements and a trading post; several episodes of *Ramar* feature a frontier-style home for Ramar and Howard, native villages strewn across the plain, and there is a trading post run by European settlers; the western features a guide-translator (like Tonto) so the whites may approach the

Native Americans, while Ramar frequently depends upon his informative comic-relief man-servant, Charlie, with an assortment of supporting (neither slaves nor drunkards) workers to approach the Africans; most importantly, Ramar, the doctor, and Howard, the research scientist, are two white men whose purpose is not to exploit but to establish, restore, and support, via the technology of modern medicine and science, the health and prosperity of the native population, and like deputies in a frontier western town, Ramar and Howard, seemingly acting as imperial managers, establish peace amongst the occasionally warring populations while confronting outlaws. Fox did not direct documentaries or newsreels about African culture; these are performance spectacles, B television productions.

Other select international and national film and television narratives produced in the 1950s invoke problematic historical and artistic issues associated with Africa and Africans. In 1950, French filmmaker René Vautier directed *Afrique 50*, a stridently anti-colonial, anti-capitalist, and consequently banned film about the subjugating presence of the French nation in Africa. Even for the postmodern audience, desensitized by the relentless flow of historical data and images of cultivated cruelty across the media, Vautier's study in exploitive power is exceptional. *Afrique 50* examines racist postwar hegemonic practices and transgressions, committed in the name of progress and civilization. Steven Ungar notes that: "*Afrique 50* satisfies several criteria of a *film à thèse* by documenting and denouncing incidents of violence perpetrated during 1949 and 1950 in conjunction with colonial policies in French West Africa and, especially, in the Ivory Coast."[21] Shortly after Vautier's suppressed production, French directors Alain Resnais and Chris Marker released their remarkable generic blending of experimental documentary and independent cinema, a unique African-centric film, *Les Statues meurent aussi* [*Statues Also Die*] (1953).

This celebration of African art transcends the typical homage and cataloging of the museum setting, as it positions the audience to see the mortality of devoured and appropriated cultural artifacts, traditionally defined by Western categorizations of pragmatics and beauty. The directors' camera placement and overall shot composition—in multiple dissolves, pans, and medium to close-up shots—create the sense of walking through African space and time. According to Matthias De Groof, "*Les Statues* sheds a critical light on the ethno- [and] historio-centric western gaze. The film takes the dispossession and transformations of African artefacts as a heuristic model in order to understand the greater dynamics of the colonial gaze,"[22] to which he adds: "The film is not satisfied with vainly trying to reproduce traditional meaning, but makes an attempt to project African art into the future."[23]

In the episodes of *Ramar* directed by Fox discussed below, antiquated tribal customs, magic, and Western progressive-technology tropes are effectively rendered, projected, as plot engagements. Fox's "Danger in Disguise" episode establishes Dr. Ramar and research scientist Prof. Howard as enlightened scientists and unofficial authority figures (recalling a previous colonial era and ideology), who combat two newly arrived botanists—actually murderers—in search of seed and extracts from plants that can be made to produce narcotics. This is a variation on the postwar "dope" admonition-hyperbolic narratives, like William Seiter's *Borderline* (Bren-Seiter: Universal Productions, 1950), André De Toth's *Monkey on My Back* (Imperial-United Artists, 1955), and Otto Preminger's *The Man with the Golden Arm* (Preminger Films: United Artists, 1955). In this *Ramar* episode, the murderers contrive to steal, in place of the actual drug, Howard's research data into exotic, indigenous plant life and then sell it to pharmaceutical conglomerates back in Western civilization, suggesting that information is the new ivory. They are detected by an old post trader who reads the native drums communicating the events, and the thieves are killed by natives in an act of justifiable revenge. The negative racial associations are clearly linked to the corrupting presence of the white men. In another *Ramar* episode directed by Fox, "Contraband," white men instigate the theft of ivory, along with the murder of natives and slaughter of elephants. This episode features the alchemical mixture of plants and herbs—good magic—and several sequences involving the conniving chicanery of an intrusive presence.

A similar plot line is developed in Fox's episode "Striped Fury," as a search for powerful medicinal plants involves confirming the astonishing ability of a plant extract to retard the deterioration of the body: marketing the youth formula. Complicating the storyline is the presence of two escaped (colonizing) tigers in the jungle, the result of a mythic "great white hunter"—another recurring postwar jungle trope— losing this shipment en route to civilization. This episode also features the abundant incorporation of stock footage of tigers, leopards, and even a water buffalo, to create a sense of visual authenticity. The tribal witch doctors inaccurately believe that Ramar is the person responsible for the menacing tigers, so they curse Ramar. A totemic figure of Ramar is stuck with pins that are smeared with poison, and Howard falls ill as he impulsively makes contact with the figure. Bad magic is put into play against Ramar's good, curative magic, and order and justice are eventually restored.

In another episode directed by Fox, entitled "Jungle Terror," Wilkins is a corrupt trader who, like the unethical agent, Silas Meacham, hawks illicit goods and spirits to the Native Americans in John Ford's *Fort Apache* (1948). Wilkins sells cheap liquor and manages to induce the African chief to steal a cache of gold. In a complementary plot, while Ramar and Howard continue in a search for the magic botanicals, a plane crash occurs in the jungle, which jeopardizes the safety of the survivors, mistakenly viewed by the natives as gods fallen from the sky. Although the pilot is killed as he attempts to steal a golden statue, the other two passengers are rescued and escape. Eventually, social order and the cache of gold will be restored. Perhaps the most interesting insight into this episode is the juxtaposition of the stock footage of chimps, lions, lizards, and even a waterfall with the out-of-place, violent white criminals: these are images of the natural world juxtaposed with corrosive human nature.

The episode entitled "Doomed Safari" is noteworthy for several reasons. Two people visiting Africa on their honeymoon, Ramar's friends, go off in search of uranium. The husband is identified as a mineralogist. Like Conrad's Marlowe on his own mission of recovery in the jungle, Ramar's friend works for the "company," but a rival has preceded him in the search for the dangerous atomic material. Although the rival has entered and escaped from the deep jungle territory, Ramar's friend is taken prisoner, but he is mistakenly identified by his rescuers as the body burning on a tribal ritual pyre; it is actually the deceased witch doctor. Cut-away shots of a wild boar and leopard engaged in a life and death struggle comment on the intrigue and uncertainty of the outcome. Although Ramar's friend is caught, tied up, and mauled by a lion, he is saved, while his rival is killed near the cremation site. The quest to locate the forbidden uranium is abandoned, and this episode, broadcast in 1953, popularizes the postwar fascination and anxiety with unknown atomic substances and their power to entice and destroy, seen in film narratives such as Robert Aldrich's *Kiss Me Deadly* (1955). In these broadcast episodes, Ramar is a signifying presence, the other in the midst—the space and time—of others. He was not alone in this unusual sociological placement in the 1950s media.

Two linked episodes of *Ramar* directed by Fox, entitled "Evil Trek" and "White Savages," also feature a powerful white woman living amidst the jungle setting and tribal way of life, only she is a corrupting interloper who, like Conrad's Mr. Kurtz, has risen to power through nefarious means and "taken a high seat amongst the devils of the land." In "Evil Trek," the first broadcast episode of the series, the audience is introduced to the progressive white researchers as they enter the environment on a slow river boat, heading to the local trading post. Instead of searching for ivory, Tom Reynolds, Ramar, and Howard seek usually forbidden sites in search of herbs and medicines, magic in the making, for Western consumption. As they travel to a very remote region, framed by Fox's cut-away shots of jungle life to establish a sense of space and time, they discover a white goddess leading the tribe (Figure 11.3). They inquire about obtaining some local poisonous plant life, which is actually the source of the magical formula. As they are unknown interlopers, the two men are made prisoners by the goddess and the tribe; eventually, they escape with a few samples and cross the river, back to civilization.

In a follow-up episode entitled "White Savages," the opening shot credit sequence reveals another side to Ramar; he fearlessly shoots a lion, establishing him as a warrior-savant for the audience. Science is a positive identity marker, but guns make peace. Two escaped prisoners-murderers enter the

Figure 11.3 "The Jungle Goddess."

jungle setting in search of illicit drug technology located in the forbidden land of the white goddess. Interestingly, the drug extract involves facilitating youthful rejuvenation, a postwar narcotic-like commodity. Eventually, the escapees make their way to the remote location where they encounter the white goddess Irma, living unhappily with the natives and desirous of escape. She feigns her fractured English to denote a false identity. In reality, she is a con artist who joins in with these criminals to fleece the natives of their natural wealth. She betrays the criminals and the tribe, but all are caught or killed as a result of Ramar's intervention. The action imagery at the beginning of the film comes full circle as Ramar is depicted both as a man of peaceful progress and a symbol of retributive justice. He shoots as well as he thinks.

As a big game hunter and symbol of forceful, armed manliness, Hathaway's Douglas-as-hunter, and frequently the "active" Ramar, also recall the popular myths of masculinity ritualized in the author Robert Ruark's *Horn of the Hunter* (1953), a literary memoir of African safaris full of blood, alcohol, and imposing signs of white male, aggressive virility. Ruark notes in a tone of near wistful elation the manly and privileged pursuits of "kills past" while on the safari:

> I believe I know what they [hunters] get out of it. There is a simple love of outdoors and of creatures . . . that drives a man to the vastnesses [*sic*] of Africa to fulfill some need of basic simplicity in himself. My friend, Selby, hopelessly lost in the jungles of so small a town as Nairobi, is Moses leading his flock when all he can see is horizons and a lion or two. The complete love and trust of his blacks are testament to this . . . These few surviving men [hunters] are largely Jasons in search of the Golden Fleece, and they don't care who brings it down . . . because the ultimate end is noble in the mind.[24]

Ruark believes that "deep in the guts of most men . . . [is] an atavistic memory of his fathers, who killed first with stone, and then with club, and then with spear, and then with bow, and then with gun, and finally with formulae," to which he adds:

> How meek is the man of no importance; somewhere in the pigeon chest of the clerk is still the vestigial remnant of the hunter's heart . . . this is a simple manifestation of ancient ego . . . because man the hunter lives basically in his belly.[25]

However primeval and romantically descriptive the passage, Ruark excludes from his charting of jungle life those who do not hunt for sport or commerce. Ramar was a doctor who used his weaponry not for sporting purposes but solely for survival or to track criminals, not to gain trophies of dead animals. The people inhabiting Ramar's enlightened jungle space and time, both men and women, avoid such rhetorical puffery and instead work toward a common good.

Ruark's fabled jungle safari also excludes women whenever possible from these rarefied sites:

> More dangerous than an angry cow elephant with a young calf . . . is the woman on safari. She is generally rich and spoiled, old and full of complaints, or young and apt to fall a little bit in love with the hunter.[26]

This is one postwar narrative's hyperbolic view of survival and experience in Africa. Ellen Burton, who is neither "shrew [n]or nymphomaniac,"[27] refutes Ruark's non-sensical assertions; in *White Witch Doctor*, although imperfect, Burton is a strong, capable, and intelligent character who works with Douglas to achieve their common goal. In fact, the safari trek is completed, and she becomes the new "big mama" practitioner for the tribe, performing rituals of white magic to restore the ill to sound medical health. As she saves a baby from death at birth and removes an impacted wisdom tooth with magical chloroform to save the chief's favorite wife, Burton discredits the black magic of her enemy, the tribal witch doctor.

In the Fox-directed *Ramar* episode "Tribal Feud," another symbolic white goddess, a kidnap victim taken from the trading post, contrasts with the evil female goddess, as the hostage is required by one of two warring tribes to create black magic to assist them in their war. Although a jealous witch doctor drugs her and she takes the ritual "fire walk," she survives. As Ramar and friends shoot their way out of the village, the evil witch doctor and nomads lose the battle, and the good king (who speaks some English) is restored to sovereignty. In these interrelated narratives about power and exploitation, it is women, more than gold, who are agencies of mystifying power and conflict as they affect and eventually control so much male behavior.

Wheeler Dixon states: "What will . . . twenty-first century viewers make of Ramar's ceaseless quest through a jungle that never existed?"[28] It is my contention that Fox's *Ramar of the Jungle* episodes, among other media staples produced in the 1950s, are contemplative, historical, often disconcerting images: problematic and imaginary entertainment spectacles that still interest the critical viewer.

NOTES

1. Wheeler Winston Dixon, *Lost in the Fifties: Recovering Phantom Hollywood* (Carbondale: Southern Illinois University Press, 2005), 43.
2. Dixon, *Lost*, 34.
3. Charles Musser, ""Why Did Negroes Love Al Jolson and *The Jazz Singer*?: Melodrama, Blackface and Cosmopolitan Theatrical Culture," *Film History* 23:2 (2011), 205.
4. Ibid., 216.
5. Donald Bogle, *Prime Time Blues: African Americans on Network Television* (New York: Farrar, Straus and Giroux, 2015), 42.
6. Dixon, *Lost*, 27.
7. This perspective, which viewed race and racism, the historical black American experience, via the perceptions of (sympathetic) white participants, was evident in such later film productions as Alan Parker's *Mississippi Burning* (Orion Picture, 1988) and Tate Taylor's *The Help* (Dreamworks, 2011).
8. The familiar sounds of the living jungle, although not produced for an African setting, are arguably best presented in David Lean's wartime epic film, *The Bridge over the River Kwai* (Horizon, Columbia Pictures, 1957). The sound landscape of wildlife and natural elements surround the construction of the infamous Burma Railway during WW2. The opening shot sequences of the film, prior to the eruptive sound of the approaching train whistle, are overwhelmingly effective, sensual, and realistic.
9. Chinua Achebe, "An Image of Africa," *The Massachusetts Review* 18:4 (1977), 782–94, 782.

10. Ibid., 783.
11. Chadwick Allen, "Hero with Two Faces: *The Lone Ranger* as Treaty Discourse," *American Literature* 68:3 (September 1996), 615.
12. "Ghost Canyon" was Episode 16 of Season 5.
13. Michael Ray Fitzgerald, "The White Savior and his Junior Partner: The Lone Ranger and Tonto on Cold War Television (1949–1957)," *The Journal of Popular Culture* 46:1 (2013), 79.
14. Ibid., 83.
15. Ibid., 94.
16. Ibid., 85.
17. This chapter refers to those eleven episodes of *Ramar of the Jungle* known to be directed by Wallace Fox which were available in several media formats, including YouTube and especially on DVD formats. On page 38 of his study, Dixon verifies that thirteen *Ramar* episodes were directed by Fox, but two were composed of recycled footage and lengthened into made-for-television films; I am excluding these re-edited broadcast episodes in this chapter, as these two productions mostly recirculate previously discussed information. I also exclude information readily available on various Internet sites which provide broadcast dates and other technical specifications.
18. These websites offer excellent reproductions of the respective paintings: <https://artsandculture.google.com/asset/the-parley-frederic-remington/qQFnS_iqcWBDEw?hl=en>; <https://www.artbasel.com/catalog/artwork/28962/Henri-Rousseau-Le-lion-ayant-faim-se-jette-sur-l-antilope> (both accessed June 15, 2018).
19. Frances P. Bolton, "A View of Africa." The Annals of the American Academy of Political and Social Science, 306, *Africa and the Western World* (July 1956), 122–6.
20. Dixon, *Lost*, 37.
21. Steven Ungar, "Making Waves: René Vautier's *Afrique 50* and the Emergence of Anti-Colonial Cinema," *L'Esprit Créateur* 51:3 (Fall 2011), 34–46, 42.
22. Matthias De Groof, "Statues Also Die—But Their Death is not the Final Word," *Image & Narrative* 11:1 (2010), 33.
23. De Groof, "Statues," 36.
24. Robert C. Ruark, *Horn of the Hunter* [1954] reprinted (Long Beach: CA, Safari Press, 1996), 80–2.
25. Ibid., 22–3.
26. Ibid., 74.
27. Ibid., 74.
28. Dixon, *Lost*, 45.

Index

Note: n indicates notes; *italic* indicates figures

CPSIA information can be obtained
at www.ICGtesting.com
Printed in the USA
JSHW051652060922
30175JS00001B/25

9 781399 505635